D1531518

University of Michigan Publications

HISTORY AND POLITICAL SCIENCE

VOLUME VI

THE GRAIN SUPPLY OF ENGLAND DURING THE NAPOLEONIC PERIOD

THE MACMILLAN COMPANY
NEW YORK BOSTON CHICAGO
ATLANTA SAN FRANCISCO

MACMILLAN & CO., Limited
LONDON BOMBAY CALCUTTA
MELBOURNE

THE MACMILLAN CO. OF CANADA, Ltd.
TORONTO

THE

GRAIN SUPPLY OF ENGLAND

DURING

THE NAPOLEONIC PERIOD

A THESIS

BY

W. FREEMAN GALPIN

New York

THE MACMILLAN COMPANY

London: Macmillan & Company, Limited

1925

Set up and printed,
October, 1925

PRINTED IN THE UNITED STATES OF AMERICA

PREFACE

THE grain trade of England has been one of the most decisive factors in that country's history. For many centuries this trade waxed and flourished to the satisfaction of a people who were preëminently interested in agricultural pursuits. And when, as a result of the Industrial Revolution, that trade shifted from an export to an import traffic in corn, it assisted to a marked degree in the rapid rise of England as the most powerful and wealthy country of the nineteenth century.

The importance of this commerce in corn, while generally appreciated, has not had the scientific study that it warrants. The contributions made by Gras, Prothero, Gonner, Slater, not to mention many others, have been concerned chiefly with the internal and domestic phases of British agriculture. Cunningham, Page, Levi, Porter and Tooke have treated of this subject only as incidental to their particular problems. Of recent date there have appeared the studies by Rose and Melvin, and the more popular work by Barker.

When I first undertook the study of England's grain supply during the Napoleonic era, I had little appreciation of the vastness of the subject. For a time the problem seemed to be centered about a mere discussion of the quantities of corn that were imported during this period. Research, however, disclosed the inadequacy of this opinion. A careful and appreciative study of the movement of grain necessitated, it was found, an examination of the various laws that regulated this trade. But having turned the numerous pages of the British statutes, I found that the operation of these laws was fairly negligible during the Napoleonic period. As a result, I undertook the task of trying to ascertain what were the factors which set aside these timeworn laws. This caused an investigation of the harvest conditions, the progress of enclosure, the balancing of political interest against personal desire, the struggles within Parliament, and, finally, the general conduct of domestic and foreign affairs.

So extensive did the problem become that definite and rigid boundaries had to be prescribed, if any results were to be obtained. In the first place, it was necessary to place a time limit upon the subject. It was decided that the fall of 1799 would best serve as the introductory date in view of the fact that the harvest conditions of that year had a distinct effect upon the year 1800; and that the year 1813 would best mark the close of this study, as it was that year which definitely terminated the Emperor's power in Europe. Again it was necessary to limit the subject to a consideration merely of the import trade in corn. The size of this volume will probably warrant the omission of the relatively unimportant export and internal commerce in corn. Some discussion, however, of both the export and the internal trade was found essential; which explains, in part, the comments on the West Indian and Canadian trade in the introductory chapter. Furthermore, it was the import trade of England primarily, and only incidentally that of Scotland and Ireland, that compelled attention.

With these general ideas in mind, the fundamental purpose of this study becomes apparent; namely, a disclosure of the general movement of grain during the Napoleonic period, and the correlation of that trade with the Continental System.

That the imperial decrees of Napoleon cut seriously into the corn supply of Britain, cannot be doubted. It did not, however, ever reach the point where the English people were brought face to face with starvation and defeat. The tremendous increase in domestic production, the numerous methods adopted to bridge the apparent scarcity by substitution and retrenchment, and the rapid exploitation of the grain fields of the United States, rendered starvation practically impossible. This was the opinion of the humble but practical corn merchant of America. It was also the view held by the Emperor himself, who even went so far as to supply his enemy with grain. As will be seen, the imperial program called for a prohibition of all export because of the terms of the Continental System, and because of several very serious harvest failures. On the other hand, it was primarily because of the bumper crops in France that export was permitted, at another time, under the agency of the Licence System.

In perfecting his Licence System, Napoleon had the experience of France's corn policy, dating from the time of Colbert. He also had a model in the well-organized system that existed in England. In the fifth chapter an attempt has been made to give, by way of suggestion, a rough idea of the inception and growth of the British licenced trade. The need for a careful account of the British Licence System is very apparent, as indeed is a volume on the origins of the November Orders in Council. In Chapter III I have hazarded a fresh interpretation of these measures, and it is my belief that further research will tend to show that economic motives first, and military needs second, prompted the appearance of these Orders. The effect of these measures upon the English grain trade, especially the trade with the United States, is one of the most interesting phases of this study. That these Orders produced decided reaction both in America and in England becomes more and more apparent from a study of the English import figures and of the manifests of clearances from American harbors.

The course of my research has placed me under obligation to several most obliging friends. I owe great thanks to Professor W. E. Lingelbach for his scholarly guidance and assistance when I was a graduate student at the University of Pennsylvania, as well as for his kindness in reading and in offering helpful counsel on the substance of this study. I am, furthermore, indebted to Professors A. B. White and N. S. B. Gras of the University of Minnesota for most valuable assistance and advice. I am also under obligation to President M. L. Burton, Dean A. H. Lloyd, and Professors C. H. Van Tyne, A. L. Cross and U. B. Phillips of the University of Michigan for their willing coöperation in ironing out some very troublesome problems that I encountered in the course of my study. Nor am I forgetful of the interest and stimulus furnished by Professor J. A. James of Northwestern University, under whose direction my thoughts were first turned towards history and this particular work. And finally, I owe unstinted thanks to those who in a humble, but in a most effective and endearing manner, furnished at a great sacrifice the inspiration and assistance necessary for the development of this volume. I am also deeply obligated to Dr. E. S. McCartney of the University of Michigan for his most careful and scholarly editing of this volume.

W. Freeman Galpin

University of Michigan
Ann Arbor, March, 1924

CONTENTS

THE GRAIN SUPPLY OF ENGLAND DURING THE NAPOLEONIC PERIOD

CHAPTER I

INTRODUCTION

The threefold purpose of the Corn Laws — The relations between these measures and the Corn Trade — The importance of the export trade — The Industrial Revolution increases the value of the import trade — The relation between the Corn Trade and the Navigation System.

THE Corn Laws of Great Britain are very numerous. In one instance the law may be a most thorough and comprehensive measure touching every conceivable phase of the corn trade; while in another case it may be no more than a mere clause tucked in among the sections of an unrelated act. Broadly speaking, these laws consist of a body of legislation dealing with every angle of an internal and an external trade in corn.[1]

A study of these laws, as well as of the forces prompting them, shows a threefold purpose: to obtain for the consumers an adequate supply at a fair and reasonable price; to foster the agricultural interests so as to benefit landlord and farmer; and to promote the general welfare of the state by a ready supply in time of war, by increased revenue, and by a larger merchant marine. The combination of purposes is illustrated in part by an examination of the various acts and reports of Parliament, as evidence of which the following may be cited:

> The COMMITTEE . . . Have, in pursuance of the Instructions which they received, proceeded to examine the Act of the 31st of the King, and to take, from the best Information they could obtain, a Comparative View

[1] Unless otherwise stated, the word 'corn' will be used as a general term covering grain, meal and flour of all kinds; frequently the word 'grain' will be used as a synonym for 'corn.'

of the Price of Labour, and of the unavoidable Expenses incident to the Farmer . . . as the best Criterion by which they might judge of what ought to be the Price of the different Species of Grain, so as to allow to the Grower such a fair and reasonable Profit as may induce him to pursue that Line of Husbandry which will the most contribute to the Production of such an ample Supply of the different Kinds of Corn and Grain, as may be sufficient for the Consumption of the Kingdom.[2]

English legislators were interested chiefly in the export of corn before the middle of the eighteenth century.[3] After that, exportation became less important until by the Napoleonic era it was a negligible matter.[4] This alteration in the corn trade seems to have been caused by the silent working of the Industrial Revolution. A rapid increase in population, chiefly within certain metropolitan districts, quickened the demand for corn, a demand, which the agriculturists were unable to equal, in spite of numerous improvements in agricultural methods, enclosures, and more bountiful harvests. To meet this lack of food, recourse had to be had to foreign corn, which in turn forced a change in the import regulations. Hence the attempt to protect the producer by an increase in the import rates was brushed aside by the demand for larger food supplies.

In 1800, the export trade of England was governed in the main by the laws of 1791 and 1793.[5] These measures prescribed a set of elaborate and highly technical regulations. Of particular interest was the grouping of the maritime counties into administra-

[2] *Parl. Papers,* 1804, No. 96, p. 3: see also Nicholson, J. S., *The History of the English Corn Laws,* pp. 12–13. A mere glance at the income derived from the import duties shows the importance of this phase of the Corn Laws: see *Accounts and Papers,* 1898, vol. 34, p. 259.

[3] Gras, N. S. B., *Evolution of the English Corn Market,* has by far the best account of the Corn Laws before the 18th century. No adequate study exists for the later period. Nicholson, J. S., *op. cit.,* and Prothero, R. E., *English Farming, Past and Present,* give suggestive résumés for this later period.

[4] For a table of imports and exports from 1697 to 1896, see *Accounts and Papers,* 1898, vol. 34, pp. 256–258. See Customs, 17: 23–28, for an account of corn shipped to Europe, Asia, Africa and America from 1801 to 1806. Exports during the Napoleonic era were of little importance; only in 1808 did this trade assume any size, and then because of the need of maintaining the British army in the Spanish Peninsula.

[5] 31 Geo. 3, c. 30; 33 Geo. 3, c. 65. These laws also governed the import trade, for which see p. 5.

tive districts, each district having an individual schedule of prices which directed the movement of grain within the district.[6] It was upon these prices that the grain trade rested in normal times. Definitely, however, it was the relation these prices bore to certain other prices, fixed by law, that determined this trade.

The export trade may, for convenience, be placed under the general heads: to foreign states, to the British possessions, and to Ireland.[7] The first and last were dependent upon the schedule of prices mentioned above, while the export to the various possessions, being of a special nature, was subject to an altogether different system. The export of corn, malt, bread and biscuit to foreigners was forbidden when the average price of British corn in the maritime districts was at or above the following rates: wheat, 46*s.*, rye, pease and beans, 30*s.*, barley, beer and bigg, 23*s.*, oats, 15*s.* per quarter, and oatmeal, 14*s.* per boll.[8] One main exception to this arrangement merits attention. Following an ancient custom, the Crown upon the advice of the Privy Council might prohibit (regardless of the price) the export of any British or foreign corn and biscuit from Great Britain.[9] The evident purpose of this exception was to stop export in times of scarcity.[10]

[6] A similar division was made of the inland counties, but this did not concern the foreign trade. The export trade was dependent upon a scale of prices that was fixed each week, the import, upon a rate which was made four times a year. These prices were printed in the *London Gazette:* see Appendix No. 5.

[7] In 1800, the trade between Ireland and Great Britain, and between Ireland and the world, was chiefly regulated by the Irish Acts 23 and 24 Geo. 3, c. 19; 32 Geo. 3, c. 20; and the British Act 31 Geo. 3, c. 30. In the main this trade followed the same lines as that of the trade of England. It should be noted, however, that both the Irish and the English enjoyed a preference over outsiders in the trade between the two islands.

[8] 31 Geo. 3, c. 30, Table B; 33 Geo. 3, c. 65, clause 15.

[9] A time limit was stated in all orders. Certain minute exceptions exist to the general statement as given above.

[10] During the first four years of the period covered by this study, ten distinct orders were issued; after that, none seem to have been made: see P. C. Reg., 154–164. The discontinuance of these orders is explained by the fact that the prices of corn uniformly prohibited all export, and permitted generally importation: see P. C. Reg., 163, Aug. 9, 1803.

This power did not include the trade to the English possessions, as set forth in the acts of 1791 and 1793. According to these measures the export to these places was left to the merchants of certain British ports, or else was handled directly by the Privy Council.

Probably the most important part of this trade was that which centered in the British West Indies and in Canada. Before 1783 American produce found a profitable as well as a legal market in these colonies. The recognition of American independence brought this trade to an end. To meet this situation, the British Government issued orders and statutes in rapid succession, which established most securely the Navigation System in respect to the trade between these possessions and the United States.[11] American commerce was distinctly limited, and the West Indies were forced to depend upon British or Canadian corn. Upon the outbreak of war with France it became plain that a new method would have to be adopted. Law or no law, American grain began to find its way into the West Indies, violating in every way the British commercial system. The complete abandonment, however, of this system did not take place at this time. Only as the occasion demanded did the British make the necessary concessions.[12]

Such in brief was the law that regulated the export of corn, a trade which was rapidly sinking into comparative unimportance. The supremacy that the English farmer had enjoyed before the Industrial Revolution was forever gone. The manufacturers, intent upon a cheap and a certain source of food, demanded and ultimately obtained a complete abolition of the various laws that stopped the import of foreign corn. This was not, however, until some time after the period covered by the limits of this volume.

Beginning with the nineteenth century, the import trade assumed unparalleled proportions. The conduct of this trade was

[11] See for example 23 Geo. 3, c. 39; 25 Geo. 3, c. 1; 27 Geo. 3, c. 7; 28 Geo. 3, c. 6; 29 Geo. 3, c. 16; and 33 Geo. 3, c. 50. See pp. 5–6 for a discussion of the Navigation System.

[12] See for example 27 Geo. 3, c. 27; 35 Geo. 3, c. 57; 47 Geo. 3, s. 2, c. 38; 48 Geo. 3, c. 125; 53 Geo. 3, c. 67.

so arranged that the volume of the imports increased as the price of corn advanced in Great Britain. Obviously, this increase in imports was in the interest of the consumer. To protect the producer and to obtain a revenue for the state, these acts incorporated the principle of the sliding scale of duties. To illustrate: whenever the price of wheat in 1800 was under 50*s.* per quarter, the import of foreign wheat was practically stopped by a duty of 26*s.* 8 2/20*d.* per quarter; if the price was at or above 50*s.*, but under 54*s.*, then a duty of 2*s.* 9*d.* was asked; while if the price was at or above 54*s.*, then a duty of 6 12/20*d.* was levied.[13] One main exception should be noted: namely, that the importer from the British possessions enjoyed preferential rates.[14]

Closely associated with the import trade were the questions of bounties, of the warehousing of corn, and of the Navigation System. For the present, the first two need not detain us.[15] It will be of decided interest, however, to note the relation of the Corn Laws to the time-honored Navigation System.

A careful study of the act of 1651, and particularly of the law of 1660, leads to certain general conclusions.[16] Grain of all descriptions might be imported into England, Wales, Ireland, or

[13] See Appendix No. 3. For various additional customs fees see 27 Geo. 3, c. 13; 31 Geo. 3, c. 30; 37 Geo. 3, c. 97; 41 Geo. 3, c. 91 (U.K.); and 42 Geo. 3, c. 27.

[14] From Oct. 16, 1799, to June 30, 1803, the Crown permitted the free import of corn in either British or neutral ships, regardless of the manner in which the latter might be navigated: see note 10. From Nov. 12, 1803, to Nov. 10, 1804, foreign and colonial wheat was subject in the majority of the maritime districts to the lowest duty, although in the London area the highest duty was in force. From then until Feb., 1814, all wheat imported into any of the districts of England paid the lowest duty: see Appendices Nos. 3 and 5.

[15] See Chapter II for an account of the bounty system. In order to promote the trade in foreign corn and to obtain a supply in times of scarcity the system of warehousing corn was adopted. For the details see 31 Geo. 3, c. 30; 33 Geo. 3, c. 65; 35 Geo. 3, c. 4; 39 Geo. 3, c. 87. The warehousing acts proper, especially 43 Geo. 3, c. 132, do not, I believe, concern the general trade in corn: see 48 Geo. 3, c. 126.

[16] See also Reeves, J., *The Law of Shipping and Navigation;* Beer, G. L., *Commercial Policy of England towards the American Colonies,* in *Columbia University Studies,* 1893, and Clark, G. N., "The Navigation Act of 1651," in *History,* VII: 282–286.

into any of the colonies from any of the colonies, or from any foreign possessions in Asia, Africa and America, provided the vessel was English or colonial in construction and ownership, and that the master and three fourths of the crew were English subjects. Again, grain of all types might be imported into England, Wales, or Ireland from Europe either in English ships as described above, or in ships of the country producing the imported goods.[17] Finally, the export of grain of all descriptions was permitted from any of the colonies to any port or place in the world.

A proper appreciation of these facts is important. Subsequent legislation for one hundred and twenty-two years in no way seriously changed the conduct of the corn trade from Europe to England. Modifications and extensions were made in respect to other commodities;[18] corn, however, remained untouched.[19] In 1782, Parliament relaxed the restrictions placed on foreign shipping by providing that any vessel might engage, under certain conditions, in the enumerated trade of Europe.[20] This smacked, however, too much of free trade for the hide-bound protectionists who were able five years later to reëstablish the principle of 1660.[21] As a consequence, European corn could be imported into Great Britain only by British ships, owned, built and navigated according to law, or in the ships of the country producing this article.[22] From 1787 to the outbreak of the French war, the European corn trade to Great Britain and Ireland rested upon these regulations. A more drastic change had taken place,

[17] If imported in ships of the country producing the corn, then the master and three fourths of the crew had to be subjects of that state. Corn was not listed among the enumerated goods of the colonial trade; it was, however, included in the enumerated list in the European trade.

[18] See 2 Wm. and M., s. 1 c. 9; 7 and 8 Wm. and M., c. 22; 15 Chas. 2, c. 7; 18 and 19 Chas. 2, c. 2; 14 Chas. 2, cc. 11, 13; 1 Anne, s. 1, c. 21; 6 Geo. 1, c. 15. By 6 Anne, c. 11, Scotland had been included in the terms of the Navigation System. Ireland had been a part since 1651.

[19] By 23 Geo. 3, c. 1, all sorts of corn might be imported into Great Britain, from any country or place in neutral or British ships: see also 23 Geo. 3, c. 9.

[20] 22 Geo. 3, c. 78.

[21] 27 Geo. 3, c. 19, as limited by 14 Chas. 2, c. 11, and 6 Geo. 1, c. 15.

[22] See Reeves, J., *op. cit.,* pp. 239–240.

however, in the conduct of the trade between the mother country and the colonies.[23]

Before 1783, America was within the scope of the Navigation Acts. American corn, therefore, might be shipped from these colonies to England, Ireland, Wales, to any of the possessions of the English king, or to any port whatsoever. This was contingent upon the vessel's being English, Welsh, Irish, or built and owned in the colonies, and navigated according to law.[24] By an act of 1696, however, all goods had been forbidden entry into Ireland unless they had first been landed in England.[25] This remained true until the reign of George the Second when non-enumerated goods — and that included corn — might once more be imported into Ireland.[26] Later, in 1766 all non-enumerated goods, if bound to a port north of Cape Finisterre, were to be landed first in Great Britain.[27] This was the situation at the outbreak of the American Revolution.[28]

After 1783, the trade between the United States and the British Empire was fundamentally changed. For a time it seemed that a liberal policy would be adopted by England.[29] Unfortunately, there was enacted a measure which gave to the Crown the conduct of the trade with the United States, a measure which

[23] See 4 Geo. 3, cc. 19 27; 5 Geo. 3, c. 45; 2 Geo. 3, c. 24; 3 Geo. 2, c. 12; 13 Geo. 1, c. 5; 15 Chas. 2, c. 7, for instances of relaxations in the Navigation Acts in respect to America.

[24] 15 Chas. 2, c. 7; 22 and 23 Chas. 2, c. 26, stopped the trade in enumerated goods between Ireland and the colonies. The act of 1663 forbade the direct export from Ireland to the colonies of everything except servants, horses, and provisions.

[25] 7 and 8 Wm. 3, c. 22.

[26] 4 Geo. 2, c. 15: see also 5 Geo. 2, c. 9, and 20 Geo. 3, c. 10.

[27] 6 Geo. 3, c. 52, clause 30; according to this, the trade in these non-enumerated goods to Ireland was stopped. This was changed so as to include Ireland by 7 Geo. 3, c. 2. 9 Geo. 3, c. 28, extended this trade, except rum, to Guernsey and Jersey.

[28] The export trade in corn from Great Britain and Ireland was very small. Any trade from Ireland was closed by 15 Chas. 2, c. 7, and 22 and 23 Chas. 2, c. 26; it was also controlled by the operations of the Corn Laws. By 18 Geo. 3, c. 55, this trade was thrown open to Ireland: see also 3 and 4 Anne, c. 7.

[29] 23 Geo. 3, c. 26: see also *Parl. Hist.*, XXIII: 602–615, 640–646, 724–730, and *Trade of Great Britain and the United States*, p. 64 *seq.*, and Bibliography.

was renewed yearly until 1797.[30] According to the terms of the orders issued under these various acts, and in accordance with Jay's Treaty, American corn might be imported into Great Britain and Ireland, in either British ships, owned, built and navigated according to law, or in American ships; provided the latter had been built in America, and were owned by subjects of that state, and had a crew, the master and three fourths of which were American citizens.[31] Jay's Treaty expired in 1806; but the principles it contained, as well as the act of 1797, were kept alive by Parliamentary action until the ratification of a definite treaty in 1815.[32]

This in brief is an outline of the Corn Laws necessary for an introduction to the study of the grain trade during the Napoleonic era. Practically, from 1804 to the Corn Law of 1814, the grain trade functioned without any great interference by these laws. It is not hard to find or to understand the cause of the failure of these laws to operate, although the importance of their non-operation has been overlooked by most writers. It is the purpose of the chapters that immediately follow to show the trend of events that made possible the virtual suspension of these and subsequent laws.

30 23 Geo. 3, c. 39; 24 Geo. 3, cc. 2, 15; 25 Geo. 3, c. 5; 26 Geo. 3, c. 4; 27 Geo. 3, c. 7; 28 Geo. 3, c. 5; 29 Geo. 3, c. 1; 30 Geo. 3, c. 11; 31 Geo. 3, c. 12; 32 Geo. 3, c. 14; 33 Geo. 3, c. 10; 34 Geo. 3, c. 5; 35 Geo. 3, c. 26; 36 Geo. 3, c. 58; 37 Geo. 3, c. 37.

31 This was a marked departure from the Navigation System, which forbade the import into Great Britain of any goods of Asia, Africa and America, except in British ships. For a discussion of Jay's Treaty, see Bemis, S. F. *Jay's Treaty* (New York, 1923), especially chaps. 2, 13.

32 37 Geo. 3, c. 97, carried into effect the provisions of the Jay Treaty. This act was kept in force by 45 Geo. 3, c. 35; 46 Geo. 3, c. 16; 47 Geo. 3, s. 2, c. 2; 48 Geo. 3, cc. 6, 85; and 49 Geo. 3, c. 59, by which it was indefinitely extended. American corn might find a legal entrance into Great Britain via Quebec: see 30 Geo. 3, c. 29, clause 2. It is to be noticed that Americans were excluded by the Navigation Acts from the trade between Europe and the United Kingdom after 1783, except during periods of war. Direct trade to Ireland from America was granted by 41 Geo. 3, c. 95.

CHAPTER II

PEACE AND A LARGE LOAF

The failure of the harvest of 1799 — Parliament enacts a far-reaching relief program — The Corn Committee of 1800 — The importance of the foreign supply, especially in relation to prices — The food shortage during the winter of 1800–1801 — Conditions aggravated by numerous riots — Speculation and monopoly — The General Enclosure Act of 1801 — The effect of the high prices and the unfavorable state of agriculture upon the movement for peace.

THE Eighteenth Parliament of Great Britain, the last by that name, was a most important body.[1] Upon the shoulders of its members had fallen the Herculean task of guiding a foreign war, soothing a turbulent Irish people, allaying the injured feelings of neutral nations, and solving a host of other problems that choked and clogged the progress of state affairs. And then, as the century drew to a close, another and far more significant question arose to aggravate, if not to imperil, a distracted nation. This problem, the maintenance of an adequate food-supply, was of fundamental importance. Upon it rested the success or failure of the Government. Irish union, American rights, yes, even the war itself, would have to be neglected, if not altogether postponed, should the administration fail to check the further growth of a nation-wide famine.

In order to obviate this catastrophe, Parliament late in September, 1799, undertook the passage of a relief program.[2] Distillation from wheat, barley, malt and all sorts of grain, meal flour, or bran was prohibited in Scotland; while the use of wheat and wheat flour by the distilleries was forbidden in England.

[1] The 18th Parliament actually opened Sept. 27, 1796, and ended Dec. 31, 1800.

[2] For a review of agricultural conditions in 1799, see *Farmer's Mag.*, I: 101; *Agricultural Mag.*, I: 217–218, 222; *Annals of Agriculture*, XXXIV: 158–160; and *Monthly Mag.*, VIII: 764.

The Crown, furthermore, was granted the power to suspend the export and to permit the free import of all kinds of corn.[3]

A recess which extended through the Christmas season enabled the members to become personally informed of the gravity of the situation. Wheat, which had sold for 49*s*. 6*d*. in January, 1799, was 93*s*. 10*d*. in December of the same year.[4] Heavy rains, cold winds and frosts had so lessened the home supply that in spite of unprecedented importations severe want and suffering had been felt, especially among the poor of the larger cities. In London, Edinburgh and elsewhere, soup-houses and public kitchens were opened. Subscriptions for the purchase of wheat to be sold to the needy at cost, the extension of the poor rates, wheatless meals and days, and many other methods were adopted whereby the period of scarcity might be bridged.[5]

During the interval the Government had not been idle. Convinced of the need for immediate economy, the Duke of Portland sent a circular letter to the lord lieutenants, mayors and bishops of the realm urging the strict enforcement of the *Assize of Bread.* The reply, generally speaking, was none too favorable. It was argued by some that the act was feasible only in times of prosperity; others stated that it would cause increased consumption and thus defeat the very purpose of the law.[6] Popular opin-

[3] 39 and 40 Geo. 3, c. 7; c. 8, clauses 2, 3, 4; and c. 9.

[4] *Reports from Committees of the House of Commons,* IX: 185–186. Hereafter this will be termed: *First Series:* see also *London Gazette,* 1799. Unless otherwise stated all prices quoted in this volume are for quarters, a quarter equalling eight bushels.

[5] *Farmer's Mag.,* I: 104; *Gentleman's Mag.,* LXX: 80–81; *British Mag.,* I: 207; *Monthly Mag.,* VIII: 931–932; *Annals of Agriculture,* XXXIV: 264–265, 285, 294, 312; *Agricultural Mag.,* I: 222, II: 13–14; and *Scott's Mag.,* LXII: 67.

[6] H. O., 42: 49, 43: 11, especially the letters to Portland from Abingdon, Jan. 4, 1800, from the Marquis Townsend, Jan. 20, 1800 and from the Quarter Sessions of Berks, Jan. 14, 1800. The *Assize of Bread* had been fixed by 13 Geo. 3, c. 62 (see also Assize of Henry 3, 8 Anne, c. 19, and 31 Geo. 2, c. 29) which provided that in times of scarcity the Justices at the Quarter Sessions might forbid the baking or selling of any bread of a quality superior to or of a higher price than the "standard wheaten loaf," i.e., a loaf three fourths of whose weight was of undressed flour, except the bran or hull. By this regulation more bread could be made from a given quantity of flour: see Prothero, R. E. *English Farming, Past and Present,* Appendix No. 3, and Webb, S. and B., "The Assize of Bread," in *Economic Journal,* XIV: 196–218.

ion asked that the measure either be repealed or submitted to a thorough investigation.

In view of these facts a committee was appointed by the Commons to make the assize of 1773 more effective, and to consider the best means of bettering the misfortunes that had arisen from the deficiency of the harvest. This committee reported early in February, 1800.[7] Its conclusions rested upon the testimony of "respectable physicians," millers, bakers, and men like Mr. Claude Scott, a leading corn-factor of London, and Arthur Young, the editor of the *Annals of Agriculture*. This body found the act of 1773 seriously out of date. It was also discovered that "scarcely any Bread is consumed in the metropolis, but that which is made from fine Wheaten Flour," and that attempts in former periods of scarcity to use a coarser kind of bread had met with uniform failure. The committee, accordingly, deemed it unwise to change the food of so large a part of the community, especially in view of a deficient harvest. To meet this condition, the report advised a personal reduction in the use of wheaten flour, and the passage of a law prohibiting the sale of bread until it was twenty-four hours old. The committee also endorsed the Government's decision not to compete with private purchases abroad. In former times of scarcity the Government had bought supplies in foreign markets, and had sold this corn in England at a direct loss to English merchants As a result, the latter were unwilling to make purchases abroad without the assurance that the Government would not become a competitor. A statement to this effect was promptly made by the Ministry.[8]

The debate on this report showed many shades of opinion. Lord Hawkesbury held that the danger had been overestimated, and asked that a more thorough examination be made before any final step be taken. He was, however, in favor of prohibiting the sale of fresh bread, and introduced a bill to that effect. It was commonly believed that as one half of the bread baked in

[7] *First Series,* IX: 67–79.

[8] *Ibid.:* see also Add. MSS., 35128, Clerk of the Committee to A. Young, Feb., 1800. On Oct. 2, 1799, Pitt had remarked in Commons that the Government had no idea of buying corn abroad. Hansard is silent as to this statement, but a contemporary account may be found in *Monthly Mag.,* VIII: 821. See also B. T., 5: 11, Feb. 24, 1800.

London was used on the day it left the ovens, this measure would lessen the consumption by one tenth.[9] Others who saw in this proposal " more of taste than reason " pointed out the relative insufficiency of the bill.[10] It was generally granted that these conditions had been caused in part by the failure of the harvest. The war also came in for its part of the blame, while others held that the Corn Laws were the cause for all the trouble.[11]

A similar state of affairs existed in the House of Lords. The Archbishop of Canterbury, holding direct legislation as unnecessary, introduced a series of self-denying resolutions which received the support of the Lords, not, however, before the Earl of Darnley had subjected these propositions to much criticism. He challenged, also, the reliability of the Commons' report on the ground that the evidence it presented rested upon the testimony of but two witnesses, one of whom was a corn-factor. Finally, he held that a careful investigation would show the absence of any great scarcity.[12]

It is difficult to see what practical value the prelate's resolutions had. That it was followed by some is shown by the remark of Lady Holland that " During this scarcity, be it natural or artificial, we adopt the regulations of the Lords; each person in the family is limited to a quartern loaf per week, no pastry, no fine bread for breakfast." [13] The value of these resolutions for us does not consist in any mathematical deduction as to the possible number of bushels to be saved; but rather as a clear expression of opinion of the danger of impending famine. With-

[9] This measure was known as the *Stale Bread Act:* see *Parl. Hist.*, XXXIV: 1490–1492; *Gentleman's Mag.*, LXX: 175; *First Series*, IX: 68.

[10] *Annals of Agriculture*, XXXV: 33; *Anti-Jacobin Rev.*, V: 238–239.

[11] *Parl. Hist.*, XXXIV: 1489–1495. The *Monthly Mag.*, IX: 31, has this remark: " Tell the legislator, that all the acts yet framed relating to grain, their ashes given to the winds would more benefit his country than any he could substitute in their place."

[12] *Journals of the House of Lords*, XLII: 370, 378, 384; *Parl. Hist.*, XXXIV: 1495–1505. The Commons' report had been brought into the upper house by Lord Auckland. The charges made by the Earl of Darnley do not appear to be altogether just: see p. 11.

[13] *The Journal of Elizabeth, Lady Holland*, II: 59: see also *British Mag.*, II: 446.

out a doubt the home production was short. Mr. Claude Scott estimated the wheat crop as being 50 per cent below normal. Although no reliable statistics exist, an examination of the reports of the various Parliamentary committees, of the records of the Board of Trade, the Home Office, the Board of Agriculture and of the current newspapers, magazines and agricultural publications places this fact beyond dispute. From these, as well as from other sources, it is also established that the foreign supply was deficient, because of the agricultural, military and political situation on the continent.[14]

This foreign supply was one of increasing importance.[15] In point of fact it may be regarded as the index to the high prices. It serves as a barometer for the British market during the Napoleonic era. Although an upward trend in the price of corn would have followed as a natural result of the crop failure, the underlying cause for the extreme high price is to be found not in the home supply, not in the growth of population or in the shifting of that population from the country to the town, not in an inflated currency, not in the speculations of the monopolist, although these were factors of importance, but rather in the shortage of the foreign supply. Yet when one considers how small the quantity imported was in proportion to the amount used, one is inclined to ask whether it was not a case of "much ado about nothing." While we of today have the advantage of knowing the relatively small amount imported, still it is of value to realize that the foreign supply was the all-determining factor. This view is constantly to be found in the many sources for our period, of which our best informant is the Englishman himself. Here one happily notes a psychological factor that at once discloses a probable explanation. Impressed by the idea of his own self-sufficiency, the Englishman became visibly excited whenever that self-sufficiency was threatened. On every hand he saw visions of impending famine. The press graphically conjured up

[14] See *The Life and Correspondence of Rufus King,* III: 136; *Annals of Agriculture,* XXXIV: 107.

[15] Prothero, R. E., *English Farming, Past and Present,* p. 270 *seq.,* contains an interesting résumé of this idea.

before his worried brain visions of rice and turnip bread. The prayers and supplications of the clergy rang continually in his ears. Although his King and Parliament belittled the scarcity, everyone told him of its presence, and soon he believed it to be true. Forgetful of the possibilities of retrenchment and substitution, not pausing to investigate the extent of the supposed failure, and believing starvation inevitable, the Englishman turned to Europe and America for relief. As long as these sources were open he was somewhat satisfied. Any interference, such as the Armed Neutrality or the threat and final appearance of the American Embargo, immediately caused the Englishman to believe that starvation stared him in the face.[16] It was, therefore, just the dependence placed upon this supply, though small in itself, just the fear that it might be interfered with, that caused the market to rise so abnormally high. This fact should be kept always in mind in this study of the grain trade of Great Britain during the Napoleonic era.[17]

In the meantime the Committee of the Commons had continued its work and early in March had made a second report.[18] As a result of this and other findings, Parliament enacted a series of measures dealing with the agricultural situation. Bounties were to be given until October, 1800, on all wheat, flour, rye, oats and rice imported into certain ports of Great Britain. For the same period the manufacture of starch from wheat was forbidden. The prohibition of distilling low wines or spirits from corn in Scotland was extended until February, 1801. The act enabling the Crown to stop export and to permit free import was continued for a time, and the export of rice was forbidden until October 15, 1800. The establishment of a new table of assize, the *Stale Bread Act*, as well as a law granting for a limited

[16] *Cf.* Home Office Privy Council, and Board of Trade Papers: see also *British Mag.*, I: 388; *First Series,* IX: 75; *Parl. Hist.*, XXXV: 608–609, 652, 695; and Consular Despatches, Bristol, Dec. 17, 1800, March 30 [1801?].

[17] This view is often expressed in the following pages. See Prothero, R. E., *op. cit.*, pp. 210–213, for a discussion of the effects of the Corn Laws and of rents upon the price of corn.

[18] *First Series,* IX: 81–86.

time the import of Swedish herring, and an act incorporating the "London Company for the Manufacture of Flour, Meal, and Bread," were other measures passed by Parliament.[19]

Coincident with this outburst of legislation came a flood of favorable reports as to the next harvest. The spring months, except in northern Britain, had been suitable for agriculture. The Government, anxious to impress the public mind with the value of this event, announced the return of improved conditions.[20]

Cautioned by the experience of the former year and determined to seek out the reliability of these optimistic advices, the Board of Agriculture circulated a letter throughout the island asking for definite information. Some seventy-five answers were received. Lord Carrington, president of the Board, decided after careful study that "the produce of the wheat harvest in the whole country will this year be considerably under the average crop." This opinion, together with an abstract of the returns, was sent to Secretary Dundas, who in turn directed them to the Board of Trade.[21] A week later Dundas forwarded a letter

[19] 39 and 40 Geo. 3, cc. 18, 21, 25, 29, 35, 53, 58, 91, 97. The bounty on rye was to last until Oct. 15, 1800. A violation of the *Stale Bread Act* is noted in the *Monthly Mag.*, IX: 399, X: 85, 581. See *Anti-Jacobin Rev.*, V: 353, for an editorial against the use of Swedish herring. The purpose of the London Company was to supply the city with a constant supply of food at a cheaper rate than that charged by the millers: see *Commons' Journal*, 55: 600, 615, 632, 658, 691, 704, 731, 784; also Walpole, S., *The Life of the Rt. Hon. Spencer Perceval*, I: 76–78 (London, 1874), and *Monthly Mag.*, X: 71. It should be noted that distillation was not forbidden in England. An attempt to encourage the use of potatoes failed because of the bitter opposition on the part of the common people. A few farmers grudgingly admitted that perhaps potatoes ". . . t'wouldn't poisson tha' pigs: " see Stirling, A. M. W., *Coke of Norfolk*, p. 176 (London, John Lane, 1912).

[20] *Commons' Journal*, 55: 793; *Farmer's Mag.*, I: 217, 232, 334–337; *Monthly Mag.*, VIII: 1024, IX: 312, 516; *Agricultural Mag.*, II: 215, 290.

[21] B. T., 1: 18, Dundas to Liverpool, July 2, 1800, with an enclosure dated June 26, 1800. As early as March the Board of Agriculture had been alarmed by the "Resolves of the County of York," March 15, 1800. These resolves had stated that the next harvest would be below normal: see Board of Agriculture Minutes, May 27, 1800, April 5, 1803. The returns from the circular letter of the Board are to be found among the manuscripts of that body.

received from a Mr. John Cochrane which reads in part as follows:[22]

> I arrived here [Edinburgh] yesterday and cannot refrain from troubling you . . . on the miserable appearance of the crop, I may say all the way from London. From London to Stamford, the crop is merely tolerable; from there all the way to Haddington I did not see a single field that could be called a middling good crop. . . . As I travelled the whole during daylight, few fields escaped my observation, and I made it a point to engage at each stage what the prospects were which I found very gloomy indeed.

A spell of intense heat, a prolonged drought, helped by the activities of the grub, had produced this result.

Throughout the summer and fall the reports continued to be most discouraging; and although prices declined slightly during the harvest, there was but a temporary respite. October averages for all England and Wales closed at 114*s.* 5*d.*; those for November, at 123*s.* 6*d.*, and for December, at 137*s.*[23] It cannot be doubted that this depressing condition had been caused by the failure of the harvest. It would be wrong, however, to insist upon its being the only or even the most important cause. For convenience these factors may be grouped under certain domestic and foreign happenings. Under the head of domestic occurrences, it should be noted that the Government, by untimely utterances and actions, had stampeded public opinion so as to make it fearful of the future. "From the best information that can be obtained of the state of this year's crop throughout the Kingdom," wrote Portland, "I am sorry to state that according to the most sanguine estimation, the produce of it is not likely to amount to more than 3/4ths of an average crop."[24] Similar

[22] B. T., 1: 18, Dundas to Liverpool, July 10, 1800: see also H. O., 42: 51, Banks to Liverpool, Sept. 11, 1800; Add MSS., 35128 Lord Carrington to A. Young, July 25, 1800; and *Letters and Papers of Charles, Lord Barham,* III: 14, *Publications of the Navy Records Society,* vol. XXXIX, 1911, for optimistic reports, which unfortunately proved untrue.

[23] *London Gazette.* Unless otherwise stated, prices quoted are for wheat.

[24] H. O., 42: 51, Portland to Marlborough, Sept. 29, 1800. Shortly after the Home Office asked the Established Church to inquire through its clergy as to the state of the harvest, and to make a report before the meeting of Parliament. The replies indicated that the crop was below the average: see H. O., 42: 52. The Board of Trade made a similar investigation during September and October, and found conditions very

letters were sent broadcast over the island, the baneful effect of which was as evident as it was astonishing. "Publication of your letter has caused an advance of 5/ per bushel in wheat and flour. Your Grace meant well but when you reported that the crop was scarce, how else could people take it." Another critic said that these letters sounded "the dreadful alarm of probable famine."[25] At the same time that Portland was casting gloom over the minds of many by these ill-advised statements, the Government issued a proclamation providing for the suppression of riots and for the protection of the corn-factors, which, though conceived in the hope of instilling confidence, was nevertheless interpreted by many to be proof of a scarcity.[26]

Another force that worked most potently in creating these tales and prices was the foreign situation. It will be recalled that during the late summer months of 1800 an acute crisis had grown between the Baltic powers and Britain. Certain overt acts caused the formation of the Armed Neutrality, which was immediately followed by the Russian Embargo of November 18, 1800, and by the stoppage of trade with the Baltic ports. The press and Commons joined in a bitter attack upon the Government for embarking upon so dangerous a foreign policy at a time when the nation was actually dependent upon these states for most of its corn.[27] Besides the Armed Neutrality, one

---

unfavorable: see B. T., 6: 139. See also *Windham Papers,* II: 161; *Dyott's Diary* (London, Constable, 1907), I: 140; *Farmer's Mag.,* I: 445, 461; and *Monthly Mag.,* X: 364.

[25] H. O., 42: 52, Anonymous to Portland, Oct. 29, 1800, I. Meanwell to Auckland, Oct. 26, 1800: see also Consular Despatches, Bristol, Oct. 10, 1800; *Parl. Hist.,* XXXV: 518–519; and *Monthly Mag.,* X: 364.

[26] P. C. Reg., Sept. 18, 1800. In conjunction with this set of causes one should note that the fall in prices during July had been too rapid, and that the importers had withheld supplies so as to obtain higher prices, and, finally, that speculation had done much to stimulate the market.

[27] Martens, G. F., *Recueil des Principaux Traités d'Alliance, de Paix, etc.,* VII: 153, 155, 236; Scott, J. B., *The Armed Neutralities of 1780 and 1800,* pp. 17, 18, 66; and Monod, G. W., *Documentary History of the Armed Neutralities* (University of London Press, 1919). See also Consular Despatches, Bristol, Dec. 17, 1800; *Parl. Hist.,* XXXV: 608–609, 652, 695; and below, pp. 128–130, for a discussion of the operation of the Armed Neutrality.

should not overlook the war with France.[28] As a result of these domestic and foreign causes, the partial failure of the crops, the overhasty and unguarded utterances of the Government, the French war, and the Armed Neutrality, corn prices rose to unheard-of heights.

Out of this unfortunate situation there grew signs which served to convince many of an actual scarcity. These were the wide use of substitutes, the public and private acts of charity, and, what was more alarming, the numerous riots that took place in the various parts of the kingdom. The practice of retrenchment had been adopted the year before. This was now continued, and usually consisted in decreasing the quantity of flour used in the making of bread, of establishing wheatless days and meals, and of limiting the use of pastries, buns and fine cakes. Other methods adopted tended to increase the consumption of fish, together with potatoes and other vegetables. The nation-wide approval of this form of substitute was urged by the Government, Church and Press.[29] The numerous and active soup-houses, together with voluntary gifts, gave still another form of relief.[30] King, the American agent at London, remarked in a letter to his Government, that were it not for the soup-houses, the vigor of the administration would be scarcely able to check public disturbances.[31] Charity, however, proved to be of little value.

Early in February and throughout the remainder of the year, riots broke out in practically every part of England.[32] At Romsey the distress and the tendency to riot became so strong

[28] See pp. 30–31.

[29] See p. 10. "Vestry Minutes, Marylebone (Middlesex)" Dec. 13, 1800, quoted by Webb, S. and B., "The Assize of Bread," in *Economic Journal,* XIV: 213; see also *Monthly Mag.,* IX: 97, 192, 310, 501, 609, XI: 79; *Anti-Jacobin Rev.,* V: 238–239; *British Mag.,* II: 446; *Scott's Mag.,* LXIII: 175; Wilberforce, R. I. and S., *Correspondence of Wilberforce,* III: 4–5; and "Report of the Manuscripts of J. B. Fortescue, Esq., preserved at Dropmore," in *Historical Manuscripts Commission,* VII: 23.

[30] *Ibid.* See also H. O., 42: 48, Monckton to Portland, Dec. 11, 1799, and H. O., 42: 49, 50.

[31] *Life and Correspondence of R. King.,* III: 198.

[32] The numerous bundles of the Home Office for these years indicate the serious attention given to this matter.

that the local officers were concerned as to the future. Especially was this true when the following notice made its appearance:[33]

DEATH TO TAKE THIS DOWN.
TAKE NOTICE.

Bakers and Bigge Donns
and beware of fire and tonges
if you do not lower the bread
you will soon lose your blood

We dont care for your Volunteers
that will not put us in any fear
we will soon put the bakehouse in
one fire
if you dont lower it to our desire

and this is sined by, we just one and twenty.

At Bath a poster announced: " Peace and Large Bread or a King without a Head." [34] At Birmingham and Nottingham the people used force to gain their ends. So serious did the affair become that the military was called upon to keep order, which it did only after several brisk encounters with the rioters. In London angry and hungry throngs paraded the streets demanding immediate relief. " Inflammatory " notices calling upon the people to take steps against a " set of mercenary slaves and government hirelings " made their appearance over night. Another proclaimed: " Bread or Blood. . . . Have not Frenchman shewn you a pattern to fight for liberty? " [35] Throughout the country the glare of burning stacks and bakehouses threw a vivid color over an exhausted nation.[36]

The problem seems to have been aggravated by the presence of ill-disposed persons who were bent upon taking this occasion

[33] H. O., 42: 49, Latham to Portland, Feb. 26, 1800; a copy of this poster is found in *Monthly Mag.*, IX: 201.

[34] H. O., 42: 49, George to Portland, March 16, 1800.

[35] H. O., 42: 51, Combe to Portland, Sept. 14, 17, 18, 22, 1800; *Commercial and Agricultural Mag.*, II: 372, III: 231; *European Mag.*, XXXVIII: 236–237, 303–304; *Annual Register*, 1800, p. 212; *Windham Papers*, II: 161; and *Report of Cases Argued and Determined in the Court of the King's Bench*, I East, 616, 617.

[36] H. O., 42: 49, 50. See H. O., 47: 25, J. Mansfield to Portland, Jan. 27, 1801, and a letter from the aldermen and mayor of Nottingham to Portland, Michaelmas, 1800, for petitions asking for pardon for persons convicted of engaging in food riots: see also *Scott's Mag.*, LXII: 139, 359, 644; *Monthly Mag.*, X: 287, 292; *Memoirs of the Life of Sir Samuel Romilly*, II: 73; and *Life and Correspondence of R. King*, III: 234.

as a fitting opportunity to embarrass the administration. Although the great majority of these were probably English, there were a few French agents whose presence gave to the affair a more significant aspect. The reported organization of revolutionary societies, with memberships supposed to be in the thousands, is further proof of the seriousness of the movement.[37] From Wilford, near Nottingham, the news reached the Home Office that "the persons who meet together are rank Jacobins and the scarcity of grain is merely a pretext. They cry out for a Revolution, and after the French fashion date their days of liberty from the commencement of these riots."[38] Not to stop to seek the truth of these stories, the fact remains that the rumor of French agents and propaganda daily gained strength, and must, therefore, be viewed as one of the contributing forces that caused these riots.

In an attempt to stop all disturbances growing out of the scarcity, the Government published in the *Gazette* an offer of reward and pardon for each instance or threat of violence. The extent to which this plan worked may well be questioned. Portland declared: "I must admit that I do not recollect an instance of any discovery having been effected by the offer of reward and pardon."[39] The insertion of this notice, however, must have withheld many from committing acts of violence. At times the Government actually used force to break up these riots. A more telling method consisted in the local authorities guaranteeing security and indemnity to those who might bring their goods to market. In every instance noted, these riots were put down without any great damage or loss.[40]

During this period — December, 1799, to November, 1800 — the export of corn and rice, except for enumerated purposes, was

[37] H. O., 42: 49, Anonymous to Lord Elden, March 31, 1800.

[38] H. O., 42: 51, Sam'l Smith to King, Sept. 16, 1800; also H. O., 42: 48, Monckton to Portland, Dec. 11, 1799.

[39] H. O., 43: 12, Portland to Wm. Baker, Aug. 24, 1800.

[40] The Crown issued, Sept. 18, 1800, a proclamation forbidding riots, and offering help to farmers and corn-factors in the marketing of their corn: see P. C. Reg., 155; and also H. O., 42: 49, Circular letter to the Lord Lieutenants, March 3, 1800, and H. O., 42: 51, Portland to Hicks, and others, Sept. 9, 12, 1800.

forbidden, and the import of corn was allowed duty free.[41] In order to stimulate the latter trade a series of measures were adopted. Neutrals were allowed to import, in any ship other than those owned by the enemy, corn from any country, even from France. British merchants, upon licence, were given the same privilege.[42] In answer, furthermore, to private petitions for governmental help in obtaining supplies, the Ministry instructed the British agents in the Barbary states to use their influence with the native rulers and traders to aid in the export of corn. Others sought similar facilities in Italy, Sicily and the Baltic, and gained assistance in one form or another. British consuls in the United States received instructions to further the grain trade to England by granting licences to ships of neutral states.[43] More adventurous persons obtained permission to live in France and to undertake a licenced trade in corn.[44]

The Government was also approached by the Board of Agriculture with the proposal that rice be imported from India. Acting either as a result of this or upon independent thought, the Ministry contracted with the East India Company for the entrance of rice duty free. Late in August, orders were sent to India.[45] Finally, by way of economy, Rose, vice-president of the

[41] See p. 5, note 14.

[42] B. T., 5: 11, Dec. 12, 1799: see also Chapter VI.

[43] B. T., 5: 11, Feb. 24, May 6, 1800; B. T., 1: 18, Feb. 28, 1800; H. O., 43: 11, Fawkener to King, Feb. 26, 1800: see also Chapter VII, and *Memoirs and Correspondence of Viscount Castlereagh*, III: 246.

[44] P. C. Reg., 154, and *Correspondance de Napoléon Ier*, No. 4436.

[45] Board of Agriculture, Minutes, June 3, 1800, April 5, 1803; *Life and Correspondence of the Right Hon. Henry Addington, First Viscount Sidmouth*, I: 264–265; *Monthly Mag.*, X: 488; B. T., 1: 18, Dundas to Liverpool, July 10, 1800. It is possible that the export of rice was forbidden during the passage of the bill: see p. 20. It is interesting to note, in view of the lateness of the season when the orders were sent to India (the contract with the company had been made before June) and the expiration of the rice bounty, Oct. 2, 1800, that very little rice was obtained. From necessity, the bounty was renewed in November and a more liberal grant made to the company. As a result over 20,000 tons of rice were imported — but only after the harvest of 1801 — becoming, therefore, a drug on the market. The Government, moreover, was obligated to pay a heavy bounty. Had the Ministry adopted the plan proposed by the Board of Agriculture early in 1800, these unfortunate results might have been avoided.

Board of Trade, persuaded most of the starch-makers and the distillers in and about London to refrain from using grain for the time being, and gained their support for the introduction of a bill for the better conduct of their industry.[46]

Notwithstanding these various activities, the extensive imports, and the national economy, the situation became very serious. Early in October, Pitt and Rose agreed that Parliament should be called so that "if no effectual measure can be taken for the relief of the country with respect to the supply of corn, or to lessen the price, that the country may at least see the subject has not been neglected."[47] Shortly after, it was agreed to call Parliament for November 11, 1800. The renewal of the starch, distillery and rice acts constituted one of the proposals that Pitt intended to submit to Parliament.[48] Other features of his program included the use of Swedish herring, the mixing of barley and wheat in the making of bread, and an increase in imports.[49]

As might be expected, this program gave the King the theme for his address to Parliament. The Crown, moreover, suggested severe punishments for all who had maliciously tampered with the market for private gain. Parliament replied by the introduction of a series of measures and by the appointment of a select committee to consider the causes for the scarcity and the high price of provisions.[50]

Within a short time this committee made several reports. The general shortage of the wheat crop was frankly admitted; while importation and economy were suggested as remedies for the

[46] *The Diaries and Correspondence of the Right Hon. George Rose,* I: 283–285. It is interesting to note that Pitt and Grenville held different ideas of the Corn Laws. Grenville was in favor of free trade, while Pitt was opposed: see Stanhope, Earl, *Life of William Pitt,* III: 247–248.

[47] *The Diaries . . . of . . . Rose,* I: 281–283; *Life . . . of . . . Sidmouth,* I: 264–265.

[48] *Ibid., Commercial and Agricultural Mag.,* III: 302–303.

[49] *Life . . . of . . . Sidmouth,* I: 264–265; *Dropmore Papers,* VI: 357–358, 371–372.

[50] *Commons' Journal,* 55: 796, 797, 802–803; *Lords' Journal,* XLII: 659. Even before Parliament had been called, interest had become intense throughout the island: see Stanhope, Earl, *Life of Pitt,* Appendix xxi; *Gentleman's Mag.,* LXX: 998; *European Mag.,* XXXVIII: 303-304.

situation. It was believed that the annual consumption in the kingdom amounted to 7,000,000 quarters of wheat. To meet this there was the harvest of 5,000,000 quarters; the remainder, therefore, would have to be gained from foreign sources. Little dependence was placed upon the continent in view of the unsettled state of affairs. From the United States, however, 580,000 quarters might be expected, as well as 30,000 from Canada. Adding to this the supposed import of 170,000 quarters since October there still remained 1,200,000 quarters to be obtained from other sources. To meet this deficit, it was hoped that the prohibition of the use of wheat in the starch and distillery concerns would produce 400,000 quarters, that the use of coarse meal and rice would yield 1,030,000 quarters, and that retrenchment would give 300,000 quarters. The increased use of fish was another form of relief suggested.[51]

The reports of the Lord's Committee covered practically the same general ground. Its analysis of the charge that speculation and monopoly had caused the nation-wide distress deserves attention. It seems that a din of discordant voices had arisen from the press and pulpit, and from private individuals accusing the corn-factor and farmer of deliberate and selfish misuse of the market.[52] The cry of fraud and graft in our own day is sufficiently common for us to recognize it under the names it then took of forestalling and regrating. What was highly displeasing, therefore, to the Government, as well as to many others was that no less a person than Lord Chief Justice Kenyon appeared to accept every rumor as fact, and went about the country instructing grand juries accordingly.[53] Lord Grenville, commenting upon this, remarked: "I really think that all the nonsense into which some of our best disposed friends and many who ought to have known better have gone headlong upon the occasion of the scarcity — more formidable than the scarcity it-

[51] *First Series,* IX: 125–128.

[52] *Commons' Journal,* 55: 796; *European Mag.,* XXXVIII: 236–237; *Farmer's Mag.,* I: 446; *Commercial and Agricultural Mag.,* II: 175–180, 258–261.

[53] Malthus, Robert, *An Investigation of the Cause of the Present High Price of Provisions,* p. 3; *Annual Register,* 1800, pt. 2, p. 23.

self." [54] Pitt termed the statements of Lord Kenyon "dangerous notions," but did not wish to condemn publicly those who held these views. He was for soothing rather than for irritating public opinion, and believed that a temperate discussion would do much to appease the indiscriminate clamor.[55] On the other hand, Lord Kenyon, Thomas Erskine, who later became Lord Chief Justice, and a large share of the laboring element insisted by word and deed that the corn trade was in the hands of grafters, "mercenary slaves and government hirelings." In a letter to Kenyon, Erskine described the situation as it appeared to him: [56]

> There are now only great landlords (the farmers) and great merchants with great capitals, in lines which were not formerly considered as the occupations of merchants. They sweep the whole country before them, in the purchase of the necessaries of life and they command the markets. I have talked with Fox who thinks all this visionary (taught, I suppose in older days, by Burke) but who has not, in the least, convinced me.

Others were of the same belief. The Earl of Warwick thought that the sale of wheat was handled by "opulent men," and that "power at present certainly is lodged where it is much abused." [57] Prices, so wrote another, would be reduced only when the laws against forestalling were revived; that there had

[54] *Journal and Correspondence of Lord Auckland,* IV: 111–112.

[55] *Dropmore Papers,* VI: 371–372; Stanhope, Earl, *Life of William Pitt,* III: 252–253; *The Manuscripts of the Earl of Lonsdale,* p. 149, *Historical Manuscripts Commission.* Arthur Young remarked in a letter to Mr. J. Symonds, Nov. 30, 1800: "Did not you rejoice with me that Sherman animadverted on those judges who thundered their anathemas against forestallers, etc.?": see Add. MSS., 35128. See *Commercial and Agricultural Mag.,* III: 208, for the comment that "a judge's robe conveys unto the wearer an infallible knowledge of political economy." See also *Windham Papers,* II: 161.

[56] *The Manuscripts of Lord Kenyon,* pp. 554–555, *Historical Manuscripts Commission:* see also, Campbell, Lord J., *The Lives of the Chief Justices* (Boston, Estes and Lauriat, 1873), IV: 84–87.

[57] H. O., 42: 49, Warwick to Portland, Jan. 1, 1800: see also H. O., 42: 50, Bazley to Portland, June 23, 1800, and H. O., 42: 51, Mitchell and Folliott to Portland, Sept. 15, 23, 1800. For an opinion by the press, see *Anti-Jacobin Rev.,* VII: 236; *Agricultural Mag.,* II: 175–180; and also *Letters of Admiral of the Fleet, The Earl of St. Vincent,* I: 298, *Publications of the Navy Records Society,* vol. LV, 1922. For instances of reported convictions for regrating, see *Commercial and Agricultural Mag.,* II: 450, III: 65; *Monthly Mag.,* X: 371.

never been a scarcity, but that thousands of quarters had been deliberately destroyed so as to keep prices high.[58]

It was only after careful study of this and other evidence that the Lords' Committee stated that "they have not been able to trace, in any one instance, any thing more than such suspicions and vague reports as usually prevail in times of scarcity;" that they "do not take upon them to determine that no abuses have been in any instance committed by individuals; but in the trade at large they have hitherto perceived no injurious system to prevail."[59] Comber, in his tract the *Inquiry,* voiced the same idea and warmly applauded the findings of the committee. Malthus was of the same opinion, and Sidney Smith stated: "This absurdity of attributing the high price of corn to the combinations of farmers and the dealings of middle-men was the common nonsense in the days of my youth. I remember when ten judges out of twelve laid down this doctrine in their charges to the various grand juries on their circuits."[60] In a similar strain Lord Holland remarked: "In this admiration of a mistaken and pernicious system, I believe that he [Kenyon] was sincere, for on such matters he was ignorant in the extreme."[61]

In arriving at a conclusion, even at this late date, one has to be very cautious. No one can examine the Home Office Papers and escape the conviction that in many instances unwarranted distress was felt by scores of unfortunate persons. That there was truth in the general charge of forestalling and regrating is very evident. But in "the trade at large," the fact remains that private manipulation could not have worked any permanent effect upon the price of corn. Especially does this seem to be

[58] B. T., 1: 19, Parkes to the Board of Trade, Nov. 12, 1800: see also *Agicultural Mag.,* II: 175–180. Wilberforce wrote in his diary that the Government seemed unable to protect the poor from the sharpers: *Correspondence of Wilberforce,* III: 11.

[59] Second Report, Lords' Committee, to be found in *Parl. Hist.,* XXXV: 840–854.

[60] Quoted by Campbell, Lord., *op. cit.,* IV: 87; Malthus, Robert, *op. cit.,* pp. 1–5. By 12 Geo. 3, c. 71, the various laws dealing with forestalling, etc., had been repealed; Lord Kenyon prosecuted on the basis of Common Law.

[61] Holland, Lord, *Memoirs of the Whig Party* (London, Longmans, 1852–1854), II: 167.

true when one considers the unprecedented imports that were then in progress, the general discredit that was placed upon these charges, and above all, the many causes that worked to further high prices.

In an attempt to lower these prices, the Crown issued a proclamation urging economy in the use of grain, and frugality in the consumption of oats by the Government horses.[62] Parliament, in the meantime, had been investigating the causes for these high prices. In all, the Commons' Committee made six reports before Christmas, and that of the Lords made two.[63] The thoroughness of these reports indicates in part the enormous labor of the committees. Wilberforce stated: "I have not for one morning omitted to take my place at the committee, and that cuts such a solid lump out of the day, as to leave the rest composed but of fragments." [64]

As a result of the recommendations of these committees, Parliament enacted a series of measures. The export of rice was forbidden, the power of the Crown over the export and the import of corn was extended, and the starch, stale bread and distillery acts of the previous session were continued. Also, bounties were granted on all imported corn and rice,[65] a table of assize was established, and the free import of Swedish herring was permitted, as well as of fish in general from certain of the British North American colonies. Finally, the manufacture of fine flour from wheat and the making of bread from fine wheat flour were forbidden.[66]

[62] P. C. Reg., 155, Dec. 3, 1800; *Commons' Journal,* 55: 882, 890: see also *Life and Correspondence of R. King,* III: 345.

[63] *First Series,* IX: 65–128; *Parl. Hist.,* XXXV: 778–786, 840–854.

[64] *Correspondence of Wilberforce,* II: 384.

[65] 41 Geo. 3, c. 10, which renewed in part the acts of 1800: see note 19, and also 41 Geo. 3, cc. 13, 34 (U. K.). The evident purpose of a bounty was to increase imports, and the determining figure at which the bounty operated served as a guaranty to the importer. For facts as to the working of these bounties see B. T., 5: 12, Oct. 3, 24, 29, and all of Nov., 1800; B. T., 6: 139, Memo. Oct. 21, 1800; F. O., 5: 33, Bond to Grenville, March 31, 1801; and *Commons' Journal,* 63: 845.

[66] 41 Geo. 3, cc. 1, 2, 3, 5, 10, 11, 12, 16, 17, 18, 19. It was suggested that the upholsterers, paperhangers, printers, and bookbinders be forbidden to use flour: see *Anti-Jacobin Rev.,* VII: 355; and also *Dropmore Papers,* VI: 406, for Pitt's attitude towards the *Assize Act.*

From the adjournment of Parliament to its meeting in February, 1801, the agricultural situation failed to improve. In spite of heavy imports, the wide use of substitutes and the continued activities of the soup-houses, the weekly average for all England and Wales rose from 137*s.* to 144*s.* 10*d.*[67] Rioting, furthermore, continued to annoy the Government.[68] To the scourge of war, the *Monthly Magazine* stated, was now added that of famine at home, which, if not caused by the war, had been greatly increased by reason of the fact that it shut off the English from almost every source of relief.[69]

Once more Parliament turned its energies to the problem. A select committee of the Commons, after a period of over four months, made seven reports. The recommendations of these reports were: the repeal of the act forbidding the making of flour from wheat; the offering of premiums for the cultivation of potatoes; the granting of bounties on all corn, pulse, flour and rice imported into Ireland; the appropriation of certain sums for the relief of the poor and more able administration of the London corn market.[70] After much discussion Parliament passed bills touching the first three of these recommendations.[71] Further, extra bounties were granted on American wheat, the distillation of spirits from corn was forbidden in Ireland, and ships laden with grain from the East Indies were allowed to enter Irish ports.[72]

This legislation dealing with Ireland had been caused by a shortage of the food supplies in that island. As early as March the situation had become so serious as to cause a proclamation

[67] *London Gazette.* At Edinburgh the Quakers imported corn, and kept soup-houses at their own expense: see *Scott's Mag.*, LXII: 845; *Parl. Hist.*, XXXV: 870; *Farmer's Mag.*, II: 80, 88–91, 95, 97, 108–109; *European Mag.*, XXXIX: 23; *British Mag.*, II: 446. At High Wycombe Lord Carrington was reported to have erected a public oven where rice pudding was sold at a penny a pound: see *Monthly Mag.*, X: 557.

[68] See also the Home Office Papers; *Diary and Correspondence of Charles Abbott,* I: 263; and the *Life . . . of . . . Sidmouth,* I: 364, 469–470.

[69] *Monthly Mag.*, XI: 71.

[70] *First Series,* IX: 129–159.

[71] 41 Geo. 3 (U. K.), cc. 1, 2, 20, 34, 92.

[72] 41 Geo. 3 (U. K.), cc. 13, 16, 37.

forbidding the export of rice, Indian corn and flour from Ireland.[73]

In the meantime the House of Lords had appointed a committee to investigate the condition of the corn market and report on the advisability of a new enclosure act. The occasion, in part, for this committee had been caused by almost a universal demand throughout the island for a more effective enclosure act. Local agricultural societies, the press, private individuals and county juries had been sponsoring this proposal for some time.[74] The Committee of the Lords reflected this sentiment by reporting, early in May, that the most effective way of avoiding another scarcity was the further enclosing of commons and waste lands.[75] The shortage of the harvests of 1799 and 1800 showed the vital need for a new and more comprehensive law. Parliament replied by passing the *General Enclosure Act* of 1801.

By the terms of this act much that had been harmful before was removed. The many fees, the unnecessary procedure, and the delay, were swept aside by the mere insertion of the clauses of the act of 1801 in any individual bill. The act, however, had a serious defect in that it dealt chiefly with common lands.[76]

[73] *Commons' Journal,* 56: 288; 41 Geo. 3 (U. K.), c. 36; fish and all provisions whatsoever might be imported duty free by this act.

[74] Early in March, 1800, the County of York had resolved that the only way of overcoming the shortage of corn was by further cultivation. Copies of this resolution were sent by the Board of Agriculture to the various counties: see Minutes, Board of Agriculture, May 27, June 26, 1800, March 17, 1801. The Grand Jury of Herefordshire adopted a series of resolutions similar to those of the County of York: see *Monthly Mag.,* IX: 406.

[75] *Lords' Journal,* XLIII: 180; see also *Monthly Mag.,* IX: 406; *Commercial and Agricultural Mag.,* III: 329–330; *Annals of Agriculture,* XXXV: 69–73. It is not my purpose to discuss the question as to whether the old system of common and open field cultivation was better than that created by the act of 1801; nor shall I examine the methods used in the passing of the many individual enclosure bills, or the results that followed. These and many other problems, such as the Speenhamland System, belong to other studies. My interest is given solely to the increase in arable land and the increase that followed in production.

[76] 41 Geo. 3 (U. K.), c. 109. Open fields were left for later legislation: see 6 and 7 Wm. 4, c. 115; 8 and 9 Vic., c. 118. For further facts see Hunter, Sir Robert, "Movement for the Inclosure and Preservation of

In spite of this no less than 300,413 acres were brought into cultivation within a year. Before the close of the Napoleonic era a total of 1,483 acts enclosed about a million acres. The importance of this increased acreage is apparent when one recalls the general European situation and the economic conditions existing in Great Britain as a result of the Industrial Revolution.

The *Enclosure Act*, although it brought about an immediate increase in acreage, was not directly responsible for the drop in prices that took place during the spring of 1801.[77] A favorable summer and fall brought a further decline; wheat, which had averaged on April 25 148*s.* 6*d.*, was listed on November 28 at 75*s.* 2*d.* This was high when compared with 47*s.* 11*d.*, the average for November, 1798.[78] The knowledge of these facts changed what otherwise might have been undue confidence into caution — a desire to prevent if possible another food shortage. Parliament reflected this feeling by the conservative way in which it dealt with the situation. The power of the Crown over the corn trade was extended for a time, and distillation from corn was forbidden in Scotland and Ireland. On the other hand the *Stale Bread Act* was repealed.[79]

It is to be noted that distillation was not forbidden in England. At once many petitions were presented to Parliament asking for an extension of this act to England. It was felt by the petitioners that agricultural conditions demanded the con-

---

Open Lands," in *Royal Statistical Society,* 1897, pp. 360–437; Marshall, Wm., *Review of the Reports of the Board of Agriculture* (York, 1808–1817). Porter, G. R., *Progress of the Nation* (London, Meuthen and Co., 1912), contains a chart showing the number of acres enclosed. Slater, G., *The English Peasantry* (London, Constable, 1907), furnishes a table of common fields enclosed by private bills. See also Gonner, E. C. K., *Common Land and Inclosure* (London, Macmillan, 1912), pp. 56–69.

[77] *Commons' Journal,* 57: 3–4; *Farmer's Mag.,* II: 454–455; *European Mag.,* XL: 236; *Life and Correspondence of R. King,* III: 473; *Monthly Mag.,* XI: 104; 287–288, 379, 564, XI: 87, 183, 379. As early as January the prospects had appeared favorable; see *Farmer's Mag.,* II: 84, 340; and also Add. MSS., 33108, ff. 407–408.

[78] *First Series,* IX: 184, and *London Gazette,* contain weekly averages for all England and Wales. See also Consular Despatches, Bristol, July 10, Aug. 27, Sept. 5, 1801.

[79] 42 Geo. 3, cc. 4, 5, 13, 15.

servation of the grain used by the distilleries. Parliament, however, denied the request on the ground that conditions in England did not warrant such a step.[80] It was for exactly the opposite reason that distillation was forbidden in Ireland, where a serious shortage of corn and potatoes existed.[81] Neither Parliament nor the Ministry gave any attention to the Irish situation until March, 1802, when a committee was appointed to consider the condition of the corn trade between Great Britain and Ireland.[82] According to the recent *Act of Union,* free trade had been established between the two islands. Unfortunately, this did not touch the corn trade, the conduct of which had been left for future action.[83] After some thought, the Committee decided to change this arrangment and submitted a bill to that effect. The new measure provided for trade in corn, subject to a schedule of rates which was dependent upon the average prices in both islands.[84]

It will be recalled that in May, 1802, the much-mooted peace with France had been settled. The question at once presents itself: To what extent, if any, did the agricultural situation influence the Ministry in arriving at peace? Evidence with regard to this is ample. One need only review the material already presented to realize that the Government had been seriously taxed in the conduct of the war by the state of the nation's agriculture. A shortage in the home production, riots of a frequent and serious nature, a stoppage of the foreign supply, and an era of high prices had argued constantly for peace.

Notwithstanding these facts, the Pitt Ministry held that the

[80] *Commons' Journal,* 57: 60, 64, 65, 70, 73, 75, 76; *Monthly Mag.,* XII: 475; *Life . . . of . . . Sidmouth,* I: 475–476.

[81] *Commons' Journal,* 56: 288, 76: 1032; Customs, I: 267, Nov. 12, 1799; *Memoirs . . . of . . . Castlereagh . . .* III: 392, IV: 15, 67, 78; *Life and Correspondence of Cornwallis,* III: 295; *Diary . . . of . . . Abbott,* I: 359–360.

[82] *Parl. Hist.,* XXXVI: 360–364; *Commons' Journal,* 57: 233. See *Diary . . . of . . . Abbott,* I: 377–379, for a possible explanation of the conduct of the Ministry in postponing action for so long a time: see also *Monthly Mag.,* XI: 286; Add. MSS., 33108, ff. 9.

[83] 39 and 40 Geo. 3, c. 67; see 40 Geo. 3, c. 38 (Irish), and *First Series,* IX: 162.

[84] 42 Geo. 3, c. 35, continued by 43 Geo. 3, cc. 14, 78, to July 1, 1804.

war had not caused the high prices. It has been insisted "that the scarcity was intimately connected with the war; but whatever speculative reasoners might contend, the evidence of facts was incontrovertibly against their system . . . [as] war had a tendency to make corn cheaper. . . ." This form of argument failed to convince the mass of the people, who had staunch defenders in the Commons. Among these was Sir Francis Burdett who "wished to point out the cause of the present distress and famine, and he had no difficulty in doing it. He had not far to look for it. It stared him in the face (looking at Mr. Pitt). It was seated on the treasury bench."[85]

Outside of Parliament the cry for peace was much greater. Thomas Grenville, in a letter to his brother, October 9, 1800, wrote: "The scarcity of bread and consequent distress of the poor, if it continues, will I believe, force you whether you will or no to make your peace with France."[86] The *Monthly Magazine* stated: "As the humane and laudable policy therefore, of *starving* the French nation cannot be realized, perhaps it would be found policy to try to prevent our own people from starving by making Peace."[87] The American consul at Bristol reported: "I . . . much fear what I have long apprehended that the war will spread still wider, unless indeed severe want of provisions should compel this Government to make peace."[88] "Let us have peace," remarked a correspondent to Auckland, "and within a month there will be reasonable prices and supplies."[89]

In the light of this evidence, it would be strange indeed if the minds of the ministers were not moved to bring to a close a war which had been extremely costly, which had been severely

[85] *Parl. Hist.*, XXXV: 504, 508, 516–517, 532–533, 539, 698. In the Lords, a motion for peace, although voted down, had brought forth the remark: "Peace is essential to diminish the present Scarcity of Corn, for that although Scarcity may be produced by scanty Crops, yet that the Danger of impending famine is chiefly to be attributed to the War: " see *Lords' Journal*, XLII: 378.

[86] *Dropmore Papers*, VI: 343–344.

[87] *Ibid.; Monthly Mag.*, X: 364–365, XI: 185.

[88] Consular Despatches, Bristol, Dec. 17, 1800; see also Melville, Lewis, *Life and Letters of William Cobbett,* I: 212, and *Parl. Hist.*, XXXV: 220.

[89] H. O., 42: 52, I. Meanwell to Auckland, Oct. 26, 1800.

criticized within and without Parliament, and which was slowly but inevitably bringing the country to a point of exhaustion. In the process of this exhaustion the scarcity and the high prices must have operated to a great extent, and in that way have furthered the cause of peace.

CHAPTER III

THE CORN LAWS OF 1804 AND 1805

Favorable agricultural conditions in 1802 and 1803 — The depression of 1804 — The landed classes denounce the existing Corn Laws — The discussions in Parliament — The passage of the Act of 1804 — The harvest failure of 1804 — Further protection is demanded by the agriculturists — The Corn Law of 1805.

WHEN Parliament reassembled in November of 1802, the agricultural situation had become greatly improved. The Crown characterized the harvest as "the bounty of Divine Providence."[1] Murray, the American consul at Liverpool, reported: "The crops in general throughout the United Kingdom are so uncommonly abundant that foreign wheat and flour are become a drug."[2] The market also reflected this outlook; wheat, which in 1801 had averaged in Great Britain 115*s.* 11*d.*, now stood at 67*s.* 9*d.* This sharp decline had caused a marked decrease in imports, wheat alone registering a 50 per cent drop.

Parliament could well afford to allow much of the former legislation to expire. It renewed, however, the power of the Crown and the Lord Lieutenant over the corn trade, and extended until July, 1804, the acts that ordered the movement of grain between Great Britain and Ireland.[3] The passage of

[1] *Commons' Journal,* 58: 10. Similar expressions may be found in *Farmer's Mag.,* I: 102; *Commercial and Agricultural Mag.,* VII: 146, 228; *Monthly Mag.,* XIV: 197, 372.

[2] Consular Despatches, Liverpool, Sept. 5, 28, 1802: see also *idem.,* Bristol, March 20, May 3, July 24, Sept. 13, 1802.

[3] 43 Geo. 3, cc. 12, 13, 14, 78. The trade to the Channel Islands, heretofore enjoyed by Southampton, was thrown open to all English ports: see 43 Geo. 3, c. 105; 45 Geo. 3, c. 68. By 43 Geo. 3, c. 68, a small ad valorem duty was placed on the export of all corn except that to the places mentioned in the act of 1791. The amount of this duty rose during the period covered by this study: see *Accounts and Papers,* 1898, vol. 34, p. 242.

these measures was accompanied by little discussion. The agricultural crisis of the previous year had become only a bitter memory, and the cry of hunger, so recently heard, was now silenced by the bursting granaries of a thankful people.

The harvest of the next year, while inferior in oats and beans, was described " as equalling if not exceeding an average." [4] The Corn Exchange in Mark Lane told the same story. When Parliament met in December, 1803, the weekly average price of wheat in England and Wales had fallen to 54*s*. 9*d*. Further decreases continued until March 3, 1804, when the price was 49*s*. 7*d*. A similar happy state of affairs existed in Scotland. In Ireland, however, a deficient potato crop had caused an unusual alarm. The Lord Lieutenant tried to help matters by prohibiting the distillation of spirits from oats and oatmeal, while Parliament assisted by passing an indemnity bill, making valid the action of the Lord Lieutenant, and by an act stopping the export and permitting the import of all corn.[5] These laws, as well as that which renewed the power of the Crown over the corn trade, were to last until March 25, 1804.[6]

In the meantime, this unfortunate state of agriculture spread to Great Britain. It was believed, especially in Norfolk and Suffolk, that this misfortune was due to the operation of the Corn Law of 1791. Petitions, accordingly, were presented early in 1804, asking for a revision of this Corn Law " upon a fair and permanent basis." [7] These petitions were referred, in time, to a select committee which made a report early in May, 1804.[8] The problem which had faced this committee had been to find a price which not only would stimulate production but which also would give to the producer a fair profit on his investment. It

[4] *Farmer's Mag.,* IV: 473, V: 102, 111; *Commercial and Agricultural Mag.,* IX: 130, 203.

[5] *Commons' Journal,* 59: 27; *Parl. Debates,* I: 1608; 44 Geo. 3, cc. 11, 12: see H. O., 43: 14, J. King to Fawkener, Oct. 18, 1803, for a copy of the Lord Lieutenant's proclamation.

[6] 44 Geo. 3, c. 4.

[7] *Commons' Journal,* 59: 83–84, 124, 187, 192. It was claimed, in view of the *Act of Union,* and the recent changes in the corn trade of Europe, that the act of 1791 was out of date.

[8] *Commons' Journal,* 59: 275: see *Monthly Mag.,* XVII: 311, 509.

was found, however, that the standard of prices as fixed by the law of 1791 was no longer a fair basis for regulating the traffic in corn, primarily because in the interim the cost of production had greatly increased. A new scale of prices seemed essential if consumers were to have a ready supply and if farmers were to have ample protection. According to the existing law of 1791, the export of wheat from Britain was to be stopped when the average price in any district was at or above 46*s.* The committee advised that this be raised to 52*s.*[9]

It was hoped that this recommendation, if adopted, would increase the quantity of domestic corn, and thus benefit both producer and consumer. Bounties were suggested as a further means of helping the farmer and of guarding his interests. As to import regulations, while no change in the rates was proposed, it was recommended that the scale of prices be radically modified. The committee also proposed, as a substitute for the existing plan, that the export and import trade of the maritime districts of England be governed by the average of the averages of these districts.[10] Certain other recommendations were made for the trade with Ireland.

And then, anticipating the arguments of a decade later, the committee declared that in former times the Corn Law had been framed so as to encourage export, which had resulted in a profitable revenue for the state and low prices for the consumer. Recently, a reversal in legislation had brought a shrinkage of exports, which robbed the state of a needed income and, what was more unfortunate, had increased importation. It was for exactly these reasons that the Committee had been led to suggest higher export and import schedules.[11]

It was not to be expected that everyone would praise this report. Doubtless the most obvious ground for complaint was to

[9] Other kinds of corn received similar advances. [10] See pp. 2–3.

[11] See *Parl. Pap.*, 1804, No. 96, for a copy of this report. The committee also questioned the advantage of giving any power to the Crown over the corn trade on the ground that an ill-advised use of this power would stop the agricultural growth of the country. No change, however, in this respect was to be made until the other recommendations of the report were accepted.

be found in the clauses dealing with the Irish trade. In sharp contrast to the existing system,[12] the Committee had proposed to increase the import rates in a fashion which would place both Irish and foreign corn practically on the same footing. Naturally, the Irish, who benefited from the preference which they enjoyed over foreigners in the corn trade to Great Britain, protested most loudly against the proposal of the Committee.[13] It was also held by the landed classes of Ireland that the new arrangement would react most unfavorably upon the agricultural development of Ireland.[14]

This defect in the report may account for its recommitment in June, 1804.[15] In less than a week a second report appeared.[16] With but two important exceptions this report followed the lines set down in the earlier one.[17] The question of the Irish trade was seemingly settled by dropping Ireland out of the proposed bill. Import from Ireland, therefore, was to be conducted as it then existed, namely as set down by 42 Geo. 3, c. 35, which gave to the Irish a distinct advantage over foreigners.[18] A new plan for the determination of prices, however, was made. The first report had proposed that the average of the averages of the maritime counties should regulate the English trade. It was now suggested that the scheme adopted by the act of 1791 be continued, and that the duties on foreign corn be governed by the average price of each district according to the proposed table of prices.

The opinions expressed in these reports seem sound from the point of view of the producer, not, however, from that of the consumer. For what cared the latter about increased acreage and supply if the result was to be a higher price? To him, foreign corn was as wholesome and was, moreover, much cheaper. According to the existing law, foreign wheat paid a duty of 24*s.*

[12] See 42 Geo. 3, c. 35.

[13] See Appendix No. 3.

[14] *Commons' Journal,* 59: 323, 333, 338, 350, 356.

[15] Of late the Irish trade had become of greater importance: see Appendix No. 8, and Consular Despatches, Falmouth, July 7, 1804.

[16] *Commons' Journal,* 59: 328, 341–343, and *Parl. Pap.,* 1804, No. 127.

[17] A slight difference in the import and export rates for barley, rye, pease and beans existed between these reports.

[18] *Commons' Journal,* 59: 342: see also 44 Geo. 3, cc. 65, 89.

3*d.*, if the price at the port of importation was under 50*s.*, and a duty of 6*d.*, if the price was at 63*s.* Under the proposed bill a duty of 24*s.* 3*d.* was to be paid whenever the price was under 63*s.*[19] Similar advances were suggested for the other kinds of corn. Whether the proposed act would increase the domestic supply or not was problematic, even though it was reasonably certain. In any event, an increase would only temporarily postpone the inevitable — increased imports, for England could not then, and can not now, be both an industrial and an agricultural state.

Late in June a bill embodying this report, modified by several amendments, was introduced in the Commons. After much discussion the measure was passed and sent to the Lords,[20] where an active opposition developed, led chiefly by the Earl of Stanhope. The striking answers of Lord Hawkesbury, however, insured the success of the bill, which after some slight change was returned to the Commons. It seems that the bill as it passed the Commons had provided that the prices should be determined by the joint prices of England and Ireland. The Lords, however, struck out Ireland. The Commons interpreted this as an attack upon its constitutional power over financial measures, and refused to accept the bill. A new measure, shorn of this objectionable feature, was introduced and passed.[21] The new law provided that the average of the averages of the English districts was to govern the trade of England, and that the average of the Scottish districts was to control the trade of Scotland. It also considerably raised the standard of prices for both import and export.[22]

Hardly had this measure passed before an upward trend appeared in the price of corn.[23] The agitation of the past two

[19] To these duties should be added the increases that had been made since 1791, for which see Appendix No. 3. Since the report did not include these additions, I thought it better not to introduce them here.

[20] *Commons' Journal,* 59: 353, 356–357, 361–363, 392–393, 396. See *Parl. Debates,* II: 782, 957.

[21] *Parl. Debates,* II: 1073, 1132, 1134–1144; Stanhope, Earl, *Life of Pitt,* IV: 211.

[22] 44 Geo. 3, c. 109: see also Appendix No. 2. A 12½ per cent increase in the import duties was made by 44 Geo. 3, c. 53.

[23] See Appendix No. 5, and *London Gazette.*

months had disturbed the market. This had been followed by "blight, rain, and high winds."[24] The supply of 1803, which the nation had tried to stretch over until the new harvest, suddenly disappeared. Voices arose condemning the Government for interfering with the accustomed regulations by the passage of the recent act.[25] The *London Times* commented: [26]

> The Corn Bill is as yet imperfectly understood by the farming interest and possibly when its object and provisions are generally known it may operate in the way that those who proposed it intended. The public, erroneously perhaps, are however of the opinion and the more rational of those who are affected . . . think it would be full as well if that article had been exempted from all regulations and left to find its own level.

Although it was most certainly true that the discussion at Westminster had disturbed the market, and had encouraged speculation, the contention that the law itself had caused this marked increase could hardly have been true, as the measure in question did not operate until the middle of November.

The charge, however, that the "subsequent advances arose . . . from the unfavorable market and the apprehensions of a defective harvest" was one that was more in keeping with the facts.[27] This was the opinion held by several of the corn-factors of London, and by certain leading periodicals.[28] As might be expected these high prices invited importation. In August the *Farmer's Magazine* stated: "Importations from abroad, chiefly of wheat and oats, have . . . gone regularly forward, which substantiates in the most satisfactory way the doctrine uniformly maintained in this work respecting the dependence which Great Britain . . . must have upon foreign countries for a supply of corn." [29] Against this inrush of foreign corn and reports of

[24] Consular Despatches, Bristol, Aug. 29, 1804; *Farmer's Mag.*, V: 475; *Cobbett's Pol. Reg.*, VI: 236; Add. MSS., 35129, Lord Sheffield to A. Young, Sept. 2, 1804.

[25] *Cobbett's Pol. Reg.*, VI: 237–238.

[26] *London Times,* Nov. 10, 1804: see *Cobbett's Pol. Reg.*, VI: 237, 305.

[27] *Parl. Pap.*, 1805, No. 154, p. 8. In January, 1805, the Board of Agriculture discussed at some length the question of the harvest of 1804: see Board of Agriculture Papers, Jan. 22, Feb. 5, 1805.

[28] *Farmer's Mag.*, V: 368, 476–477; *Scott's Mag.*, LXVI: 642.

[29] *Farmer's Mag.*, V: 368.

a favorable harvest, the market not only resisted any bearish attacks, but on the contrary steadily mounted to greater heights. On November 10, 1804, the weekly average for England and Wales was 76*s.* 10*d.;* on December 8, 1804, it was 86*s.* 11*d.;* and on January 12, 1805, it was 86*s.* 6*d.*

Throughout the winter months of 1804 and 1805, prices continued to climb upward. Late in February, 1805, a petition was presented by the manufacturers of Stockport, condemning the recent act and praying for its instant repeal.[30] Tradesmen, laborers, manufacturers, chambers of commerce, town and city officials were represented by a series of petitions from Middleton, Bolton, Wigan, Lanark and many other towns.[31] All, however, without a voice of protest were laid on the table. It may be that Parliament proposed to test the act of 1804 before registering disapproval. This may be deduced from a remark of the Secretary of War who declared that the petitioners complained of evils which had not come into existence.[32] This was perfectly true. By the terms of the much abused act, the export of wheat was forbidden when the price was above 54*s.*, although the weekly maritime average at that time was 92*s.* 4*d.* The effect of this high price had been to close the ports to the export of wheat. If the Secretary had any idea that a public statement would throw discredit upon any further petitioning, he was greatly mistaken, as fresh complaints continued for some time.[33] These appeals should have convinced the Government that the country was disturbed. And while public opinion was probably at fault in connecting the act with the high prices, still the fact that there were high prices should have aroused the Ministry to action.[34]

[30] *Commons' Journal,* 60: 83.

[31] *Ibid.*, 97, 110, 115, 119.

[32] *Parl. Debates,* III: 706.

[33] *Commons' Journal,* 60: 122, 124, 138, 141.

[34] The Home Office Papers, as well as the current newspapers, fairly echo with the accounts and rumors of food riots: see, for example, *London Times,* May 13, 1805. Leeds, Manchester and other towns asked for the repeal of the act: see *Commons' Journal,* 60: 161, 172, 174, 176, 201. Parliament did renew the power of the Crown and Lord Lieutenant over the corn trade: see 45 Geo. 3, c. 26. It should be noticed that the Government encouraged imports by a further development of the Licence System: see p. 92.

During the period that these petitions were flooding the tables of Parliament, the market, under the stimulus of a favorable harvest, gradually steadied, the average price staying about what it had been for the past quarter. It was not, however, until May that Parliament took any step, and then only after Lord Hamilton had moved the appointment of a select committee.[35] Pitt, Coke, Western and Foster, all of whom had been on the former committee, stoutly defended the act of 1804. Protection, they declared, was vital and essential; without it, the farmer would be driven from the market by the foreigner. Furthermore, these men held that the increase in imports and the decrease in prices had been caused by the act of 1804.[36] Exactly what effect this measure could have had is rather hard to see. Prices were much in advance over those stated in that act or in any law of the last two decades. Importation, therefore, had come about as a result of these high prices and not because of any law.

It may have been this fact which caused sixty-three members of the Commons to rally to the support of Lord Hamilton as opposed to the protests of forty others who followed the views of Pitt.[37] The Committee appointed as a result of this vote lost no time in making a report. This body found from a study of the petitions that all condemned the act, especially the advance that had been made in the export and the import rates and the change that had taken place in the mode of fixing the average prices. Some few petitions stated that the extra duties on warehoused corn taken out for home use was unjust. Others, especially those from Scotland, pointed out that the separation of Scotland from England in the fixing of prices had shut the Scottish ports to imports, although the market price in western Scotland was above the import average. The Scottish petitioners also felt that the ports were open for too short a time (three months) to allow imports to come from Canada, and that Irish corn was withheld until the price had equalled the rate at which foreign corn might be entered at the lowest duty.[38]

[35] *Commons' Journal,* 60: 260; *Parl. Debates,* IV: 740.

[36] *Parl. Debates,* IV: 740–742.

[37] *Ibid.,* 742.

[38] *Ibid. and Commons' Journal,* 60: 260, 333. Western, Coke, Foster,

An examination of these findings and of the evidence presented by the committee are of interest. It was found that, although the act of 1804 was partly responsible for the high prices, the chief cause was the unfavorable harvest. No particular fault can be found with this statement, although it is likely that had the harvest been normal an increase would have followed by reason of the protective features of the act. Again it seems true that the acts of 1791 and 1804 had withheld a supply by forcing foreign warehoused wheat to pay double duties when taken out for home consumption, and that this wheat might be exported even though the export of British wheat was forbidden. The claim that the act had closed the Scottish ports when under the former law they would have been open is substantiated by the reports of the Receiver of the Corn Returns.[39] These reports, however, do not show the same result for the next quarter.[40] It must not be lost sight of, however, that the average price for November controlled the imports until February. Consequently, the act of 1804 had stopped import when the price in Scotland was above the rate of 1791 which law would have allowed import at the low duty. If it worked this way in one quarter, might it not do so again in the future? The petitioners from Scotland thought so, and, for that reason, did not hesitate to condemn the act of 1804. It was suggested by way of substitute that the prices in Great Britain be fixed by the average of the averages of all the districts of England and Scotland. In this way, a free exchange of grain might take place between the two, and above all, the ports would open and close more in conformity to actual conditions than they did under the act of 1804. As for the charge that larger supplies might be brought from Canada, it would seem that, had the amount of corn available for shipment in Canada been larger, the charge might have been well founded.[41]

Russell, Sinclair and Scott, among others, were on this committee: see *Parl. Pap.,* 1805, No. 154, for a copy of this report.

[39] This office had been created by the act of 1791.

[40] See the *London Gazette* for the average prices.

[41] See Appendix No. 8; and also 31 Geo. 3, c. 30; 33 Geo. 3, c. 65. Under these laws the import price was fixed four times a year. It is quite likely, although the report had little to say, that Irish wheat was withheld for personal gain.

On the basis of this report, however, a bill was introduced in the Commons, which within a month became law, although it did not go into effect until August, 1805.[42] This measure provided that the entire trade of Great Britain was to be governed by the average of the averages of the English districts. Exportation was to be forbidden from any district if the price of any grain was above the import average for the previous week. Beyond this the measure did not go. It had settled the chief complaints from Scotland, but it had not lowered the rates by which the export and import trade was regulated. Even if the act had lessened these rates, there would have been no marked change in the prices, as economic forces and not legislation determined these prices.

Other measures of the session dealing with the corn trade provided for the renewal of the previous acts and for an increase in the duties on all corn.[43] The quarterly average price of wheat in November of the same year was 78*s*. 8*d*., according to which wheat paid a duty of 7 13/20*d*., which in no way checked the heavy import of wheat. " There never was," the *London Times* stated, " a greater importation into [the] Shields in so short a space of time than took place last week. . . ." In October the same paper reported that " the importation of wheat alone last week amounted to about 15,000 quarters. . . ." [44] Not since the days of 1800 and 1801 had the country seen so large an influx of foreign corn. These imports, together with the reports of a favorable harvest, caused a drop in the prices.[45] By February, 1806, the quarterly average price of wheat had fallen to 72*s*. 8*d*. The agricultural situation continued to improve. Amid this wave of prosperity, Parliament modified the act of the previous year to read that it in no way applied to the coastwise trade or to the shipments to those places mentioned in the acts of 1791 and 1793. It also extended the time limit of the act permitting the Crown to regulate the corn trade.[46]

[42] 45 Geo. 3, c. 86.

[43] 45 Geo. 3, cc. 29, 68, 80.

[44] *London Times,* July 19, Oct. 21, 1805.

[45] *Ibid.,* Nov. 1, 1805; *Monthly Mag.,* XX: 391; and Consular Despatches, Bristol, Aug. 30, 1805.

[46] 46 Geo. 3, cc. 11, 29.

CHAPTER IV

CORN VERSUS SUGAR

Economic and political conditions in the spring of 1806 — The American Embargo and the French Decrees — The Continental Closure — The West Indian Interests seek relief — The Tory Ministry and the Orders in Council — The question of distillation from corn or sugar — The debates of 1808 — The Distillery Act of 1808 — The discussions in Parliament over the renewal of this act in 1809 and 1810 — The attitude of the agriculturalists — The passage of the Distillery Acts of 1809 and 1810 — The favorable harvest of 1810.

THROUGHOUT the Napoleonic era the English watched with great interest the rise and fall of the price of wheat. This was particularly true in February, 1806, when the market took a decided downward turn. This pleasing situation, unfortunately, was blasted by certain foreign complications. Prussia, forsaking a policy of neutrality, allied itself with France, seized Hanover, and closed its ports to the British. By way of retaliation, an English fleet blockaded the Ems, Weser, Elbe and Trave. A state of war became imminent. "The mysterious conduct of the Prussian Monarch . . . instantly caused a rapid advance upon wheat and oats."[1] Mark Lane underwent violent changes; wheat advancing, April 14, 15*s.* per quarter.[2] A decided drop in imports followed. Whereas in 1805, 559,628 quarters had been entered from Prussia, but 51,523 quarters were imported the next year. Everyone, excepting members of Parliament, seemed greatly concerned.

With the exception of declaring the corn trade between Great Britain and Ireland free from all restrictions, little seems to have been done.[3] Nor does there appear to have been any signal cause

[1] *Farmer's Mag.*, VII: 249.

[2] *Ibid.*, VIII: 29, 409; *London Times,* April 15, 1806.

[3] 46 Geo. 3, c. 97; *Parl. Debates,* VII: 514–515, 520–522; *Parl. Pap.,* 1813, No. 184, p. 18; but see p. 93 for an extension of the Licence System to this area.

for alarm. The fear that might naturally have existed was offset by the heavy imports from other countries, by the harvest of 1806, and by the favorable condition of the young crops.[4] Throughout 1807 the reports were generally pleasing. An uncertain and damp spring had been followed by a more seasonable summer and autumn, which resulted in a fair, though not overstocked, harvest.[5] Increased cultivation, due to the high prices and the process of enclosure, as well as to the extensive imports, forced prices downward so that by November 7, 1807, the average price for all England and Wales was 66*s.* 1*d.*[6]

During the winter of 1807–08, the corn market stayed about the same.[7] Various factors made this possible, chief of which were the import of foreign corn and the harvest of 1807.[8] There was doubt, however, whether the domestic supply would hold over the summer months. Reliance upon Northern Europe as a source of supply had been destroyed by the growth of the French Empire. It was natural, therefore, that the corn merchants should view with dismay the growing difficulties with America. The large imports thence during the past year had encouraged the belief in the permanency of this seemingly inexhaustible granary. Unfortunately for England, America had certain definite ideas of her own. It was not to be expected that America would complacently allow her men-of-war to be fired upon, her vessels condemned and her diplomats made to feel the insignificance of their country. Retaliation followed of necessity, and took the shape of an embargo measure which passed Congress one month after the appearance of the November Orders.

The result was at once apparent. "The news," so wrote

[4] Consular Despatches, Bristol, March 24, May 21, 1806. The harvest of 1806, except for barley and oats, fulfilled all expectations: see *Farmer's Mag.*, VI: 523; *Dropmore Papers,* VIII: 139, 266.

[5] *Athenaeum,* I: 555, 675, II: 216–217; *Monthly Mag.*, XXIII: 103, 306, 407, 511, 617, XXIV: 102, 215, 312, 511; *Farmer's Mag.*, VIII: 519; *Agricultural Mag.*, I: 158, 232; *Morning Advertiser,* Jan. 1, April 3, June 1, Sept. 1, 2, 1807; *Morning Chronicle,* Oct. 2, 1807; *Parl. Pap.*, 1808, No. 178, pp. 122–123.

[6] *London Gazette.*

[7] *Ibid.*

[8] *Farmer's Mag.*, IX: 131–132; *London Times,* Jan. 5, 6, 8, 11, 25, Feb. 2, 16. 1808.

Murray, "of the Embargo has occasioned a considerable advance in the value of many articles of the produce of the United States."[9] It was not without reason, therefore, that the merchants viewed the future as most discouraging. Oddly enough, the quarterly average price of wheat in February, 1808, was but 2*s.* 1*d.* higher than that of the past quarter. It was, however, the knowledge that prices would rise that prompted the anxiety among the merchants over the relations with America.[10]

In the meantime Parliament had met and had directed its attention to continental affairs. As a consequence of Tilsit and the Milan Decree, European markets had been closed to England, whose merchants and manufacturers at once began to complain. Probably the loudest and most prolonged wail of distress arose from those whose interests were bound up in the sugar trade.

The condition of this very important trade had become most serious. For some time past the sugar market had been frequently disturbed, chiefly on account of the general European situation.[11] Early in April, 1806, a well attended meeting of the West Indian planters had protested against a proposed increase in the sugar duty.[12] The planters held that the war was gradu-

[9] Consular Despatches, Liverpool, Feb. 6, 1808: see Chapter VIII for a more detailed account.

[10] Consular Despatches, Liverpool, Feb. 6, 1808; *Farmer's Mag.*, IX: 127. It will be recalled that the unusual activity in America before the *Embargo* had cleared many a ship, and that these arrived early in 1808 in time to bolster up the market.

[11] In 1799 the merchants of Liverpool and Lancaster obtained a loan from Parliament to relieve them from financial ruin, which had been caused in part by the closure of European markets, and by the large amount of sugar on hand: see *Commons' Journal,* 55: 27, 34, 36, 40–42, 44, 46, 47, 48; and 39 Geo. 3, c. 5. Ever since 1791 a marked increase had taken place in the amount of sugar imported into Great Britain. The amount on hand in 1799, after deducting all re-exports, was 2,772,437 cwt., while in 1798 it had only been 1,576,552 cwt.: see *Parl. Pap.,* 1808, No. 178, pp. 304, 305. From 1799 on the West Indian interests received more and more attention from Parliament: see *Commons' Journal,* 57: 857, 942, 61: 771; *Parl. Debates,* IX: 90–100; *Monthly Mag.,* XVII: 509.

[12] *London Times,* April 12, 1806. This increase amounted to 3*s.* per cwt.; other increases had been made since the outbreak of the war: see *Commons' Journal,* 61: 181–182; *Parl. Debates,* VI: 571; *Accounts and Papers,* 1898, vol. 34, p. 216. The proposed duty received royal assent,

ally depriving them of their accustomed markets, that their market in England had become overstocked, and that the proposed duty was most unjust.[13] A memorial, accordingly, was presented to the Government, setting forth these grievances. Upon the receipt of this paper, Grenville sent it to Auckland with the following remark: [14]

> As you have not work enough, I send you a memorial from the W[est] I[ndian] planters . . . we cannot abandon our duties nor give up the people of this country to the monopoly of these gentlemen. Perhaps if you have no objections to go through the form of seeing these people at the Committee, that might be the best course; but I suspect the real object of the whole is to lay ground for jérémiades about the slave trade.

Acting upon this advice Auckland received a group of planters at the office of the Board of Trade. Far from being a mere "form," the meeting was the first of a series of conferences held during June and July. At these meetings accounts and papers were called for, sugar refiners were summoned and interviewed, while the planters themselves deluged the Board with numerous resolutions and petitions.[15] A study of these sources shows that the West Indian merchants, after ably presenting their miserable

---

May 5, 1806: see 46 Geo. 3, c. 42. See also Dowell, S., *History of Taxation and Taxes in England* (London, Longmans, 1884), vol. II, Book II, chaps. 9, 10, vol. IV, chap. 4.

[13] Opposition was also voiced in Commons: see *Parl. Debates,* VI: 635. Total imports of sugar for 1805 and 1806 were 3,178,788 cwt. and 3,815,175 cwt. Total sugar exports for these years were 1,102,685 cwt. and 1,103,435 cwt., leaving on hand 2,076,103 cwt. for 1805, and 2,801,740 cwt. for 1806: see *Parl. Pap.* 1808, No. 178, pp. 185, 305; and also *idem.,* pp. 243, 244–245, for the amount left on hand in London, Liverpool, Bristol, Leith, Whitehaven, Lancaster, Hull and Glasgow. It is of interest to note that the price of sugar was steadily falling. In Jan., 1805, the price was 55*s.* 1¾*d.* per cwt.; in Jan., 1806, 48*s.* 6¾*d.*; and in Jan., 1807, 38*s.* 0½*d.*: see *Parl. Pap.,* 1808, No. 178, pp. 180, 317.

[14] *Dropmore Papers,* VIII: 162–163; and also p. 181. Whatever idea the planters may have as to the slave trade, there can be no doubt that by the summer of 1806 the chief cause for their condition was the partial stoppage of the trade to Europe. The West Indian interests frequently complained of the coolness of the Ministry toward their lot: see *Parl. Debates,* IX: 89–100; *London Morning Chronicle,* March 13, 1807. For a general account of the West Indies, see Tilby, A. W., *Britain in the Tropics* (London, Constable, 1912), chap. 2.

[15] B. T., 5: 16, June 6, 13, 16, July 2, 1806.

lot, asked for certain changes in the duty and the drawback on sugar. As for any change in the duty, the Board had distinctly stated that none would be made. Early in July, however, in answer to the repeated demands of the planters, the Board communicated with the Treasury about certain changes in the bounty.[16]

During the summer and fall of 1806, as has been noticed, the European situation drifted from bad to worse. The rapid extension of French power had shut the markets to the British sugar trade. This caused renewed interest on the part of the West Indian merchants who agreed to present another memorial to the Ministry.[17] Early in December this memorial was read before the Board and discussed at great length. One part of this paper contained a sketch of the deplorable state of the West Indian trade and the imperative need for relief. Another section suggested a bounty on the export of sugar. A third read: [18]

> That the measure of encouraging a further home consumption of sugar by substituting its use for that of grain in the distilleries and breweries appears to be called for no less by the present circumstances attending the sugar planters, than by the reasonable apprehension there is of a scarcity of grain in Europe.

After a discussion, which extended throughout the remainder of the year, the Board agreed to several resolutions which were at once sent to the Treasury for its consideration. One of these resolutions provided, among other things, that the question of distillation be referred to the House of Commons,[19] which had been agreed upon only after repeated meetings with the planters, the excise officers, and " some very intelligent distillers." " It is true," wrote Auckland, " that they have about 80,000 hogsheads of British sugar in our warehouses, and are suffering

[16] B. T., 5: 16, July 4, 1806. This matter was later taken up in Parliament: see *Commons' Journal,* 61: 495, 510, 517, 522, 530, 535, 556, 560; and 46 Geo. 3, c. 109.

[17] *Dropmore Papers,* VIII: 454, 456.

[18] B. T., 5: 16, Dec. 9, 1806. The memorial itself, adopted Dec. 5, may be found under that date in B. T., 1: 31.

[19] These resolutions may be found in B. T., 5: 16, Dec. 29, 1806. A summary is given in *Dropmore Papers,* VIII: 489–490: see also 46 Geo. 3, c. 109, and note 16 of this chapter.

greatly under the stagnation. The distillery, I find, cannot take above 12,000 hogsheads this year, nor above 24,000 in any year, even if it should be thought right to confine the distillers to sugar."[20] In shifting the settlement of this matter to Parliament, the Board felt that the question would be brought before the nation. In this way public opinion might exert its influence in the manner desired.

Late in December, therefore, Lord Temple moved the appointment of a select committee of the Commons to inquire into the expediency of permitting the use of sugar and molasses in the distilleries and breweries. Lord Temple estimated that there were from 150,000 to 160,000 hogsheads of sugar in the various ports of England; but explained that, however imperative the case of the planters might be, it should be understood that the proposed measure would not exclude grain; rather was it to allow the use of both sugar and grain upon the principle of fair competition, not of exclusion.[21]

The committee, having been appointed, undertook its task and in February, 1807, made a report.[22] Nothing more is heard of it until March 24, when it was taken from the table and given to a Select Committee on the West Indian Planters' Petition.[23] This body had had its inception as a result of a series of petitions which had been presented, late in the spring, over the condition of these islands.[24]

[20] *Dropmore Papers,* VIII: 469, 471–472, 474: see also B. T., 5: 16, Dec. 17, 19, 1806.

[21] *Parl. Debates,* VIII: 238–239; *Commons' Journal,* 62: 24.

[22] *Parl. Pap.,* 1807, No. 83, *Report of the Sugar Distillery Committee.* This report shows that the increased quantity of sugar on hand had been caused by the loss of European markets, by reduced prices in England, by the hazards of the war, and by the increased cost of production. The distress, however, did not warrant the use of sugar in the distilleries, as such a measure would not give any material help to the planters, and would be, furthermore, contrary to the interests of the agricultural classes. If the future should bring about no relief to the planters, a proposal of this nature might then be found necessary. This veiled promise was eagerly seized upon by the West Indian merchants: see *Parl. Debates,* IX: 99. As pointed out by "Z" in *Cobbett's Pol. Reg.,* XI: 132–133, the cost of sugar was then greater than the cost of barley: see also *Commons' Journal,* 62: 37, 57, 58, 82, 133–134.

[23] *Commons' Journal,* 62: 283.

[24] *Ibid.,* 62: 188–189, 236, 248, 281; *Parl. Debates,* IX: 140–141. Peti-

Briefly, these petitions set forth the following ideas. First, the wealth of these islands was of paramount importance to the mother country. This was illustrated by the large sums of British capital invested there, by the great share these islands had in the total trade of Great Britain, and by the fact that the commerce of the West Indies had been a fruitful nursery for English seamen. Second, this prosperity had been created by the Navigation System. Of late, this system had been seriously weakened by the Government's policy of placing the conquered islands on the same footing as that of the British islands; by allowing neutrals to carry foreign colonial produce to the enemy; by stopping, in part, the trade to the continent; and by the heavy import duties on sugar.[25] Third, the Government had recently passed certain relief measures, which, though greatly appreciated, were but temporary forms of relief. Fourth, in view of the foregoing factors, the economic position of the islands was extremely uncertain, cultivation being carried on with little or no profit. Fifth, adequate relief could be had only by lowering the sugar duties, by freer relations with the United States, and finally by allowing the use of sugar in the distilleries and breweries.[26]

Although these petitions and the report of the Distillery Committee had been given to the Committee on the West Indian Planters' Petitions, nothing seems to have come of it. This was

---

tions relative to the slave trade, in which reference is made to the sugar trade, may be found in *Commons' Journal,* 62: 129, 143, 146–148: see also *Parl. Debates,* VIII: 512.

[25] *Parl. Debates,* VIII: 807–808. The importance of the American trade to Europe is shown by the 45,097 hhds. of sugar imported into Amsterdam in 1806: see *Parl. Pap.,* 1808, No. 178, p. 260, and Pitkin, T., *Statistical View of the Commerce of the United States,* pp. 123, 135–137, 157–158.

[26] Distillation by sugar was to last as long as the depressed state of the sugar market continued, and as long as no injury was inflicted on the corn market. In one petition the desire was for the "preferable consumption of sugar;" another called for "competition with grain." Any loss in revenue through the lowering of the sugar duties would be offset by the increased income gained through the use of sugar. Freer relations with America would allow the West Indies to exchange their goods for timber and provisions.

probably due to the fact that the Distillery Committtee had disapproved of the use of sugar, and because the Government was then engaged in the discussion of other relief measures.[27]

In the meantime the Board of Trade had continued its investigation of the matter. It will be recalled that late in December a series of resolutions had been sent to the Treasury. This office answered early in 1807 to the effect that a bill would be introduced shortly in Parliament providing for bounties on sugar and additional import duties on brandy. Later in the same month the Board gave its approval to a measure providing for a bounty on refined sugar.[28] As a result of these steps, Parliament passed in March, 1807, two measures which placed a bounty on sugar and an excise duty on brandy.[29] In addition the Board busied itself with the question of distillation. Matters came to an abrupt end, however, by the fall of the Whigs, late in that month.[30]

Henry Adams in his admirable *History of the United States* refers to the appointment of a Committee on the state of the West Indian commerce as foreshadowing the November Orders.[31] If this is true, considerable criticism may be made of the authors of

[27] Probably another retarding force was the growing opposition among the landed classes: see *Morning Advertiser,* Jan. 6, 1807.

[28] B. T., 5: 17, Jan. 6, Feb. 13, 1807.

[29] 47 Geo. 3, s. 1, cc. 22, 27; *Commons' Journal,* 62: 130, 133, 137, 144, 150, 161, 196, 201, 205, 231, 246; *Parl. Debates,* VIII: 851. These proposals were endorsed by Lloyd's Coffee House: see *Literary Panorama,* I: 1347. At the same time a bill dealing with the Irish trade of rectifying spirits was passed: see 47 Geo. 3, s. 2, c. 19. The following table is of interest:

Brandy imported into Great Britain from

	France	Spain
1805	2,662,544 gallons	405,399 gallons.
1806	1,417,920 gallons	263,161 gallons.
1807	2,166,889 gallons	155,541 gallons.

See *Parl. Pap.,* 1808, No. 178, p. 208.

[30] B. T., 1: 32, Joseph Pinsent to Auckland, Jan. 8, 1807, in which the idea is expressed that the adoption of sugar by the distilleries would not injure agriculture. See also B. T., 1: 32, Wm. Manning to the Board, Jan. 28, 1807; *Commons' Journal,* 62: 281; B. T., 5: 17, Jan. 20, 26, Feb. 6, 9, 1807; and *Cobbett's Pol. Reg.,* XI: 24–28, 179–185, 222–224, 337–339.

[31] Adams, Henry, *The History of the United States,* IV, chap. 4.

these measures; further it reduces to a minimum the retaliatory idea which is set forth in these orders. In addition to the material gathered by Adams certain other facts may be presented.

The entire question of neutral trade, particularly that of America, made its appearance upon the outbreak of war in 1793. The favorable position of the United States with respect to the French West Indies at once transferred the bulk of the carrying trade of these islands to American merchants. Direct trade between these islands and France was declared unlawful by Great Britain. It was perfectly legal, however, for Americans to bring colonial produce to the United States. Once imported, this became part of the national stock of that country and might be exported thence to France. This irregular trade caused a breach to exist in the commercial system held by European states, namely, that foreigners were excluded from the colonial trade. For very apparent reasons, however, neither France nor the United States cared at all for this system. Consequently, England applied the Rule of 1756, and proclaimed the doctrine of continuous voyage. But in spite of these rules, the January Orders, the bitter decisions of the British Admiralty Courts, and the attacks by British men-of-war, Americans continued to supply the enemy with colonial produce.

Small wonder was it that the British looked upon this situation as unjust. Why should a neutral be allowed to engage in so profitable a trade, when the docks and warehouses of England were jammed with the produce of the British West Indies? This idea appears constantly in the petitions that were presented to Parliament and to the Board of Trade. The West Indian merchants of Glasgow wrote:[32]

> We take leave to add that there appear to us no remedies immediately applicable to those evils and calculated to remove them to any extent, but restraining the neutral carrying trade, so as to afford us a fair competition with the other nations of Europe. And above all — increasing the home consumption of sugar by permitting its use in the distilleries and breweries under such regulations as may be best adapted to promote the general advantage.

[32] B. T., I: 32, Wm. Manning to the Board, Jan. 28, 1807: see also B. T., 5: 17, Feb. 6, 1807; *Literary Panorama,* II: 665.

In Parliament, Mr. George Hibbert voiced the same idea: [33]

> . . . how far the welfare and very existence of our own colonies were endangered by the consideration which we persist in paying to the claims of neutrals, in forbearing to impede, as in time of war we might, the transit of our enemy's colonial produce to the European markets under all the advantage and security of neutral flags, thus taking away the inducement which the enemy might have to except colonial produce from the rigour of his general exclusion of our commerce.

Measures of relief had been passed, but as long as Europe kept faith with the Berlin Decree, the sugar interests had no effective or permanent outlet for their goods. Temporary assistance might be obtained either by allowing the use of sugar in the distilleries or by changing the January Order so as to create a market in Europe.[34] The Ministry of All Talents had shown that it was against distillation from sugar; it had also consistently opposed any change in the January Order. The attitude of the Tories, although not clearly established, had been sufficiently shown to foreshadow the substitution of sugar for corn, and the adoption of a more drastic commercial policy.

On April 8, 1807, the Portland Ministry, with Perceval as Chancellor of the Exchequer, came into office. For the remaining few weeks of the session nothing was done beyond the addition of two members to the Committee on the West Indian Planters' Petition.[35] Early in the next session activity was resumed by the appointment of a Committee on the Commercial State of the West Indian colonies.[36] This body made a report

[33] *Parl. Debates,* IX: 100. Mr. Hibbert was a member of Parliament from Seaford and took an active part in these debates. Personal reasons probably explain this interest, as he was a partner in two houses trading to Jamaica and the Barbadoes: see *Parl. Pap.,* No. 178, p. 166.

[34] Lloyd's Coffee House issued this statement, May 20, 1807: "Until the northern ports are again open to receive our colonial produce, there is no likelihood of a change for the better": see *Literary Panorama,* II: 665.

[35] *Commons' Journal,* 62: 362. Parliament adjourned April 27; the new session opened June 22, 1807.

[36] *Commons' Journal,* 62: 668. Rumors of a Swedish attack upon Hamburg had bolstered the market in April: see *Literary Panorama,* II: 440. It is interesting to note that sixteen out of the original committee had served on the Committee on the West Indian Planters' Petition, and that eight of these had been on the Distillation Committee.

late in July, 1807, but once more matters lagged. Other affairs demanded prior consideration; and although occasional reference was made to the colonies, nothing resulted. During the last days of the session, however, the Ministry pledged itself to make an investigation and report at the next sitting of Parliament.[37]

During this interval, indeed ever since Perceval had taken office, the lot of the planters had grown worse. An overstocked British market was constantly becoming more glutted, and prices were naturally being forced downward.[38] At the same time the West Indian interests were arousing and agitating public opinion with the view of compelling the Government to adopt a drastic program of relief. For the present the planters and their friends were content to demand the stoppage of the neutral trade to the continent.[39] Nor was the Ministry ill disposed towards such a

[37] *Commons' Journal,* 62: 668, 764, 770, 835; *Parl. Debates,* IX: 735, 742, 1151–1153, 1170. The report is to be found in *Parl. Debates,* IX: Appendix, and in *Parl. Pap.,* 1807, No. 65. The main facts of the report may be grouped: since 1799 the cost of production in the West Indies had greatly increased, while the profit from the sale of colonial produce had decreased; relief might be had by reducing the sugar duty, by a bounty on the re-export of sugar, and by stopping the neutral trade in colonial goods; the present trade in provisions between the islands and the United States might be handled in part by the British North American colonies; and immediate action was highly imperative. Note the absence of any clause asking for distillation from sugar.

[38] *Monthly Mag.,* XXIII: 305, 509, XXIV: 100, 212, 310; *Cobbett's Pol. Reg.,* XIII: 60–64, 96, 147. The average price of sugar was 36*s.* 9¾*d.* per cwt., for January, 1807; for July, 34*s.* 9½*d.*; for December, 32*s.* 10¼*d.*: see *Parl. Pap.,* 1808, No. 178, p. 183. On July 13, 1807, a total of 425,148 cwt. of sugar was either in the warehouses of London or afloat at the West Indian docks in the Thames: see *Parl. Pap.,* 1808, No. 178, p. 315.

[39] *London Times,* Sept. 29, Oct. 6, 27, 1807; *Cobbett's Pol. Reg.,* XII: 690–702; *Parl. Debates,* IX: 686. "Why then," said Lord Howick, June 30, 1807, "not substitute for that order in council which has been thought so weak and futile, another of more vigour, and able to effect all that the present ministers, when in opposition had said it ought to effect?" See also *Literary Panorama,* II: 457–470, 1129–1144; Stephen, James, *War in Disguise* (London, 1805); and the same writer's work, *Dangers of the Country* (London, 1807). Note the flat denial by Mr. Hibbert that planters were unprincipled: see *Parl. Debates,* X: 679–680. The cost of freight and insurance for carrying a cargo of sugar from the foreign West Indies to the United States and thence to Holland amounted to £6 13*s.* 6*d.*; while the cost from the British islands to London and thence to Holland equalled £13 6*s.*: see *Parl. Pap.,* 1808, No. 178, p. 257.

policy. Early in October, Perceval and Castlereagh were in correspondence over this matter.[40] From then on until the appearance of the November Orders, the Ministry diligently worked on a program which would cripple an energetic enemy, ruin a neutral trade, and afford relief to the planters. It seems very likely, therefore, in estimating the causes of these Orders one should place greater stress upon the neutral trade than upon the idea of combating the French decrees. That retaliation in some form or other was inevitable is not questioned; but the retaliation as outlined in the November Orders concerns a neutral as well as an enemy.

Upon the initial, though delayed, appearance of these measures, much misunderstanding arose as to their exact meaning. Concerning this we are not now interested. Suffice it to say that according to the accepted interpretation the direct and indirect trade in foreign colonial produce to Europe was totally forbidden. In this way one of the chief complaints of the planters had apparently been met. In an attempt, however, to soften the sting to the neutral it was provided that certain articles of foreign colonies might be entered in Great Britain and thence exported under tax and licence fee to special ports on the continent. In short the depressed British sugar market was given another source of supply, and an important object of the orders, namely, a European market for British West Indian produce, was partially missed. Especially was this true when the Milan Decree shut still more tight the ports of the continent to the British.[41]

The recommendation of Lord Sidmouth, in his answer to the Lords Commissioners' speech, that the Ministers investigate the distressed state of the West Indies, and give them proper relief, was, therefore, not unexpected.[42] Late in February, 1808, the Commons appointed a committee to inquire into the wisdom of limiting the distilleries of the United Kingdom, or a part

[40] *Memoirs . . . of . . . Castlereagh,* VIII: 87.

[41] For the text of these orders, see the *London Gazette,* Privy Council Register, and *Parl. Pap.,* 1808, No. 5. For Auckland's comments see *Dropmore Papers,* IX: 143, 147; *Parl. Debates,* X: 677.

[42] *Parl. Debates,* X: 15.

thereof, to the use of sugar and molasses.[43] While this body was at work, the question of the planters came up several times. Considerable stress was laid upon the effects of the November Orders: those favoring these measures graphically foretold a favorable future for the colonies; while those opposed pointed to a dull sugar market and to overflowing warehouses.[44] Ill feeling had also grown among the agriculturists who saw in this proposal an attack upon their interests.[45]

Although this discussion waxed exceedingly warm, it does not seem to have stopped the work of the Committee, which tried to lull discontent by denying the rumor that it had decided to allow distillation from sugar.[46] In less than three weeks the Committee made a report in which there was a recommendation to stop the use of grain in the distilleries. The colonies, so the report stated, were in the throes of a business depression caused largely by the lack of a foreign market and by the competition of foreign sugar in Britain.[47]

[43] *Commons' Journal,* 63: 102, 137; *Parl. Debates,* X: 712–713. The reports of Feb. 17 and July 24, 1807, were given to this committee. Because the report of February, 1807, had argued against distillation from sugar, it does not follow that distillation was inexpedient in 1808.

[44] *Parl. Debates,* X: 733, 1236–1237, 1239–1240. During this period the export and bounty bills were renewed: see 48 Geo. 3, cc. 16, 17; and also 48 Geo. 3, c. 69.

[45] *Morning Chronicle,* March 3, 1808; *London Times,* March 25, 1808; *Cobbett's Pol. Reg.* XIII: 605–608. The *London Times,* March 3, 1808, reported that sugar had taken a 4*s.* per cwt. rise in view of the proposed measure, while the *Morning Chronicle,* April 14, 1808, remarked that the act proposed to " sterilize the country for one year."

[46] *Parl. Debates,* X: 1256. The Board of Agriculture was inclined to view the rumor as true: see Board of Agriculture Papers, April 8, 1808.

[47] Other causes mentioned were the excessive freight charges and the increased cost of production. See the evidence submitted by Mr. T. Kemble, *Parl. Pap.,* 1808, No. 178, pp. 24–25. Mr. Kemble stated that sugar rose 3*s*. per cwt. in expectation of Parliamentary help. The report showed the following facts:

	Cwt.
Quantity of sugar annually remaining for consumption in the United Kingdom, upon an average of four years ending 1807	2,636,658
Average export thence to foreign parts for the same four years	972,220
Imports for year ending Jan. 5, 1808, excluding that into Ireland	3,651,686
Amount left for home consumption	2,521,152
Amount left, after exportation to foreign parts	1,130,534

The Committee felt that these conditions in the colonies warranted the use of sugar in the British distilleries for the period of a year.[48] It was believed that the substitution of sugar for corn would not injure the barley interests as the quantity of barley sown that year could not be unsown and " as there is no

---

Should there be no export in 1808, a quantity equal to that exported in 1807 would be thrown upon the home market, to which there should be added Danish sugar. The result, therefore, would be a drop in the price of sugar.

The annual consumption of sugar in the United Kingdom for five years ending 1785 amounted to	1,422,024
Annual consumption upon an average of four years ending 1807	2,636,658
Increased consumption	1,214,634
Average import for four years ending 1807	3,608,878
Amount with the import from foreign colonies deducted, taking 1807 as average	581,881
Average annual import from the old British colonies	3,026,997
Average annual consumption in the United Kingdom	2,636,658
Average annual surplus above consumption	390,339

According to these figures one notes that the year 1807 had an increase both in exports and imports. It was reasonable to expect that the next year would have an increase in imports and a decrease in exports, because of the continental closure which would greatly increase the surplus. Now what might this surplus be? For the four years ending 1807 the average surplus had been 390,339 cwt. from the British West Indies, to which should be added the average surplus of 581,881 cwt. from conquered islands, which made an annual surplus of 972,220 cwt. Hence the surplus in 1808 would probably be greater than that of 1807. Note, however, the fact that the average remaining for consumption for the four years was greater than that left for consumption in 1807. The fact, however, remains that there was a surplus in 1807, and that there would be a larger one in 1808. The facts so presented warranted, therefore, the contention of the Committee that the planters were in dire straits, even though this view casts much doubt upon the efficiency of the November Orders. The report is found in *Parl. Debates,* XI: Appendix; the report together with the evidence is given in *Parl. Pap.*, 1808, No. 178. It contains 318 pages of report, testimony and evidence. The examination of forty-five witnesses covered the period from March 1 to April 6, 1808. A careful study of the evidence tends to create the impression that the Committee took its task very seriously.

[48] For certain reasons molasses was left out: see the report. The amount of corn used in the distilleries of the United Kingdom was 300,000 cwt. in England, 169,000 cwt. in Scotland, and 311,000 cwt. in Ireland. There was considerable illegal distillation in Ireland, which the Government seems to have been unable to stop. For this and other reasons the Committee left Ireland out of the proposed bill.

ground to suppose that a similar measure will take place next year, the very re-opening of the distilleries to the produce of his industry cannot but do away with any evils occasioned by the effect of a temporary alarm on the minds of the farmers."[49] Besides, corn imports had been altogether too large, the average for the past five years being 770,000 quarters, not counting that from Ireland. On the other hand 470,000 quarters, chiefly barley, were used by the British distilleries. The Committee, after balancing these figures, found that this unfavorable trade might be done away with if grain were not used in the distilleries.[50] Further, as the barley interests gave but one sixteenth of their total crop to the distilleries, the loss of that market would be offset by the gain of others. Finally, the Committee stated that—

> . . . the permanent adoption of this measure would be attended with great evils to the agriculture of the country; they feel it incumbent on them to state that nothing . . . but the strong case so clearly made out by the West Indian interest . . . could prevail upon them to advise even this slight temporary interference . . . with an established system of agriculture.

Although the Committee had clearly shown the need of giving help to the West Indian interests, it does not seem, at first glance, that the method suggested was altogether expedient. One very naturally questions the view held by the Committee that the barley growers would not sustain a loss in case the distilleries were closed to them.[51] What assurance did the Committee have that, if the volume of corn imports were reduced, the British

[49] The Committee frankly admitted that there would be a protest from the agricultural classes, but pushed it aside for the reasons given above.

[50] Note that this rests upon the dangerous assumption that barley could be used as food instead of wheat; it ignores, furthermore, the loss in revenue that would follow from a decrease in corn imports.

[51] It was the belief of men like Claude Scott, Arthur Young and Edward Wakefield that distillation from sugar would not injure the corn then growing, but that there would be a decided fall in prices of all grain, especially if the harvest was abundant. Mr. George Chalmers, clerk of the Board of Trade, believed that the landed classes had no cause for alarm, but that the stoppage of grain in the distilleries would create a popular clamor which would result in higher prices: see *Parl. Pap.*, 1808, No. 178, pp. 81–85, 89–90, 111, 114.

people could or would use barley as a food,[52] or that the proposed measure would not discourage the sowing of barley for the next year?[53] The life of the measure, to be sure, was limited to one year, but if the British sugar could not find a Continental market in 1808, might not Europe be closed in 1809? If this were to take place, then the sugar interests would ask for a continuation of the act, in which case the barley growers would incur a serious loss. On the other hand, it seems that the loss of the market in the distilleries could be offset, in part, by selling barley for feed. Further, in some parts of England oats, instead of barley, might be cultivated, with no harm to the soil.[54] Finally, one should remember that of the total barley crop but one sixteenth was used by the distilleries.

Another question demanding attention was that of how much sugar the distilleries could actually use; for unless it could be shown that sufficient quantities would be used, there was no reason for depriving the farmers of an accustomed market. Auckland estimated that not more than 12,000 hogsheads or 168,000 cwt. of sugar could be used by the distilleries in 1806, and that no more than 24,000 hogsheads or 336,000 cwt. could be used in any year.[55] The facts given by the Committee showed that one quarter of corn, and two cwt. of sugar would yield a given amount of wash. Now if 470,000 quarters of corn were annually used in the British distilleries, 940,000 cwt. of sugar would have to be consumed in case the distilleries were closed to corn. Contrasting this amount with the surplus of sugar in 1807, one notes that practically the entire amount could be used by the distilleries.[56]

[52] Arthur Young pointed out that actually no gain would be made by prohibiting the use of corn in the distilleries, as such an act would decrease the total demand for domestic corn: see *Parl. Pap.*, 1807, No. 178, p. 81.

[53] It probably would have lessened the amount sown in 1809 had the barley growers known that the distilleries would also be closed in 1810: see *Parl. Pap.*, 1810, No. 67, pp. 16, 17.

[54] See *Morning Chronicle*, April 28, 1808; *Cobbett's Pol. Reg.*, XIII: 641–648; *Parl. Pap.*, 1808, No. 178, p. 85.

[55] See p. 47, and *Parl. Debates*, X: 733. Auckland made this estimate when a member of the Whig Ministry.

[56] It would not, however, take care of the surplus of 1808: see *Morning Chronicle*, March 3, 1808, and *Cobbett's Pol. Reg.*, XIII: 696–698.

In view of these facts it would seem that the proposed bill was justified. The injury likely to be borne by the barley counties [57] would be slight in comparison to that which had been sustained by the West Indian interests. Nor need the agriculturists, or the nation, have had any fear as to the food supply. The prospective harvest was in the fields, and would be reaped, distillation or no distillation. Regardless of the proposed act foreign corn would, moreover, enter Great Britain in proportion to the demand for corn. Furthermore, very little barley was imported; and as barley could not be used satisfactorily as a substitute for wheat,[58] the total import of wheat would not be lessened by a surplus barley crop. Finally, it was the duty of the Government to give help to all forms of industry and commerce. A short time before Parliament had passed a general enclosure act and several new corn laws which had helped the farmers and landlords. Assistance was now being asked for by the West Indian interests. It would seem, therefore, but right for the agriculturists to shoulder a part of the burden imposed upon the empire by reason of the war.

There was, however, another course which if adopted might have satisfied both parties; namely, to permit the neutral, for the period of the war, to trade freely with the enemy in both foreign and domestic sugar. This, of course, would have aroused the commercial classes, and in any event would have forced a drastic change in the Orders in Council — a step which would have been quite contrary to the ideas of the Tory Ministry.[59]

To return to the Committee's report, no sooner had it been presented than the charge was made in the Commons that it was only a majority report. One member declared it to be a party measure as no one from the barley counties was on the Committee. Another believed that, although the colonies were entitled to consideration, it should not be at the expense of another

[57] The loss would be the greatest among the barley growers of Norfolk.

[58] Contemporary opinion sustains this idea: see *Parl. Pap.*, 1810, No. 67, pp. 53, 122.

[59] This idea was expressed at that time: see *Parl. Debates*, XI: 818. Exactly what would have been the attitude of Napoleon is, of course, problematic.

branch of industry. The Committee answered by stating that the farming interests were adequately protected by the clause in the proposed bill which permitted the instant repeal of the act in case of any sudden fall in the price of barley. The absence of any members from the barley counties was explained by pointing out that a member from Norfolk would have been named had any then been present in Parliament. The Committee insisted, finally, that the proposed measure was justified because of the unfortunate situation of agriculture both in Europe and in England.[60]

This last argument was exceedingly clever. It has already been shown that, although the harvest of 1807 was not normal, still it was by no means a failure.[61] The fact that it was not normal, coupled with the recent drop in imports and the unsettled state of the English market, led the Committee to view the future with much concern. It was, however, altogether too early to be predicting definitely the harvest of 1808.[62] One may question, moreover, as Perceval did at a later date, the wisdom of such a prophecy, as any public statement of this type was quite apt to stampede popular opinion.

This is exactly what took place. Through fear of impending disaster, a disturbed country joined with the farmers and landed classes in denouncing the proposed measure. Meetings of protest were held at Norwich, Walden, Chelmsford, Colchester, and Braintree.[63] Early in May petitions poured into Parliament. The petitioners agreed, in view of the present state of the market, that it was an ill-chosen time to introduce an act which was certain to cause the most injurious effects to agriculture. It was also declared that the "depression of our produce for the benefit of our own distant colonies, appears . . . both impolitic and unjust" and that if you lessen the demand for grain you decrease

[60] *Parl. Debates,* XI: 55–59.

[61] See p. 44.

[62] Varying reports, as was usually the case, as to the harvest of 1808 were made before April of that year: see *Agricultural Mag.,* II: 156. The grain interests themselves denied the existence of a scarcity: see *Parl. Debates,* XI: 494, 816.

[63] *London Times,* April 22, 1808: see also *Cobbett's Pol. Reg.,* XIII: 673–686, and the *Morning Chronicle,* April 14, 1808.

the amount grown.[64] On the other hand an equal number of petitions were presented in favor of the report, most of which came from Liverpool, Glasgow, Greenock and other commercial and manufacturing towns, whose citizens saw in the bill a new source of grain.[65]

In the meantime the Ministry had introduced a series of recommendations containing, in general, the chief points of the report. In the discussion which followed, several interesting points arose. According to the report, the proposed law was to last from the first of July, 1808, to the first of July, 1809. This differed from the Ministry's recommendation, which called for no distillation from the first of July to the first of October, 1808. Immediately the question arose: Why make such an absurd proposal, as during the months suggested by the Ministry the distilleries do little business?[66] The Government answered this charge by stating that its recommendations provided for the continuation of the prohibition, under certain circumstances, until July, 1809.[67] Again, the original report suggested that the measure be limited to Great Britain, while the Ministry now asked for prohibition in the United Kingdom. This change seems to have been caused by the unfortunate condition of the crops in Ireland.[68]

Doubtless the Ministry thought that these changes would make the bill more acceptable to the agricultural classes. So pro-

[64] *Commons' Journal,* 63: 294–295, 316, 339–340, 343, 352, 357–358, 386, 407. On May 12, 1808, a petition was presented asking that a thorough inquiry be made before any action be taken; this was denied on the ground that immediate relief was necessary for the planters: see *Parl. Debates,* XI: 160.

[65] *Commons' Journal,* 63: 320, 340, 357, 365, 379, 386, 394: see *Monthly Mag.,* XXV: 185, for an article supporting the West Indian merchants

[66] *Parl. Debates,* XI: 438, 448, 705–706. The charge seems to be true: see *Parl. Pap.,* 1808, No. 178, p. 27.

[67] The clause provided that after Sept. 1, 1808, the measure might be continued by proclamation until forty days after the next session of Parliament. This was interpreted by the Ministry, and accepted by the opposition, to mean from July to July: see *Parl. Debates,* XI: 441. The operation of this measure, however, rested upon royal order; the mere knowledge that it would not work otherwise probably softened the sting to the landed classes.

[68] *Parl. Debates,* XI: 431.

nounced was the opposition to these recommendations that it was with difficulty that the Ministry mustered one hundred and twenty-two members to carry a motion to commit, over the protest of one hundred and eight.[69] Commenting on this close vote, the *London Courier* remarked:[70]

> With so small a majority, we should think Ministers will see the necessity of not pressing the measure. . . . If the West Indian interests want relief, relieve them, but not at the expense of the Mother Country, of the landed interests. . . . Such a measure as the stoppage of the distillation from grain can only be justified upon one ground — a real scarcity of grain.

Exactly what took place in the Committee of the Whole House is not known, although the matter was debated into the early hours of the next morning. Evidently the opposition was conducting a determined resistance. The Government, however, had the greater strength as is shown by the vote on a motion to commit.[71] The arguments advanced during the course of the debate on this vote, while showing better thought and preparation, disclosed no new ideas. Those favoring the measure held that the landed interests would sustain no great loss, and that the sugar merchants and planters would receive positive benefit; those opposing denied the right of the Government to legislate for one group at the cost of another, and above all at the cost of the agriculturists who could ill afford any change in their accustomed trade.[72]

The matter came up again on the twenty-seventh of May, when a series of resolutions were reported by the Committee of the Whole House. The first one provided that all distillation

[69] *Commons' Journal,* 63: 349; *Parl. Debates,* XI: 448. It seems that the Ministry explained the substitution of the Committee's report by their own recommendations, on the ground that conditions had changed since the Committee had reported: see *Parl. Debates,* XI: 430–431, 434, 437, 439, 440–441. The debate on commitment may be found in *Parl. Debates,* XI: 428–448.

[70] *London Courier,* May 20, 1808: see also issue for May 24, 1808.

[71] *Parl. Debates,* XI: 493, 538. See comments in the *London Courier,* May 24, 1808; *London Times,* May 27, 1808; and *Monthly Mag.,* XXV: 571.

[72] *Parl. Debates,* XI: 493–538, especially the speeches by Mr. Barham and Mr. Western.

in the United Kingdom should be stopped from July 1 to October 1, 1808. Another allowed the Crown to continue this prohibition from October 1 to thirty days after the beginning of the next session of Parliament. Finally, it was proposed that during this prohibition the excise duty on spirits made from sugar should be regulated in the United Kingdom, so that together with the custom duty on sugar it would not exceed the duties on malt and spirits made from grain.[73]

Although the hour was late, the Commons went into a committee to discuss the first two resolutions, from which it did not arise until early the next morning. After several amendments had been made to the Committee's report, the resolutions were accepted and given to another group to frame into a bill. Contrasting these resolutions with the set as first introduced, one notes the following changes: distillation was to be forbidden after June 10 in England, after June 15 in Scotland, and after June 20 in Ireland, and to extend throughout the United Kingdom until December 31, 1808; the Crown, moreover, was empowered to stop, after September 1, 1808, the operation of this law, or to continue it from December 31, 1808, until thirty days after the next meeting of Parliament.[74] The change in the first resolution had doubtless been made so as to stop the increased distillation from corn which was then in progress. In this way the sugar merchants would not be robbed of the proposed market for their goods. The change in the second resolution probably had been made so as to weaken the opposition by permitting immediate redress in the event of an abundant harvest in 1808.[75]

The Corn Distillery Bill, as it was known, was introduced by Mr. Huskisson on May 30, 1808.[76] A few days later the second

[73] This resolution was given to the Committee on Ways and Means: see *Commons' Journal,* 63: 377; and also *ibid.,* pp. 416, 417, 425–427, 430, and 48 Geo. 3, c. 152.

[74] *Commons' Journal,* 63: 377. The votes on these amendments seem to have been very close: see *Parl. Debates,* XI: 706.

[75] *Parl. Debates,* XI: 704.

[76] The next day, the second report from the Committee on the West Indies was made and laid on the table; on June 10, a third report was dealt with in the same fashion, and on June 22 a fourth report received the same treatment: see *Commons' Journal,* 63: 388, 422, 461–462. The

reading passed by a vote of 90 to 39, which indicated clearly that the cause of the opposition was lost.[77] The third reading was carried, June 13, by a vote of 74 to 34, after which the bill passed the Commons.[78] After a short discussion in the Lords, the measure was accepted and became law June 30, 1808.[79] The joy of the West Indian interests seemed complete. On the other hand, the agriculturists deeply resented this attack upon their vested interests, and straightway made plans to stop any further inroads.

Three other acts dealing with the corn trade were passed by Parliament. The power of the Lord Lieutenant over the corn trade was extended until March, 1809.[80] Growing difficulty with America and the distress among the West Indies caused Parliament to allow the export of sugar and coffee from these islands to any European port south of Cape Finisterre, and to permit in

---

reports are to be found in *Parl. Debates,* XI: Appendix; the reports together with the evidence are found in *Parl. Pap.,* 1808, Nos. 278, 300, 318. The second report condemned the licenced trade in foreign brandies, and advocated the discontinuance of these licences, or a decided increase in the import duties. Parliament answered by placing a 10*d.* increase: see 48 Geo. 3, c. 80, and 48 Geo. 3, c. 119, for a further increase. Nothing was done to disturb the Licence System. The third report advised that the West Indies be allowed to barter sugar and coffee, as well as rum and molasses, for lumber and provisions of neutral states; also that stronger methods be adopted to stop the commerce between the enemy colonies and the United States. Nothing, however, came of these suggestions: see *Parl. Debates,* XI: 1056–1062. The fourth report called for a reduction in the import duty on refined sugar and closed with this remark: ". . . nothing has occurred since their appointment which has opened the prospect of any improvement in the West Indian Body."

[77] *Commons' Journal,* 63: 405. The arguments may be found in *Parl. Debates,* XI: 816–824; see also *London Times,* June 4, 1808.

[78] *Commons' Journal,* 63: 429. The Lords introduced no new ideas in the course of the debate; a sharp dissent, however, was entered on the journal: see *Lords' Journal,* XLVI: 760; *Parl. Debates,* XI: 999–1001.

[79] 48 Geo. 3, c. 118. In the meantime Mr. Barham and Mr. Hibbert had tried to commit the second and third reports of the West India Committee. The Government, however, was able to defeat this move: see *Parl. Debates,* XI: 973, 1056–1062. In addition to the *Distillery Act,* duties on warehoused coffee, when taken out for home consumption, were lowered by 48 Geo. 3, c. 120.

[80] 48 Geo. 3, c. 27. This did not extend to the trade to Great Britain.

turn the import of corn from these ports or from the coast of Africa. For the same reason, rice, grain and flour of any foreign colony in North or South America might be imported by certain West Indian ports, while a few articles of the United States might be entered, provided they had first been exported to Canada.[81]

During the passage of these acts the general trend of the market had been upward, due in part to the late discussion in Parliament.[82] A drop in imports and a scarcity at home were factors of greater importance. The spring and summer of 1808 had been none too favorable to the growing crops. This unfortunate situation had been followed by a series of fogs and rains which lasted throughout the fall. A more unfavorable season could hardly be imagined. By Christmas the full extent of the harvest was known. Rye, barley and oats seemed to be normal, but wheat, beans and pease were all below the average.[83] Parliament, which had recently met, at once renewed the power of the Crown and the Lord Lieutenant over the corn trade of the United Kingdom.[84]

The principal discussion of the session, however, centered about the question of distillation. Parliament had met January 19, 1809, and within two weeks Perceval threw the landed classes into fright by proposing the renewal of the *Distillery Act*. This law, he argued, had brought much benefit to Great Britain, but not to Ireland. The inability of the Irish Government to enforce the law had allowed the use of grain in the distilleries. In view of this and an overbundant potato crop, Perceval deemed it unwise to include Ireland in the proposed act. In case, however, the price of corn rose in Great Britain, the bill would be extended to Ireland by royal proclamation. After some further talk it

[81] 48 Geo. 3, cc. 69, 125.

[82] *London Examiner,* 1808, p. 327; *Farmer's Mag.,* IX: 386: see also *London Gazette,* 1808.

[83] *Farmer's Mag.,* IX: 527; *Monthly Mag.,* XXV: 189, 383, 479, 575, XXVI: 199, 299, 401; *Repository,* I: 51; *Agricultural Mag.,* II: 156, 469; *Athenaeum,* IV: 564.

[84] 49 Geo. 3, cc. 23, 31. The *Distillery Act* was extended until forty days after the beginning of the next session of Parliament: see P. C. Reg., 178, Nov. 16, 1808.

was agreed that a bill should be brought in covering these suggestions.[85]

Within a week this bill was introduced and read twice.[86] It was not, however, until the end of February that the matter received further attention. During this interval the opposition had not been silent. A storm of protest arose throughout the kingdom.[87] In Commons the talk grouped itself about the exclusion of Ireland, which was viewed as an unwarranted attack upon the agriculture of the country.[88] After a determined stand, the Ministry was forced to yield, and Ireland was included within the terms of the bill.[89] Shortly after, the measure passed both houses.[90]

It is interesting to note, in view of the discussion of 1808, that the cause for the renewal of the act was not merely the favorable results experienced by the planters, but also — probably primarily — the increased price of corn and the drop in imports.[91] That the price had risen and imports had fallen is perfectly true. Early in March, Vander Horst had remarked that the winter had —[92]

> continued very mild until nearly the close of the year when it became cold with much snow and a most unusual fall of rain accompanied by an almost constant succession for nearly two months of the most boisterous weather within my recollection, in consequence of which the country was greatly flooded, and the shipping not only in our coast, but even in many of our harbours have suffered in a degree beyond all former precedent. . . .

[85] *Parl. Debates,* XII: 240–241; *Commons' Journal,* 64: 18, 696. The proposed bill also had a clause stopping the trade in spirits between the two islands.

[86] *Commons' Journal,* 64: 22, 29.

[87] *Commons' Journal,* 64: 44, 54, 62, 64, 70, 78, 98, 99. Some of the petitions called for a renewal of the measure; others opposed this, while still others objected to the omission of Ireland.

[88] *Parl. Debates,* XII: 374–377. Foster declared that not one hogshead of sugar had been distilled in Ireland, and Eden denounced the Orders as the cause of all the trouble.

[89] *Parl. Debates,* XII: 1044–1051, 1127–1134; *Commons' Journal,* 64: 88, 100.

[90] *Commons' Journal,* 64: 106, 120, 131; 49 Geo. 3, c. 7: see also, 49 Geo. 3, cc. 8, 10, 11, 31.

[91] The act of 1808 had been extended to Feb. 28, 1809: see P. C. Reg., 178, Nov. 15, 16, 1808, and *Athenaeum,* IV: 564. On that date corn was used by the distilleries, which at once caused a drop in the price of sugar: see *Monthly Mag.,* XXVII: 215.

[92] Consular Despatches, Bristol, March 4, 1809; see p. 65, note 83.

Nevertheless, this boisterous weather does not seem to have harmed the young crops. During the summer, the fields looked favorable in spite of the heat. A heavy rain, however, spoiled matters; the harvest was clearly below the average.[93] The effect of this is to be seen in the price of wheat. On January 7, 1809, wheat had averaged 90*s*. 4*d*. in England and Wales; on June 10, it was 88*s*. 6*d*.; on September 2, it stood at 98*s*. 8*d*.; on December 30, 102*s*. 2*d*.[94]

Without doubt this sharp increase during the autumn had been due in part to the American *Non-Intercourse Act*, which, as Murray wrote, had " considerable effect on the value of American Produce." [95] Prices current at Liverpool, August 19, 1809, listed American wheat at 13*s*. to 13*s*. 9*d*. per seventy pounds, and flour at 45*s*. to 50*s*. per barrel. A similar list, September 13, showed wheat selling from 15*s*. to 16*s*. and flour from 50*s*. to 56*s*.[96] On the other hand the volume of imports was slightly greater than that of the past year. The fear, therefore, of a complete stoppage of the foreign supply and the partial failure of the home crops had caused these high prices.

This in brief was the situation facing Parliament when it met, January 23, 1810. Within two weeks a series of petitions from Scotland appeared asking for the renewal of the *Distillery Act* on the ground that the measure had been very helpful and because of the rumor that there was a scarcity of corn. On the other hand the Irish petitioners felt that the act had stopped the growth of agriculture, which was so essential at that time for the welfare of the entire nation.[97]

The debate was opened, February 13, 1810, by Rose who

[93] *Athenaeum,* V: 383; *Farmer's Mag.,* X: 112, 253, 271, 401, 424, 430, 546, 557; *Monthly Mag.,* XXVII: 110, 423, 645, XXVIII: 242, 347; *Literary Panorama,* VII: 350; *Repository,* I: 396–397; *Dropmore Papers,* IX: 323; *Life and Correspondence of R. King,* V: 124, 144, 150, 171; Consular Despatches, Bristol, Sept. 23, 1809.

[94] These are weekly averages.

[95] Consular Despatches, Liverpool, Sept. 13, 1809.

[96] *Ibid.*

[97] *Commons' Journal,* 65: 27, 33, 40, 49, 78, 84, 85. In the fall of 1809 the Ministry had its attention called to the question by a series of petitions asking for relief against sugar distillation: see B. T., 5: 19, Aug. 24, Sept. 27, 1809. The Board answered these by writing that distillation from sugar was to be continued, and a proclamation to that effect was shortly

moved the commitment of the act of 1809 to the whole house. At once Parnell sprang to his feet. With telling effect he called upon Perceval to show why the Ministry had required an investigation of the agricultural situation in 1808 before passing the distillation bill, but why no inquiry was now made. The causes, Parnell declared, for the act of 1808 had been twofold: the distress of the West Indies and the failure of the harvest. These, he insisted, did not exist in 1810. The sugar merchants were no longer in need of relief as the price of that article had risen from 32*s*. per cwt. in 1808 to 56*s*. in 1810. Nor were the present high prices of corn to be explained on the ground of scarcity, but rather because of an inflated paper currency. The entire proposition was an unwarranted and dangerous attack upon the agricultural interests of the state. Finally, if the report were true that the act was not to include Ireland, then the omission of that island would constitute a violation of the *Act of Union*.[98] In closing, Parnell proposed an amendment which called for an inquiry into the agricultural condition of the kingdom. Similar ideas were held by Newport, Hutchinson, Gratton and others from the farming sections of England. Rose and Perceval replied to these charges by condemning the amendment. They believed that, if carried, it would cause an unnecessary alarm throughout the realm.[99] Again, they insisted, with much truth, that the harvest of Great Britain had been a failure, and that this, rather than a disorganized currency, had forced prices up. Nor was there any violation of the *Act of*

---

issued which extended the act until March 5, 1810: see B. T., 5: 19, Oct. 31, 1809; P. C. Reg., 183, Nov. 1, 1809. See also B. T., 1: 48, for a letter from a Wm. Young, Nov. 3, 1809, depicting the favorable condition of the crops and asking for a repeal of the recent act. See also the resolutions of the Cotton Manufacturers of Glasgow favoring the use of sugar; B. T., 1: 49, Feb. 12, 1810.

98 The supposed violation of the *Act of Union* existed in the proposal which was to stop the trade in Irish distilled spirits between the two islands.

99 It will be recalled that the inquiry in 1808 had caused an alarm over the question of scarcity; to what extent Perceval had profited by the experience gained in 1808 can not be determined. Probably such an investigation was not now suitable to his immediate plans.

Union, for unless Irish spirits were kept out of Britain, British corn would find a market in the form of Irish spirits. The Ministry announced, moreover, that the proposed measure was not to include Ireland, as that island had a most bountiful harvest, a statement which was apparently true.[100] The result of this rather heated discussion favored the Government, as Parnell's motion was decisively defeated and the order for commitment carried.[101] The next day a bill incorporating the main ideas made by Perceval was read for the first time.[102]

This bill concerned only Great Britain, a fact which did not altogether please the British landlords. From various parts of Britain petitions appeared for and against the bill. In support of those condemning the proposed act, Mr. Western asked the Ministry to show cause for the continuance of the measure. With great force and skill he declared that the old story of distress among the West Indies was no longer heard, and that the friends of the measure had found refuge in a supposed scarcity. Wheat alone, he maintained, had risen in price since 1808.[103]

Whether the West Indies needed any help or not, does not seem to have been considered by the Ministry. The question was viewed solely from the point of view of the corn market, and there seems to be no reason for doubting the wisdom of this opinion. If in 1808 the Government felt that the colonies were entitled to relief, it does not necessarily follow also that the cause for that relief had to exist in 1810 in order to justify a similar act. In 1810, the sugar interests were fairly prosperous, thanks to the *Distillery Act.* Repeal that act and the West Indies would straightway be where they had been in 1808. Although doubtless aware of this likely condition, the Ministry nevertheless felt that the act ought to be continued because of the harvest failure of 1809. Prices, contrary to Western's statement, were higher than they had been for the past two years.[104]

[100] *Parl. Debates,* XV: 393.

[101] The vote was 58 to 17: see *Parl. Debates,* XV: 390–399; *Commons' Journal,* 65: 91. The report of this committee favored prohibiting the distillation of corn in Britain.

[102] *Commons' Journal,* 65: 95.

[103] *Parl. Debates,* XV: 499.

[104] This was not true for oats, beans and pease. See *Cobbett's Pol. Reg.,* XVII: 240–242, for an attack upon Parnell.

An attempt by Parnell and Western to postpone action by placing the matter on the table was crushed by a vote of 155 to 54.[105] Two days later, the measure was warmly debated in the Committee, where an attempt was made to extend the measure to Ireland. In introducing an amendment to that effect, Lord Hamilton asked: " . . . if there was such a superabundance of grain in Ireland how . . . [did it happen] that special licences were granted to import grain into this country from France?" This was a fair question, and, as far as the debates show, no attempt was made to answer it. On the contrary the Ministry sought to prove that the bountiful crops of Ireland ought to be distilled so as to further the growth of corn in that island. In England, however, where there was a scarcity, distillation from corn was to be forbidden so as to save every possible bushel of corn. In spite of these conflicting ideas, the Government defeated Lord Hamilton's motion and passed the bill as first introduced.[106] In the Lords, the landed classes bitterly attacked the measure, but were not able to overcome the majorities of the Government and the bill became law.[107] They were able, however, to enter a dissenting resolution and to obtain the appointment of a committee to inquire into the question of distillation from sugar.[108]

[105] *Commons' Journal,* 65: 109; *Parl. Debates,* XV: 499–500. Notice the forecasting of the alliance of 1814 and 1815.

[106] *Parl. Debates,* XV: 541–552; the vote on Hamilton's motion was 110 to 68. See the *London Times,* Feb. 17, 23, 1810. At the same time a bill to stop the import of Irish and British spirits into both islands was introduced; later, this bill was joined to the distillation bill and became part of 50 Geo. 3, c. 5. During this period, several petitions dealing with distillation were received: see *Commons' Journal,* 65: 91, 92, 93, 95, 96, 103, 108. Even after the measure was passed petitions continued to be presented: see *ibid.,* 65: 276, 307, 345, 348, 357, 373, 457, 489, 495. These were all from Scotland and desired the repeal of the act. See also B. T., 5: 20, Sept. and Oct., 1810, for frequent mention of petitions; see too B. T., 5: 20, Dec. 13, 20, 1810.

[107] 50 Geo. 3, c. 5.

[108] *Parl. Debates,* XV: 642–644, XVI: 1. In view of the discussions of 1814 and 1815 this dissent is of interest. The contents of this document may be grouped as follows: first, the bill had been rushed through without a careful examination having been made; secondly, that the bill harmed the farmers; thirdly, that it injured the West Indies as it gave but a temporary form of relief; fourthly, that the bill was contrary to the interests of the mass of the people who depended upon grain for their food;

In brief the arguments of the Lords were that any injury inflicted upon the farmers and landlords would cause a decline in agricultural activity, and that any decrease in the supply would create a serious problem for consumers who could ill afford to pay the increased cost which would naturally follow. In general, the truth of this opinion can not be denied. But did the act harm the agricultural interests; and if it did to what extent?[109] That a relatively unimportant branch of agriculture would suffer can not be questioned; but was that injury, though little, justified? The Ministry insisted that it was, because of the scarcity of corn. It is of interest to note that this scarcity, according to report, was not sufficiently large to check distillation, had corn been used; further, it was not proved that the barley so saved by the distillation from sugar could be used as food for man. Hence as barley was practically the only corn saved by the distillation bill, it is not altogether clear how distillation from sugar would provide extra supplies of corn for consumption. Again, it would seem that the omission of Ireland from the act was actually a blunder on the part of the Ministry as the distilleries of Ireland used not merely barley, but oats and wheat as well. Why should this be allowed, when England was suffering from a scarcity? Why, also, should the nation pay toll to France by licencing corn imports when Ireland had such large supplies? The answer, possibly, to this question may be found in the West Indian problem. The Continental System had robbed these

---

see *Lords' Journal,* XLVII: 496–497. This shows the growing concern on the part of the agriculturists for the need of further protection. Indeed, the Lords' Committee, appointed the same day the bill became law, was ordered to inquire into the "Effect likely to be produced by a further Continuation of the Prohibition of Distillation from Grain, and generally into the Circumstances which may tend to the Encouragement and Protection of the agricultural Interests of the United Kingdom:" see *Lords' Journal,* XLVII: 502. During the debate in the Lords numerous petitions were presented; see *Lords' Journal, ibid.,* 481, 486, 487, 488, 491, 535, 558, 594, 599, 611, 621, 662, 686, 695. For copy of this report see *Parl. Pap.,* 1810, No. 67.

[109] The evidence submitted by Messrs. Coke, Curwen, W. M. Hill and Beecher, all of Norfolk, was that the closure of the distilleries to corn would ultimately harm agriculture, especially if the measure were continued in the future: see *Parl. Pap.,* 1810, No. 67, p. 4.

islands of an accustomed market. To make good this loss, the Government had passed the *Distillery Act,* which helped the West Indian interests at the expense of the barley growers; a cost, however, which was small in contrast to that which had been borne by the sugar interests. Once more, the problem practically narrows itself down to the November Orders and the French Decrees; and the question of their repeal or change rested upon other and possibly more important matters.

One can not but wonder, in view of the past conduct of Western and his fellow landlords, to what extent these gentlemen were prompted by a desire to help the consumers. For the time, at least, it was but natural that both producers and consumers should join in opposing an act which they thought harmful to their interests. Which of the two would first withdraw from this alliance was to be clearly seen in the passage of the laws of 1814 and 1815.

The session of 1809 and 1810, to return to the matter at hand, closed without any serious change in the Corn Laws.[110] Prices of wheat and rye were higher than ever before, while other grains showed a slight drop.[111] On March 17, 1810, the average price of wheat in England and Wales was 102*s.* 3*d.;* by August 11, 1810, it was 115*s.* 2*d.* Various factors had produced these prices: the failure of the harvest of 1809, the foreign situation, and the unseasonable weather in the first part of 1810,[112] the interference with the supply from Europe and America, and the inflation of the currency. Prospects were very gloomy. During the summer, however, the weather steadily improved.[113] By the middle of

[110] See 50 Geo. 3, c. 19.

[111] The lowest duty on imports was collected during this period; the total amount collected equalled £56,268; see *Accounts and Papers,* 1898, vol. 34, p. 259.

[112] See p. 67; and also *Monthly Mag.,* XXVIII: 113, 200, XXIX: 103, 199, 307, 405; *Cobbett's Pol. Reg.,* XVII: 935, 936; *London Times,* Feb. 17, July 21, 1810. Contrast these prices with those given by Smart, Wm., *Economic Annals of the Nineteenth Century,* I: 225.

[113] *Monthly Mag.,* XXIX: 519, 620; *Cobbett's Pol. Reg.,* XVII: 113, 200; *London Times,* July 13, 1810. Note the repeated rumor of a scarcity in Ireland, and the keen remarks made about it and the *Distillery Act* of 1810, in *Cobbett's Pol. Reg.,* XVII: 137, 178, and *London Courier,* July 26, 1810.

September prices began to tumble as definite news told of a favorable harvest. A situation the reverse of the past quarter was now thankfully reviewed by the nation. Favorable reports were sent in from all parts of the kingdom. The year closed amid a "harvest of golden grain," and most pleasing prospects for the future.[114]

[114] B. T., 6: 177, Petition from Ranoff, Sept. 28, 1810; *Farmer's Mag.*, XI: 514, XII: 396–397, XIII: 115; *Literary Panorama,* VIII: 782, 948, 955, 1181, 1391; *Cobbett's Pol. Reg.*, XVIII: 214. See P. C. Reg., 189, Oct. 17, 1810, for an order in council providing for a general prayer of thanksgiving in the United Kingdom. The weekly average price of wheat in England and Wales was 105*s.* 8*d.* on Sept. 29, 1810; on Nov. 3, 1810, 99*s.* 11*d.*; and on Dec. 29, 1810, 94*s.* 7*d.*: see *London Gazette.*

CHAPTER V

AN ERA OF HIGH PRICES

The Commercial and Industrial crisis of 1811 and 1812 — The Committee on Commercial Credit — The high prices of 1812 — The Luddite Riots — The break-up of the Continental System in 1813 — The fall in prices.

IT was during this period of bumper crops that a commercial and industrial crisis took place which shook the kingdom to its very foundations. The steady growth of the Industrial Revolution, overspeculation in the golden bubble of South America, the Orders in Council and the impending American war were factors that had caused this crisis. "For a few months past," wrote Vander Horst, "commercial failures to a vast amount have been almost daily occurring at Liverpool and in its neighborhood."[1] Manufacturers, burdened by overproduction and worthless credit, were forced either to stop all production or to run along on the narrowest possible margin. The merchants, deeply indebted to the manufacturers by reason of the ill-conceived South American trade, had a stock of unsold goods. In the meantime the brokers and bankers who financed these merchants found themselves in a serious dilemma.

As this wave of depression grew, firm after firm crashed and declared itself bankrupt.[2] Factories closed down; and labor roamed the country in quest of work and food. Universal distress camped in Great Britain where the Imperial eagles could not. The situation in the manufacturing and commercial districts became most acute. It was stated that over a thousand persons in Carlisle were out of work. In Liverpool some 16,000 were kept alive by charity during the winter of 1811–12.[3] These

[1] Consular Despatches, Bristol, Oct. 25, 1810.
[2] *Annual Register,* 1811, p. 24.
[3] *Parl. Pap.,* 1812, No. 210, p. 365.

figures may seem small when contrasted with the dense populations there today. We should recall, however, that the entire population of Great Britain in 1811 was but 12,353,000 and that Liverpool had only 94,376 people.[4]

In an attempt to give relief, the Government appointed a Committee on Commercial Credit. This body, urged on by the thought that something must be done, made within a week a report which was enacted a month later into law. This measure provided for the advance of Government bills, upon sufficient collateral, to those who wished this assistance. The Ministry extended a helping hand to the bankers, merchants and manufacturers, but turned a cold shoulder towards the laboring classes who largely bore the burden of it all.[5] Small wonder was it, therefore, that the unemployed wagged their heads and questioned the cause for this unemployment and the shortage of food. Their vision, considerably blinded by a narrow perspective and by the presence of hunger in their homes, caused them to place the chief blame upon that " detestable " source of all trouble — the power-loom. Producer after producer, understanding the value of these time- and labor-saving machines, had placed them in their factories. The result was inevitable. Large numbers of workers were discharged, who naturally looked upon the power-loom as the chief cause for their distress.

Closely akin to this in the list of grievances was the high price of food. That the harvest of 1811 was short, is beyond all question. A single quotation will illustrate this fact: [6]

> The weather during the last three months has been uncommonly capricious, constantly running into extremes, thereby giving much trouble and

[4] *Ibid.*, No. 316, pp. xxviii, 160.

[5] 51 Geo. 3, c. 15; *Parl. Debates,* XIX: 123–129, 249–260, 328–350, 416–422, 529–538, 662–664. See Hammond, J. L. and B., *Skilled Labourer* (London, Longmans, 1919), for a review of the condition of the factory hands. The Home Office Papers are crowded with vivid accounts of this situation.

[6] *Farmer's Mag.*, XII: 538. The *Monthly Mag.* stated that the wheat crop was one third under the average: see XXXI: 304, 399, 503, 604, XXXII: 101, 205, 309. The *Literary Panorama,* IX: 605, 1007, X: 356, 568, and *Bell's Weekly Messenger,* Jan. 5, 1812, estimated the crop to be one fourth short. See also B. T., 5: 21, Nov. 28, 1811 and B. T., 1: 61, Dec. 2, 1811.

vexation to the corn farmer. . . . The Wheat crop is less or more a defective one in every district, but more so in some districts than in others. According to our accounts it can rarely be estimated above five-eighths of an average crop; though, what is surprizing, the quality of the grain is generally good. . . . Indeed as the failure this season was not, in many instances, occasioned by mildew (at least in Scotland) the grain that was in the ear arrived at complete maturity without being stunted of nourishment. The deficiency evidently proceeded from wetness in May, from cold frosty nights in June, from boisterous winds when the plant was under the blossom process, and from want of sun and heat when the grain was formed in the ear of the plant.

The effect of these factors upon prices had been most pronounced. The year opened with wheat averaging for England and Wales 94*s.* 7*d.*, and closed at 106*s.* 7*d.*[7]

During this period Parliament gave but scant attention to the agricultural state of the country. The *Distillery Act* was allowed to die; and no important change was made in the Corn Laws. In general, export was stopped, except that to the enumerated places, and import was permitted at the lowest duty.[8]

The failure of the harvest of 1811 prompted Parliament to

[7] These are weekly averages. For a detailed account see Appendix No. 5.

[8] See Appendix No. 5. It seems that the Ministry tried to foster a bill that would permit the use of both sugar and grain in the distilleries. This was a marked concession to the agriculturists. It failed, however, to satisfy either the landed or the West Indian interests, both of whom wanted the complete monopoly of the distillery trade. In general, the West Indians rallied to the support of the measure, while the landed classes opposed it. The debate lacked much of the fire of the previous years, and in the Commons the bill passed without great opposition. In the Lords, however, the matter was postponed for six months because of the strength of the agriculturists. The bill did not provide for equal duties on corn and sugar wash; rather, sugar was given a distinct preference: see *Commons' Journal,* 66: 205, 215, 218, 223, 225, 228, 234, 236, 242, 247, 250, 256, 257; *Lords' Journal,* XLVIII: 202–203, 204, 205, 212, 217, 226, 241, 242–243; *Parl. Debates,* XIX: 321–325, 357–360, 687–690, 753–754, 789–795, *Farmer's Mag.,* XII: 117, 265; *Anti-Jacobin Rev.,* XXXVIII: 330; see also 51 Geo. 3, c. 42; *London Times,* Dec. 18, 20, 1810. During the fall and winter of 1810, the Board of Trade received fifteen petitions against the continuation of the *Distillery Act* and thirteen petitions in favor of the law. The arguments of those opposed were that (1) the present crop was very abundant, especially of oats and barley; (2) the reasons for distillation that existed before were now of no value; (3) the continuation of this act would be harmful to the agriculture of the United Kingdom. Those in favor argued that (1) foreign affairs warranted a renewal of the law; (2) the high prices of corn showed the relative scarcity of corn; (3)

action.[9] Early in January, 1812, Perceval introduced a series of resolutions providing for distillation from sugar. He deemed the adoption of these most imperative in view of the comparative failure of the crop.[10] These resolutions aimed at the revival of the *Distillery Act* of 1809 and of the act suspending the trade in spirits between Ireland and Great Britain. Little or no debate followed, and both resolutions became law early in February.[11]

By the terms of the act, distillation from grain was not forbidden in Ireland, but by March it became clear that this had been a mistake. An overuse of grain by the distilleries and a failure of the potato crop had caused a rapid rise in prices. Late in the next month, therefore, distillation from grain was stopped in Ireland.[12] As a further check against the excessive use of grain, a measure was passed which forbade the use of wheat and other

---

the act had been of great help to the West Indies; (4) business conditions did not warrant any tampering with the trade of the colonies: see B. T., 6: 177; also B. T., 1: 53, Dec., 1810, for a copy of a resolution signed by ten distillers of Essex, Surrey and Middlesex, that they would not distill from corn until the sense of Parliament had been obtained. It is also significant that during 1811 the licenced trade was seriously checked, especially to France and Holland; in this way a source of food was closed. See pp. 118–119.

[9] Late in 1811, the Board of Trade received a group of petitions against the use of grain in the distilleries on the ground that the harvest was a failure: see B. T., 5: 21, Nov. 28, 1811; B. T., 1: 61, Nov. 20, Dec. 2, 1811; cf. *London Times,* Nov. 20, 1811, for an editorial calling for distillation from sugar.

[10] The purposes of these resolutions were (1) to prohibit from Feb. 1, 1812, until Dec. 31, 1812, the making or brewing from oats, barley, or any other corn, grain or malt, flour or bran, or any mixture of the same, for distillation in Great Britain; (2) to prevent distillation after Feb. 15, 1812, from any of the foregoing articles in the form of wash or worts; (3) that after Oct. 1, 1812, the prohibition might be stopped by proclamation (not less than 30 days after date of proclamation) or might be continued from Dec. 31 until 30 days after the next meeting of Parliament. Other resolutions dealing with corn and sugar were proposed, but these concerned the revenue. These are to be found in *Parl. Debates,* XXI: 147–150; *Commons' Journal,* 67: 34–35.

[11] 52 Geo. 3, c. 3; for the debates see *Parl. Debates,* XXI: 286–292, 320–326, 490–492; and also *Commons' Journal,* 67: 28, 34, 37, 42, 50–51, 56, 68. It seems that the causes for this act were the failure of the harvest of 1811 and the general scarcity of corn.

[12] 52 Geo. 3, c. 47; *Parl. Debates,* XXII: 31–36, 232–234, 239–243, 708–716, 857–858; *Commons' Journal,* 67: 306, 312, 315, 328: see also 52 Geo. 3, c. 118.

articles of food in the manufacture of starch, hair powder and glue.[13]

By this time, however, a crisis had been reached. The favorable prospects of early 1812 disappeared as an unseasonable summer progressed.[14] Rich and poor alike felt the pinch of scarcity — but not hunger, for that was the privilege of the poor. The former were forced to give up their pastry, and frequently mixed rice with flour in making bread. This was very laudable, but was small by way of sacrifice as compared to that which the poor were called upon to make. If the well-to-do had their wheatless days, they at least had milk, meat, cheese and many other articles of food. On the other hand, rice-bread, oatmeal and water furnished a meagre diet for the laborer in either the country or city.[15]

Added to this was the rapid drop which had taken place in imports. According to many, this had been caused by the November Orders.[16] This was by no means a new idea. As early as 1808 the charge had been made that these measures had withheld food supplies.[17] Again, to judge from facts presented on the eve of the war with America, there can be no doubt but that the distress in Leeds, Manchester and other industrial centers had been caused in part by these Orders; especially, as they had seriously interfered with the grain trade. Broughman presented this idea when speaking of the scarcity: "Have you not taken away the only remedy for this scarcity; the only relief to which we can look under a bad harvest — by closing the corn market

[13] 52 Geo. 3, c. 127, to extend to Nov. 1, 1812; *Commons' Journal,* 67: 426, 429, 506, 508, 514: see also *Parl. Debates,* XXII: 273–278; *London Times,* Oct. 27, 1812. A renewal of the licenced trade with France and Holland was allowed in 1812: see p. 120.

[14] *Monthly Mag.,* XXXIII: 96, 307, 403, 500, 595, XXXIV: 95–96; *Bell's Weekly Messenger,* Feb. 2, July 5, 1812; *Literary Panorama,* XI: 178, 945, 946. Weekly prices had risen from 106*s.* 7*d.* on Jan. 4 to 140*s.* 9*d.* on July 4, 1812.

[15] *London Times,* Nov. 9, 1811.

[16] *London News,* April 26, May 10, 1812; *Diary . . . of . . . Abbott,* II: 376.

[17] *Parl. Debates,* XII: 85, 376, 780: see also *ibid.,* XXII: 435, 438, 1095; *Athenaeum,* V: 192; *Repository,* I: 52; *London Examiner,* Jan. 24, 1808; and *Parl. Pap.,* 1808, No. 119.

of America? . . . Why, Sir, to deny that these measures [the Orders in Council] affect the scarcity is . . . absurd."[18] A mere glance at the import figures will convince one of the truth of this statement. To add still more to the seriousness, fear as to the harvest and the effect of the American declaration of war forced prices upward.[19] By August 15, 1812, the weekly price of wheat for England and Wales reached 155*s*.

The effect of these prices, and of the failure of the harvest of 1811 and the unsettled weather of 1812, as well as of the industrial and commercial stagnation, is to be seen in the riots that broke forth in various parts of the realm. At Bristol, Carlisle and Glasgow these grew to an alarming size. At Sheffield the flour dealers were forced by a mob of men and women to sell their grain at stated prices. The following notice, found among the Home Office Papers, shows the seriousness of the situation. It was addressed to a Mr. Douglass who seems to have owned a mill near Manchester: [20]

> If you do not advance the wages of all your workmen at Holywell, you shall have all your mills burnt to the ground immediately. It is harder upon us here than upon those who receive parish relief. We are starving by inches by reason of our small wages and provisions so high.
>
> The Poor cry aloud for bread
> Prince Regent shall lose his head
> And all the rich who oppress the poor
> In a little time shall be no more.

Troops were sent to this and other parts of the country. One may feel sure, however, that the favorable turn of the weather in August, with the subsequent fall of prices, was more effective than the military in quieting these disturbances.[21]

It is not our purpose, nor is it altogether necessary, to go into an exhaustive study of these riots, commonly known as the Lud-

[18] *Parl. Debates,* XXIII: 492, 496: see also *ibid.,* XXII: 435, 438, 1095.

[19] *Farmer's Mag.,* XIII: 427; Consular Despatches, London, Aug. 3, 1812.

[20] H. O., 40: 1, Wm. R. Hay, Police Officer at Manchester, to Ryder, May 6, 1812.

[21] *Annual Register,* 1812, "Chronicle," pp. 55–58; *Life . . . of . . . Sidmouth,* III: 89–90; *Memoirs of Sir Samuel Romilly,* III: 46; *London Times,* April 11, 17, 20, 24, Aug. 21, 25, Sept. 28, 1812; Consular Despatches, London, Aug. 14, 29, 1812.

dite Riots. The details of this organized movement, the frame-breaking by the strikers, the mysterious meetings and oaths, and the ultimate result have been well told by J. L. and B. Hammond in *The Skilled Labourer*. Our interest in this movement is chiefly one-sided, namely, the extent to which the agricultural situation aided in causing these riots.

According to the facts given by a committee appointed to inquire into these disturbances, it was found that the high price of corn was but a contributing cause. Greater emphasis was placed by all examined upon the want of trade and work. When conditions were compared with the first two years of the century, the witnesses unanimously said that the want of food was far more severe than in 1811. At the earlier date there had been both work and money; at the time in question, there were a limited supply of food and very little money. The inevitable result had been rioting and bloodshed.[22]

Similar expressions may easily be found in contemporary literature.[23] Whether there would have been any riots had the agricultural condition been favorable, is quite another matter. General Maitland, in charge of the military in the disturbed area, believed that the Luddite Riots would never have happened had the harvest been better and had trade been free with America. This is also the view of the Hammonds in *The Skilled Labourer*.[24] Without a doubt there is much truth in this conclusion. The high prices showed the presence of a scarcity as well as a bridgeless gap between the laborer's purse and a loaf of bread. Had the harvest of 1811 been better, had the weather been more favorable during 1812, and had trade been free with America, there is nothing to indicate that the course of these riots would not have been far different. To declare, however, that there would have been no riots is to ignore the bitter hate in the laborer's mind towards the power-looms that had robbed him of work. Further, such a view overlooks the November Orders whose longevity can best be explained by their success.

[22] *Parl. Debates*, XXIII: 496; *Parl. Pap.*, 1812, No. 210.

[23] See for example *London Times*, April 14, 1812.

[24] H. O., 42: 129, quoted by Hammond, J. L. and B., *op. cit.*, p. 323. See also H. O., 40: 1, Report from Maitland, May 6, 1812, and Maitland to Ryder, May 11, 1812, and Maitland to Sidmouth, June 19, 1812.

These very measures, by checking commerce with Europe, had decreased the trade with the United States. Again, it should be borne in mind that the industrial crisis that had its climax in the Luddite Riots had its beginnings not in 1812, but late in 1810 and early 1811, during which period one notes a steady drop in food prices. This drop, it will be recalled, had been caused by the bountiful harvest of 1810, and the large volume of imports of that year, and the early, though false, reports of a favorable crop in 1811. Vander Horst, writing late in June, 1811, remarks: "Agricultural pursuits now employ a great number of those who at other seasons of the year [are] occupied in the different manufactures of the Kingdom."[25] Hence, by way of résumé, it may be stated that the chief cause for the riots of 1812 can not be found in the agricultural situation, although it was a factor of importance, but rather in a combination of the agricultural and the other causes noted. Finally, it should be observed that General Maitland felt that the discontent had been fomented by those interested in the doctrines of the French Revolution. "I have no doubt," he wrote, "there is a most mischievous spirit abroad, aiming at nothing more or less than the subversion of the Government of the country and the destruction of all property."[26]

Throughout the remaining months prices steadily fell, wheat averaging for England and Wales December 5, 1812, 121*s*. 5*d*. During harvest time, however, cold winds, heavy rains and frosts tended to harm the quality of the crops, as well as to cause much damage to the young plants.[27] An early winter of unusual severity followed. This was the winter which buried the Grand Army in Russia. Nature, it seemed, was equally bent on disabling England.

The harvest of 1812, therefore, while by no means as poor as

[25] Consular Despatches, Bristol, June 25, 1811. See Smart, Wm., *Economic Annals of the Nineteenth Century,* I: 226–227, 263–275, and Tooke, Thomas, *History of Prices* (London, Longmans, 1838–1857), I: 303 ff., for a discussion of this industrial crisis.

[26] H. O., 40: 1, Maitland to the Home Office, May 6, 1812.

[27] *Farmer's Mag.,* XIII: 536; *Bell's Weekly Messenger,* April 5, Sept. 27, 1812; *Literary Panorama,* XII: 528, 722; *Monthly Mag.,* XXXIV: 95, 191, 285; *Life and Correspondence of R. King,* V: 274; *Diary . . . of . . . Abbott,* II: 408.

that of 1811, still was below the average; wheat, fortunately, suffered the least of all. Grave doubt was expressed as to the condition of the young crops. Anticipating the worst, the Crown proclaimed the continuation of the *Starch Act,* while Parliament, as soon as it had met, extended this law until October 1, 1813.[28] Distillation from grain was also stopped in the United Kingdom until January, 1814.[29]

The opening of 1813 marked the break-up of Napoleon's power. From that time the European sources of grain were thrown open to the English. The Continental System was a thing of the past. Thus far in our study the Continental System has been dealt with only incidentally. It is the purpose of the remaining chapters of this volume to show the relationship between that system and the grain trade of Great Britain.

28 53 Geo. 3, c. 2, repealed by 53 Geo. 3, c. 23: see also *Commons' Journal,* 68: 859.

29 53 Geo. 3, c. 7.

CHAPTER VI

THE LICENCED TRADE

The genesis of the Licence System — Its growth and development up to the Peace of Amiens — The renewal of war in 1803 — The Licence System and the Navigation Acts — The Orders in Council of June and August, 1805 — The rapid extension of the Licence System after the February Order, 1807 — The Tory Ministry and the Orders of November, 1807 — The attempted restriction in the spring of 1809 — The harvest failure of 1809 — The French and Dutch Licences of 1809 and 1810 — The temporary restriction of 1811 — The War of 1812 — The downfall of Napoleon and the abandonment of the Licence System, 1813 — An appreciation of the Licence System.

IT is believed, in the light of the foregoing account, that the effect of the operation of the old-time Corn Laws during the Napoleonic era was negligible. The extent to which these measures directed the grain trade may, therefore, be questioned. Economic and political causes set these laws to one side, and placed in their stead a most interesting substitute. Out of conditions peculiar to a state of war, there had grown a system of licences by means of which all trade might be undertaken.[1] It is the purpose of this chapter to show, so far as is possible, the origin and growth of this substitute, *The Licenced Trade*. Fortunately, our problem disposes itself into several divisions: the period before the Peace of Amiens; the years after that until 1807; the time between the Orders of January, 1807, and those of April, 1809; and finally, the era from April, 1809, to the close of 1813.

At the outset one is met by the question of the meaning and scope of the term, *The Licenced Trade*. The word 'licence' implies a permission, given by one constitutionally entitled to grant it, to undertake an act which is forbidden by statute. By

[1] It should not be inferred that the need of guarding a foreign supply had caused these licences, or that the use of them was limited to the grain trade.

'trade' is meant all forms of foreign commerce and navigation. For our purpose this is limited to the grain trade, although frequent reference will be made to trade in general. The immediate objective, therefore, is an analysis of the licenced trade in its relation to the movement of grain.

Necessity and necessity alone had caused the Government to licence a trade in corn. The inability on the part of the agriculturists to grow sufficient corn had forced the Ministry to seek for additional supplies in foreign countries. As has been already shown, this situation preceded the French War.[2] The advent of this struggle made the problem infinitely more acute. Ordinary and accustomed methods adapted to conditions of peace broke down, forcing the Government to suspend, in part, the Navigation Acts, and to allow a limited trade with the enemy.

Hardly had the fiction of peace with France been shown by the outbreak of war in 1793, when the trend of events clearly foreshadowed the system of licences as it later developed. Early in May of that year, in an attempt to inflict a telling blow upon the enemy, Parliament passed the *Traitorous Correspondence Bill*. This law forbade, during the war, the selling, supplying, contracting for or delivering, on the part of anyone in Great Britain, military stores, commercial paper or specie of England, forage, foodstuffs, raw and finished articles of clothing, to or for the use of the French Government or places annexed to or under the influence of France, its armed forces or agents. This measure applied to both Britishers and neutrals in Great Britain, and aimed at the total stoppage of export trade with the enemy in any of goods enumerated in the act.[3] The evident impossibility of enforcing this law clearly impressed the Ministry, which is shown by a clause within the act which permitted the export of these articles to the enemy by anyone in Great Britain, provided a licence had been obtained from the Crown.[4] Thus as early as 1793 there was a legal basis for a

[2] See p. 2.

[3] Only by implication can it be stated that this act served as a basis for import licences, an idea which is strengthened by 39 Geo. 3, c. 98: see also 34 Geo. 3, c. 34.

[4] 33 Geo. 3, c. 27: see also 34 Geo. 3, cc. 9, 79. Corn, grain, meal and

licenced export trade with the enemy. No further changes were made until 1796, when anyone in Great Britain was allowed by licence to sell or ship certain articles of the growth, production or manufacture of Great Britain or of any foreign country. It was, also, understood that these goods were destined to or for the use of persons in the United Provinces, the Austrian Netherlands, or Italy, provided the goods were exported under bond and in neutral ships.[5] Two years later the act of 1793 was extended to the United Provinces, Switzerland, and, in 1800, to Spain.[6] Without doubt this was a direct, though legal contravention of the object of the war in that it allowed trading with the enemy. To do otherwise, however, was clearly impossible.

The first definite signs of import licences appear in the Orders in Council of October 5, 1796, and April 25, 1798. These measures permitted, under certain conditions, a licenced export and import trade between Great Britain and Flanders, France and the United Provinces, of enumerated goods, among which were listed corn, grain, meal, or flour.[7] A more definite and comprehensive measure, doing away with individual orders or acts, was adopted in the summer of 1799. According to this, one might import into the United Kingdom from any place in neutral ships any of the goods named in any order, notwithstanding any

---

flour, as well as other goods, were listed among the prohibited articles. Licences were asked of all subjects going to France or to places under its control. Any insurance issued in Great Britain upon French ships bound to a port of France was null and void. Heavy penalties were stated for any violation of this act.

[5] Order in Council, Sept. 3, 1796; this order was based upon the acts of 1793 and 1794. All licences issued under this order were to expire when the order did, Dec. 25, 1796. The articles to be exported were to be named within the licence, and were not to include any naval stores or supplies for the army, or any article prohibited by law. Minor custom regulations also existed.

[6] 38 Geo. 3, cc. 28, 45, Orders in Council, Oct. 5, 1796, April 25, 1798, March 14, 1800: see also 38 Geo. 3, c. 79. No further changes were made before the Peace of Amiens.

[7] By 39 Geo. 3, c. 98, Spanish wool might be imported under licence from any place in neutral ships. At a later date, the principles of the Orders of 1796 and 1798 were extended to Spain: see P. C. Reg., 154, March 14, 1800. See Appendix No. 6 for typical licences in which a full list of the enumerated goods is given.

law to the contrary.[8] Supplementing this, an act passed early in 1800 permitted a licenced import trade between the United Kingdom and European possessions in America. This trade might include any raw or manufactured goods or produce, not forbidden by law, provided they were imported in neutral ships.[9] Early in December of the same year, the Council ordered that all neutral vessels importing supplies from ports, blockaded or unblockaded, should not be touched by any British ship or privateer.[10]

The sovereign power of Parliament to pass these measures cannot be disputed. It should be noted, however, that these acts contravened the object of the war and seriously relaxed the time-honored Navigation System.[11] Frequent changes of the latter had been made early in the war. In 1795, as a result of diplomatic negotiations with the United Provinces, Dutch property coming direct thence was allowed to be warehoused in Great Britain. This property might be imported in any vessel, navigated in any fashion whatsoever. About the same time the privilege of warehousing was given to goods belonging to Dutch, British, or neutral subjects going from a neutral state to a Dutch port in neutral ships or those of British or Dutch subjects.[11a] The authority for this trade, however, was an order in council, and not an act of Parliament. By way of indemnification, two measures were passed which, having granted protection to all ships that had availed themselves of these orders,

[8] 39 Geo. 3, c. 112, to last until Nov. 4, 1799. It was continued by 39 and 40 Geo. 3, cc. 9, 17, and 41 Geo. 3, c. 20, and revived and continued until six weeks after the next session of Parliament by 41 Geo. 3, c. 19 (U. K.). These acts seriously changed the Navigation System, a fact which did not meet with the approval of the Board of Trade: see B. T., 5: 11, Feb. 8, 1800; 5: 12, Nov. 26, Dec. 5, 1800; and Nov. 27, 1801.

[9] 39 and 40 Geo. 3, c. 34, limited to Sept. 29, 1801. Only British subjects might engage in this trade, and then only upon the express provision that goods in such proportional value as directed by the Crown had been exported to these countries.

[10] P. C. Reg., 155, Dec. 10, 1800: see 39 Geo. 3, c. 87.

[11] For other instances see 33 Geo. 3, c. 26; 35 Geo. 3, c. 100; 36 Geo. 3, c. 4; 37 Geo. 3, c. 8; 42 Geo. 3, c. 16; 37 Geo. 3, c. 84; 38 Geo. 3, c. 25; 39 Geo. 3, cc. 95, 98; 39 and 40 Geo. 3, cc. 34, 64; and 36 Geo. 3, c. 113.

[11a] Orders in Council, Jan. 16, 21, 1795.

provided: first, for a continuation of this trade; secondly, that all goods so warehoused might be taken out of storage either for sale in England or for reëxport; and thirdly, that Dutch ships might, under certain conditions, be placed in English registry for the European trade.[12] As the act did not mention licences, considerable doubt arose as to whether these papers were necessary. Certain officials believed that a British subject did not have to secure a licence for this trade, while others held that a licence was required. After some time it was decided by the Admiralty, and later by the Court of the King's Bench, that a licence was required of all subjects trading with the enemy either in British or neutral ships.[13]

The need for these various acts is so apparent that no further comment is demanded. Suffice it to say that on the basis of these acts and orders a fairly well regulated trade was created. No licences were required of a neutral to import grain from enemy or non-enemy territory in neutral ships and on neutral account. This interpretation, although not stated in any given act or order, nevertheless was held to by the Privy Council and the Board of Trade. A licence was demanded, however, for British subjects in neutral ships to import grain from hostile territory on British account, and for a British subject to engage in any form of trade. Needless to say, no licence was necessary for a British subject to import from a neutral place.[14]

In general these licences had certain features in common. All

[12] 35 Geo. 3, cc. 15, 80. The next year these acts were renewed until Feb. 22, 1797, and from then by a series of renewals to Jan. 1, 1804: see 36 Geo. 3, c. 76; 37 Geo. 3, c. 12; 38 Geo. 3, c. 9; 39 Geo. 3, c. 12; 39 and 40 Geo. 3, cc. 9, 11, 65. By 42 Geo. 3, c. 80, the provisions of these acts were repealed and others substituted. This act was to expire Jan. 1, 1804, but was continued by 44 Geo. 3, c. 30, to eight months after the ratification of peace.

[13] The Case of the *Hoop,* Feb. 13, 1799, Robinson, *Report of Cases* ..., I: 197–219: see also Potts against Bell and others, in error, *Term Report* (London, 1802), 8: 548–561.

[14] B. T., 5: 11, Dec. 12, 1799: see also P. C. Reg., 156, the Council to Mr. Nepean, Nov. 17, 1800, and P. C. Reg., 154, the Council to Mr. Thompson, April 25, 1800. By enemy territory was meant, before the Peace of Amiens, France, the United Provinces, the Austrian Netherlands, Spain, Italy and Switzerland.

applications had to be made to the Privy Council which, after an examination, might order the granting of a licence. Ordinarily, these papers mentioned no definite article. Instead, a list of goods was inserted within the body of the licence, permitting the import of any of those articles, among which was listed "Corn, if importable according to the provisions of the Corn Laws." [15] All licences bore the name and the address of the person or persons to whom granted, the date of issue, and the length of time the licence might be used. In this way more than one voyage was possible. Each application was supposed to give the name of the vessel and its master. This, however, was not always possible, as often the applicant had no particular ship at hand. Often the licence did not state the place to or from which the trade was to be limited. Frequently, the trade was from "any port of Holland" or "France" to "any port of Ireland," England, or to a series of ports in the United Kingdom.[16] At times licences were issued to ships in Great Britain to trade to and from the continent; at other times, to ships in continental ports to trade to and from Great Britain. The first type was known as 'export and import' licence; the second as 'import and export' licence. Often the route of the vessel was marked out in advance. This had been found necessary because of the proximity of the enemy to the continental port, or because of some apparent fraud.[17] Again, though the ship's

[15] The P. C. Reg. does not always list the article or articles in its record of licences. Usually the clerk stated that a licence had been granted for a "General Cargo." In the actual licence and order the goods are always given.

[16] The following European ports were usually mentioned, those *underscored* being the more frequent: *Rotterdam, Amsterdam, Dordt, Cherbourg, Boulogne, Charente,* Calais, Dieppe, Dunkirk, Fécamp, Nantes, Havre, Bilboa, Seville and Morlaix. London, Liverpool, Bristol and Aberdeen were often given as the port of destination. Often licences were granted permitting the import of corn from the "Mississippi" or "New Orleans:" see P. C. Reg., 157, Jan. 3, March 5, 1801. During the period of the Armed Neutrality a licenced trade was allowed with the Baltic powers: see pp. 128–129. As neutral ships were generally used it is of interest to note that those most often employed were Prussian, American, Danish, Swedish, or ships of Papenburg, Oldenburg, Kniphausen and Mecklenburg.

[17] See P. C. Reg., 154, Feb., 1800; 158, July 28, Aug. 27; 159, Sept. 7, 1801, for licences given to traders who evidently were furnishing the French fleet at Brest with provisions.

papers might show that the vessel had left a hostile port "for a neutral port," nevertheless the possession of a licence protected that ship from capture.[18] Finally, it should be noted that licences were granted permitting importation from a blockaded port.[19]

These features and peculiarities seem quite mild when compared with the elaborate licenced trade of a later date. It is important to notice, however, that the system, as it has been given, furnished the groundwork for the later scheme as it existed after the Peace of Amiens. It is also significant to note that this rather mild form contained neither the wide scope nor the abuse that attended the licences issued after 1807. An attempt to regulate and control the extent and the number of licences granted is characteristic of the early period and not of the years that followed the November Orders.

THE PERIOD FROM THE PEACE OF AMIENS TO JANUARY, 1807

The short-lived Peace of Amiens ended in May, 1803. Recent events had shown only too well the hollow mockery of that treaty, as well as the avowed purpose of both belligerents to wage a war to the finish. The first overt act, on the part of Great Britain, came on May 16, when a general embargo was placed upon French shipping. At the same time letters of reprisal were issued against the enemy.[20]

At once a sharp reaction appeared among the mercantile classes. The renewal of war meant a stoppage of all trade with the French. To many this foreshadowed serious financial stringency. Fearful of the future and desirous of obviating all unnecessary losses, they gave immediate attention to the question of relief. The experiences of the late war suggested a return to the system of licences. On the very day, therefore, that

[18] The port might be neutral, or one under French influence. See Appendix No. 6 for the form of a licence agreed to by the Advocate General.

[19] See P. C. Reg., 156, Dec. 3, 1800, for a licence granted to the neutral brig, *Francis and Elizabeth,* to import a cargo of wheat from Havre, then blockaded.

[20] See P. C. Reg., 162, May 16, 1803; also 162, May 23, 1803, and 163, June 22, 1803.

the embargo was announced a group of London merchants petitioned the Council for a licenced trade on the ground that it alone could forestall failure. Within forty-eight hours an answer was given: licences would be issued permitting the import, and the export of goods of the same general type as had been allowed during the recent war, to and from France, Spain and Holland. This, as it was stated, was to be "considered as a general Rule with respect to exportations and importations to and from France, Spain, and Holland until further order of this Board."[21]

Licences, chiefly of the "general" type, were immediately issued.[22] The evident value of these papers consisted in the protection they afforded both the ship and the cargo from capture and condemnation. Strictly speaking, they did not safeguard any vessel from a violation of any navigation or revenue act, as the authority for these licences did not rest upon any Parliamentary action. Late in June, therefore, the Council decided to remedy this defect by the introduction of a bill legalizing all licences that had been granted and provided for their future use on the basis of 36 Geo. 3, c. 76, and 39 Geo. 3, c. 112.[23] After some delay a measure to that effect passed Parliament.[24]

The imperative need for giving help to the British people justified this measure. Its provisions were as follows: first, that Italian organzined thrown silk, with certain exceptions, might be imported by anyone from any neutral place in any vessel; second, that flax and flaxseed might be imported by anyone from any place in any neutral ship; third, that the

[21] P. C. Unbound Papers, Council Minute, May 18, 1803. Among the Unbound Papers for June, 1803, there is a suggestive résumé of the Council's policy entitled, "Proceedings in Council relative to Trade with France, Holland and Spain during the present war."

[22] See Appendix No. 6 for typical licences.

[23] P. C. Reg., 163, Council to Vansittart, June 29, 1803; see also P. C. Unbound Papers, "Proceedings in Council. . . ."

[24] 43 Geo. 3, c. 153. This was to last until six months after the ratification of peace. It was repealed in part by 52 Geo. 3, c. 119; see also 54 Geo. 3, c. 81; 55 Geo. 3, c. 8; 59 Geo. 3, c. 110; and *Commons' Journal*, 58: 643, 652, 658, 659, 664, 679, 683, 692, 693.

Turkey Company might import goods of Turkey, Egypt and the Levant, from any place, either in British, Irish, or neutral ships; fourth, that goods heretofore imported from any European place within the Straits, except from the dominions of the Grand Seignior, might be entered by anyone in either British, Irish, or neutral ships; fifth, that all goods warehoused under any order in council might be taken out for domestic use or for reëxport; sixth, that pitch, tar, deal-board, fir and timber might be imported from any German port in British or Irish vessels; seventh, that the export to Europe of copper suitable for naval purposes might be stopped by royal act; eighth, that salt might be imported by anyone from Portugal in neutral ships; ninth, that wool, cotton-wool, barilla, Jesuits' bark, linen yarn, hemp, indigo and cochineal might be imported from any place whatsoever in any neutral ship; tenth, that licenced imports from hostile countries, made by virtue of any order, were valid, and that any articles named in any order might be imported in neutral ships.

A striking parallelism exists between this act and the measures used before the Peace of Amiens. It is very evident that the act of 1803 was by far the more comprehensive. This is shown by the more extensive list of goods that might be imported. It should also be noticed that the act, except in one instance, concerned an import trade, and, with the exception of the Levant and German trade, might be entered into by anyone in a neutral ship from any place outside of the Straits.[25] Again, it is worthy of attention that the act constitutes a most extensive relaxation of the Navigation System in that it allowed neutrals to become the carriers for the British import trade. Finally, that a licenced trade with enemy states might be entered into by either neutrals or British subjects.[26] In this

[25] It did not, therefore, with the exception of copper, concern an export trade. Licences, however, for the reasons mentioned above, were issued: see p. 90. In all cases import was understood to mean import into the United Kingdom.

[26] The act expressly referred to 12 Chas. 2, c. 18, and to several others as in no way checking the operation of this measure. One should also note the renewal and continuation until eight months after peace of 42

fashion the English had access to Europe in spite of the energetic steps taken by Napoleon to keep them out of the continent.

On the basis of this act, an order was issued September 14, 1803, which permitted until further notice the import of certain enumerated goods, neutral or British property, in neutral ships from unblockaded ports of France and Holland. Both British subjects and neutrals had to have a licence to engage in this trade.[27] A further extension came as a result of another order issued June 29, 1805. This measure is of great importance: in the first instance, by reason of the detailed list of articles that might be imported from and exported to unblockaded ports of France, Holland and Spain; secondly, because neutral ships carrying these goods for British subjects, even without a licence, were not liable to seizure; and thirdly, because this order provided for the insertion within the body of the licence of the phrase which allowed a trade "directly or circuitously" from and to the continent.[28]

This last arrangement had been caused by recent happenings in Europe. Prussia, after a period of questionable vacillation, recognized the power of France by closing, March 5, 1806, her ports and those of Hanover to the British. Great Britain answered on April 5 by placing an embargo on all Prussian shipping and by declaring eleven days later a blockade of Europe

Geo. 3, c. 80, by 44 Geo. 3, c. 30; also that until May 5, 1805, hides, calfskins, tallow, horn, wool, excepting cotton-wool might be imported in foreign ships: see 44 Geo. 3, c. 29; continued by 45 Geo. 3, c. 80, and 48 Geo. 3, c. 24, until three months after peace: see also 39 Geo. 3, c. 87.

[27] P. C. Reg., 163, Sept. 14, 1803. French lawns and cambrics were added by Order of April 23, 1804, and lace by Order of April 19, 1805: see P. C. Reg., 165, 167, and P. C. Unbound Papers, "Proceedings in Council. . . ."

[28] P. C. Unbound Papers, Council Minute, May 31, 1805; P. C. Reg., 167, June 29, 1805. See also P. C. Reg., Aug. 15, 1805, for order allowing the entry in neutral ships without licence of enumerated goods that were neutral or British property: see also B. T., 5: 15, July 18, 1805. The Order of Aug. 15, 1805, was extended by Council Minute, Dec. 10, 1805, so as to permit the import of goods not mentioned in the August Order, but which were definitely named in the licence. Licences, although not required by the August Order, were still being issued as merchants continued to seek them in the belief that they were necessary. Under the terms of the December Order any article not forbidden by law might be imported.

from the Elbe to Brest, with the exception that this blockade was not to stop the departure of any ships then in process of loading, or those sailing under the Danish flag.[29] By interpretation as well as by fact, Prussian territory was thus understood to be under French influence, and as such was governed by the act of 1803. The import of corn, grain, meal, or flour, therefore, might take place from this area as well as from other hostile sections. Proof of this is seen in the large number of "general" licences which were granted for this district.[30]

Most of the licences granted for import were given to neutral carriers. In a number of instances the neutral ship was American; more frequently, it was a Dutch vessel, or some other ship sailing under the flag of Kniphausen, Papenburg, Oldenburg, Bremen, or Hamburg.[31] As has already been shown, these ships might trade between certain ports of the United Kingdom and those of France, Spain, Holland and Prussia.[32]

This, in brief, was the state of the licenced trade upon the eve of the January Order of 1807. That the neutral had ample cause for complaint in the commercial policies established since the Peace of Amiens cannot be questioned. Further, the most important neutral, America, had become visibly concerned over the West Indian program of Great Britain, as was shown by the Essex Decision and the proposed Treaty of 1806. All of which merely foreshadowed a more oppressive policy, disastrous in its effects, upon both neutrals and belligerents.

29 See P. C. Reg., 169, for these orders.

30 See P. C. Reg., 169.

31 The ships of these minor states had received special dispensations from the effects of the Prussian blockade. The trade, furthermore, to and from the ports of the Jade was open to all British and neutral ships: see P. C. Reg., 169, 170, 171, for the Orders of April 16, May 14, 24, June 5, Nov. 19 and Dec. 16, 1806. American ships were given the same rights: see P. C. Unbound Papers, Council Minute, Feb. 18, 1807.

32 See Appendix No. 7 for the number of general licences that were issued. Licences were frequently granted for trade with Leghorn and the river Weser.

THE PERIOD FROM 1807 TO APRIL, 1809

In a direct, though considerably delayed, answer to the British blockade of the Elbe came the well known Berlin Decree.[33] By way of retaliation there appeared the Order in Council of January 7, 1807.[34] The substance of this order was the Rule of 1756, according to which a trade which was unlawful in time of peace could not become legal in time of war. This principle had been applied by the British to the French colonial possessions upon the outbreak of war in 1793. The extension of this rule to the coast trade of France was the avowed object of the January Order.[35]

It is important to note that this measure nowise changed the Licence System. Indirectly, however, a distinct change had taken place. Neutral vessels had heretofore engaged in the coastwise trade of the enemy. An American ship, for example, having discharged its cargo at Brest might carry freight thence to Fécamp, and sail from there to London with a cargo of importable goods; here a consignment of manufactured articles would be obtained and the ship would then clear for America. The January Order stopped this very profitable trade; it did not, however, prevent a neutral from trading directly between an enemy port and the United Kingdom. An American, having landed a cargo in France, might sail directly to the United Kingdom with a cargo of lawful goods. Mild as this measure was when contrasted with later orders, it was still too severe and drastic. Licenced ships, therefore, laden with importable articles

[33] This decree is to be found in *Correspondance de Napoléon, Ier*, No. 11283, and *Le Moniteur,* Dec. 5, 1806. For a convenient summary see Melvin, F. E., *Napoleon's Navigation System,* p. 7.

[34] The inception of this order is to be found in *Dropmore Papers,* VIII: 468, 473, 485, 490; *Parl. Debates,* VIII: 39; and the *Morning Chronicle,* Jan. 5, 1807. Among the Unbound Papers of the Council there may be seen the rough drafts of this order, together with the form given by the Advocate General, Jan. 5, 1807. The order itself may be found in P. C. Reg., 172, Jan. 7, 1807; also in *Parl. Pap.,* 1808, No. 5. See *London Times,* Jan. 9, 11, 12, 1807, and Melvin, F. E., *op. cit.,* p. 15.

[35] This measure had a marked effect on the then pending treaty with America, and caused a decided opposition from that nation. A neutral might still trade directly between France and its own ports.

were allowed to go from an enemy's port via England to the port of destination regardless of whether that port was in the hands of the enemy or not.[36]

Further concessions were sought by the mercantile classes, which is shown by a letter the Council received from Mr. John Irving, a prominent grain merchant of London. Having stated that there was considerable shortage of corn in England, and that recent happenings in Europe had decreased the available supply from the Baltic, Mr. Irving remarked: [37]

> These considerations lead me to suggest . . . that possibly considerable supplies may be obtained from the dominions of the enemy. I mean particularly France, where there is a great superfluity of wheat, and not withstanding the laws of prohibition it occurs to me that the differences of price in the two countries . . . [would] induce merchants to run the hazard of importation. But it will be necessary before any attempt is made to know that Government will give every facility and protection to such adventures.
>
> Upon the premises stated I beg leave, therefore, to ask of your Lordship . . . whether I could calculate on the entry into blockaded ports of neutral vessels in ballast and their exit, laden with wheat and other grain and whether such ships bound to ports of this kingdom shall be permitted to go free and unmolested even though the property should belong to the enemy. . . .

It is at once apparent that this request exceeded any privilege given by the June Order or by any order. Since August 15, 1805, neither neutral nor British merchants had to have a licence to import any of the enumerated goods in a neutral ship from an unblockaded port. Mr. Irving, on the other hand, asked that a neutral ship be allowed to go, in ballast, to a port actually blockaded, there to load a cargo of wheat and clear with foreign papers which showed beyond all doubt that it carried an enemy cargo. Further, although it was not stated, it was, however,

[36] P. C. Unbound Papers, Jan. 7, 1807. In a bundle of that date there is to be seen a piece which contains many interesting comments on the January Order. This piece has been endorsed: "This order has been relaxed," and cites an instance of nineteen Spanish ships laden with wine which were allowed to proceed under licence to Holland. From the wording of this piece, it would seem that these ships had first entered an English port.

[37] P. C. Unbound Papers, Jan. 13, 1807: see also *ibid.*, Letters of J. W. Lubboch and J. Irving to the Council, Jan. 9, 1807.

probably well known that no ship could leave a French harbor unless bound to a neutral or to another French port. Not merely did Mr. Irving desire that the principle of strict blockade be thrust to one side, but also that the enemy's property might actually be imported, seemingly on the enemy's account. All licences heretofore granted had stated that the imported goods were to be entered either for neutral or British account. Without a doubt the thought in the mind of the petitioner was to protect his clearance from a port, strictly blockaded, with a cargo which appeared to be the property of the enemy, destined to an enemy or neutral port. In short Mr. Irving had hit upon a plan to evade the French decrees, but which if granted would cause a marked departure from the policy laid down by the various orders and acts. And what was the answer of the Ministry? After a short time, the Council granted the request on the understanding that, before a licence would be issued, Mr. Irving should be able to prove that the wheat could be exported from France. Evidently he was able to do this, since in February a licence was granted.[38]

Shortly after the action taken on Mr. Irving's letter, the Ministry decided to make a change in its entire program, which change appeared in the Order of February 4, 1807. The chief points of this measure were: that the British navy and privateers were not to stop neutral ships laden with importable goods going to the United Kingdom, provided they had not cleared from a port actually blockaded; that in case of seizure, a vessel was to be released at once; that no licence was required for neutral ships engaged in this trade; and that among the enumerated commodities that might be imported was listed corn of all descriptions.[39] Contrasting this order with that of August, 1805, one notes that although in both instances neutral ships were given

[38] *Ibid.:* see the endorsement, dated Jan. 16, 1807, to Mr. Irving's letter of Jan. 13, 1807. See also P. C. Reg., 172, Feb. 24, 1807.

[39] P. C. Reg., 172. This order did not mention licences, the implication being, therefore, that none were required. This seems to have been the case before the order: see note 41. See also P. C. Unbound Papers, 1807, for an endorsement by the Advocate General, Feb. 5, 1807, on the letters from Mr. Lubboch and Mr. Irving, *op. cit.*

the right to import, without licence from unblockaded ports, articles for neutral or British account, the February Order, by not mentioning to whom the cargo might belong, allowed neutral ships to import these goods from unblockaded ports, even though the goods seemed to be " enemy's property."

The need for this change from the former policy had been caused by Napoleon's blockade of the British Isles. This did not prevent French or neutral merchants from trading between French and neutral ports. If a neutral, therefore, could clear from one French port for another French port or for a neutral port, why might not this vessel, in spite of all French papers accompanying the vessel, go to a British port? This, indeed, seems to have been the object of the February Order.[40] Imports under this measure greatly increased, and in most cases, by means of licences. These, of course, were not needed; nor had they been required by the late order. An opinion to this effect was given by the Advocate General, which reads in part as follows: [41]

" . . . that the ground on which these licences had been granted, was not for the purpose of placing foreign trade under the control of the executive, but to permit British subjects to trade with the enemy. In 1805 a General Order in Council had been issued, to

[40] This order did not prevent the capture of any ship engaging in the coastwise trade of the enemy. As will presently be seen, the sailing in ballast from one port of the enemy to another was not looked upon as a violation of the January Order.

[41] *Parl. Debates,* X: 924–925. Contrast this with the report of the speech as given in the *Morning Chronicle,* March 8, 1807: " . . . to carry on a trade which was contrary to law. This has been done also, not only by the issuing of Licences in individual cases, but by general orders of the Privy Council, as by the order June, 1805, of which any merchant was at liberty to avail himself without a licence. It so happened, however, that merchants had, notwithstanding this order, continued to apply for licences to carry on that trade which they might have carried on without a licence in consequence of the order, from an idea perhaps of obtaining a further security to their transactions." See also P. C. Council Minutes, 1807, July 7, 1807, directing the Admiralty not to molest neutral ships sailing in conformity with these two orders. A study of the admirable work by J. Reeves, *The Law of Shipping and Navigation,* pp. 358–370, substantiates in the main the general idea given above as to the use of licences by neutrals and Britishers.

enable British merchants to trade with the enemy, in certain articles of great importance to agriculture and to manufactures. In Feb., 1807, an extension of that Order had been made; but the merchants had nevertheless continued voluntarily to take out licences, although they had been repeatedly told that they were unnecessary."

It is important to notice that this trade was limited to unblockaded ports. Licences, notwithstanding, were granted for trade with ports strictly invested by the British navy.[42] And, as the French power expanded, trade was allowed with blockaded and unblockaded North Atlantic and Baltic ports. It should also be recalled that the Fox Blockade, though relaxed by the February Order, was still in force.[43] On February 11, 1807, two vessels of Bremen were licenced to import grain from the Elbe; somewhat later, another licence allowed ships of Hamburg, Bremen and North Germany to trade to and from the United Kingdom, whether these ports were in the hands of the French or not.[44] The following month, the Council, having permitted the export of coffee, sugar and colonial produce to the blockaded area, granted licences to import thence corn and other enumerated goods.[45] Again, in a letter to the Admiralty, June 29, 1807, the Council directed that ships laden with British coal might pass the blockade of the Ems, Weser, Elbe and Jade, and return with corn and other provisions.[46] In August, further changes took place when it was decided that ships of less than sixty

[42] See P. C. Reg., 172, March 6, 19, 30, 1807, for licences to trade with France; also see the licence issued to Reed and Irving, P. C. Reg., 172, Feb. 24, 1807, and one to James Currie, April 14, 1807, a copy of which is given in Appendix No. 6. Other instances may be found in later volumes. On April 22, 1807, a licence was granted to four British ships, formerly Prussian, to import corn from any port of France, blockaded or not, and regardless of any documents accompanying the ship or the nationality of the crew.

[43] This order, though removed for the period of the Franco-Prussian War of 1806, was reëstablished after Jena and Auerstadt: see B. T., 5: 17, March 13, 1807.

[44] P. C. Reg., 172, March 18, 24, 25, 26, April 9, 24, 1807: see also P. C. Council Minutes, Feb. 18, 1807.

[45] P. C. Reg., 172, the Council to Mr. Marsden, March 17, 1808: see also P. C. Reg., 172, March 17, 28, May 18, 1807. On June 17, 1807, ships of Hamburg and Bremen were allowed to trade freely with British ports.

[46] P. C. Reg., 173; P. C. Unbound Papers, Council Minute, July 7,

tons sailing from a British or neutral port might enter this zone with non-contraband articles, and return to a neutral or British port, provided the cargo might legally be imported into Great Britain.[47]

Certain other changes in the Licence System should be noted. Neutral ships generally were allowed to return unmolested to any unblockaded European port.[48] Further, in all export licences the name of the ship, the tonnage, and the port of clearance were inserted within the licence, and the time of clearance endorsed by a customs official.[49] Also, in all import licences, the British port of destination was given in the licence.[50] Again, in all licences issued for import from the Baltic a condition within the paper stated that all ships having a cargo of naval stores were to sail, unless under convoy, to Dundee or Leith, and there obtain a fresh clearance for the port of ultimate destination.[51] All import licences granted for ships sailing under the French flag limited the freight to naval stores, timber, raw materials, wines and corn or flour.[52] Another feature was the provision that there should be inserted within the licence after the list of importable goods, the clause " . . . and all such other articles as are not prohibited by law to be exported . . . or imported." This had been found necessary in order to check the continual litigation, expense and delay which had been caused by the slightest variation in the articles specified.[53] Again, neutral ships sailing from French ports, blockaded or not, to the United

---

1807. I noticed that from May 7 to July 25, 1807, sixteen licences were granted to thirty-four ships to pass this blockaded area with "general" cargoes.

47 P. C. Reg., 173, the Council to Viscount Fitz-Harris, July 10, Aug. 8, 1808: see also B. T., 5: 17, April 27, 1807, for an earlier statement.

48 See for example, P. C. Reg., 173, May 7, 11, 22, June 1, 1807.

49 P. C. Unbound Papers, Council Minute, April 8, 1807.

50 P. C. Unbound Papers, Council Minute, March 4, 1807. It is of interest to note that this rule had to be renewed in 1808: see P. C. Council Minutes, March 4, April 5, 1808.

51 P. C. Unbound Papers, Council Minute, March 7, 1807. Note that these regulations did not apply to Swedish ships or to those bound to Liverpool, Hull, or Newcastle.

52 This marks the beginning of an important phase of this trade: see P. C. Unbound Papers, Council Minute, June 16, 1807.

53 P. C. Unbound Papers, June, 1807. No other date is given.

Kingdom, might, before August 10, 1807, stop at some neutral port for fresh clearance and then go to the port of destination, provided that no contraband had been brought into the blockaded port. After that date this feature was withdrawn and the ship was ordered to sail direct to the United Kingdom. Finally, all licences were ultimately to be deposited in the Customs office.[54]

In the meantime the Whigs had been replaced by the Tories whose policy was admirably shown by the November Orders of 1807.[55] The avowed object of these measures was that of retaliation against both enemy and neutral. Now retaliation implies that an injury has previously been inflicted upon the one who retaliates. In the case of Great Britain this injury had been caused by the Berlin Decree. When one investigates the case of the neutral, he finds that no injury seems to have been committed; unless, indeed, one feels inclined to accept the rather lame excuse given by the Tories, that as the neutral had not taken any drastic step to resist the French decrees the conclusion was that the neutral accepted the enemy's program.[56]

Turning to the measures themselves, one is at once perplexed by their number and the carelessly worded and indefinite phrases. These orders "multiply so rapidly," wrote Auckland, "that I cannot yet find time to consider them; and I only know that the acknowledged necessity of so many explanations proves, at least, that the first measure was ill-considered." [57]

Out of this bewildering maze of instructions and counter instructions, one may glean the object and motive of the Minis-

[54] See P. C. Reg., 173, Aug. 3, 1807, for a licence for three neutrals to pass the Ems, though blockaded; also a licence granted Aug. 8, 1807, for a general cargo from Cadiz then invested by a British fleet. It was stated that on the outward voyage a ship might stop at Tönning or some other neutral port: see P. C. Council Minutes, 1807, Aug. 10, 1807; and also P. C. Unbound Papers, Council Minute, Aug. 7, 1807; P. C. Reg., 173, Aug. 7, 1807; and P. C. Council Minutes, 1808, April 8, 1808.

[55] P. C. Reg., 174, Nov. 11, 18, 25, 1807. As to the origins of these measures and their relation to the West Indian Trade, see pp. 47–50: see also *Dropmore Papers,* IX: 143, and *London Times,* Sept. 29, 1807.

[56] Considerable opposition on the part of the Whigs greeted the advent of these measures.

[57] *Dropmore Papers,* IX: 153: see also *ibid.,* 158, 168.

try.[58] In the first place, there was a blockade of France and all countries under its control. According to this, all trade to and from this area was forbidden; and all enemy property found upon any vessel was subject to capture. Certain exceptions should be noted: neutral ships leaving the United Kingdom, Gibraltar or Malta might sail to a port mentioned in their clearances; neutral vessels, also, might go direct from a European blockaded port to the United Kingdom; in neither case, however, was a ship to enter or leave a port actually blockaded or to have a cargo of enemy property. All of this seems highly contradictory. On the one hand there is a statement that there should be no trading with the blockaded districts; on the other, a statement that a ship might sail to and from these blockaded ports. It should be noticed, however, that a clear distinction is made by these orders between a port blockaded by an order in council and a port blockaded "in the most strict and vigorous manner." That is, a blockaded port was one which was merely declared to be in a state of blockade, while a port actually blockaded was one strictly invested by the British navy. By means of this distinction, a neutral ship might sail to and from an enemy's port that was not actually invested by the British navy.

The phrase "enemy property" is equally indefinite. A very literal interpretation would doubtless mean that the proof of the ownership of the cargo was based upon the ship's papers. This view was not held by the British, as a clause in the November Orders reads:

> Nothing in the above order [that is, the order declaring France and its dependent states in a state of blockade] . . . shall extend . . . to repeal or vacate the additional instructions of the 4th of February last, directing that neutral vessels laden with cargoes consisting of articles therein enumerated, coming for importation to any port of our United Kingdom (provided they are not coming from any port in a state of strict and vigorous blockade) shall not be interrupted.

As has been shown, the February Order allowed the use of papers and documents which seemingly proved the cargo enemy

[58] It is not necessary from the point of view of this study to treat the various phases of these orders except as they concern the movement of grain.

property. The November measures, therefore, expressly allowed a continuation of this scheme; an interpretation which is borne out by an examination of the licences granted after November. This idea is also strengthened by the Instructions of November 25, 1807, which forbade the stopping of neutral ships going direct from a port not actually blockaded to the United Kingdom with goods, no matter "to whomsoever the goods . . . may appear to belong."[59] Another definite purpose of the November Orders was to permit the import in neutral ships of all articles referred to in 43 Geo. 3, c. 68, which greatly extended the number of importable articles.[60]

And what of licences? They were not required for the import of corn and other lawful articles from ports not actually blockaded. The only need for a licence seems to have been the desire "to secure the neutral master, crew and vessel from detention in the case of any sudden embargo and consequent hostility . . . and to [permit him to] return with his vessel and crew to some port not blockaded."[61] The granting of licences to trade in lawful goods between unblockaded ports and the United Kingdom became, however, the normal practice. It was somewhat different in respect to those ports actually blockaded. It would seem that the British would have absolutely enforced this blockade, and indeed, this was probably the hope of the Ministry. Stern necessity caused exceptions to be made, and so, to obviate capture from the blockading squadron, the Government issued the protecting licences.[62]

59 These instructions, being of a later date than the blockade order of Nov. 11 and the instructions of Nov. 17, in which comment is made on the February Order, would seem to show that the Ministry recognized an inconsistency between their orders and that of February, 1807, and at once changed theirs to suit the earlier one.

60 "An Act to repeal the Duties of Customs payable in *Great Britain*, and to grant other Duties in lieu thereof."

61 P. C. Reg., 174, Nov. 28, 1807.

62 See P. C. Reg., 175, Jan. 4, 1808, for a licence permitting James Campbell to import in three neutral ships, wines and other articles "from Cadiz (notwithstanding the blockade) to Great Britain and notwithstanding such vessels may have carried provisions or produce of the United States into Cadiz or may sail under a Certificate in lieu of a Register:" see also licences granted Jan. 20, 23, Feb. 29, 1808. As extra precaution, the Admiralty granted passes: see P. C. Reg., 175, Jan. 20, 23, 1808.

During the remainder of 1807 an important extension of the November Orders was made. The position of the Channel Islands to the French coast made this an easy way into the enemy's country. The governors of Guernsey and Jersey, therefore, were allowed to grant licences to neutral ships of not over one hundred tons burden for an export and an import trade with ports not actually blockaded. These licences, generally, conformed to those granted by the November Orders.[63]

From then on until April 26, 1809, a steady increase took place in the number of licences granted, which is of interest in view of the Orders of June and August, 1805, and February, 1807.[64] Of greater importance is the fact that an increasing number were issued for trade with ports actually under a strict blockade.[64a] In either case licences were granted to the following classes of persons: first, to merchants interested solely in the export trade to the continent; secondly, to those interested in merely importing cargoes of lawful goods from Europe; thirdly, to persons who engaged in an export trade to, and an import trade from, Europe; and fourthly, to those who were interested in an import trade from, and an export trade to, the continent. The goods which might thus be imported into the United Kingdom were limited to those given in the Customs Act of 1803.[65] This, however, was altogether too large a list to be practical, and so in the summer of 1808 a reduction in the number of

[63] P. C. Reg., Dec. 18, 1807: see also Dec. 9, 15, 18, 1807, for references to the Russian trade. The licenced trade of the Channel Islands was stopped in 1810 because of the large quantities of brandy which had been imported from France: see P. C. Reg., 189, Nov. 6, 1810.

[64] P. C. Unbound Papers, a bundle marked "Various." There is no date given to this bundle, but, to judge from an examination, it must have been written before April, 1809. This bundle furnishes a list of licences then being granted, and the various conditions attached to each.

[64a] See Appendix No. 6: see also P. C. Reg., 179, Feb. 7, 1809, for a licence for the *Celte* to sail with grain from Brest; also a licence issued April 5, 1809, P. C. Reg., 180, which allowed the *Fortuna* to go from a blockaded or unblockaded Baltic port to the United Kingdom. 48 Geo. 3, c. 37 (April, 1808), permitted licences for trade "from any Port or Place from which the *British* flag is excluded, in any Ship or Vessel belonging to any Country, whether in Amity with His Majesty or not."

[65] 43 Geo. 3, c. 68. This list included corn, grain, meal, or flour.

articles took place.[66] In March, 1809, a change was made whereby a larger number of articles might be imported from France and Holland.[67]

Before April, 1809, neutral ships flying any flag, except the French, were given all the privileges of the licenced trade.[68] At times, however, a neutral flag merely disguised a French or British vessel; often the French flag was used, and that under express provision in the licence. Originally, of course, this had been forbidden, but the merry game of give and take between the two belligerents had dulled the sharpness of the measures. The mercantile classes, therefore, were not at all surprised to find in February, 1808, that licences were being issued permitting a great change over the earlier and original system. For example, on February 12, 1808, a licence was issued to one William Tooke, allowing him to import certain lawful goods in British ships, under Prussian colors, from the Baltic. Again, on August 20, 1808, a licence was granted a British ship to go to Riga under the American flag. The mere fact that the name and nationality of the vessel were often left blank at the time the licence was granted would tend to show that, in conjunction with a French licence, a neutral or French ship might enter a British port under a neutral flag.[69] Nor was it an unusual

[66] P. C. Council Minutes, 1808, June 17, 1808. This did not restrict the import of corn in any ship belonging to any country whatsoever, notwithstanding any law in force.

[67] Corn was still included: see P. C. Unbound Papers, Council Minute, March 11, 1809. At the same time it was decided that applications and licences for import from Holland and France should give the articles to be imported, a requirement which had been found necessary in view of the late frauds: see P. C. Unbound Papers, Council Minute, March 6, 1809. After Feb. 10, 1809, Spanish wool might be imported in British, Spanish, or neutral ships from ports on Spain, not to the east of St. Andero: see P. C. Unbound Papers, Feb. 10, 1809. Bottles, lace, French cambrics and lawns were no longer allowed from Holland: see P. C. Unbound Papers, Council Minute, April 12, 1809. At the same time, it was stated that in the future no cargoes might be brought from Holland to the United Kingdom for the purpose of paying duty and then proceeding to any other country.

[68] See P. C. Reg., 175, Jan. 4, 1808, for a licence issued to one Alexander Rose, permitting the import of a general cargo from France: see also P. C. Council Minutes, 1808, June 17, 1808.

[69] This was true of import, and import and export licences.

affair for an English man-of-war to permit a vessel flying the French tricolor to sail by in peace. The Council Minute of June 17, 1808, distinctly stated that in cases where a ship had exported a cargo of British manufactured or colonial produce from the United Kingdom to the enemy's country, the return cargo might be imported "under any colours, not even excepting those of France."[70]

As has already been mentioned, it was not always found practical to give in the application for a licence the name or nationality of the vessel. The Council, probably, had been forced to accept this irregularity, because the applicant had found it necessary to have a ship which could meet the French as well as the British regulations,[71] and to obtain such a ship often took considerable time. It was necessary, however, to have inserted within the licence a statement of the British port of destination, and a clause stating that the ship would sail direct from the European port to the United Kingdom.[72] A stricter policy existed in the trade to Holland, in which both the application and the licence were to give the port of clearance.[73] In any case, upon the departure of a vessel from Europe, the tonnage, the name, and the time of clearance were to be endorsed on the licence.[74]

The requirement that the port of destination be given was frequently waived so as to allow the ship to change its course whenever it was found necessary. For instance, a neutral ship might be at Fécamp chartered to load a cargo at Dunkirk.

[70] 48 Geo. 3, c. 37, allowed the use of any flag: see also P. C. Reg., 176, May 5, 1808, and *ibid.*, 179, Feb. 7, 1809, for instances of the use of the French flag; also P. C. Reg., 180, March 22, 1809, for a licence granted to the British ship *Neptune* to sail to Archangel under any flag and under any name. It should be noticed that, when the French flag was used, the licence stated that the flag was not to be shown beyond the ports of France. In any event it was clearly stated by the licence that ships of France built or manned by a French crew were nowise protected from capture: see Bundle, "Various," 1809, and P. C. Reg., 179, Feb. 1, 1809.

[71] A natural result of this policy was to stimulate speculation in Europe in British licences.

[72] P. C. Council Minutes, March 4, April 5, 1808.

[73] *Ibid.*, June 29, Aug. 6, 1808: see also P. C. Reg., 178, Sept. 1, 1808.

[74] The applicant was always asked at the time of application whether he then knew the port of clearance: see P. C. Council Minutes, June 29, 1808.

This of course was contrary to the British orders. To avoid this, it was stated in the licence that the vessel might proceed in ballast from one port to another, provided the latter was not in a state of strict blockade and that, having secured its cargo, it should sail directly to the United Kingdom.[75] Again, a ship was permitted to stop at a neutral port and obtain fresh clearances,[76] a procedure which was very common in the Baltic trade. At various times, neutral ships sailing under any flag except that of France were allowed to import certain goods into a British port and, having paid the duty, to clear to some designated neutral port on the continent.[77]

The entire matter of routing a vessel seems to have been the burden of considerable thought on the part of the Council. Ships from a port of France west of Havre were to sail to a port between Portsmouth and Falmouth; those from a port east of Havre, to an English port between Dover and Harwich. In either case a convoy was necessary.[78] A vessel laden with naval stores from Russia and the Baltic, if bound for a port south of Hull, was ordered, unless under convoy, to touch at Dundee or Leith, and to obtain there a fresh clearance, and to sail thence under convoy to the port of destination. If this port was Liverpool or any place in Ireland, then the ship was directed to sail north and proceed down the western coast of Scotland.[79]

[75] See, for example, the licence granted to Alexander Rose, P. C. Reg., 175, Jan. 4, 1808. This principle was clearly stated in a letter to the Admiralty, May 15, 1809: see P. C. Reg., 181.

[76] P. C. Council Minutes, 1808, April 5, 1808.

[77] See P. C. Reg., 179, Feb. 1, 1809, for a licence to Mr. Irving permitting twelve ships laden with grain to go from Denmark to Norway via England: see also P. C. Reg., 179, Jan. 21, 1809. This privilege was denied to all Dutch ships in 1809: see P. C. Unbound Papers, April 12, 1809.

[78] In Bundle, " Various," it is stated that a ship with a cargo of brandy and wine had to stop at Plymouth for convoy: see also P. C. Unbound Papers, Council Minute, Feb. 10, 1809.

[79] When convoyed, a vessel was supposed to stay with the convoy as long as the latter was ordered to guard the ship. Vessels so routed and licenced might of course import corn: see Bundle, " Various; " P. C. Unbound Papers, June 21, 1808, Feb. 18, 1809; and P. C. Council Minutes, 1808, March 7, 1808.

Many of these regulations had become necessary by reason of the French decrees. Napoleon had insisted that every ship, before clearance, should have in its possession papers showing that it was going to a neutral or allied port. The British Ministry, consequently, had to protect its licenced imports from France, and inserted within the licence the clause that the vessel, though sailing with French papers, was not subject to capture.[80] Finally, vessels having unloaded their cargoes might clear to any unblockaded port in Europe.[81]

These peculiarities, generally present in some form or other in the import licences, were also usually found in the 'export and import' and the 'import and export' licences. Licences of this latter type were granted for trade to Holland, Germany, the North Baltic, or Russian ports. As in the import licences, the time limit was usually six months. In the case of ships trading to and from Holland, the licence might be used for any number of trips within the time stated in the licence.[82] The export and import, as well as the export licences, allowed the export of British manufactures and colonial produce according to the November Orders.[83]

The continental ports most frequently mentioned from which import occurred were Antwerp, Rotterdam, Amsterdam, Bordeaux and Charente; often the phrase was 'any unblockaded or blockaded port' of France, Holland, Prussia, Russia, or the Baltic. During the first half of 1808 the trade was largely limited to France, Holland and Spain; but in the latter part of that year the trade from Holland, Russia and the Baltic became more com-

80 See P. C. Reg., 178, Sept. 1, 1808, for a licence to Samuel Joseph: see also vols. 176, 179, May 5, 1808, and Jan. 21, 1809, for licences to James Currie and certain London merchants.

81 See P. C. Reg., 175, Jan. 4, 1808, for a licence for six ships to trade from Holland to Ramsgate.

82 See P. C. Reg., 178, Sept. 1, 1808, for a licence to Samuel Joseph. As for the Russian trade, it is to be noted that from Sept. 23, 1808, until the end of the year licences were issued for nine months: see P. C. Unbound Papers, Sept. 23, 1808. From Bundle, "Various," it would seem that licences for trade with France might be used for more than one trip.

83 See P. C. Reg., March 10, 1808, for a licence granted to John Hull for a trade to and from the Baltic in a vessel belonging to the state of Papenburg: see also P. C. Council Minutes, 1808, June 17, 1808.

mon. Occasionally licences were granted for trade to the continent via Heligoland; nor was it uncommon for licences to be issued allowing a trade with the United States.[84] In the case of Spain, it is to be noticed that after the Spanish revolt against the French the English hostility towards Spain ceased. The result, therefore, was the opening of a new market for British commerce, and the blockade, except in those places directly under the control of France, was no longer operative.[85]

Another factor that merits attention is a change in the matter of granting licences, which was made through the illness of George III. Heretofore, all licences had been granted under His Majesty's Sign Manual, and signed by one of the principal secretaries of state, as well as by the Crown.[86] In an act passed in June, 1808, it was stated that upon order in council all licences might be granted upon the signature of one of the Crown's chief secretaries.[87]

THE PERIOD FROM APRIL, 1809, TO THE CLOSE OF 1813

By the spring of 1809 it had become apparent that the Licence System needed repair. It will be recalled that Perceval had condemned Napoleon, and incidentally all neutrals, to humiliation and defeat by the November Orders. Whether this object could ever have been realized or not, is a matter of conjecture, as the rapid growth of the Licence System completely frustrated these measures. Trading with the enemy had become the normal course, the orders notwithstanding. It was this situation, so con-

[84] In view of the American *Embargo,* it had been found necessary to licence trade with the United States: see P. C. Reg., 175, Feb. 3, 1808, for a licence for six neutral ships to trade between the United Kingdom and the United States; see also the licences granted, Jan. 2, 20, 25, 30, and Oct. 3, 1809. In a licence granted Oct. 7, 1809, mention is made of Amelia Island.

[85] See P. C. Reg., 177, July 4, 1808, for an order declaring Spain no longer in a state of blockade; Cadiz was expressly mentioned as not being blockaded: see P. C. Reg., 177, July 15, 1808.

[86] The almost childish signature of George III, "George R," is often seen in the upper left hand corner of the licences issued before 1808.

[87] 48 Geo. 3, c. 126. All licences so granted were to have attached a duplicate of the order in council: see P. C. Reg., 177, July 14, 19, 27, 1808.

trary to the spirit and the letter of the Orders, that the Government tardily recognized by undertaking a thorough examination of the Licence System.

A new program was announced by Order in Council, April 26, 1809. According to this measure, the Orders of November 11 and 25, December 18, 1807, and March 30, 1808, were revoked. Instead, a blockade was declared of all ports under the French control from the Ems to Northern Italy.[88] A week later a supplementary measure repealed the Instructions of June 29, 1805, of November 18 and 25, 1807, and of February 24, 1808; and also the Order of February 4, 1807, in respect to all trade to and from ports actually blockaded and those subject to the April Order of 1809.[89] As a result of these new measures, the further use of licences within the restricted area was totally forbidden.[90] Articles mentioned in the February Order of 1807 might still be entered by neutrals in neutral ships from any unblockaded port even though the British flag was excluded.[91] Licences for this trade, although not required by the Orders of April and May, 1809, and February, 1807, continued to be granted. The mercantile classes, evidently, felt that complete protection by the British navy could be had only through the use of licences.

There can be no doubt that the licenced trade had been thoroughly overhauled. Trading with the enemy was to be reduced to a minimum. The success of this program, however,

[88] P. C. Reg., 180. By Order in Council, May 17, 1809, this blockade was extended to the eastern as well as to the western mouth of the Ems: see P. C. Reg., 181.

[89] P. C. Reg., 181, May 3, 1809. Licences issued before April 26, 1809, were still good: see P. C. Reg., 181, May 2, 1809.

[90] This was before the Erskine Agreement, news of which reached Canning May 22, 1809. Although this treaty was disavowed, a temporary suspension of the April Order was allowed so as to protect all ships which might have sailed under this treaty: see P. C. Reg., 181, May 24, 1809.

[91] During the summer of 1809, licences for trade with Northern Germany, Russia and the Baltic were issued: see P. C. Reg., 181, 182, 183. Probably the restricted list of importable goods was still in force. Export trade to these places was allowed. The Fox Blockade was still in force: see *American State Papers, Foreign Relations,* III: 356, Wellesley to Pinckney, March 26, 1810.

would rest upon the degree to which these orders would be enforced. Unfortunately, this purpose was never realized. Exceptions were made from the very first, simply because the Ministry was trying to do the impossible. English and neutral merchants cared little for the virtuous resolves of the Government; they were interested in profits, big profits, and sought, therefore, to cause a change in this new program. So great was the effect of public opinion, that by the end of May the Ministry was forced to grant licences, allowing any ship under any flag, except the French, to import a cargo of lawful goods from "any port of Holland north of the island of Walcheren and west of the island of Juist."[92] Early in June, a further extension was made when neutral vessels of not over twenty tons were licenced to trade under any flag, except the French, from Heligoland to a Dutch port north of Walcheren and west of Juist.[93] At the same time licences good for three months were granted for trade to and from Heligoland to any port east of Juist and to the Eider river inclusive.[94] During the course of the next few months these Jade or Norden licences, as they were called, become most common.[95]

It is to be noticed that these changes did not concern France. Evidently the Ministry intended to keep a rigid blockade of the French coast. In May, the Council proudly stated that not a single licence had been granted for trade with France since the appearance of the April Order,[96] a record which remained unbroken throughout the summer of 1809.

[92] P. C. Reg., 181, May 29, 1809: see this and other volumes for numerous instances.

[93] P. C. Unbound Papers, Council Minute, June 6, 1809. These licences were to be effective until Sept. 10, 1809.

[94] *Ibid.* At a later date the military commander at Walcheren was allowed to licence a trade between and including the rivers Swin and Meuse: see P. C. Unbound Papers, Sept. 13, 1809. In October the import of corn from Walcheren was allowed: see B. T., 5: 19, the Board of Trade to Mr. Cooke, Oct. 9, 1809.

[95] These licences were so named because the port of Norden and the river Jade were usually referred to in them.

[96] P. C. Reg., 181, May 15, 1809. In the same source is found the interesting remark that occasionally manuscript licences were issued: see P. C. Reg., 182, July 27, 1809. By 49 Geo. 3, c. 60 (June, 1809), the import from

What would have been the ultimate result of the April Order cannot be determined. For some time after that measure, British manufactures and colonial produce, and even neutral goods that had paid import duty in the United Kingdom, had been smuggled into the continent. Imports, moreover, of European naval stores and foodstuffs had been made since the spring of 1809. It would seem that the British Government must have sensed that any further change would make the late order a dead letter. And yet, in spite of this knowledge and the strict blockade of the French coast, the Ministry finally allowed a complete reversal of their program.

What was the cause for this change? The answer is simple, and is to be found in the state of the harvests in France and Great Britain. The failure of the British crops caused the Government to seek foreign grain. Distance, as well as growing hostility, prevented any immediate help from America. From the Baltic little might be had, by reason of the Continental System and the increased demands for food made by the French armies in that region. Where, then, might a supply be had? Only from France, where there was an overabundance of corn.[97] The combined force, therefore, of these two factors, scarcity in Great Britain and overabundance in France, set at naught the good intentions which the Ministry had had in the spring.

On September 28, 1809, the Council agreed to grant licences for the import of grain, meal, or flour and burr-stones from the ports of France and Holland; and also for the export of British manufactures and colonial produce to these ports within the following districts: first, from any port between Sluys and Calais; secondly, from any port between Boulogne and Le Conquet; thirdly, from any port between Brest and Bayonne; and fourthly, from any port of France within the Straits.[98] This

---

any port of Europe or Africa, of lawful goods, the growth or produce of any country, was allowed until the close of the war. This act made valid all trade that had existed before its passage.

[97] See pp. 66–67 for proof of the scarcity in Britain; for conditions in France, see pp. 168–170; also Melvin, F. E., *op. cit.*, pp. 82–91.

[98] P. C. Unbound Papers, Council Minute, Sept. 28, 1809. This order also allowed any ship, except a French, to sail in ballast if necessary from

amounted, actually, to a licenced trade with any port between Sluys and Bayonne both inclusive. Extension of this area rapidly followed. Early in October a licenced trade was allowed between Great Britain and Europe via Walcheren. These were called Dutch licences, and permitted any vessel bearing any flag, except the French, to sail in ballast from any enemy port north of Walcheren to a Dutch port and to carry from any Dutch port north of Walcheren or west of Juist a cargo of corn to an English port north of Dover.[99] Norden licences to trade by way of Heligoland also continued to be granted for the import of corn and other lawful articles.

This condition remained unchanged until the middle of October, when the district for importing corn from Brest to Bayonne was limited to the area from Brest to Bordeaux. Norden licences, however, were extended so as to include all trade from Emden, while export and import Walcheren licences were to last for three months after issue.[100]

The next month the licenced trade was considerably checked. The British Government, believing that the import licences already granted for corn from France and Holland were numer-

---

any port in Holland or France to a place within the restricted area. Brest had been blockaded since 1803, and the entire district by the April Order of 1809. The third district was narrowed at a later date to include only the area between Brest and Bordeaux: see P. C. Unbound Papers, Council Minute, Oct. 11, 1809. The following is of interest:

NUMBER OF LICENCES ISSUED

Date	District I	II	III	IV	Total
Sept. 28					22
Sept. 30	10	12	14	0	36
Oct. 2	7	13	11	4	35
Oct. 3	6	15	11	1	33
Total	23	40	36	5	126

99 P. C. Reg., 183, Oct. 12, 1809. From that date until Oct. 26, a total of seventy-six Dutch licences was granted on eleven different days.

100 P. C. Unbound Papers, Oct. 11, 1809; by these licences British manufactures and colonial produce might still be exported in return for corn. Licences to trade to and from the Baltic were issued as before: see for example P. C. Reg., 183, Oct. 27, 1809.

ous enough to obtain the available supplies in these states, decided to grant no more.[101] It was generally understood that those issued and still unused would cause extensive imports. It should be noticed that this decision in no way checked the licenced trade to and from the Baltic, Russia, Norden and the island of Walcheren.[102]

Although the Council had forbidden the further use of licences for trade with France and Holland, subsequent events showed that this was but temporary in nature. From November, 1809, until March, 1810, but two licences were granted for this trade.[103] During this period, however, considerable import took place, due, in part, to the fact that the action of the Council had not been retroactive.[104] Accordingly, the licences whose time had not expired were honored by the British authorities. Another fact which shows continued import was the decision the Council made to extend the time limit of these licences, in view of certain difficulties encountered by many ships in clearing from France. In all cases the extension of time was to date from February 21, 1810, when an order appeared carrying into effect this extension.[105] At the end of the new limit, a fur-

101 P. C. Unbound Papers, Council Minute, Nov. 6, 1809. In the margin of this minute there is written that up to Nov. 1, 1809, a total of 1741 corn licences had been granted under the September Order; this agrees with the figures as given in *Parl. Pap.,* 1813, No. 184, p. 42. It is to be noticed that in these licences the various rules and peculiarities mentioned before still existed.

102 During November and December, 1809, American licences were granted in large numbers. Certain minor changes were made in the Norden and Baltic trade: see P. C. Unbound Papers, Council Minute, Nov. 9, 22, Dec. 13, 1809.

103 See P. C. Reg., 184, Dec. 4, 1809, for a licence granted to a Mr. J. Athens allowing the import of corn from any port between Boulogne and Le Conquet. In P. C. Reg., 185, March 3, 1810, the total number of licences issued from Jan. 1, 1809, to March 3, 1810, is given as 1743.

104 During January and February, 1810, licences were frequently issued permitting ships that had brought grain from France and Holland to return in ballast to any port of Holland.

105 See P. C. Reg., 185, Feb. 21, 1810, for an order extending the time limit as follows: five weeks for those for trade between Brest and Bordeaux; and four weeks for those for trade between Boulogne and Le Conquet, Sluys and Calais, and Holland to ports north of Walcheren and west of Juist. Notice of this extension was posted Feb. 20. A copy of it

ther extension was found necessary; consequently all unused licences were to last until June 10, 1810.[106]

Before this date, however, the Government, yielding probably to pressure from the mercantile classes and anticipating another crop shortage, granted new licences for trade with France and Holland.[107] On May 17, 1810, the following notice was posted at the Council office:

> Licences will be granted for the Importation of Grain, Meal, Flour and Burr Stones in Vessels bearing any flag but the French, from the following districts, such Licences to be in force till the 10th of November next: From the River Ems to Boulogne both inclusive, and from Boulogne to Nantes both inclusive. Licences will be granted for export to the above [places] in vessels that have brought in grain from either district.

Exports were to consist of colonial produce, East Indian and Prize goods, British manufactures, and all forms of lawful articles excepting cotton-wool.[108]

---

is to be found among the P. C. Unbound Papers in a group called "Orders and Notices." On May 23, 25, 1810, the Lords called for information on all licences issued, and requested that all orders and notices that had been posted at the Council office should be sent to them. These were returned to the Lords, June 7, 1810: see *Lords' Journal,* XLVII, 689, 699–700, 746. Evidently, the group marked "Orders and Notices" was a copy of a part of the return to the Lords. The original orders and notices may be found in a group marked "A Group of Papers;" the marks of the stickers can readily be seen. These orders and notices are also to be found scattered through the Council Minutes.

[106] P. C. Reg., 186, the Council to the Customs, April 9, 1810, directing the admission of all licenced ships coming from France and Holland with corn, which had cleared before the expiration of the time as set by the Order of Feb. 21, 1810: see also, P. C. Unbound Papers, "Orders and Notices;" also Council Minute, April 24, 1810. The order extending the time of these licences to June was issued May 2, 1810: see P. C. Reg., 186.

[107] See P. C. Reg., 186, April 26, 1810, for a letter from the Council to Messrs. Roberts and Co., refusing their request for a licence to trade with France: see, however, P. C. Reg., 186, May 15, 1810, for a licence granted for trade with France.

[108] P. C. Unbound Papers, "A Group of Papers," May 17, 1810. This notice stated that all corn licences whose time limit had been extended to June 10 might be renewed and continued until Nov. 10, 1810, upon application and payment of a stamp tax. See also P. C. Unbound Papers, "Orders and Notices." All licences granted under the authority of the Order of March 2, 1810, were extended to Aug. 10, 1810: see P. C. Reg., 187, June 23, 27, 1810. See also Melvin, F. E., *Napoleon's Navigation System,* p. 266.

Immediately a great rush for these licences took place. On May 18 forty-two licences were issued permitting three hundred and forty-two ships to sail in ballast from any port in France or Holland to any port from the Ems to Boulogne, and to return with a cargo of grain.[109] In October, however, a decided drop in imports seems to have taken place, which caused a check in the further use of these licences.[110] Shortly after, the pendulum swung the other way, and import again took place even though at that particular time the export of corn was practically forbidden in France.[111]

In the meantime corn had been imported from other parts of Europe. Most of this seems to have come from the Baltic, the port of Norden, and the island of Heligoland. Early in January, 1810, the Council licenced the import from the Baltic of certain articles with the exception of German linens, stock-fish and oil; these licences were to be effective until September 29, 1810.[112]

109 P. C. Reg., 186. Ten other licences were granted the same day for fifteen ships to trade between Ostend, Groningen, Amsterdam, Nantes, Calais, Rotterdam, and a port from Boulogne to Nantes both inclusive, and the United Kingdom. The following is of interest:

Date	Number of licences	Number of ships	Port
May 21, 1810	2	17	between Ems and Boulogne
May 28, 1810	5	12	between Ems and Boulogne
May 29, 1810	14	24	various French ports
May 30, 1810	12	25	various French ports

From June 1 to 13 inclusive, forty-eight licences allowed one hundred and sixty-five ships to trade with any port between Ems and Boulogne, and Boulogne and Nantes both inclusive: see P. C. Reg., 187. On June 1, vessels were permitted to sail in ballast from a French or Dutch port to a port between Boulogne and Nantes inclusive. See P. C. Unbound Papers, Council Minute, June 18, 1810, directing licences for a trade from Nantes to Bordeaux inclusive. The form and detail of these French and Dutch licences corresponded to those granted in 1809.

110 P. C. Unbound Papers, Council Minute, Oct. 29, 1810. The reason assigned for this measure was that the import of corn for the last quarter had been "very considerable."

111 P. C. Reg., 189, Nov. 6, 1810.

112 P. C. Unbound Papers, Council Minute, Jan. 16, 1810. This had been foreshadowed by a notice posted Jan. 15, 1810: see P. C. Unbound Papers, "A Group of Papers." German linens were removed after May 31, 1810: see 50 Geo. 3, c. 26, and P. C. Unbound Papers, Council Minute,

In June of the same year the Privy Council extended the licenced trade to the Baltic. All ships, except those of France, might import corn and other lawful goods from any unblockaded Baltic port. Again, any such vessel might sail in ballast from a port north of the Scheldt to an unblockaded Baltic port, and import thence a similar cargo. In either case the possession of papers representing a destination other than that of the United Kingdom did not invalidate the licence. The cargo, moreover, might be represented as belonging to anyone.[112a]

Shortly before the close of 1810, the Government stopped issuing these Baltic import licences, and refused to extend the time for those licences still unused. This decision did not prevent licences from being granted solely for the import of corn. Grain might also be imported by all holders of export licences to the Baltic, provided application for this privilege had been made when the licence was granted.[113]

Licences for trade with Norway and with Danish ports outside the Baltic had frequently been granted, as well as for trade to and from the continent by the way of Heligoland and Norden.[114] In March " General " licences were issued for trade to and from Heligoland to any Danish port between the Eider and the Bay of Kiel.[115] Several months later Heligoland was

---

May 31, 1810. Licences granted under the Order of Jan. 16, 1810, were called Baltic import licences, and were issued in large numbers during the remainder of that year: see P. C. Reg., 184–189. On July 13, 1810, an extension of time was granted on all Baltic licences until Jan. 1, 1811; at the same time new licences were issued for a similar period: see P. C. Unbound Papers, " A Group of Papers."

[112a] P. C. Reg., 187, June 1, 1810.

[113] P. C. Unbound Papers, Council Minute, Dec. 4, 1810. The export licences to the Baltic were to last until June 25, 1811.

[114] P. C. Unbound Papers, March 26, 1810. The import licences for Norway and Danish ports outside of the Baltic were to last for four months. The licences to trade via Heligoland and Norden had been issued on the basis of the Order of Jan. 16, 1810; these licences were to be good for six months: see P. C. Unbound Papers, " Orders and Notices," March 20, 1810.

[115] P. C. Unbound Papers, " Orders and Notices," March 29, 1810; see also, under same date, " A Group of Papers." Shortly before, it had been decided to grant no more licences to import corn from Denmark to touch and pay duty at Leith, and then to sail to Norway. Repeated instances of

struck out of the licences, and from then on importable goods were to come direct from this district to the United Kingdom.[116]

There existed yet another type of licence which proved of value in the grain trade. It will be recalled that on March 1, 1809, the United States had passed the *Non-Intercourse Act*, which stopped all trade between America and both belligerents.[117] In order to obviate this act and to insure a supply of corn, the British extended the Licence System to the United States.[118] At the same time, licences were issued permitting the entrance of American grain into the Spanish Peninsula, where large numbers of British soldiers were stationed.[119]

It should be noticed that the American licences conformed in general to those granted for the European trade. In either type there was a fundamental difference between the export and the import licences. In the export, as in the export and import licences, it was uniformly required that the name of the ship, its tonnage, and usually the master's name, should be inserted within the body of licence. In the import, as in the import and export licences, this requirement had not been found practical. It was stated that the name of the master, the tonnage of the boat, and the time of clearance should be endorsed on the licence at the port of clearance. Consequently, if in the export, or in the export and import licences, the name of the

---

fraud doubtless explains this step: see P. C. Reg., 191, April 24, 1811; and also P. C. Unbound Papers, "Orders and Notices," March 20, 1810.

[116] P. C. Unbound Papers, Council Minute, Aug. 13, 1810. From June 1 to 13, 1810, a total of one hundred and eighty-two licences had been granted to six hundred and one ships to trade between the United Kingdom and Russian, Baltic and Scandinavian ports: see P. C. Reg., 187.

[117] See p. 108 for instances of licences granted for the American trade in 1808.

[118] P. C. Reg., 183, Orders in Council, Oct. 3, 7, 1810. A favorite point for smuggling seems to have been Amelia Island: see P. C. Unbound Papers, Council Minute, Feb. 15, 1810; a licence was also granted to Mr. Zimmerman, a copy of which is given in Appendix No. 6.

[119] P. C. Unbound Papers, "Various." During 1811 licences were granted for the export of corn from France to Lisbon: see P. C. Reg., 190, March 12, 1811. Trade between the Baltic and Lisbon was forbidden; probably because of the distance and the danger present from the French privateers: see P. C. Reg., 191, May 15, 1811.

vessel, its tonnage, and the name of the master were not given in the licence, the British naval and Customs officers were to consider such a licence a forgery.[120]

During the next three years the Licence System continued to operate on the same basis as that established in 1809 and 1810. The following changes, however, should be noted: On February 27, 1811, the phrase then common to all licences, "a vessel bearing any flag except the French," was made to read, "a vessel sailing under any flag except that of France or except a vessel belonging to France or subjects thereof or belonging to the subjects of any territory, town or place annexed to and forming a part of France."[121] This was a decided step in the direction of limiting the use and abuse of licences. A further restriction was made in April, when the Order of February 4, 1807, was revoked.[122] This left the Fox Blockade, the January Order of 1807, and the April and May Orders of 1809 as the basis for the trade with the enemy. All trade within the area included by these measures was forbidden by reason of the strict blockade that was supposed to be in force. It was, probably, because of this blockade and its apparent enforcement, that the licenced trade with this district became a negligible matter. Licences, however, were still granted for trade with Russia and with ports within and outside the Baltic. Further restriction occurred when it was determined to issue no more licences for ships to sail in ballast from ports north of the Scheldt, unless the name and the tonnage of the vessel had been definitely given in advance.[123] Again, it was declared that no licences would be

[120] These facts are clearly stated in a letter to the Admiralty: see P. C. Reg., 188, Aug. 28, 1810. In the same letter there is a descriptive list of twenty different types of licences then used. Most of these permitted the import of corn; they have been mentioned in this study. See also P. C. Reg., 188, Sept. 5, 1810.

[121] P. C. Reg., 190, Feb. 27, 1811. This did not invalidate licences granted before Feb. 20, which seems to have been the date when the foregoing decision was made.

[122] P. C. Reg., 192, Order in Council, April 11, 1811.

[123] P. C. Unbound Papers, Council Minute, Feb. 23, 1811. In cases where these details were not given, ships were allowed only from ports north of Tönning: see P. C. Unbound Papers, Council Minute, Feb. 16, 1811, for a similar restriction on the trade to the White Sea.

issued for ships to proceed in ballast for French or other blockaded ports, unless proof had been furnished that the ship had entered such a port under a British licence.[124]

About the same time the Council called for a descriptive list of all licences then used. This report seems to have been made July 31, 1811, and showed a total of eighteen different licences.[125] Those touching the grain trade may briefly be summarized. First, the Baltic and White Sea licences. These were granted for an export and import trade, and protected all goods that legally might be exported to and imported from these places.[126] Second, licences for trade with Norway and Sweden outside the Baltic. These were limited to the import trade and were to be effective for four months.[127] Third, 'import and export' licences, permitting trade between Heligoland and Europe on the one hand, and on the other between Norden and the Eider, both inclusive. Vessels so protected might trade either to the east of Juist, or westward between Juist and Borcum, or from a port east of Juist to the Eider. Fourth, Norden licences. These were limited to an import trade and followed a route from a point between Norden and the Eider to a port north of Dover. Fifth, the American licences. These were granted to neutrals for import purposes only.[128] Sixth, licences for the import of wheat only, in ships above one hundred tons, from certain ports within Denmark, Holstein and Jutland, outside the Baltic.[129]

[124] P. C. Unbound Papers, Council Minute, April 16, 1811.

[125] *Ibid.*, July 31, 1811.

[126] These licences were to last until Jan. 1, 1812.

[127] By order, Sept. 13, 1811, these licences were placed upon the same footing as the Baltic and White Sea licences.

[128] From July 8, 1811, to Jan. 20, 1812, fifty-five licences had been granted for British-owned ships to import American produce, timber, corn and tobacco from the United States to the United Kingdom: see P. C. Unbound Papers, 1812.

[129] This was ordered Aug. 26, 1811. P. C. Unbound Papers, Council Minute, Nov. 13, 1812, directed that ships of one hundred tons, not sailing under either the French or American flag, might import corn from Zeeland, Jutland, Schleswig and Holstein to special ports in the United Kingdom. A bond of £4,000 was required if the name of the ship and its tonnage were not given, and a bond of £3,000 if these requirements were fulfilled.

During 1811 the Government, as has already been shown, tried to restrict the use of licences. This attempt proved to be a failure, as during 1812 there was a decided return to a licenced trade with the enemy. Licences were granted, for example, for the import of grain from the Jade district, France, Flanders and Holland.[130] It should also be noticed that the Council endorsed the licences issued by Sir James Saumarez, British admiral stationed in the Baltic, for the import of corn.[131] This was also the case with the licences granted by Admiral Sawyer, stationed at Halifax, for the carrying of American corn to the Spanish Peninsula. Upon the advent of war with the United States, 'export and import' licences were granted to neutrals sailing under any flag except the French or American, to trade with the Peninsula and also with the United Kingdom.[132]

By this time, however, the Continental System was rapidly falling into ruin, bringing down with it the Napoleonic Empire. Section after section of the European coast that had been directly or indirectly under the French shook off this foreign domination, and declared its ports open to the British. The further operation of the British orders was thus gradually rendered unnecessary. One by one the various blockades were removed.[133] And so the year 1813 came to a close with a marked decrease in the extent to which the Licence System was employed.

[130] This was true of all forms of import and export, or export and import licences: see P. C. Unbound Papers, Council Minute, Nov. 13, 1812. Trade with France once more became active. Large quantities of manufactures and colonial produce were sent to France in return for wines, brandies and silks: see Melvin, F. E., *Napoleon's Navigation System*, pp. 291, 325.

[131] B. T., 1: 73, for a list of licences granted by Saumarez from June to Oct., 1812. See also *Letters of Sir T. B. Martin*, II: 26–27, 74–75, *Publications of the Navy Records Society*, 1898, vol. XII.

[132] P. C. Council Minutes, March 30, 1813. In these, as well as in all licences granted since 1811, the various requirements mentioned before were still in force. For a discussion of the Peninsular trade, see the author's article "The American Grain Trade to the Spanish Peninsula, 1810–1814," *American Historical Review*, October, 1922.

[133] P. C. Reg., 195, Orders in Council, Nov. 30, Dec. 13, 1813. See P. C. Unbound Papers for an interesting endorsement on a letter to Thornton, Aug. 7, 1812: see also P. C. Unbound Papers, Council Minute, March 20, 1813.

Throughout the period of the French War, and particularly during the Napoleonic era, the Licence System proved to be one of the most outstanding features of British policy. The Licence System permeated the entire life of the nation. Privy counselors and clerks, Lord admirals and seamen, ambassadors and consuls, all busied themselves in countless ways in carrying out the many details of this system. British manufacturers and agriculturists, East and West Indian merchants, exporters and importers, producers and consumers, all watched with great interest the growth and extension of a system that played so important a part in their very existence.

In the main the Licence System tended to articulate with the general trend of the war, especially with the French decrees; and resulted ultimately in an almost complete suspension of the Navigation Acts. Critics arose who condemned the use of these licences. England's wealth, strength, and resources, so they argued, had been built upon a time-tested foundation, the Navigation System. Why, then, thrust this system to one side, and permit the future of the state to rest upon so uncertain a basis as the Licence System; a system, moreover, which ran counter to the very purpose of the war, and which permitted friend and foe to gain handsome profits at the expense of loyal Englishmen? The landed classes claimed that the Licence System was an unwarranted attack upon the growth and extension of agriculture.[134]

This view, however, overlooks the problem that faced the British Government and nation. Not since the days of Louis XIV, probably not since the Armada, had England been called upon to fight such a desperate battle for existence. The mere conduct of the war was in itself a task which demanded unusual effort and attention. The war, however, could not be won simply by an army and a navy, especially when Britain was fighting so capable a foe as Napoleon. Neither England nor France was able to bring their armies and navies to bear upon each other in a constant manner. If they had, the issue might have been settled long before Waterloo. As it was, the British

[134] See for example *Farmer's Mag.*, X: 547, XI: 101.

fleet completely dominated the sea and kept Napoleon's Grand Army out of the British Isles. On the other hand, the British fleet could not keep the Grand Army from ruling the continent. What did it avail Great Britain, then, if she did have control of the seas, but Napoleon controlled the continent? Europe, then as today, was England's foremost market for manufactured goods. This market, however, had been closed to the British by the Continental System. Europe also had food supplies which were believed to be absolutely necessary for England's growing industrial life.

The problem facing the British Government of conducting a gigantic war, and, at the same time, of keeping its subjects contented by industrial activity and by a constant food supply, was most difficult indeed. It was a problem, moreover, which called for immediate solution, or else the enemy might win the war. Brushing to one side, therefore, the pointed criticisms of Englishmen and neutrals, the British Government hit upon the Licence System as a method of winning the war. British manufactures and colonial goods found a market in Europe with or without Napoleon's consent. By the same method the English Government imported unparalleled amounts of corn, the absence of which might have been highly dangerous to the existence of the British nation.[135] To the extent, therefore, that the Licence System made possible the sale of British goods abroad and the import of corn from Europe and America, it may safely be stated that the Licence System justified its existence.[136]

[135] The British trade to and from the continent was made less difficult by the French Licence System.

[136] It has not been the purpose of this chapter to treat the Licence System in its larger aspects, this being reserved for future study. The immediate object has been to show the relation between this system and the grain trade. The definite connection between the actual movement of corn and the various orders and decisions dealing with licences will furnish the theme, in part, for the remaining chapters of this volume.

CHAPTER VII

THE GRAIN TRADE, 1800 TO 1802

The Industrial Revolution and its effects upon British Agriculture — The important European and American sources of supply — The imports from Germany and Prussia — The relation between these states and Russia to the Armed Neutrality — The situation in France and Holland — Economic, rather than political, forces control the corn exports from Europe to England.

THE eighteenth century was preëminently a century of revolutions. Political and economic forces of great magnitude shook a self-satisfied Europe to its very foundations. Thirteen colonies won independence from an England which but a few years before had withstood the might of half of Europe. The Grand Monarchy of Louis XIV reluctantly resigned in favor of a Greater Britain. These were significant achievements, pregnant with meaning for the future. Of greater importance and far more reaching in its effect was the Industrial Revolution. Like the other forces mentioned, this world-embracing movement had its beginnings in the last quarter of the eighteenth century and had, for an immediate objective, the disestablishment of the Ancient Régime.

The Old Order, which for several centuries had dominated man, was doomed to everlasting destruction. Fundamentally, the Industrial Revolution was chiefly responsible for this change. With the appearance of the factory system, the division of labor, and the rapid growth of towns and cities, new and important problems arose for immediate consideration. The most pressing of these, for England, was the question of the nation's food-supply. The shifting of population from the country to the town, together with a marked increase in the birth-rate of the town, resulted in an ever increasing demand for food.[1] To meet

[1] A marked increase in the total population of the kingdom had followed the Industrial Revolution.

this condition, attention was turned towards the growth of domestic production; but with the opening of the nineteenth century, with its wars and rumors of war, the interest of thoughtful men was directed to the task of increasing the import of corn.

England obtained her foreign corn chiefly from certain agricultural parts of Europe and North America. As to the former, the Mediterranean basin may be left out of consideration, since the grain-producing states at that time were confined to those regions bordering on the Atlantic, the North Sea and the Baltic. Of these the most favored was Prussia, which for some time had been the center of the European grain trade. Among the many cities of this kingdom which engaged in this trade, by far the most important was Dantzic. This city was the emporium of an extensive and highly productive district, by reason of its location on the lower Vistula, down whose waters floated flat-bottomed boats and loosely constructed rafts loaded with grain. The rich soil of the Vistula basin extended over large parts of Prussia, Poland, Volhynia and Galicia. The productivity of this area, together with a cheap and abundant supply of labor, made it the granary of Northern Europe. Though strategically located, Dantzic had no seaport of its own. This defect had been overcome by the building of an out-port, Newfahrwasser, from which the Dantzic merchants shipped during the summer and early fall large quantities of grain, chiefly, it is believed, to England.[2] The rye trade, however, was practically limited to Holland, although some went to England, and even to Spain and Portugal when the market was especially attractive.[3]

Königsberg, like Dantzic, had no natural port; the presence of

[2] *Parl. Pap.*, 1814–1815, No. 26, pp. 35, 36. Total exports of wheat from Dantzic to England equalled 253,333 lasts from 1794 to 1806 inclusive; during the same time, 79,153 lasts were exported to other states. The source gives no comparative figures before 1794, and nothing at all from 1806 to 1814: see *Parl. Pap.*, 1826, No. 159, p. 90: see also *ibid.*, pp. 50–51, 126–128. For a contemporary account of the grain trade of Dantzic, see Oddy, J. P., *European Commerce,* I: 244–250.

[3] *Rijks Geschiedkundige Publicatien, Gedenkstukken der Algemeene Geschiedenis Von Nederland,* edited by H. T. Colebrander, VI de deel II stuk, De Stassart to D'Alphonse, March 11, 1812. Hereafter, this source will be cited as *R. G. P.*

a bar at the mouth of the Pregel kept ships of more than six-foot draft from the city proper. Königsberg, therefore, made use of Pillau as a port of shipment. The Pregel drained parts of Poland and Russia which grew large quantities of wheat and oats, most of which was exported to England.

The other ports of Prussia played relatively a minor rôle in the grain trade. Memel, the farthest north, and Stettin may be left out of consideration. Corn was shipped to England from Greifswald, Stralsund, Elbing, Libau and Barth only under exceptional circumstances.[4] Cologne, which had played so large a part in the English trade during the Middle Ages, had lost all importance in this respect. In times of unusual demand, however, supplies for Britain were sent from Cologne down the Rhine to Antwerp, or more often to Rotterdam. It should be recalled that Holland produced little more than was needed for its own use, and often had to import supplies.[5] It was only in times like the Napoleonic era when the British market was very attractive and when the harvests in Europe were abundant, that the merchants of Antwerp, Amsterdam, Ghent and Ostend exported corn which had been obtained from the Dutch provinces, Cologne, Frankfurt and other inland cities.

Second to Dantzic, the leading port of Northern Europe was Hamburg, situated on the north bank of the Elbe at its junction with the Alster, some sixty miles from the sea. This distance was no serious handicap, as ships drawing fourteen feet of water could with little difficulty dock at Hamburg. The position this city had in the grain trade was due to its location on the Elbe, whose fertile basin extended over seven hundred miles in length. North of Hamburg, Bremen was the center of the trade of Hanover, Brunswick and Hesse-Cassel, whose soil was not well suited for extensive cultivation. Rye was the chief article exported, though oats were occasionally shipped to England. Bremen, however, did not and could not rival either Hamburg or Dantzic. Lübeck on the Trave and Emden on the Ems engaged to some

[4] See Oddy, J. J., *op. cit.*, I: 153, for an account of the trade of Libau.

[5] *R. G. P.*, VI de deel, I stuk, Rapport du Conseiller Real, July, 1811, chap. 5, and *Parl. Pap.*, 1826, No. 159, p. 51.

extent in the grain trade, especially during the period covered by this study. Rostock and Wismar, ports of Mecklenburg, were of minor importance.

The Russian towns of Riga and St. Petersburg were not of great significance, as the severe and prolonged winters of this country usually locked these harbors for more than a third of the year. Archangel occasionally shipped large quantities. Odessa, obtaining its supplies from Kiev and Podolia, exported little corn to England; rather did it confine its trade to Mediterranean ports.

The ports of Leeuwarden and Groningen usually sent to England a small supply of oats and, during periods of demand, some wheat. The French towns of Douai, Nantes, Morlaix and Bordeaux were of little importance in the grain trade of England. Though France was a country of decided agricultural wealth, it grew but little more than it actually used. The policy, furthermore, of the Ancient Régime had been to check exportation. During the Napoleonic wars the exports of France assumed larger volume. Of the Mediterreanean ports Leghorn alone sent occasional cargoes to England.

In the New World, the ports of New York, Philadelphia, Baltimore, Alexandria and Norfolk were of increasing importance. The agricultural possibilities of the United States were well known, New York, Pennsylvania and Virginia producing the larger share of the nation's supplies, although the country to the west of the Alleghanies was rapidly pushing to the front. Most of the surplus of America was shipped to the West Indies, Canada, Great Britain and the Spanish Peninsula. In Canada, Quebec monopolized the grain trade, which, however, never assumed any size during the Napoleonic era.[6]

After this preliminary survey, attention may be given to the trade itself. Fortunately, the period covered by this study falls into several groups which may be conveniently used. That which first demands consideration is the period from 1800 to 1802 inclusive. It will be recalled that this was a time of great scarcity,

[6] These facts were taken chiefly from *Parl. Pap.*, 1813–1814, No. 339; 1814–1815, No. 26; 1826, No. 159; 1826–1827, Nos. 27, 83, 157; 1828, No. 258: see also McCullock, J. R., *A Dictionary of Commerce* (London, Longmans, 1859), and Oddy, J. J., *op. cit.*

high prices and extensive imports, factors which warrant its being studied apart from the years which followed.

The precarious condition which England faced in the first few years of the nineteenth century increased the import of corn. Low duties, often suspended, combined with liberal bounties had flooded British markets with unprecedented supplies of foreign corn. Out of a total of 3,336,949 quarters of wheat imported from 1800 to 1802 inclusive, 2,424,718 quarters came from Prussia, Russia and Germany. The grand total of all corn amounted to 5,829,180 quarters of which 1,819,242 quarters had come from Prussia.

The importance of Prussia as a source of supply was well known by the English. For over a quarter of a century Prussian wheat had figured conspicuously in the British markets. From 1792 to 1798 inclusive, 3,987 ships entered London with cargoes of corn, timber, linen and yarn.[7] When questioned by the Corn Committe of 1800 about the probable source of foreign corn, Mr. Claude Scott replied: " . . . our principal source . . . may be looked for this year from the Baltic, and chiefly from Poland." [8] The granting of bounties on Prussian wheat is further proof of the value attached to this trade. So effective had this inducement been that the harvests of Galicia and Olmütz found their way to England, the difference in domestic prices and those in England being more than enough to cover the cost of freight and insurance, and still leave a handsome profit for the importer.[9]

During these years the agricultural situation in Prussia and Germany had been, generally speaking, very satisfactory. Unsettled weather conditions in the first quarter of 1800 had caused a flurry in the British market, and for some time there was doubt whether any supplies might be had from Prussia. King remarked in a letter: " It is apprehended that no considerable succor can be obtained from the North of Europe, where from the same cause [the weather] there is likely to be a failure of

[7] *First Series,* XIV: 492–495.

[8] *Ibid.,* IX: 75.

[9] See *Parl. Pap.,* 1814–1815, No. 26, pp. 34–35; 1826, No. 159, p. 52; 1826–1827, No. 333.

crop."[10] The Prussian Government, aware of the danger, had, early in 1800, placed an embargo on all foodstuffs, excepting wheat.[11] In March this embargo was extended to wheat. Fortunately, this restriction on wheat was removed within a week, and export was again permitted.[12] The embargo on other grain was continued until May, 1801.[13]

In spite of these difficulties, as well as the unfavorable harvest of 1800, the exports of that year and of 1801 were very large.[14] It is to be noticed, however, that there had been a drop in 1801, which probably had been caused, in the main, by the activities of the Armed Neutrality. Prussia had been drawn reluctantly into this confederation, the effect of which had been to stop all trade with England. In order to checkmate the plans of the Emperor Paul, as well as to insure a constant supply of corn, the British minister, Carysfort, issued licences protecting Prussian ships carrying grain to England.[15] When news of this

[10] *Life and Correspondence of R. King,* III: 136–138; *First Series,* IX: 75; F. O., 64: 57, F. C. Lentze to Grenville, March 2, 1800. Lentze was British consul at Stettin.

[11] *First Series,* IX: 75; *British Mag.,* I: 388. This embargo did not include Dantzic. The export of all corn, except rye, was allowed until Sept., 1805; rye exports had been forbidden during the summer of 1800 when it was feared that there might be shortage of that grain: see *Parl. Pap.,* 1826–1827, No. 157, pp. 25, 26. Because of the excessive demand in England the old export tax of 14*d.* per quarter was for the time raised to 8*s.* 2*d.* per quarter for wheat. After 1800 the tax was lowered to its former rate, where it remained throughout the period covered by this study: see *Parl. Pap.,* 1826–1827, No. 157, p. 26.

[12] F. O., 64: 57, Lentze to Grenville, March 2, 1800, and Garlike to Grenville, Aug. 9, 1800. News of this was sent to Mr. Scott: see P. C. Reg., 154, April 3, 1800. Garlike was the British ambassador at Berlin.

[13] During this period a heavy export duty was placed on wheat: see F. O., 54: 61, Hawkesbury to Carysfort, May 8, 1801; F. O. 64: 58, Carysfort to Grenville, Aug. 9, 1800; F. O., 64: 57, Drusina to Grenville, Aug. 1, 1800. During 1800, two hundred and twenty-six ships cleared from Königsberg for England, of which number but forty-five were British.

[14] F. O., 64: 57, Drusina to Grenville, Aug. 1, 1800; F. O., 64: 59, Drusina to Hammond, Nov. 25, 1800: see also J. Williams to S. Bourne, London, April 3, 1801, Bourne MSS.

[15] F. O., 64: 60, Carysfort to Grenville, Feb. 18, 1801. The day before Carysfort had written: "There is nothing to be feared but from the stoppage of the present supply of corn, and I am happy to hear from what I think good authority that the Prussians themselves are taking the most

reached England, the Ministry at once endorsed these licences and informed Carysfort that they would be respected even in the event of war.[16] The following day the Council drafted an order guaranteeing protection to all Russian, Swedish, Danish and Prussian ships importing grain, provisions and naval stores belonging to the subjects of these states, of Great Britain, or of a neutral state, to the United Kingdom. This protection, moreover, was extended to the return voyage as well.[17] Early in March a copy of this order was sent to Carysfort, together with directions permitting him to grant further licences.[18] A little later the entire affair was made public by an order in council. During the remainder of March and all of April, this order seems to have been used to a great extent. On April 14, Drusina, British consul at Königsberg, wrote Hawkesbury that he had granted passports for twenty-four ships laden with 27,690 quarters of wheat, 60 tons of hemp and 270 tons of flax, all bound for London. Two months later Drusina reported that thirty ships had cleared for London from Elbing with 30,000 quarters of wheat.[19]

In the meantime Nelson's victory at Copenhagen and the death of Czar Paul had tempered the Prussian Government to undertake a friendly policy towards England. Early in May the export of barley, pease, rye and oats was allowed. This was followed by a definite statement on the part of Baron Jacobi, Prussian minister at St. James, that there were no restrictions

---

effective measure, that is by giving large bribes to obtain leave for the exportation of it." In March, Drusina asked whether the British Government intended to grant licences: see F. O., 64: 60, March 24, 1801.

16 F. O., 64: 60, Grenville to Carysfort, March 3, 1801.

17 B. T., 5: 12, March 4, 1801: see also B. T., 1: 19, March 3, 1801; P. C. Reg., 157, March 17, 1800, for a copy of this order.

18 F. O., 64: 60, Grenville to Carysfort, March 10, 1801.

19 F. O., 64: 61, Drusina to Hawkesbury, April 14, June 26, 1801. In view of the rumor that Denmark intended closing the Sound to all licenced ships, many of these ships cleared for Lisbon and Emden. At the same time Carysfort informed his Government of the licences he had granted to ships bound to England from Dantzic and Stettin. He also added that the American consul at Stettin had been very active in granting licences: see F. O., 64: 60, Carysfort to Grenville, March 26, 1801, and F. O., 64: 61, Carysfort to Grenville, April 8, 1801.

on the trade between Prussia and England.[20] This announcement removed the need for any more licences. As a result of the action of the Prussian Government and the favorable harvest in Prussia, the corn trade was greatly increased.[21] During the remainder of 1801 and throughout 1802 exportation from Prussia was entirely free. The total amount imported by Great Britain, however, was much lower than in the previous year. This decline, as has been stated, was caused by improved conditions in Great Britain.[22]

Although a member, and the principal one, of the Armed Neutrality, Russia gave England large supplies of wheat during this period. In 1801, for example, a total of 204,654 quarters of corn had been imported, of which 174,337 quarters were of wheat. Much of this must have found its way through ordinary channels, but during the life of the Armed Neutrality, the British Order of May 17, 1801, must have covered and protected much of this trade. In June of that year, trade was declared to be free and unrestricted.[23] Of the total export from Russia during the first three years of the century, over one half found its way to England, the remainder being marketed in France or in ports of the Mediterranean.[24] The existence of high prices in Eng-

[20] F. O., 64: 61, Hawkesbury to Carysfort, May 8, 1801; *ibid.*, Drusina to Hawkesbury, June 26, 1801. On May 18, 1801, ships were allowed to clear from Great Britain for Hamburg or any other place on the Elbe: see P. C. Reg., 158.

[21] See F. O., 64: 61, Drusina to Hawkesbury, June 26, 1801.

[22] What was true of Prussia was also largely true of Germany. Large supplies from the German states, not including Prussia, were sent to England during the years 1800–1802. Although this trade was not seriously checked by the Armed Neutrality, it was nevertheless affected by the unsettled weather and harvest conditions, common to Europe at that time. See J. J. Kalckoff to Bourne, Oberlahnstein, June 11, 1802, Bourne MSS.; Consular Despatches, Hamburg, Nov. 3, Dec. 8, 1800; *Parl. Pap.*, 1826, No. 159, p. 163; *ibid.*, No. 258, p. 71.

[23] P. C. Reg., 158, June 4, 1801.

[24] *Parl. Pap.*, 1826–1827, No. 27. This source contains a table of prices in the various ports as well as the amounts exported; all of which shows a fair harvest. In 1802, a total of 13,354 millions of rubles worth of corn and flour was shipped from Russia. In the same year, 25.8 per cent of the ships that left Russia were British, 26.5 per cent were German, and 7.2 per cent, Russian: see Kovalevsky, M. M., *La Russie* (Paris, 1900), pp. 691, 696, and Oddy, J. P., *European Commerce*, I: 89.

land, together with a liberal bounty, had been quite sufficient to overcome the export duty of 5*s.* per quarter for wheat and the cost of transportation from Russia to Great Britain.[25]

The harvest conditions in England had also stimulated the trade from the Scandinavian states, a region that ordinarily did not ship much corn to England. This trade, probably, would have been larger had it not been for the unsettled weather in 1801 and for the Armed Neutrality. As it was, 141,990 quarters of corn were shipped during these years to Great Britain.[26]

The situation in France for the same time had been none too favorable. The harvest of 1799 had been below the average, while those for 1800 and 1801 were even more disappointing. Prices became abnormally high, especially in the *Départements* of the South and Southeast. In the district of Basses-Alpes, the average for the three years 1800–1802 was 36 fr. 25 c. per hectolitre, while that for the entire country was 22 fr. 35 c.[27]

The French Government was fully alive to the situation and tried to give such relief as was possible. Fortunately for the people as well as for the Consulate, Paris had been well stocked through the energy and foresight of Napoleon, who dreaded bread riots.[28] As a result, Paris had no extreme suffering during

[25] The Russian tariff of 1798 also provided for an export tax of 3*d.* per quarter for rye, and 8*d.* for oats, and a 6*d.* duty for barley. This continued the rule until 1811, when export was allowed duty free: see *Parl. Pap.*, 1826–1827, No. 221, No. 53.

[26] Trade with Denmark and Sweden was declared free, June 4, 16, 1801: see P. C. Reg., 158. See also F. O., 22: 36, Merry to Grenville, Feb. 1, 15, 22, 1801; *Parl. Pap.*, 1826–1827, No. 83, p. 11; *ibid.*, No. 27, pp. 15–18, for prices of wheat in Sweden: see too Oddy, J. P., *op. cit.*, II: 13, 14. During the period 1791–1801, Sweden had several successive harvest failures, and so great was the distress that a large part of the population was compelled to use the bark of trees as a substitute for rye and wheat, which usually came from Prussia: see *Parl. Pap.*, 1826, No. 159, p. 52.

[27] *Documents Statistiques sur la France,* 1837, pp. 7–15: see also *R. G. P.*, III de deel I stuk, The First Consul to Talleyrand, Dec. 16, 1800. Prices were raised by harvest failures, forestalling and undue speculation; many interesting references may be found in Aulard, A., *Paris sous le Consulat,* especially No. DCCVI, Nov. 28, 1801, which is a copy of an inscription written on the walls of Paris: "Vive Louis XVIII. Donnez nous du Pain." See also *Cobbett's Pol. Reg.*, I: 700, 766.

[28] Chaptal, J. A., *Mes Souvenirs sur Napoléon* (Paris, E. Plon, 1893), p. 285. See also Levasseur, E., *Histoire du Commerce de la France* (Paris,

the crisis of 1801 and 1802. Elsewhere, conditions became most acute. The Government met this condition by sending agents into Belgium and into the Rhenish states to buy grain, and by prohibiting the export of corn.[29] The effectiveness of this latter measure and of the scarcity itself is shown by the fact that, from 1800 to 1802 inclusive, a total of but 2,786 quarters of corn was shipped from France to England. It was due to no fault of the Government that these few thousand bushels found a market in Great Britain. The vigilance of the most active administration is seriously taxed and frequently baffled by illegal trading. Much of this trade came as the direct result of British agents who openly bought French corn.[30] Posing as the emissaries of the Consulate, these agents were able now and then to convince a few of the value of an English pound. This was the exception, and not the rule, as the hawk-like eye of the prefect and police officer had the uncanny faculty of spying on every action of all involved in the corn trade.[31]

This, however, does not seem to have been the case with Holland. The trade from this state seems to have rested largely

---

A. Rousseau, 1911), II: 50–51. For an account of the harvest of 1801, and the method suggested to bridge the scarcity, see "Procès-Verbal, VI frimaire, an X," Archives Nationales, A. F. IV: 1058, piece 13, quoted by Jaurès, J., *Histoire Socialiste,* VI: 252–253; also "De la Récolte des Blés de l'Approvisionnement de Paris," IX frimaire, an X, Archives Nationales, A. F.[4] 1318, quoted by Jaurès, J., *op. cit.,* p. 255, and Aulard, A., *op. cit.,* under the general head of "Ministère de la Police, Tableau de la situation de Paris."

[29] *Cor. de Nap.,* No. 5095: see also, Jaurès, J., *op. cit.,* pp. 255–258, Aulard, A., *op. cit.,* and *Annuaire de L'Économie Politique,* 1849, p. 337, for a statement of the activity of the Government in 1802 to provide the country with supplies. During 1802, agricultural conditions improved: see *Monthly Mirror,* XIII: 432.

[30] *Cor. de Nap.,* No. 4436. For a similar account see "Procès-verbal, VI frimaire an X," Archives Nationales, A. F. IV: 1058, piece 13, quoted by Jaurès, J., *op. cit.,* VI: 252. Passports were frequently used by the British who thereby entered France for the purpose of purchasing corn: see P. C. Reg., 154, Feb. 7, March 15, 18, 1800.

[31] Jaurès, J., *op. cit.,* VI: 248–249: see also, *ibid.,* pp. 244–263, and Aulard, A., *op. cit.* The total number of British licences issued during these years must have been small: see P. C. Reg., 154–157; also 157, Feb. 10, 1801, for a licence granted to import grain from France under Danish colors.

upon the attitude of her neighbor to the south. When the century opened, the export of corn, meal and flour was forbidden.[32] In the light of the export figures, one may well question whether the law was enforced or not.[33] General Marmont, who was stationed in Holland, informed Napoleon in the spring of 1800 that large quantities of corn were being sent to Great Britain, while his fellow-soldier, Augereau, asked for reënforcements so as to patrol the entire coast and stop the exit of corn.[34] Napoleon at once instructed Augereau to demand from the Batavian Republic a strict adherence to its obligations to France.[35] In November of the same year, the Batavian Government asserted its independence once more by refusing to renew the law forbidding the export of corn. This defiance aroused Bonaparte to action. He promptly commanded that the law be renewed and that fresh measures be adopted to prevent the export of corn.[36] Only after much effort was Semonville, the French agent, able to force the Batavian Government to accede to the wishes of Napoleon.[37] The effectiveness of these measures seems to have been limited to the paper on which they were written. Exports for 1801 were larger than in 1800, but during 1802 they were

[32] The States General, July 31, 1725, had issued a placaat providing for an import, but not an export, duty on corn. On Dec. 12, 1799, the export of corn was forbidden, and a little later in the same month this prohibition was extended to meal and flour. These orders were extended to Nov., 1800, by orders of Feb. 24, July 1, 1800: see *Verzameling van Placaaten enz., voor Vriesland,* vierde deel derde stuk, p. 303, vierde stuk, pp. 370–371, and vijfde deel eerste stuk, p. 1. See also *Parl. Pap.,* 1826–1827, No. 157, p. 15.

[33] See Appendix No. 8.

[34] *R. G. P.,* III de deel I stuk, Marmont to the First Consul, April, 1800.

[35] *Cor. de Nap.,* No. 4734.

[36] *R. G. P.,* III de deel I stuk, Semonville to Talleyrand, Nov. 14, 1800: The First Consul to Talleyrand, Nov. 22, 1800, Talleyrand to the First Consul, Nov. 25, 1800, and Talleyrand to Semonville, Nov. 30, 1800.

[37] *Verzameling van Placaaten enz.,* vijfde deel tweede stuk, Nov. 29, 1800, pp. 143–147; this decree was continued until April, 1802: see *ibid.,* zezde deel, eerste stuk, pp. 31, 41, and *Parl. Pap.,* 1826–1827, No. 157, p. 15. See also *R. G. P.,* III de deel I stuk, Semonville to Talleyrand, Dec. 4, 1800, Semonville to the First Consul, Dec. 4, 1800, the First Consul to Talleyrand, Dec. 16, 1800: see also *Monthly Mag.,* X: 586–587, for British opinion.

smaller. French influence grew at a most rapid rate: the reins were tightened and the commercial classes whipped into partial submission. Wheat exports rapidly fell, dropping from 93,824 quarters to but 1,309 quarters. It should be remembered that improved conditions in Great Britain had lessened the demand for foreign corn, a fact which doubtless worked to decrease the volume of the imports from Holland.[38]

As it was, Holland furnished large supplies to Great Britain; wheat alone amounted to 153,541 quarters for the three years, a sum that was greater than the combined imports from Ireland, France, Norway and Denmark. Holland, moreover, exported more rye to England than did any other state, excepting Prussia and Germany, while approximately one fourth of the entire barley imported came from Holland. Over a half of a million quarters of oats, as well as large quantities of beans and pease, were exported to Great Britain.

During the first three years of the nineteenth century, therefore, the grain trade of England was not seriously interfered with by Napoleon. Only in France and Holland does it appear that any attempt was made to check corn exports to Great Britain, and even in these two countries the motive which prompted this prohibition on exports was due primarily to economic causes. Elsewhere in Europe the volume of exports to England depended on political and economic factors, over which Napoleon appears to have had little control.

[38] Agricultural conditions in Holland seem to have been the same as in France: see *Parl. Pap.*, 1826–1827, No. 27.

CHAPTER VIII

ANGLO-AMERICAN GRAIN TRADE, 1800 TO 1813

The American harvests of 1799 and 1800 — Large exports during 1801 — The depression caused in the American Trade by the Peace of Amiens — The renewal of war, 1803 — The exports of 1805 and 1806 — The Embargo and Non-Intercourse Act — The Erskine Agreement — The War of 1812.

IN the history of the British import trade in corn, no country looms more important than the United States.[1] This was particularly true during the Napoleonic period when the British people were brought face to face with the stern fact that they were dependent upon outside sources for an ever increasing amount of corn. During the scarcity of 1799 and 1800, Englishmen cast anxious eyes towards America where a large surplus of corn existed. The American harvest of 1799 had been very abundant, news of which had been sent home by the British consuls.[2] At once a mad scramble for these supplies took place in England. Parliamentary committees urged and secured the passage of measures providing for liberal bounties on American corn.[3] In June, 1800, it was reported that over fifty ships had cleared from Whitehaven for America, chartered to return with

[1] During the Napoleonic era, Canada was never a dependable source of supply. The imports from Canada from 1800 to 1814 inclusive amounted to but 363,938 quarters. Often, as during the War of 1812, Canada imported British corn; more frequently she imported supplies from the United States. See *Farmer's Mag.*, VII: 112, IX: 397; B. T., 5: 22, Aug. 12, 30, 1813; B. T., 5: 23, March 1, 1814; *Parl. Pap.*, 1808, No. 178, p. 114; *Select Documents of the Canadian War of 1812,* I: 155, 191, 236–237 (Toronto, Champlain Society, 1920); *Canadian Archives,* 1921, pp. 177–178; and *Memoirs of J. C. Herries* (London, J. Murray, 1880), I: 51.

[2] F. O., 5: 30, John Hamilton to Hammond, Norfolk, Va., Jan. 2, 1800: see also F. O., 5: 30, John Wickham to Grenville, Philadelphia, Feb. 5, 1800. Claude Scott seems to have received similar advice through private channels: see *First Series,* IX: 75.

[3] *First Series,* IX: 83: see also p. 27.

flour and rice.[4] The next month the British consul at Philadelphia wrote that 22,678 barrels of flour had left that port for the United Kingdom, and that many other ships were then loading.[5] All in all, 77,609 quarters of wheat were imported from the United States in 1800.

The next year this rose to 245,371 quarters.[6] The causes for this increase are as follows: a scarcity in England coupled with high prices and liberal bounties; a favorable harvest in America; the absence of an export tax in the United States; and finally, the generally accepted opinion that American flour was of a quality superior to either British or European flour. Aware of these conditions, the Commons' Committee reported that "according to the latest information, the Crop in the United States, has been uncommonly productive, and has been nearly free from the ravages occasioned in former years by the Hessian Fly."[7] British and American merchants viewed the future with great delight. Ships were in constant demand, and that in spite of the high freight charge of 17*s.* 6*d.* a barrel. Bond, the British consul at Philadelphia, called the attention of his Government to the fact that larger amounts would be exported but for the scarcity of ships. "Almost every large ship upon her arrival in the Delaware is taken up for the purpose of conveying flour to England."[8] The effect of this increased trade was to

[4] *British Mag.*, I: 589. The demand for rice caused an advance in the price of that article in America: see *Annals of Congress,* 6th Cong., p. 60.

[5] F. O., 5: 30, Wickham to Grenville, July 30, 1800: see also his letter of Aug. 15, 1800. It is of interest to note the amounts reported to have been exported from New York and Baltimore in 1800: 100,000 barrels of flour from Baltimore, and 296,476 barrels of flour, rye-flour and Indian-meal from New York: see *Columbian Centinal,* Jan. 14, 17, 1801; and also, *Mass Hist. Coll.,* 7th Series, vol. I, pp. 69–70, and *American Antiquarian Society Proceedings,* N. S., vol. XXVII, T. B. Adams to Wm. S. Shaw, Aug. 16, 1799.

[6] Customs, 17: 23, shows that by far the greater share came from New York, Pennsylvania, Maryland and Virginia. From New York there came 253,486 cwt. of flour and 21,032 quarters of wheat.

[7] *First Series,* IX: 126. For favorable harvest reports see F. O., 5: 30, Wickham to Grenville, July 3, Aug 15 1800; F. O., 5: 33, Bond to Grenville, Jan. 20, 1801.

[8] F. O., 5: 33, Bond to Grenville, March 11, 1801: see also his letters of Jan. 20, Feb. 10 and March 31, 1801, and *Farmer's Mag.,* II: 465.

be seen in the steady rise of prices in America. Bond termed it a "monstrous price," while another declared it "amazing."[9]

In the meantime, the British Government issued, February 4, 1801, an order allowing the granting of licences, by the British consuls in America, to Danish and Swedish ships for the import of corn on British or American account.[10] Copies of this order were immediately sent to these consuls who received them late in April. Thomas Barclay, consul at New York, sent copies of this order to the Chamber of Commerce of that city, and had notices of the order inserted in the daily papers. It was his belief that the British need not expect any great returns, as there were but few vessels in American ports entitled to sail under this measure.[11]

During the summer months little corn was exported to Great Britain. This may be explained by the fact that the surplus of 1800 had been largely exhausted, and that the West Indies were offering attractive prices.[12] By the fall of 1801, the opinion was often expressed that a heavy trade might be expected in the future. This was due to the abundant harvest of that year.[13] Late in November, when American merchants were expecting handsome returns for their bumper crops, the rumor was noised about that England and France were discussing terms of peace. A contemporary writes: "It instantly operated almost like the

[9] F. O., 5: 33, Bond to Grenville, March 1, 1801: see also *Leven-Powell Correspondence,* in *The John P. Branch Historical Papers of Randolph-Macon College,* I: 245. Superfine flour sold at Alexandria, Va., at $10.83 a barrel: see *Alexandria Advertiser,* June 27, 1801.

[10] P. C. Reg., 157, Feb. 4, 8, 1801.

[11] F. O., 95: 24, May 1, 1801: see also F. O., 5: 33, Barclay to Hammond, May 3, 1801, and Bond to Grenville, May 3, 1801. For a notice of this order, see *Columbian Centinal,* April 25, 1801. The order was also published by Bond: see *Alexandria Advertiser,* April 27, 1801. The same paper for May 5, 1801, contains a copy of the Bounty Act of March 25, 1801.

[12] F. O., 5: 33, Bond to Hawkesbury, July 31, 1801: see *Alexandria Advertiser,* April 11, 1801, for an account of the exports from that city for the quarter ending March 31, 1801: see the same paper, April 16, 1801, for exports from New York to the United Kingdom, March 1 to April 1, 1801.

[13] F. O., 5:33, Bond to Hawkesbury, July 13, 1801: see *Columbian Centinal,* July 22, Oct. 17, 1801.

hand of death upon all business. . . . Wheat, corn, and flour have been constantly on the fall."[14] Throughout the winter and spring months that followed, the American market was decidedly unfavorable. In April a turn for the better was experienced, caused in the main by the "reported scarcity of provisions in England, France and Holland," and the rumor that the peace negotiations had failed.[15] Prices at once began to pick up, only to fall as rapidly upon the news that the Treaty of Amiens had been ratified. Writing to Captain Legburn the Virginian firm of Ellis and Allan remarked: "From the definite treaty being finally ratified, tobacco and flour are both rather dull."[16]

The situation failed to improve by the summer, and by the autumn the American farmer and shipper saw on the one hand "a most luxuriant harvest," and on the other, a deplorable trade condition. Eagerly they scanned every news despatch that incoming vessels might bring from England. Disappointment invariably was experienced. Each returning supercargo had the same tale to relate of the bountiful harvest in Britain. And while prayers of thanksgiving arose throughout that kingdom, the American farmer and shipper prayed that "France and England get at Loggersheads," for then "the chance would be good."[17]

[14] *Life and Correspondence of R. King,* IV: 27–28: see also Ellis and Allan to R. C. and W. G. Latimer, Nov. 26, 1801, and *American State Papers, Foreign Relations,* III: Madison to King, Dec. 10, 1801.

[15] Ellis and Allan to Legburn, April 14, 1802. During April, 1802, there was an increase in export from Alexandria; corn, most of which was in the form of flour, to the value of $151,369.96 left that port for Britain, especially Liverpool: see Customs Records, Exports, Alexandria.

[16] Ellis and Allan to Legburn, May 19, 1802: see also *Columbian Centinal,* Nov. 21, Dec. 16, 1801; *Gazette of the United States,* Dec. 8, 1801; *Washington Federalist,* Jan. 28, 1802. "No earthquake I suppose ever produced a greater crush than peace has amongst the merchants."—Geo. Jefferson to Thos. Jefferson, Jan. 16, 1802, *Mass. Hist. Coll.,* 7th Series, vol. I, p. 113. Exports to England fell in value to $78,637.75 at Alexandria: see Customs Records, Exports, Alexandria. Customs, 17: 23, 24, shows that imports of flour from Virginia fell from 167,800 cwt. to 33,218 cwt., and from New York, from 253,486 cwt. to 91,901 cwt.

[17] Ellis and Allan to Gold and to Legburn, Sept. 15, Dec. 28, 1802; also to Wilson and to Capt. Legburn, Feb. 9, 28, 1803. See also *Mass. Hist. Coll.,* 7th Series, vol. VI, p. 234. Diary of Noah Webster, *circa Oct.*

Nor, thought they, were their prayers unanswered, for in May of the next year the mailed fist again shook over Europe and the " chance " became exceptionally " good."

The renewal of war in May, 1803, brought considerable distress to the commercial classes of the United Kingdom. England's misfortune proved to be America's opportunity. The agricultural and commercial interests of the United States were delighted over the prospects for the future.[18] The merchants of New York, Baltimore and Alexandria were besieged by an endless throng of traders who impatiently demanded freights for England. The value of this trade waxed greater day by day. American grain and flour flooded the docks and crowded the warehouses of London, Liverpool and Glasgow.[19] Practically one fourth of the total wheat imported in 1803 came from the United States.

This profitable trade was shattered by the British harvest of 1803. American corn became a drug on the market. Towns like Alexandria had a violent business depression. On top of this, the weather turned foul, causing much damage to the young crops. Early in 1804 clients were advised that " the prospects in regard to Flour are rather clouded for the present, the quantity this year is certainly small, and the foreign demand extremely limited. . . ." [20] To Messrs. Heathcote of London, Ellis and Allan wrote: " Our crop of wheat is now got in but not without

---

1, 1802, MSS., and J. Watson to Gansevort, Dec. 10, 1802, General Peter Gansevort MSS., both at New York Public Library. The extent to which America had profited during the late war is well shown by the report of the Dutch Ambassador to the United States for which see Hoekstra, P., *Thirty-Seven Years of Holland-American Relations,* pp. 16–18.

[18] Favorable reports concerning American produce in England were sent to the United States by American consuls: see Consular Despatches, Falmouth, June 9, 1803; also Ellis and Allan to Edward Johnston, July 6, 1803.

[19] *Farmer's Mag.,* IV: 482, V: 110. In 1803, 97,971 barrels of flour were exported from Alexandria: see *National Intelligencer,* Feb. 22, 1804; and also Customs, 17: 25.

[20] Ellis and Allan to Messrs. Caruthers and Patton, Jan. 31, 1804: see also Stuart to Monroe, Richmond, April 14, 1804, Monroe MSS., New York Public Library; *The John P. Branch Historical Papers of Randolph-Macon College,* III: 46; and *Columbian Centinal,* July 27, 1803.

considerable damage from the great quantity of Rain that fell at reaping time we suppose the loss in Virginia to be a third of the crop, and yet a large crop is made but the grain very much injured."[21] As a result of these forces only 4,259 quarters of wheat were exported to Great Britain in 1804, as contrasted with the 109,131 quarters of the previous year.[22]

Late in 1804 news reached the United States that England needed grain.[23] Americans who ventured to answer this call found to their sorrow that the British market was by no means as bad as had been supposed. Prices in Britain actually fell, and as they declined a sharp fall took place in America. "The fall in the price of flour had occasioned amongst a number of merchants the keenest distress. Gilbert Robertson of New York has failed for a large amount, Robertson and Brown of Norfolk likewise, and six houses in Norfolk, though not much had followed this. . . ."[24] Fortunately this did not last, as the British harvest of 1805 proved to be below the average. In consequence American shipments greatly increased. Although the year 1805 closed more favorably than it had begun, the total wheat exports to Great Britain equalled but 13,453 quarters.

As the year progressed, repeated orders from England stimulated increased activity, a condition which lasted well into the summer. The American merchant viewed the future with great satisfaction. A remarkably fine and abundant harvest promised handsome profits,[25] especially as Prussia had shut its ports to

[21] Ellis and Allan to Heathcote, July 6, 1804: see F. O., 5:46, Bond to Hawkesbury, Jan. 1, 1805.

[22] This was all in the form of flour and came almost entirely from New York, Maryland and Virginia: see Customs, 17: 26.

[23] Consular Despatches, Cork, Dec. 31, 1804.

[24] Ellis and Allan to Heathcote, July 29, 1805. This decline in America had been hurried by favorable harvests: see F. O., 5: 46, Bond to Mulgrave, Sept. 27, 1805. Exports from Alexandria were limited to but one shipment, valued at $28,589.00: see Customs Records, Exports, Alexandria.

[25] Ellis and Allan to Heathcote, June 24, 1806: see also *The Writings of Thomas Jefferson* (ed. Bergh) XI: 121; Lawrason and Fowle to Pearce and Walker, June 24, 1806, to Samuel Smith, June 27, and to John Tabor and Son, July 7, 1806; and *Literary Panorama,* I: 604–606, for a letter from Warburton, Maryland, July 10, 1806.

the British. It was, however, too pleasing to be lasting. The arrival of the sloop *Liberty* put a decided crimp in these expectations. Docking at New York, the master of this ship brought the unwelcome news that England and Prussia had come to terms. Commmenting on this, Ellis and Allan stated that this —[26]

> insures to England . . . immense supplies by the person she wants them. Such a measure leaves us little hope that the price will be any better. If it should continue at 7/0 and 7/6 which we think is very doubtful, the immense crop that's made and the present situation in Europe — we are led to believe will prove disadvantageous to the price of the present crop; and yet the situation in Europe may be totally reversed. . . . Everything you know depends upon the will of Napoleon. . . .

As is well known, the "will of Napoleon" blasted the short-lived hopes of both Prussia and England. Jena and Auerstadt sealed Prussian harbors and opened those in America at the same time. Imports from Prussia fell; those from the United States steadily rose. The volume of the American wheat trade to England for 1806 exceeded that from any other country, excepting Ireland.[27]

These large shipments caused a rise in the American market. "Flour," so wrote the Virginian firm of Lawrason and Fowle, "is generally scarce, but never was known to be so much so as at this time, the cause of it is the want of Rain previous to the commencement of Harvest, and the large quantities lately shipp'd to Europe and the Indies, nearly 30,000 Bls. has sail'd from this port within the last three weeks."[28] The unfavorable weather lasted throughout the summer. Late in August a slight rain brought a small measure of relief, but it was not until September that conditions improved and saved what otherwise would have been a ruined harvest. As it was, the crop of 1806 was clearly below the average.[29]

[26] Ellis and Allan to J. H. Cocker, July 24, 1806.

[27] See *London Times,* Feb. 25, 1807; *Farmer's Mag.,* VIII: 116; and Customs, 17: 28.

[28] Lawrason and Fowle to Pearce and Walker, July 11, 1806.

[29] *Ibid.,* to Luke Baldwin & Co., Aug. 2, to John Tabor and Son, Aug. 21, and to Pearce and Walker, Aug. 30, 1806: see also Ellis and Allan to Heathcote, Dec. 6, 1806, and "Advice from Nominy," June 22, 1807, Lloyd MSS.

To the Englishman, this was most unfortunate, as his own supply was very short. Europe, moreover, had been closed by the French decrees. Prices accordingly rose throughout the island and tempted the American farmer and shipper to part with his corn in spite of adverse conditions in the United States.[30]

Early in February, 1807, the American commercial and agricultural world was thrown into a feverish state by the Berlin Decree. "The arrival of Bonaparte's decree relative to the Blockade of England has put business at a Stand," wrote Lawrason and Fowle to John Pearson, "tho' it has not yet affected the price of Flour much."[31] Contracts which had been made before the decree were fulfilled. Indeed, the American seems to have sensed that Napoleon could not stop his trade to England. And though the trade was temporarily checked, it soon resumed its former activity. "Vessels of every description are in demand. 10/0 and 10/1 stg. is given to England, and there is now not a Vessel in port unengaged nor do we know of any that are expected for freight."[32] This condition lasted throughout May, and even as late as June 2, 1807, Lawrason and Fowle wrote to John and Robert Follett of Portsmouth, New Hampshire: "We regret your not ordering the Ship direct to this port as we could have procured a freight of flour immediately for a port in [the] English or Irish Channel." Shortly after, the trade to Britain declined, chiefly because of political troubles. Prices, moreover, had already taken a tumble in England as a result of the large influx of American wheat.[33] A similar drop took place in America.

[30] Lawrason and Fowle to Capt. S. Chauncey, Jan. 29, 1807; also their letters of the same date to Thomas Clark and to Daniel Tucker, and their letter to Morrils and Tudkins, Feb. 5, 1807: see also *London Times,* Feb. 25, 1807.

[31] Lawrason and Fowle to J. Pearson, Feb. 18, 1807.

[32] *Ibid.,* to J. P. Thurston, March 23, 1807: see also their letters to J. Tabor and Son, March 4, 1807, and to Henry Sharpe, March 23, 1807. The *Farmer's Mag.* VIII: 268, 397, 408; *Morning Advertiser,* May 14, 1807; and *London Times,* April 30, May 7, June 16, July 14, 16, Aug. 11, 1807, contain interesting accounts of this trade. Customs Records, Exports, Alexandria shows the trend of the export trade during 1807.

[33] Lawrason and Fowle to Isaac McLellan, June 6, 1807: see also *Farmer's Mag.,* VIII: 383.

Rumors from Great Britain of political difficulties only added to the unfortunate lot of the American grain trade. Lawrason and Fowle refused to make purchases until it was known what steps " our Government intend taking." [34] It will be recalled that Anglo-American relations had become seriously strained through the restrictions that had been placed upon American commerce. Monroe and Pinckney, moreover, had been sent to London to arrange a new treaty of commerce (the Jay Treaty having expired) in which American rights might be given better protection. Hardly had these commissioners come to an understanding with the British when Napoleon upset everything by the Berlin Decree. The British Government at once changed its policy towards America. Because Napoleon had outraged English opinion and had threatened dire fate to all ships sailing between the British Isles and Europe, the Ministry informed the American agents that unless the United States either forced France to modify her acts, or join with Great Britain in resisting Napoleon, that American commerce would be interfered with as before. Not waiting, however, for the United States either to hear or to answer these proposals, the British issued the January Order of 1807. From then on every American ship might be stopped, visited and searched by any British vessel. Brought into port, with his cargo condemned or held for further investigation, the American captain often put to sea minus his cargo and part of his crew. Protest followed protest. American patience was at length exhausted by the attack upon the half-equipped *Chesapeake* by the British man-of-war *Leopard.* " In consequence of the late Outrage Committed by the British, Business is at a perfect stand and the opinion here is that war will be the result." [35]

Fortunately for England, as well as for the American farmer,

[34] Lawrason and Fowle to E. Cruft, June 30, July 2, 1807.

[35] *Ibid.,* to Dillaway and Baker, July 8, 1807: see also *Writings of Thomas Jefferson,* (ed. Bergh), XI: 270. At a later date, Isaac Brownson of New York remarked: "If the Government had done as much mischief with their artillery as they have with their stationery, the enemy would have sued for peace long ago." — Brownson to David Daggett, Feb. 8, 1814, Daggett MSS.

the corn trade for that year had practically been completed. And although the latter joined with his fellow-citizens in a righteous protest against the latest act of Britain, neither the attack nor the protest harmed America's trade for the time being. Their fortune rested upon what the Government might do and upon the ultimate state of their crops. For the time, the American farmer had plenty to do without attempting to decide the fate of the nation. Rain had fallen in torrents throughout Virginia. Planting had been seriously checked, while the mud-soaked roads greatly delayed the marketing of corn.[36] The harvest of 1807, in spite of these misfortunes, was " great beyond example," but the effect of the political disturbances had dulled the market to a considerable degree.[37] It became even more lifeless upon the arrival of further news from England.

Hints and rumors of new orders in council, more drastic than those of January, had for some time caused much talk from Portsmouth to Savannah. Flour rose or fell according to the temper of these reports. This is shown by a letter of Lawrason and Fowle to Edward Cruft, November 21, 1807:

> Within a few days past flour experienced Several rapid Changes in Consequence of the Variety of Accts. respecting our affairs in England; from the 9th to the 13th it was 40/, the 14th, 34/, and to-day it is 34/5 and on the rise of Course.

The next month the same firm listed flour at 35*s*., and remarked that: "Considerable ship'ts have lately been made to Portugal; about 4,000 [barrels?] sailed yesterday for that quarter." [38]

About the same time Congress met to discuss the question of war with Great Britain. As the session dragged on, it became more and more apparent that Jefferson had decided to humble England by a method as ingenious as that of Napoleon's decree.

[36] Lawrason and Fowle to John Holland, Oct. 12, 1807. Somewhat earlier there had been a drought which had caused many mills to shut down: see Howard and John Hampton to Lloyd, Sept. 17, 1807, Lloyd MSS.

[37] *Writings of Thomas Jefferson, op. cit.,* XI: 387; Thomas Hill to Lloyd, Aug. 5, 1807, Lloyd MSS. Earlier in the year the prospects had seemed very dismal: see *The John P. Branch Historical Papers of Randolph-Macon College,* III: 49.

[38] Lawrason and Fowle to Tucker, Dec. 7, 1807.

To compel the common enemy to respect their rights, both aimed blows at England's commerce: Napoleon, by the Berlin Decree, Jefferson, by an embargo. The mere rumor of an embargo caused a rapid drop in the American market. Merchants were urged to sell or ship their supplies at once.[39] Shortly before Christmas, 1807, Congress passed the expected embargo. "In Consequence of this measure," so wrote Lawrason and Fowle, "flour will be very low, probably under $4."[40] The export trade for 1807, however, had been completed; consequently this measure did not affect the commerce for that year. Out of a total of 404,946 quarters of wheat imported in 1807 into Great Britain, 249,712 quarters came from the United States.

The effect of the *Embargo* and of a supplementary law of January, 1808, upon the grain trade was very great. Lawrason and Fowle wrote to Captain W. Hutchins: "In Consequence of the embargo, flour has declined very much, the nominal price now is 4/4 to 4/3 but holders of that article sell only from necessity and the principal part of what comes in from the Country is stor'd."[41]

In Great Britain the *Embargo* caused a rapid rise in price.[42] Any dependence upon America as a source of supply was said to be out of the question.[43] Whatever effect this measure may have had upon other trades and industries, there can be no doubt as to its effects on the grain trade.[44] Only 12,836 quarters of wheat entered Great Britain from America in 1808. Doubtless most of this must have left the United States during the rush that followed the first rumor of an embargo, or else have left America for Great Britain in violation of the law. Instances of the

39 *Ibid.*, to Dillaway and Baker, Dec. 21, 1807.

40 Lawrason and Fowle to E. Cruft, Dec. 23, 1807: see also their letter to Dillaway and Baker, and to many others under the same date.

41 *Ibid.*, to Hutchins, Jan. 12, 1808; also to Mathew Cobb, Feb. 16, 1808: see also Gabriel Smither to Lloyd, May 30, 1808, Lloyd MSS. The harvest of 1808 was generally a success: see F. O., 5: 59, Bond to Canning, July 5, 1808.

42 Consular Despatches, Liverpool, Feb. 6, 1808.

43 *Farmer's Mag.*, X: 112: see also *ibid.*, IX: 276, 397.

44 Customs Records, Exports, Alexandria, shows but six clearances in 1808 for Great Britain; none of these were entirely composed of grain.

latter were probably not very numerous, but were numerous enough to result in the passage the next year of additional laws enforcing the *Embargo*.[45] The temptation to violate these laws was made most attractive by the constant reports of scarcity in England and Europe.[46] Furthermore, as has already been noticed, some corn may have been imported by means of the British licences granted to neutral ships.[47]

This illegal trade was continued when, upon the repeal of the *Embargo*, Congress passed the *Non-Intercourse Act* of 1809. With a harvest "much superior to any crop in the last three years," [48] many an American probably shut his eyes to the law and engaged in a most profitable trade.

Close upon the heels of the *Non-Intercourse Act* came the Erskine Agreement, whereby the British ambassador at Washington promised the repeal of the obnoxious orders. Madison accepted this as final, and threw open the trade with Great Britain. For over a month shippers outdid themselves in their frenzy to export goods. "There is not a ship in port unengaged," wrote Lawrason and Fowle to Mr. S. Smith, April 24, 1809. Vessel after vessel sailed, loaded with corn and other supplies.[49] Everything seemed most satisfactory, when suddenly England disavowed the act of Erskine and announced that, after a period of time, all ships found violating the orders would be seized as before. Madison could do no more than place the *Non-Intercourse Act* into operation once more. Feeling in the United States towards this step on the part of England is shown in part by the following: [50]

[45] *U. S. Statutes at Large,* II: 453–454, 473–475. It is possible that a fraudulent use of Jefferson's *flour certificates* may have permitted the shipment of grain to Great Britain.

[46] Consular Despatches, Bristol, Oct. 11, Dec. 6, 1808.

[47] See p. 108.

[48] Ellis and Allan to C. Ellis, June 14, 1809, to Heathcote, July 5, Sept. 29, 1809: see also Lawrason and Fowle to E. Cruft, July 20, 1809. A report not so favorable is found in F. O., 5: 65, Bond to Canning, Aug. 1, 1809.

[49] For British opinion as to the favorable results that might be expected from the Erskine Agreement, see *Farmer's Mag.*, X: 271, 401, 430.

[50] The Journal of the Life of Amos Wheeler, Aug. 14, 1809: see also

> Great Britain in refusing to ratify the treaty concluded by Mr. Erskine and Smith has lost the confidence of all parties in the United States. They have now sent out that villain Jackson who prepared the scaffold for innocent thousands at Copenhagen to America to practice infamy and fraud upon us.

To the American corn merchant these events did not seem so dangerous as to the trader in other commodities. None of his shipments to Great Britain had been or would be condemned by the English. The worst sting the *Non-Intercourse Act* might inflict was that the corn merchant might be forced into an illegal trade if he wished to continue his usual business.[51] There can be no doubt, however, that the trade to England was checked to a great extent, and that the export of 170,939 quarters of wheat would have been larger but for the *Non-Intercourse Act*.[52]

---

his entry for Nov. 3, 1809, as to business depression at Wilmington, N. C. This diary is in manuscript and may be found in the Yale University Library.

[51] Many shippers had sent freights before the passage of the act: see Lawrason and Fowle to Samuel Smith, Aug. 3, 1809. See also Customs Records, Exports, Alexandria, 1809.

[52] *Parl. Pap.*, 1814, No. 26; *London Times,* July 12, 16, Aug. 7, 1810. See *Boston Gazette,* May 7, 1810, for a bitter attack on this measure. Customs, 4: 5, contains these interesting figures on the import of corn in 1809:

	Wheat		Flour	
	British Ships	Foreign Ships	British Ships	Foreign Ships
	Q. B.	Q. B.	Cwt. Q. B.	Cwt. Q. B.
Imports into London				
New England ...	0 0	0 0	0 0 0	1,176 1 10
New York	488 0	3,347 0	785 0 16	38,302 3 15
Pennsylvania	0 0	435 0	1,032 2 20	25,728 0 2
Maryland	0 0	0 0	0 0 0	32,051 0 26
Virginia	0 0	0 0	0 0 0	28,027 0 19
S. Carolina	0 0	0 0	0 0 0	1,784 0 2
N. Carolina	0 0	0 0	0 0 0	0 0 0
Imports into the Out-ports				
New England	0 0	0 0	0 0 0	4,220 2 17
New York	1,869 1	20,643 3	9,853 0 16	94,496 2 21
Pennsylvania	0 0	0 0	5,457 1 12	46,628 0 0
Maryland	1,212 2	5,477 5	7,811 3 22	87,398 3 19
Virginia	0 0	397 4	3,017 3 18	42,570 0 27
S. Carolina	0 0	0 0	0 0 0	33,377 0 23
N. Carolina	0 0	0 0	0 0 0	133 3 7

tedly much of the export from America left for a port anish Peninsula, but was finally sold in Great Britain. ain David Snow, Ellis and Allan issued instructions, er 18, 1809, to carry a cargo of flour from Norfolk to Lisbon and there to dispose of it if at all possible; if not, then to London where their agent Charles Ellis would take it.

During 1810 the American trade greatly decreased.[53] This was not altogether due to the strained relations that existed between the United States and Great Britain, but rather because Napoleon had turned corn merchant and was actively engaged in shipping enormous amounts of corn to his enemy. What trade existed between America and Britain was, of course, in violation of the law of the United States. The method used by the Americans who engaged in this trade is well shown by a report of the American consul at Bristol: [54]

> American subjects will continue to arrive at our different ports with the produce of the United States after (in general) first touching at Ferol, Madeira etc., getting Portuguese Papers, changing their names and also that of their masters, and then proceeding in the double capacity of both nations with registers and other documents of each. . . . You will observe one of these in the British Mercury enclosed, registered for Lisbon under the name of 'Neuston Senora dor Nanto L. J. N. . . . Mastre.' This ship loaded with tobacco, flour etc., at Bermuda Hundred in Virginia, called at Madeira, underwent the usual transformation, came here where her cargo was landed and sold, is in fact the American ship Bristol Trader, Captain Gilbert belonging to New York, between which Port and this port she has been employed for several years past.

The evident failure of the *Non-Intercourse Act* and the added danger of capture by French privateers caused a repeal of that act and the passage of the Macon Bill. This measure offered American friendship to the country which first revoked its decrees, and promised to reëstablish non-intercourse with the other power, if within a certain time it had not also withdrawn its measures. Napoleon seized upon this opportunity and in August,

[53] But one shipment, valued at $10,017, left Alexandria in 1810 for Great Britain: see Customs Records, Exports, Alexandria.

[54] Consular Despatches, Bristol, May 24, 1810: see also B. T., 1: 52, Hamilton to Fawkener, Aug. 7, 1810, enclosing letter from Mr. Jackson, New York, July 10, 1810, in which reference is made to size of the trade to England.

1810, told the American Government that his decrees would be revoked November 1, 1810, if by that time Great Britain had repealed its orders, or the United States had forced her rights to be respected by Great Britain. Madison, accepting this ambiguous offer as a statement of the repeal of the decrees, notified England that, if the orders were not withdrawn within three months, the United States would reënact the *Non-Intercourse Act* against her.

Throughout the remainder of the year American shipments of grain to England declined, although they increased to the Spanish Peninsula.[55] The failure of the British agents at Washington to reëstablish good relations with America forced both countries gradually to drift towards a state of war. In vain did Foster tell Madison that the French decrees had not been withdrawn; in vain did Madison answer that Napoleon had kept faith with America. Finding that England would not repeal her orders, Madison laid the matter before Congress. An appeal to arms was demanded by the younger members of Congress, and finally after an outburst of oratory, war was declared, June 18, 1812.[56]

American corn exports to Great Britain rapidly dwindled into insignificance, and not until the return of peace did the grain and flour of the United States find a market in England. The absence of American produce during the period of the War of 1812 was keenly felt in Britain. Nor was it then forgotten that the American trade had assumed unparalleled proportions and

[55] Consular Despatches, Liverpool, Sept. 13, 1809. For a discussion of the American trade to the Spanish Peninsula, see my article in *American Historical Review,* Oct., 1922. Since the appearance of that article I have found definite proof of the truth of Randolph's charge that the French Government, through its minister at Washington, actually tried to influence the Administration to stop corn exports to the British forces in the Peninsula: see Transcripts of the French Ministers, MSS., Washington, D. C., Serrurier to the Minister of Foreign Affairs, Oct. 23, 1811, Jan. 2, March 22, 31, April 15, Oct. 14, 1812.

[56] The American harvest of 1811, while none too favorable in the earlier part of the year, improved as the year closed. During 1811 and 1812, the crops were very full and abundant: see Lawrason and Fowle to E. Cruft, Aug. 9, 1811, to F. W. Sargent, June 8, 1812; F. O., 5: 89, Barclay to Hamilton, Feb. 1, 1812; *Writings of Thomas Jefferson* (ed. Bergh), Jefferson to Monroe, March 8, 1811, also to Monroe May 5, 1811.

had furnished a needed supply when the continent was closed by the French decrees. From the United States during the period covered by this study, 1800 to 1813, a total of 1,317,249 quarters of all kinds of corn, grain, meal and flour had been imported into Great Britain.

CHAPTER IX

THE CONTINENTAL CLOSURE

The growth of French influence in Germany and Prussia — The conditions in Holland — The Dutch Decree of May, 1805 — The strict prohibition of all exports in France — The Berlin Decree — The marked drop in exports — The Continental System is accepted by Europe.

BY the opening of the nineteenth century the British Government was quite aware of the value of the American grain trade. This became more apparent during the period covered by this study. Certain disadvantages, however, such as the distance to America and a keen sense of national rivalry, made this trade less attractive than that from the continent. Prussia, as has been mentioned, stood first among the many European states that furnished Great Britain with corn. The rapid growth of French power in Northern Germany, as indicated by the Treaty of Basle, seriously interfered, however, with this trade. Misfortune followed misfortune, from which Prussia tried only half-heartedly to withdraw. Nor can she be blamed altogether for not doing more, as the problem facing her was not an easy one to solve. Probably the simplest way out would have been to join the coalition in its war against Napoleon. This called for determination and strength, and Prussia had none to spare. Instead, she adopted a policy of cultivating the good will of the coalition, without harming at the same time her alliance with France. Watchful waiting, it was hoped, would allow Prussia to join her true friends without endangering her position in respect to France.

In order to checkmate this move, Napoleon very cleverly gave Prussia the Duchy of Hanover.[1] For a time Prussia beamed

[1] See Servières, G., *L'Allemagne Française sous Napoléon Ier*, chap. 1, for an account of the French occupation of Hanover.

upon her benefactor until she sensed the real plans of Bonaparte. Cautiously she tried to retrace her steps, only to find a French soldier at every road, nook and lane. A way out of this delicate situation, however, appeared when the Imperial eagle flew over Ansbach on its way to meet the Russian bear.[2] A Bismarck would have declared war; and had Prussia taken this step, there might then and there have been a Waterloo. As it was, all that was done was to place an army in Napoleon's rear, and to enter into negotiations with the crafty Talleyrand. Seizing this unexpected opportunity, the Emperor shattered the coalition at Austerlitz and forced an utterly bewildered Prussia to accept the Treaty of Paris.

During these years Napoleon did not seriously meddle with the Prussian grain trade. Nevertheless, the volume of corn exports for 1803 was much lower than what it had been in 1802. This was not due to any harvest failure, as the Prussian crop was "wonderfully abundant." Prices naturally fell. Dantzic wheat dropped from 54*s*. 2*d*. in 1802 to 46*s*. in 1803, while the export duty was lowered from 8*s*. 2*d*. to 14*d*.[3] Prices, likewise, had fallen in England where a favorable harvest had been reaped. Exports, however, for 1804 rose in volume, chiefly because of agricultural conditions in England. Doubtless larger amounts would have been sent but for a shortage in the rye crop. Conditions stayed unchanged until September 16, 1805, when, as a result of a partial harvest failure, the Prussian Government placed an embargo on corn exports from Dantzic.[4] Economic and not political causes, therefore, had directed the course of the Prussian grain trade since 1803.

Austerlitz, however, was the first of a series of happenings which brought ruin to the Prussian landlord and farmer. Beginning with 1806, Napoleon forced Prussia to shut down on all

[2] For a contemporary statement, see Consular Despatches, Amsterdam, April 22, 1805.

[3] *Diaries and Letters of Sir George Jackson,* I: 516: see also *Parl. Pap.,* 1826, No. 159, pp. 90, 91, 129; 1826–1827, No. 157, p. 26.

[4] *Parl. Pap.,* 1826, No. 159, p. 128. See *London Times,* Oct. 21, 1805; *Parl. Pap.,* 1826–1827, No. 20; also No. 157, p. 25, and *Diaries and Letters of Sir George Jackson,* I: 314.

trade with England. This had been followed by the occupation of Hanover, which closed the Ems, Elbe and Weser to the British, to which England answered by the Fox Blockade.[5] The effect of these various measures was pronounced. The *London Times* for April 15, 1806, reported that wheat had risen 15*s.*, and flour, 8*s.*, because of the expected rupture between Prussia and Britain.[6] Obviously, the direct cause for this rise in the British market was to be found at Paris and not at Berlin, although one should not forget that the harvest, especially in East Prussia, had been none too favorable.

It was at this point that Frederick William plunged his state into a war with Napoleon. For a period, altogether too short to be of any value, there was free trade between Prussia and Great Britain. The smashing victories of Jena and Auerstadt, followed as they were by the Berlin Decree, reaffirmed with telling effect the closure of Prussian ports.[7] At least this was the purpose in the mind of Napoleon. For a time trade was at a complete standstill. With the departure, however, of the Emperor for the East, matters readjusted themselves and a regulated trade was created. Licences were frequently granted by the British to neutrals, as well as to subjects of Bremen, Hamburg, Papenburg and Prussia, to trade between the ports of England and Prussia.[8]

The effect of the continental closure and the constant occupation of Prussian soil by the French armies, nevertheless, prac-

[5] See Martens, G. F., *Nouveau Recueil de Traités,* I: 435; *Literary Panorama,* I: xvii; *Cobbett's Pol. Reg.,* IX: 639; and P. C. Reg., 169, April 5, 1806. See also *Parl. Pap.,* 1826–1827, No. 83, p. 35, and No. 20.

[6] See also *Farmer's Mag.,* VII: 249.

[7] It will be recalled that the cession of Hanover to Prussia in 1805 had not included Bremen, Lübeck and Hamburg. After the defeat in 1806, southern Hanover was given to Westphalia, while the northern part, together with these three cities, was incorporated within the limits of the French Empire. The British Customs Records lists the imports from these cities as coming from Germany, and not from France.

[8] On May 14, 1806, all ships of Hamburg, Bremen, Oldenburg and Papenburg that had cleared from a European port before March 28, 1806, were allowed to go in safety: see P. C. Reg., 170. For frequent references to licences, see P. C. Reg., 170, 171. The ships of these states were also allowed to trade between the United Kingdom and unblockaded ports of Holland: see P. C. Reg., 171, Dec. 16, 1806.

tically stopped the export of corn to the United Kingdom. Wheat exports dropped from 51,523 quarters in 1806 to 11,465 quarters in 1807; similar decreases took place in other grain. Most, if not all, of this trade must have been licenced, as the system of the previous year was used in 1807.[9]

Generally the situation in Germany during this period was much like that in Prussia.[10] The rapid occupation of Germany by the French placed it at the disposal of the Emperor. Harburg, Stade, Cuxhaven, Verden and the Duchy of Lauenburg were seized by the troops under Mortier. In this fashion Bonaparte sealed the Elbe and the Weser.[11] By way of answer, the British blockaded these rivers in June and August of 1803.[12] Small wonder was it, therefore, that the corn exports fell in 1803.[13]

During 1804 and 1805 the exact reverse was the case. Hamburg swarmed with British agents who were untiring in their attempts to buy supplies.[14] Napoleon must have been well in-

[9] See p. 98 for a discussion of the licenced trade to Prussia: see also P. C. Reg., 171, 172, 173, for instances of the use of these licences. The trade from Dantzic and Elbing seems to have been small by reason of the war: see *Parl. Pap.*, 1826, No. 159, pp. 90, 91, 128; 1826–1827, No. 83, pp. 35–36. Neither of these sources shows the export of a single bushel of wheat in 1807, although British import figures show that wheat did enter England: see *Parl. Pap.*, 1826–1827, No. 157, p. 25, and Appendix No. 8; and also F. O., 54: 77, Drusina to Canning, Memel, June 19, 1807.

[10] During the period of this study, Hamburg had no export tax on corn; a five per cent tax was levied at Bremen either on the bulk in kind, or on the value according to the market price; at Rostock and Wismar, a town duty was placed on all corn exported; small duties were also collected at Oldenburg, Lübeck and Holstein: see *Parl. Pap.*, 1826–1827, No. 221, pp. 38–40.

[11] Mortier had also ordered Hamburg and Bremen to place an embargo on all British shipping: see Servières, G., *L'Allemagne Française sous Napoléon Ier*, pp. 52–59; see also *Cor. de Nap.*, No. 6822.

[12] *London Gazette.*

[13] Another factor of importance in causing this drop in prices was the improved state of the British market: see Consular Despatches, Liverpool, Sept. 5, 1803. The effect of these forces is to be seen in the price of wheat at Hamburg: see *Parl. Pap.*, 1826, No. 159, p. 163; for Emden and Bremen, see *Parl. Pap.*, 1828, No. 258, pp. 71, 81.

[14] Consular Despatches, Bristol, Aug. 29, Dec. 22, 1804: see also Ernest d'Hauterive, *La Police Secrète du Premier Empire,* I, No. 1000, and Servières, G., *op. cit.*, p. 62. See too F. O., 22: 50, Fenwick to Mulgrave,

formed concerning this, although he did little to stop this violation of his decrees. What is more, he allowed certain Rhenish towns to ship flour to Hanover, which was probably intended for the use of the army, but some of which seems to have been sent on to England.[15] And yet, Hamburg itself did not profit, as the corn which heretofore had been exported from this city now found an outlet by way of Tönning, Lübeck and Denmark.[16]

In 1806, doubtless because of an increase in production, large quantities of oats were sent to England; all other grain showed a marked decrease. The demands made upon Germany by the French must have consumed a large part of the available supply.[17] With the departure of the French army into Poland, however, export again took place, especially as the customs officials were open to bribery.[18] Not until after Tilsit was Napoleon able to stop this graft and corruption.

In no other country did Napoleon meet with so much dishonesty as in Holland. As had already been shown, the Dutch proved most unwilling subjects to France. During the Peace of

---

Jan. 25, 1806, for an account of the grain trade through the Sound in 1805. (The first work will be referred to hereafter simply as *La Police Secrète*.)

[15] Duvergier, J. B., *Collection Complete des Lois, Décrets, Ordonnances, etc.*, XV: 139; *La Police Secrète*, II, No. 703; *Parl. Pap.*, 1826–1827, No. 157, p. 20: see *Parl. Pap.*, 1826, No. 159, p. 163, for the rapid rise in prices at Hamburg. In 1803, wheat averaged 55*s.* 7*d.*, in 1804 it stood at 57*s.* 2*d.*, and in 1805, it sold at 79*s.* 4*d.* At Emden the price on St. Martin's day was 46*s.* 8*d.* in 1803, in 1804, 65*s.*, and in 1805, 73*s.* 4*d.*: see *Parl. Pap.*, 1828, No. 258, p. 81.

[16] Servières, G., *op. cit.*, pp. 64–65: see also Matthiessen and Sillem to Dutilh, Hamburg, Oct. 15, 1805, Dutilh MSS.

[17] See *Cor. de Nap.* for Oct. and Nov., 1806, for several references to the gathering of supplies for the army.

[18] Licences to trade with German ports were frequently granted in London. See Fisher, H. A. L., *Studies in Napoleonic Statesmanship, Germany*, p. 337, for a discussion of the cruel extortions of food, money and supplies by the French at Hamburg, Lübeck and Bremen. Early in 1807, Marshall Brune had allowed neutrals to trade in grain with Hamburg, provided they had not communicated with the enemy: see Servières, G., *op. cit.*, pp. 113–114. The effect of these various factors in 1806 and 1807 had been to lower the price of corn at Hamburg and Emden: see *Parl. Pap.*, 1826, No. 159, p. 163; 1828, No. 258, p. 81.

Amiens matters improved somewhat, chiefly because of the increase that had taken place in Dutch commerce and industry. When it was rumored that this peace was likely to be broken, the Dutch were completely bewildered. Liston, the British agent, reported: [19]

> It would be difficult for me to give . . . an adequate idea of the grief and consternation which has overspread this unfortunate country since the people became acquainted with the existing danger of a rupture between Great Britain and France. Here may be said — for the moment — to be an end to all trade. The merchants have ordered their vessels to return from England immediately, loaded or unloaded and none of their ships can quit the harbors of the Republic, because the underwriters refuse to insure them at any price.

On the day before the outbreak of war, the Batavian Republic received orders to place an embargo on all British ships within its ports.[20] The next month, Semonville, anticipating the designs of his master, personally undertook to stop the export from Holland of all foodstuffs. French officers and soldiers, at his direction, were placed at certain points to obtain the prompt enforcement of this measure.[21]

As will be recalled, the export trade in corn to the enemy had been forbidden in Holland before the Peace of Amiens.[22] In

[19] F. O., 37: 61, Liston to Hawkesbury, March 19, 1803: see also his letter to Hawkesbury, March 29, 1803. Advices received by Wm. Bayard, of London, showed in equally graphic terms the effects of the war rumors: see Gerrits and Son to Wm. Bayard, Rotterdam, May 13, 1803; Bayard-Campbell Correspondence, MSS., New York Public Library; and also Wm. Willnick to Wm. Bayard, Amsterdam, May 20, 21, 27, 28, July 2, 1803. Prices fell at Rotterdam: the average for 1803 was 54*s*. 7*d*. per quarter of wheat; in 1802 it had been 82*s*. 3*d*. For these prices and others at Dordt and Amsterdam, see *Parl. Pap.*, 1826–1827, No. 27, pp. 28–45.

[20] *Cor. de Nap.*, No. 6743. After a delay of several days this order was complied with: see *R. G. P.*, IV de deel II stuk, Semonville to Van der Goes, May 17, 1803, and Van der Goes to Semonville, May 19, 1803; and also Hoekstra, P., *Thirty-Seven Years of Holland-American Relations*, p. 20, and F. O., 37: 61, Liston to Hawkesbury, May 25, 1803. On May 19, 1803, England had placed an embargo on all Dutch ships: see P. C. Reg., 162.

[21] *R. G. P.*, IV de deel I stuk, Semonville to Talleyrand, June 27, 1803: see also Lanzac de Laborie, L., *La Domination Française en Belgique*, II: 42.

[22] See p. 133.

April of 1802, however, the Dutch law of July 31, 1725, permitting the export and the import of corn, was reëstablished. Semonville, therefore, had stopped the clearance only of British ships laden with grain; neutrals might still trade directly between Holland and England. In the light of the improved state of agriculture in England, this trade was not so large in 1803 as it had been the year before. Had there been a scarcity in England, larger quantities would doubtless have been shipped, as in other articles a " contraband most scandalous " seems to have existed.[23] Without question it was this state of affairs that prompted the decree of July 5, 1803. This measure forbade the export of all foodstuffs to the enemy, but placed no restrictions upon the sale of this produce to neutrals, who of course carried these goods direct to Great Britain.[24] The Dutch Government, uncertain as to Napoleon's reason for favoring neutrals, asked for an explanation, to which the Emperor answered by promising to look into the matter at a later date.[25]

In the meantime the Dutch and French agents winked at the export of corn to England, where a high price made the market very tempting.[26] Semonville, determined to end this, ordered the closing of all ports to the British. Steps were also taken to stop all trade directly or indirectly with the enemy and to forbid the export of all butter, cheese, grain and flour, except that allowed by law. Further, Semonville required that all certificates permitting any trade were to be visaed by the French officials.[27] Shortly after, Napoleon endorsed what had been

[23] *R. G. P.*, IV de deel I stuk, Semonville to Talleyrand, June 27, 1803.

[24] This decree also regulated the export of naval stores and the import of neutral goods: see Hoekstra, P., *op. cit.*, pp. 21–24. The British assisted materially by licencing imports: see P. C. Reg., 162, 163, 164.

[25] *R. G. P.*, IV de deel II stuk, Gespreck der deputatie met dem Eersten Consul, July 23, 1803. It seems that a trade between Holland and Spain existed in 1804, which must have made it easy to export grain to England: see Consular Despatches, Bordeaux, Dec. 11, 1804.

[26] In 1804 the exports of wheat rose from 525 quarters to 25,861 quarters, and that of oats almost doubled the amount of the previous year. British licences were in constant demand: see P. C. Reg., 164, 165, 166.

[27] *R. G. P.*, IV de deel II stuk, Semonville to Van der Goes, Oct. 1, 1804, and Van der Goes to Semonville, Oct. 6, 1804: see also *La Police Secrète*, I, No. 372.

done, and ordered the complete stoppage of all trade with the enemy.[28]

Early in the spring of 1805, Counsellor Miot was sent by the Emperor into Belgium to examine the general situation, particularly in regard to the contraband trade. Miot found that those interested in this trade shipped their supplies to England by way of the North German ports, under the pretext of being destined for the French army in Hanover.[29] This report, together with abundant evidence furnished Napoleon by his secret police, resulted in the decree of May 31, 1805. This measure repealed all former decrees, and foreshadowed in many ways the Berlin Decree.[30] By the terms of this new order the export of corn was limited to licenced ships bound for neutral ports. In order to prevent any trade with England, the Dutch shipper, not the neutral carrier, was heavily bonded to ship his cargo to a neutral port. Even this privilege was taken away in December from ships sailing for a neutral port between the Elbe and the Weser.[31]

As a result of this drastic policy a decided drop took place in the export of oats and wheat to Great Britain. In 1804 a total of 169,614 quarters of oats and wheat had been shipped to England; the next year this fell to 68,140 quarters.[32]

During 1806 the Batavian Republic was changed into the Kingdom of Holland, with Louis Napoleon as ruler. For a time the new broom swept clean; all trade with England was strictly forbidden. As a natural result the export of corn rapidly declined. In 1805 a total of 72,516 quarters of corn was shipped

[28] *Cor. de Nap.*, Nos. 8142, 8315, and *R. G. P.*, IV de deel I stuk, Caesar to Frederick William, Nov. 29, 1804.

[29] Lanzac de Laborie, L., *op. cit.*, II: 43–50.

[30] *Le Moniteur,* June 19, 1805. This decree is also to be found in *Verzameling van Placaaten enz.*, achtste deel, pp. 33–46, and in *Cobbett's Pol. Reg.*, VIII: 94–96, 127–133.

[31] Hoekstra, P., *Thirty-Seven Years of Holland-American Relations*, p. 34.

[32] See Appendix No. 8, and *R. G. P.*, IV de deel I stuk, Serrurier to Talleyrand, June 22, 1805. Agricultural conditions in England as well as the presence of the army in Holland probably account in part for this decrease. It would seem, to judge from the marked rise in prices in Holland, that agricultural conditions were none too good: see *Parl Pap.*, 1826–1827, No. 27, pp. 31, 36.

to Great Britain; the next year this had dwindled to 29,949 quarters, of which all but 800 quarters were oats.[33]

In the meantime, Napoleon had been hurling thunderbolts right and left. Austria, Prussia, and finally Russia, were forced to admit defeat and accept the Continental System. From the point of view of this study, the Treaty of Tilsit is of prime importance. It shows that before November, 1807, the Russian trade with Great Britain had not been interfered with by the French decrees. The story of this trade during the first three years of the nineteenth century has already been told. In 1803 exports of wheat and rye had slightly risen, only to drop in 1804. The next year matters were reversed, as a total of 154,903 quarters of wheat was sent to England. In 1806, however, it dropped to 56,732 quarters.[34] This decrease must have been caused, not only by lessening of the British demand for corn, by also by the exigencies of the war and the occupation of Poland by the armies of Russia and France.[35]

To direct our attention to France, one is impressed by the strictness with which the laws against export seem to have been enforced. It is to be noted, however, that these measures were interpreted as applying solely to the direct trade with England. In 1804 Napoleon allowed the export of corn from twenty-one ports of France and Southern Germany to Spain, Portugal, Holland and Germany.[36] At first glance, it might seem that

[33] Agricultural conditions in England also had an effect. British licences for trade to Holland declined in number during 1806: see P. C. Reg., 169, 170, 171. It would seem that in Holland the harvest of 1806 was better than that of 1805: see *Parl. Pap.*, 1826–1827, No. 27, pp. 31, 37. The *Farmer's Mag.*, VII: 407, reported in July that several cargoes of Dutch oats had entered England under Kniphausen colors.

[34] Prices during these years appear to have been moderate, a condition that indicates a series of fair harvests: see *Parl. Pap.*, 1826–1827, No. 27.

[35] See *London Times*, Jan. 6, 1807; Mazade, C., *Correspondance du Mal Davout*, I: 338–339, 344, 346–347, 387. The Polish harvest of 1806 was none too favorable: see Mazade, C., *op. cit.*, II: 64, and Handelsman, M., *Napoléon et la Pologne*, p. 209.

[36] Duvergier, J. B., *Collection Complete des Lois, Decrets, Ordonnances, etc.*, XV: 30, 122: see also *Parl. Pap.*, 1826–1827, No. 157, pp. 7, 11, 19. From Aug. 29, 1789, the policy of France had been to forbid the export of corn. This had been changed in 1804. French export figures for

this law might have made it very easy for ships to slip quietly into British ports. This, however, does not appear to have been the case, as only 156 quarters of corn are recorded as having entered Great Britain from France in the two years 1803 and 1804.[37] Nearly as good a record was made in 1805, and that in spite of those who risked the wrath of the Emperor for the sake of a few British shillings.[38] These figures are especially interesting in the light of harvest conditions in France. Prices were lower than they had been for some time. In the departments of Haute-Marne and Haute-Saône, the crops were so large that requests were made for the right to export the surplus, particularly to Switzerland.[38a]

Active steps were taken by Napoleon to stop all illegal trading. Ships were frequently seized, and suspected persons forced to submit to a most careful examination.[39] At Neudorf, on the Rhine, the people for a time successfully defied the French agents, but with a few such exceptions, the desires of Napoleon seem to have been enforced.[40] Even during 1806, when harvest conditions were good and when Napoleon was busy in diplomatic and military undertakings, only 2,786 quarters of corn entered Britain from France.[41]

1804 show a large trade with other states: see *Documents Statistiques sur la France, Commerce,* 1838, p. 6; and *La Police Secrète,* I, Nos. 359, 789, 1578.

[37] Oats only.

[38] *La Police Secrète,* I, No. 374: see also *Parl. Pap.,* 1826–1827, No. 157, p. 7. A continuation of trade between France and Spain took place in 1805. In that year a law similar to that of 1804 permitted under certain conditions the export of corn to Spain and Portugal. The American consul at Bordeaux was greatly concerned over the activities of his fellow-citizens in this trade, and finally refused clearances to those who wished to carry grain from France to the United States and from there to the West Indies. The evident impracticability of this trade showed on the part of those interested an ulterior purpose. See Consular Despatches, Bordeaux, Wm. Lee to General Armstrong, April 15, 1805, and General Armstrong to Wm. Lee, April 20, 1805: see also *Parl. Pap.,* 1826–1827, No. 157, p. 19, and *La Police Secrète,* I, No. 886.

[38a] *Documents Statistiques sur la France,* 1837, p. 14; *La Police Secrète,* II, Nos. 12, 49.

[39] *La Police Secrète,* I, Nos. 426, 437, 745, 1057.

[40] *Ibid.,* Nos. 1171, 1462.

[41] Only a relatively small number of licences were issued during these

From the Scandinavian states a total of 148,898 quarters of corn were sent to England from 1803 to 1806 inclusive, the larger part coming from Denmark and Norway. This is of interest as it was then generally understood that these states grew barely enough for their own use; especially was this true of Sweden, where export was forbidden before 1812.[42] It is probable, however, that the high prices in England caused some of the merchants of these countries to engage in trade with Great Britain. It is also quite certain that some of the corn of Northern Europe found an outlet to England by way of the Scandinavian countries.

Another source of great value for the English was Ireland. Large quantities of corn, especially of oats and wheat, were sent to Great Britain. The steady and increasing demand for corn in Britain and the establishment of free trade between these two islands account in part for the rapid growth of agriculture in Ireland.

In general, therefore, it may be stated that before 1807 Napoleon had made a decided attempt to stop corn exports to Great Britain. In Northern Europe this was generally done by the occupation of the country by the French, an occupation not altogether accomplished until 1806. Holland and Southern Europe had passed into Napoleon's hands at an earlier date; Germany in part, by 1804, while Prussia, the granary of Europe, was not controlled until after Jena, and Russia, until the Treaty of Tilsit.

From Jena the Emperor had hurried to Berlin, where he startled the world with the famous Berlin Decree. It is important to note that it was not until Tilsit that any serious attempt was made to enforce this decree. That it had been partly en-

---

years for a trade with France; most of those issued were "general" in nature: see P. C. Reg., 162 to 171 inclusive. A gradual increase in the licenced trade took place in 1806. For evidence of favorable agricultural conditions in France in 1806, see *Documents Statistiques sur la France,* 1837, p. 14, and *La Police Secrète,* II, No. 1495.

[42] Export of all grain from Denmark was free from Feb. 1, 1797, to 1802; after that date an export tax of 7½*d.* per quarter for wheat existed until late in 1819: see *Parl. Pap.,* 1826–1827, No. 157, p. 30; No. 221, pp. 36–37.

forced before is known,[43] but in the main British goods entered Prussian ports as in time of peace. William Hall, a merchant trading with Europe, testified before a Parliamentary committee in 1809 that at " the latter end of February we received information that the decree had not been acted upon, and . . . when we resumed our shipments in March we did it on a moderate scale, but they increased till August; they then got to a greater extent than at any former period." [44] James Bowdoin writing to G. E. Erving from Paris, January 25, 1807, remarked: "With respect to the imperial decree it appears as to have produced no effect in England, on the contrary all our vessels which have been visited by the British ships upon this coast have been treated with the greatest respect." [45]

Aware of these infractions, Napoleon ordered a most rigid enforcement of his decree. " Cousin," he wrote in a letter to Berthier, ". . . write to the Prince of Ponte Corvo, Governor of the Hanseatic towns, to second M. Bourrienne . . . and recommend them both to keep watch, that my decree as to the blockade be strictly executed, that not one English letter pass through to the post." [46] Several months later Bernadotte was ordered to extend his lines of communication " on the left bank of the Weser in the territory of Oldenburg and as far as the border of East Frisia. This extension will . . . afford better opportunity of surveillance as to the execution of the imperial decree relative to the blockade of the British Isles." [47]

So well was this decree enforced, as regards the grain trade, that not a single bushel of corn entered Britain from Prussia in 1808.[48] Early in that year Drusina had informed the British Government that there would be little chance for any trade with

[43] For illustration see Picard, E., *Correspondance Inédite de Napoléon Ier*, No. 934.

[44] *Parl. Pap.*, 1808, No. 119, pp. 109, 116: see also Consular Despatches, Hamburg, Jan. 30, 1807.

[45] *Mass. Hist. Soc. Coll.*, 7th Ser., vol. VI, pt. 2, p. 364: see also *R. G. P.*, V de deel I stuk, Dupont-Chaumont to Talleyrand, Dec. 28, 1806.

[46] Picard, E., *op. cit.*, Nos. 1247, 1431.

[47] *Ibid.*, No. 1417.

[48] See *Parl. Pap.*, 1826, No. 159, pp. 90, 91, 128; 1826–1827, No. 83, p. 35; also *Morning Advertiser*, April 21, 1807.

Königsberg. The French consul at Dantzic, he continued, had been ordered to Paris to answer charges of having allowed a vessel from Liverpool to clear as though it had come from New York. Another factor which probably helps to explain the stoppage of the trade was the lack of grain in Prussia. The harvest of 1808 had not been overabundant. The constant drain, moreover, made upon this limited supply by the French military and by the cities must have aggravated the situation to a marked degree.[49]

Equally important was the operation of this closure upon German exports. This is shown by the prices at Hamburg. In July, 1806, wheat sold for 90*s.* 11*d.* At the outbreak of the French war, it fell to 67*s.* 11*d.* In March, 1807, the price was 59*s.* 7*d.*, while the average for that year was 60*s.* 2*d.*[50] Similar decreases took place at Emden and Bremen.[51] The exports for 1808 tell the same story: 29,999 quarters of corn were shipped to England as compared with 141,536 quarters in 1807.[52]

In France a marked drop occurred in the volume of the exports to England. This decrease was due chiefly to the strictness with which the imperial decrees were enforced, and that in spite of the urgent demand in England for the cheap and abun-

[49] F. O., 64: 78, Advices from Drusina, Feb. 20, July 26, 1808, and F. O., 64: 79, for a copy of a letter from Elbing, June 18, 1808, and Gibsonne to Mr. J. Bremen, May 31, 1808. Martens, G. F., *Nouveau Recueil de Traités,* I: 113–124, furnishes several conventions providing for supplies for the French armies. See also Mazade, C., *Correspondance du M[al] Davout,* II: 158–159, for an account of the extreme conditions in Königsberg.

[50] *Parl. Pap.,* 1826, No. 159, p. 163. During 1807 large supplies were sent from Germany to the East for the French armies: see *Memoires et Correspondance du Roi Jérôme,* II: 405–411, 457.

[51] *Parl. Pap.,* 1828, No. 258, pp. 71, 79. It will be recalled that these imperial cities and the neighboring country had been occupied by the French after the Prussian defeat, and that the Elbe and the Weser had been shut to the British: see *Cor. de Nap.,* No. 11267, and Servières, G., *L'Allemagne Française sous Napoléon Ier,* chap. 11. See Hoeniger, R., "Die Kontinentalsperre und ihre Einwirkungen auf Deutschland," in *Volkswirtschaftliche Zeitfragen,* No. 211, p. 26, for a discussion of the decline of the corn trade of Memel.

[52] "General" licences were issued in small numbers by the British for the Prussian and German trade: see P. C. Reg., 175 to 179 inclusive.

dant crops of France.[53] A certain part of that which did reach England probably was smuggled out of the country. Boulogne seems to have been a favorite point for this illegal trade. Barrels of the kind usually used for brandy, when filled with flour, had little trouble in passing the customs until a severe storm strewed the Boulogne coast with evidence of this contraband trade.[53a] During the same year, 1807, many neutral ships protected by British licences left Morlaix and other French ports for Tönning, but sailed into English ports.[53b] It is also likely that some of the corn listed as having come from Holland and Germany may have had its origin in France, which of course was possible under the law of 1804.[54] In spite of these evasions, the total amount exported decreased, especially during 1808 when a distinct tightening of the reins took place.[55]

During the summer and fall of 1808, the French farmers reaped a most bountiful harvest. Prices dropped in every part of the country; the average for the entire nation being but 16 fr. 54 c. per hectolitre.[56] In England, on the other hand, the weekly price of wheat had risen from 69*s.* 5*d.* on Jan. 2, 1808, to 91*s.* 9*d.* on Dec. 31, 1808. The demand for foreign corn grew daily throughout the island. In view of these facts, one might expect extensive exports from France to Britain. The exact opposite, however, was the case, as only 4,588 quarters of corn entered Great Britain from France in 1808. The explanation for this is altogether simple: Napoleon was strictly enforcing the prohibition of corn exports to the enemy.[57]

[53] Wheat averaged 18 fr. 88 c. per hectolitre in 1807 as compared with 19 fr. 33 c. in 1806: see *Documents Statistiques sur la France,* 1837, p. 14. See also *La Police Secrète,* III, No. 923.

[53a] *La Police Secrète,* III: Nos. 441, 494.

[53b] *Ibid.,* Nos. 664, 700, 1163.

[54] The *Farmer's Mag.,* VIII: 260, remarked that it was a generous act of the French to give the British their "daily food."

[55] For a time in 1807 some doubt existed as to the state of French agriculture: see *Cor. de Nap.,* Nos. 11583, 11695. As has been seen above, the harvest of that year was normal.

[56] *Documents Statistiques sur la France,* 1837, p. 14.

[57] A few licences were granted for the French trade: see P. C. Reg., 175 to 179 inclusive. The export of corn from France to Spain for the use of the French troops did not weaken the enforcement of Napoleon's decrees: see *Cor. de Nap.,* No. 13638.

In Holland there was a similar state of affairs. Late in November, 1806, when the commercial situation was steadily going from bad to worse, and when the grain trade was dwindling in size and importance, the Dutch Government received official news of the Berlin Decree.[58] Louis promptly ordered the execution of this measure —[59]

> . . . in East Friesland, Oldenbourg and other possessions formerly belonging to Prussia, but which were then occupied by Dutch troops. Within the kingdom [of Holland] itself the decree was to be executed only " in so far as the measures already adopted shall not be sufficient to effect the general blockade of the enemy's country." In other words, it was his intention to leave the law of 1805 unchanged and to consider the Berlin Decree a dead letter.

Two days later, Napoleon ordered the customs agents and the *gens d'armes* in East Friesland and Emden to stop all trade with the British, an indication of his mistrust of Louis. " I hope," he stated to his brother, " that you have taken the same measure for Amsterdam and Rotterdam, and that there will be thus no more correspondence with England in any part of Holland." [60]

In these letters and in the Berlin Decree, Louis saw the ruin of his downtrodden kingdom. Had it been possible, he would probably have defied his brother. As it was, he accepted the inevitable and, with a show of resistance, issued a new decree for Holland, December 15, 1806. According to this measure, no ship was to leave the kingdom without a specal certificate signed in person by Louis, and then only upon bond that the cargo was not going to an enemy port. All incoming vessels were to be seized at once, and released only upon royal order.[61]

Had this measure been enforced, it seems very likely that not a single bushel of corn would have been exported to the enemy.

[58] *R. G. P.*, V de deel I stuk, Talleyrand to Dupont-Chaumont, Nov 23, 1806.

[59] Hoekstra, P., *Thirty-Seven Years of Holland-American Relations*, p. 43.

[60] Rocquain, F., *Napoléon Ier et le Roi Louis*, Napoleon to Louis, Dec. 3, 1806.

[61] R. A. Staats Secretaire, Orig. Koninklijke Decreten en Besluiten, deel 90, No. 2, quoted by Hoekstra, P., *op. cit.*, p. 44. See also *R. G. P.*, V de deel I stuk, Dupont-Chaumont to Talleyrand, Dec. 28, 1806.

As it was, 237,523 quarters were shipped in 1807 to Great Britain. Louis, clearly, had taken advantage of his brother's absence and had allowed his subjects to trade with the British, who were suffering from an unfortunate harvest. Napoleon was fully aware of this trade, and repeatedly wrote Louis to obey his decrees.[62] Louis, however, quietly did as he wished. During March, 1807, he licenced without bond the export of foodstuffs for neutral ports. In a statement on the Dutch ports it is said that they remain "fully open to neutral vessels even those which have touched in England, and it seems that our government is more and more inclined to favor trade and commerce."[63] So active did this trade become that Louis allowed his Minister of Finance to sign the many licences that were granted.[64]

Tilsit, however, sounded the knell for much of this trade. With hurried steps Bonaparte returned to Paris and indignantly demanded the instant stoppage of this illegal trade. Completely cowed, Louis published a decree, September 4, 1807, prohibiting all trade with England.[65] Further attacks and outbursts of anger by Napoleon gradually tended to produce a situation more in keeping with the imperial program.[66] Total corn exports to Great Britain, however, in 1807 were nevertheless very large. Doubtless much of this must have been shipped before September, as during the latter part of that year a scarcity arose in Holland, caused largely by a partial harvest failure and by the heavy export trade.[67]

[62] Rocquain, F., *op. cit.,* Napoleon to Louis, Jan. 13, Feb. 25, 1807, and Louis to Napoleon, March 11, 1807. See also *R. G. P.,* V de deel I stuk, Dupont-Chaumont to Talleyrand, Jan. 22, 1807.

[63] Taylor MSS., Backer to Taylor, March 28, 1807, quoted by Hoekstra, P., *op. cit.,* p. 46.

[64] R. A. Staats Secrete, deel 359, letter Z, quoted by Hoekstra, P., *op. cit.,* pp. 46–47.

[65] *R. G. P.,* V de deel I stuk, Dupont-Chaumont to Champagny, Sept. 4, 1807, and Serrurier to Champagny, Sept. 9, 1807: see also *Cor. de Nap.,* Nos. 13051, 13065. A decided decrease in the number of British licences issued took place after this decree.

[66] *Cor. de Nap.,* Nos. 13230, 13241; Rocquain, F., *Napoléon Ier et le Roi Louis,* Napoleon to Louis, Oct. 9, 1807.

[67] *R. G. P.,* V de deel I stuk, Gogel to Louis, Sept. 4, 1807. Rocquain,

From Italy, Spain and Portugal, during 1807 and 1808, but 7,147 quarters of corn were imported, of which 4,095 quarters were of Indian corn, which probably had come from America. From the Scandinavian countries 74,318 quarters were obtained, of which all but 305 quarters came from Denmark. During the same period Ireland sent 1,059,966 quarters to England, not including 211 quarters of foreign-grown corn. From the Channel Isles 8,916 quarters were sent, most of which must have been French in origin. Scattering amounts also came from various unimportant states, as well as from prizes taken at sea. In general, Napoleon had no control over the imports from these places and from America. In Europe, however, the imperial decrees cut seriously into the corn exports to England. The Continental System, economic in nature, had thus become a most effective military weapon in the gigantic struggle between Napoleon and Great Britain. It would seem, therefore, that by the close of 1807 an imperial policy of forbidding corn exports had become a well established part of the general Napoleonic plan of humbling Great Britain.

F., *op. cit.*, Napoleon to Louis, April 25, 1808. During 1807 the average prices of all grain were slightly lower than what they had been in 1806, a condition which showed the presence of a more favorable harvest: see *Parl. Pap.*, 1826–1827, No. 27.

CHAPTER X

AN ERA OF LICENCED IMPORTS

The bountiful French harvest of 1808 and 1809 — The inception of the French Licence System — The Imperial Decree of July 3, 1810 — The harvest failures in France during 1810 and 1811 — Exports forbidden in France — Conditions in Holland — The annexation of Holland by France — The extension of the French Licence System throughout the Empire — The Russian campaign — The Continental System and Sweden — The fall of the Empire, 1813.

BEFORE 1809 the prohibition to export corn to England was a characteristic feature of the Napoleonic system. Agricultural conditions earlier in the century had caused the adoption of this program. The presence of war between France and Great Britain, moreover, implied the stoppage of all trade between these states, while the recently conceived Continental System strictly forbade all communication with the enemy. Wherever the French tricolor waved, or wherever French influence was uppermost, a drastic curtailment took place in the corn exports to Britain.

Beginning with 1809 a decided change took place. And why? The answer is altogether a simple one, and is found in the bursting granaries of the ever industrious French farmer, who since 1806 had reaped bumper crops.[1] Although Napoleon's military program had cut into these supplies, a huge surplus still remained. On top of this surplus had come the remarkable harvest of 1809 which, together with the results of the British orders and French decrees, had forced prices downward. The average price for France in 1809 was but 14 fr. 86 c. per hectolitre.[2] In Great Britain, however, prices were unusually high,

[1] For an account of agricultural conditions in 1807, see P. C. Unbound Papers, Mr. J. Irving to the Council, Jan. 13, 1807: see also p. 95.

[2] *Documents Statistiques sur la France,* 1837, pp. xiii, 14.

caused in the main by the partial stoppage of the foreign trade and by repeated harvest failures at home. It was probably this situation, abundance in France and scarcity in England, that caused Napoleon to allow the export of corn to his enemy. Had there been merely a bountiful crop in France, the lot of the French farmer would not have been very promising, as the ever watchful British navy would have stopped any export trade in corn. Or if there had been merely an unusual demand for corn in England, the English people would have gone hungry so far as Napoleon was concerned. The very fortunate combination, however, of demand and supply had created a condition which neither belligerent could ignore. The British Government, hoping to quiet the pangs of hunger among its subjects, rapidly extended the Licence System, and Napoleon, ever on tiptoe when the French peasant voiced a demand, introduced a system of licences for France.[3]

It was in March, 1809, that the French Government first undertook to issue licences for trade.[4] By means of these papers, French wines, brandies, corn and other enumerated commodities might be exported in return for certain specified articles. The demand for these licences was large, too large indeed for the very modest program then held by Napoleon. By July the system had far outgrown its original size, and yet the French agriculturists were not satisfied. The situation, however, remained unchanged throughout the summer and fall, although an increase in the number of licences did take place.[5] As a result of the French licences, and also as a result of the British licences which were being issued in large numbers, 25,058 quarters of wheat were shipped in 1809 to Great Britain from France.[6]

[3] Another motive which probably caused Napoleon to grant licences was the financial gain that would follow: see pp. 192–193.

[4] For the origin and the details of this measure, see Melvin, F. E., *Napoleon's Navigation System,* chap. 3.

[5] Melvin, F. E., *op. cit.*, chap. 4: see also *Farmer's Mag.,* X: 401, 547; *Monthly Mag.,* XXVIII: 443, for references to the import of wheat from France.

[6] 20,623 quarters were imported from Flanders, of which 20,198 consisted of wheat. See Customs, 4: 5, for an account of the imports into London and the various outports.

In contrast to former years this was a record trade; it failed, however, to satisfy the French farmer and merchant who still had large supplies on hand. Late in October, 1809, the house of Dubois Viollette of Nantes in a letter to the French Government, described the harvest as so extraordinary "as to be almost a calamity," and asked for an extension of the Licence System.[7] This petition was warmly endorsed by Montalivet, Secretary of the Interior, who at length induced the Emperor to issue a new type of licence early in December, 1809.[8] According to the terms of these licences three fourths of the export cargo had to consist of French corn, wine, and other agricultural products; the other fourth might include a number of enumerated articles. The import trade was also extended, and the time of each licence was placed at six months. As might be expected the licenced trade grew most rapidly; by February 13, 1810, a total of three hundred and fifty-four licences had been granted.[9]

The recent study by Melvin has established the fact that the French Licence System was but an important part of Napoleon's grand scheme of a French Navigation System which was announced July 3, 1810. Among the many clauses of this new decree was one which concerned the licence trade. According to this clause, all French ports were divided into two groups: the first embraced twenty ports on the Atlantic ocean and the English Channel; the second included nine Mediterranean ports. To each port Napoleon gave two hundred licences which were to be effective for six months and which were to be visaed by Montalivet before every clearance from France. Attached to the licence was a written statement of the ultimate destination of the vessel and the length of the proposed voyage. In the body of the licence there were to be inserted the names of those to whom the licence had been granted, the tonnage of the ship, and the name of both the captain and the vessel. Antwerp, Ostend,

[7] A. F.[12], 2057, Oct. 24, 1809, Transcripts, University of Pennsylvania.

[8] Melvin, F. E., *op. cit.*, pp. 120–121.

[9] A. F.[4], 1341[a], quoted by Melvin, F. E., *op. cit.*, p. 122. On Feb. 14, 1810, a new decree was issued which for certain reasons never was put into operation: see Melvin, F. E., *op. cit.*, p. 125 *seq.*, and *London Times*, Feb. 27, 1810.

Dunkirk, St. Valery sur Somme, Dieppe, Havre, Rouen, Caen, Cherbourg, Granville, St. Malo, Morlaix, Quimper and L'Orient might export corn and other lawful articles, provided one sixth of the cargo was of French wines and brandies. Nantes, Marans, La Rochelle, Charente, Bordeaux and Bayonne might export corn and other lawful goods provided one half of the cargo consisted of French wines and brandies. On the other hand, Agde, Cette, Marseilles, Nice, Savona, Genoa, Leghorn, Cività Vecchia and Ostia might export corn without any restriction.[10]

In the meantime, rumors were afloat that "40 millions" of grains had been exported since August, 1809, and that the harvest of 1810 was a failure. Napoleon, touched to the quick, ordered, July 16, 1810, the immediate stoppage of corn exports.[11] Nine days later, however, the Emperor, having satisfied himself as to the state of the harvest, allowed a limited licenced export of corn from certain French ports.[12] Exportation, therefore, which had been permitted by the Decree of July 3, and forbidden by the instruction of July 16, might now take place by means of a licence. In this way, Bonaparte hoped to crush all evasions of his order forbidding export, a policy which was altogether in keeping with the recently announced Navigation System.

During this period, the British had undertaken the further import of corn from France, a policy which continued throughout the remainder of the year, with the exception of a few days in October.[13] The combined use, therefore, of British and French licences practically freed the grain trade of all restrictions and allowed the export of 225,710 quarters of wheat to England.[14]

[10] A. F.iv, 463, Transcripts, University of Pennsylvania. This measure was modified on July 5, and 25, 1810: see Melvin, F. E., *Napoleon's Navigation System,* pp. 202, 205–206.

[11] Lecestre, L., *Lettres Inédites de Napoléon Ier,* vol. II, No. 652; Loyd, M., *New Letters of Napoleon,* No. 272; *Cor. de Nap.,* No. 16561. The *London Times,* July 12, 13, 1810, refers to the imperial decrees of June 22 and July 3, 1810. See *Literary Panorama,* VIII: 794, for an account of the adverse crop conditions in France; and also *London Times,* June 22, 25, 1810.

[12] See Melvin, F. E., *op. cit.,* pp. 205–206; and also *ibid.,* pp. 237–238, for a full account of this decree.

[13] See p. 115.

[14] From Flanders 167,153 quarters of wheat were also imported. From

Although this trade was of great value to England, it was an actual curse to France, where the harvest of 1810 had turned out to be far below the average.[15] As a natural result, corn exports stopped[16] and prices rose. In 1809, wheat had averaged 14 fr. 86 c. per hectolitre; the next year it stood at 19 fr. 61 c., and in 1811 it was 26 fr. 13 c.[17] As the situation failed to improve, attempts were made to buy corn in Northern Europe and Africa, where the harvest had been more favorable. At the same time licences were granted for the import of rice and corn from the United States.[18] By February, 1812, the price of flour

---

1800 to 1808 inclusive only 30 quarters of corn had been imported from Flanders. For a contemporary account of the trade from France, see *Monthly Mag.*, XXIX: 405, and *London Times*, June 4, 1810. The following data for 1810 are of interest:

	Imports into London from France		Imports into Outports from France	
	In British Ships	In Foreign Ships	In British Ships	In Foreign Ships
	Q. B.	Q. B.	Q. B.	Q. B.
Barley	0 0	4 0	0 0	0 0
Barley, warehoused	0 0	250 0	0 0	0 0
Beans	0 0	0 6	0 0	0 0
Pease	0 0	37 2	0 0	0 0
Wheat	0 0	111,051 0	0 0	50,429 0
Wheat, warehoused	0 0	3,655 4	0 0	2,560 6
Wheat, free	0 0	0 0	0 0	948 3
		Cwt. Q. B.	Cwt. Q. B.	Cwt. Q. B.
Flour	0 0	146,673 3 6	.636 3 19	.48,311 1 6
Flour, warehoused	0 0	2,375 0 25	0 0	0 0
Flour, free	0 0	0 0	0 0	1,734 2 0

This material is to be found in Customs, 4: 6: see also *Parl. Pap.*, 1814–1815, No. 26, Appendix No. 19, and *London Times*, June 4, 1810.

[15] A. F.[iv], 1058, quoted by Lanzac de Laborie, L., *Paris sous Napoléon*, V: 186.

[16] And yet the British figures show the presence of a trade after October: see *Parl. Pap.*, 1814–1815, No. 26, Appendix No. 19, p. 184.

[17] *Documents Statistiques sur la France*, 1837, p. 14: see also Consular Despatches, Bordeaux, Sept. 9, 1811.

[18] See B. T., 5: 21, Nov. 21, 1811, and Goulier, Lucien, *Le Commerce du Blé*, pp. 50–53, for a brief account of the grain trade under the Empire. See A. F.[iv], 1342, Transcripts, University of Pennsylvania, and Melvin, F. E., *op. cit.*, pp. 258–259.

was 92 fr. per sack in Paris; by April it was 150 fr. To combat these high prices, Napoleon created a reserve supply of wheat and flour which was to be sold to the Parisians as the price of corn rose.[19] This, however, only made matters worse, as the people interpreted this act by the Government to mean that a crisis had not as yet been reached. The Government then proceeded to stop all distillation in France and to set a maximum price for wheat.[20]

Unfortunately, Napoleon was not able to do more, as the Russian campaign demanded his entire attention. Occasionally from his camp in Russia he wrote about the agricultural situation in France, which, although much improved by the harvest of 1812, was not sufficiently bettered to warrant any changes in the existing laws.[21] As a result of these economic factors, fewer than 5,000 quarters were exported to Great Britain in 1811 and 1812.[22]

Conditions very similar in nature had existed for some time in Holland. It will be recalled that during the greater part of 1807, Louis had wilfully toyed with the imperial decrees. As a result, large quantities of corn were shipped to Great Britain. Not until September of that year was this profitable trade brought to an end, and then only upon the direct command of Napoleon. Early in January, 1808, Louis had very obediently proclaimed the Milan Decree. It was one thing to proclaim, however, and quite another thing to enforce, and Louis appears to have made very little effort to carry out his brother's wishes.[23]

[19] *Cor. de Nap.*, Nos. 18485, 18561, and Pasquier, E. D., *Memoirs, A History of My Times* (New York, Scribners, 1893), I: 528–541.

[20] *Archives Parlementaire,* 2d Series, vol. XI: 231, 232, 254, for an account of the harvest of 1811: see also Levasseur, P. E., *Histoire du Commerce de France* (Paris, 1912), II: 52; *Parl. Pap.,* 1826–1827, No. 157, p. 7, No. 27, p. 57; Duvergier, J. B., *Collection Complete des Lois, Decrets, Ordonnances, etc.,* XVIII: 232, 237. See *London Times,* March 25, April 22, 24, 1812, for an account of the scarcity in France. Prices in 1812 and 1813 were 34 fr. 34 c., and 22 fr. 51 c. per hectolitre: see *Documents Statistiques sur la France,* 1837, p. 14.

[21] *Archives Parlementaire,* 2d Series, XI: 254, 256–257.

[22] But two quarters of corn came from Flanders during these three years.

[23] The Dutch Decree of Jan. 8, 1808, may be found in Martens, G. F., *Nouveau Recueil de Traités,* I: 458.

At once Napoleon thundered a sharp reprimand, and on the twenty-third of the same month Louis again went through the form of closing Dutch ports to the ships of all nations.[24] Numerous evasions, however, followed, which the trained eye of the Emperor did not fail to see. Couriers were posted in haste, and Louis once more ordered the complete stoppage of all trade.[25] All in all, the volume of exports for 1808 was considerably lower than what it had been in 1807.

In the meantime the agricultural situation throughout Holland had become most promising. A more auspicious season could hardly have been expected. By early autumn a bumper crop was reported from all parts of the state. The agriculturists demanded a market for this unprecedented harvest. Especially was this the case when a rumor reached Holland that Napoleon had allowed export from France. This report, of course, was not true, although the Emperor at that time was taking the matter into consideration. Thoroughly impressed, however, by this rumor, as well as by the bountiful harvest, the Dutch Government asked for an extension of the right of export to Holland.[26]

Napoleon, however, turned a very deaf ear to the Dutch request; whereupon Louis, late in March, 1809, audaciously opened his ports, and allowed, under certain conditions, the export of various agricultural products.[27] When Röell, the French agent,

[24] *R. G. P.*, V de deel II stuk, Valckenaer to the King, Jan. 25, 1808. The decree may be found in *Documents Historiques et Réflexions sur le Gouvernement de la Hollande,* II: 195–198; an English translation appeared in *Cobbett's Pol. Reg.*, XIII: 349–350.

[25] Decrees of Oct. 13 and Nov. 27, 1808. The Decree of Oct. 13 may be found in *Cobbett's Pol. Reg.*, XIV: 800, 832, under the date of Oct. 18, 1808. See Hoekstra, P., *Thirty-Seven Years of Holland-American Relations,* pp. 64–76.

[26] *R. G. P.*, V de deel I stuk, Larochefoucauld to Champagny, Dec. 12, 1808; and *ibid.*, VI de deel II stuk, Gogel to Montalivet, Aug. 21, 1810, for a table of exports of oats from Frisia, Groningen, and the Department of the North for the years 1803 to 1809: see also Rocquain, F., *Napoléon Ier et le Roi Louis,* Louis to Napoleon, March 16, 1809. Wheat averaged 44*s.* 4*d.* per quarter at Rotterdam in 1809, the lowest it had been for the past ten years; oats averaged but 15*s.* 6*d.* Similar prices existed at Dordt and Amsterdam: see *Parl. Pap.*, 1826–1827, No. 27, pp. 31, 37.

[27] *Documents Historiques,* III: 55–60. A free translation may be found

protested, Louis boldly answered that he was doing only what his brother was doing.[28] As a result, the export of corn took place at a tremendous rate. The bountiful crops of that year, together with the increasing demand for corn in England, caused 307,957 quarters to enter British ports from Holland.[29] British licences, together with a willingness on the part of Louis to help the Dutch farmers, had thwarted the will of Napoleon.[30]

In the meantime, the Emperor had taken two very important steps affecting the commerce of Holland. The first was a treaty with Holland, March 16, 1809, and the second was the creation in the same month, as we have seen, of the Licence System. The belief that this system, made in the first instance for France, would be extended to Holland was very common, especially when it was known in Holland that the first article of the recent treaty with France provided for an extension of the licence trade to Holland. When it was learned, however, that Napoleon had taken no steps towards carrying out this clause, the Dutch Government expressed great concern over the matter. Repeated inquiries at length forced Napoleon to promise that Dutch licences would be granted. Characteristically, Napoleon qualified this promise by requiring that all petitions for licences be forwarded to Paris for approval.[31] It was not, however, un-

---

in *Cobbett's Pol. Reg.*, XV: 574–576. Among the articles that might be exported were oats; wheat was one of the thirty-two articles that might be imported. See *Farmer's Mag.*, X: 401, for reference to imports of oats from Holland.

[28] *R. G. P.*, V de deel II stuk, the King to Röell, April 7, 1809. Exportation was declared free by the Dutch law of Dec. 29, 1809: see *Parl. Pap.*, 1826–1827, No. 221, p. 44.

[29] See Appendix No. 8. The greater part of this trade entered London; no British ships were used in this trade: see Customs, 4: 5.

[30] It is possible that Napoleon was not deeply concerned over this violation of his decree. A bountiful harvest necessitated the export of Dutch corn as well as French, and although Bonaparte was aware that any export from Holland was illegal, he may have believed it better merely to protest against such a trade and not to attempt to enforce his decrees. Again, the Emperor was buried in foreign affairs at this time.

[31] *R. G. P.*, VI de deel I stuk, The Emperor to Lebrun, July 22, 1810: see also V de deel I stuk, Larochefoucauld to Champagny, April 16, 1809, VI de deel I stuk, Lebrun to the Emperor, July 19, 1810, and *Cor. de Nap.*, No. 16701, and Loyd, M., *New Letters of Napoleon*, No. 263.

til March, 1811, that a decree fulfilling this promise was issued.[32]

It was during this discussion that Bonaparte very suddenly, though not without many warnings, made Holland an integral part of the French Empire. Existing Dutch regulations concerning export were swept aside, and the French Decree of July 16, which forbade the export of corn, came into force.[33] The French Decree of July 25, which allowed a licenced export, did not apply to Holland, as none of the cities named in that measure were within the Dutch borders. Exportation of corn, therefore, was still forbidden in Holland.

This fact is borne out by the constant appeals that were made at that time for an outlet for the surplus of Dutch corn, for example, the letter forwarded by Gogel to Paris. In this letter great stress is placed upon the large exports of oats from the departments of the North, Frisia and Groningen during the years 1803 to 1809 inclusive, a trade which Gogel estimated to have an annual value of four million francs.[34] No change, however, was made, and the Decree of July 18 remained the law in Holland. Nevertheless, 266,811 quarters of corn were exported to England during 1810.[35] Evidently the French

[32] It is of interest to note that on Sept. 8, 1810, Montalivet forwarded to Gogel for his consideration a rough draft of a decree regulating the trade of Holland, of which article one concerned the grain trade. A sliding scale was to determine the export of wheat, barley, oats and pease. This draft was returned by Gogel with comments; nothing further, however, appears to have then happened. On October 18, 1810, a decree was issued which allowed the export of corn subject to a progressive duty whenever the price was below 24 fr. per hectolitre, provided no special decree was issued forbidding export. At that particular time exportation was forbidden: see *Parl. Pap.*, 1826–1827, No. 157, p. 20; and also *Archives Parlementaire,* Second Series, XI: 29–40. See *R. G. P.*, VI de deel II stuk, Montalivet to Gogel, Sept. 8, 1810, Gogel to Montalivet, Sept. 10, 1810, and the footnotes to Montalivet's letter of Sept. 8, 1810: cf. Melvin, F. E., *Napoleon's Navigation System,* p. 252.

[33] After the withdrawal of the French, Dec. 7, 1813, the Dutch laws were reëstablished and continued to operate until Dec. 1, 1816: see *Parl. Pap.*, 1826–1827, No. 157, p. 15; No. 221, p. 45.

[34] *R. G. P.*, VI de deel II stuk, Gogel to Montalivet, Aug. 21, 1810, Van der Capellen to Lebrun, Sept. 20, 1810.

[35] It is of interest to note that every bushel so imported was brought to England in foreign ships, and that most of it entered London: see Customs. 4: 6.

decrees were not rigorously enforced. Exportation took place with or without the knowledge of the French officials by means of British licences, which then were being granted in large numbers.[36] So extensive did this trade become that British public opinion protested on the ground that this import was the direct cause for the miserable condition of the corn market.[37]

Whatever fear Englishmen then had as to foreign corn was totally dispelled by the happenings of the next three years, as not one single bushel of corn seems to have entered Great Britain from Holland during these years. This was due to several factors. In the first place, the export of corn was forbidden in the French Empire, of which Holland was now a part; secondly, the agricultural situation in England was by no means as acute as it had been; and thirdly, harvest conditions in the Empire called for the conservation of the domestic supply and the import of foreign corn. During the earlier part of 1811 conditions in Holland were not so bad as elsewhere in the Empire. In the provinces of Frisia, Groningen and the Ems the harvest had been very abundant.[38] As exportation was forbidden, a prosperous internal trade developed with the less fortunate parts of the country which were actually importing foreign corn.[39] During 1812, the need for further help from the

36 See p. 114. The opportunity for illegal trading was very great in the neighborhood of Walcheren and the Zuider Zee.

37 *Farmer's Mag.*, XI: 100–101.

38 *R. G. P.*, VI de deel II stuk, Verstolk to D'Alphonse, March 5, 1811; De Celles to the same, March 20, 1811; Wichers to the same, April 25, May 25, 1811; and Pycke to Lebrun, July 19, 1811. On July 12, 1811, Montalivet instructed certain officers in Holland to report on the state of the agriculture; this report shows that the harvest throughout Holland was generally favorable: see *R. G. P.*, VI de deel II stuk, D'Alphonse to the Prefects, Oct. 3, 1811; Montalivet to D'Alphonse, Aug. 25, 1811; and the editorial comments on p. 1394 of the same volume.

39 *R. G. P.*, VI de deel II stuk, D'Alphonse to Lebrun, Feb. 26, 1811. See also *Idem,* Montalivet to D'Alphonse, March 3, 1811; De Celles to D'Alphonse, April 10, 1811; Lebrun to the Emperor, May 15, 1811. From the second quarter of 1809 to the beginning of 1814, the market at Amsterdam reported no imports from Poland: see *Parl. Pap.*, 1826–1827, No. 27, p. 31. It was possible, however, to get supplies from Germany. Information about this trade from Germany seems to have reached England which immediately placed her warships in the North Sea to stop all grain en route to Holland: see B. T., 5: 21, Mr. Hamilton to the Board of Trade, Nov. 21, 1811.

outside continued, as the failure of the French harvest of 1811 drew large supplies out of Holland to France.[40] Prices steadily rose, particularly of wheat, although oats remained more or less normal because of the large stock on hand. French officers in Holland were forced to ask for more pay so as to meet the ever advancing price of wheat.[41] These prices, probably, had been caused by the shortage of the harvest and by the excessive use of corn in the distilleries. It will be recalled that in February, 1812, a decree had been issued forbidding distillation in France, but not in Holland. This limitation had caused a rapid rise in the price of wheat, which the Dutch Government tried to stop by ordering the closing of all distilleries which had not been operating before February, 1812.[42]

During that year harvest conditions do not seem to have been as bad as they had been in 1811. The increased demands, however, made upon Holland by the rest of the Empire, as well as the continued prohibition on export, accounts for the absence of any active trade during 1812.

In the meantime, what of Germany and Northern Europe? It will be recalled that during 1808 Napoleon had most effectively decreased the volume of corn exports from Germany. The next year, however, 169,451 quarters were exported.[43] In order to understand this astonishing increase, one should keep in mind the political happenings of that year. As a natural result of foreign and domestic matters, Bonaparte was unable to give as much time to German affairs as otherwise he would have done. Without his guidance and oversight the enforcement of the Continental System was not as rigid as it would have been. French officers frequently yielded to the temptation placed in their way by the ever active British merchants who were most zealous in their attempts to ply a very profitable trade. British licences, accordingly, were issued in large numbers. And

40 *R. G. P.*, VI de deel II stuk, De Celles to D'Alphonse, Jan. 15, 1813.

41 Picard, E., *Correspondance Inédite de Napoléon Ier*, No. 4398.

42 *R. G. P.*, VI de deel II stuk, D'Alphonse to Montalivet, Sept. 1, 1811; De Stassart to D'Alphonse, Feb. 23, 1812; D'Alphonse to Collin de Sussy, Feb. 27, 1812; Collin de Sussy to D'Alphonse, March 18, 1812; De Stassart to D'Alphonse, May 5, 1812.

43 See Appendix No. 8.

yet in spite of this trade, prices for grain in the various cities of Germany were relatively low, a situation that indicated the presence of a large supply of corn. At Hamburg, Emden and Bremen the price of wheat and rye was lower than it had been in 1807. Oats and barley, on the other hand, were higher, doubtless because of the heavy export of these articles and their normal use in Germany.[44]

Of decided interest, during these years, is the active trade that had grown up between Great Britain and Europe by way of Heligoland. The importance of that island as a base for smuggling goods into Europe is now generally appreciated. It should also be noticed that Heligoland served as a means for obtaining supplies from the continent. Early in the year 1808 a cargo of corn entered London from Heligoland.[45] This was but the beginning of a very active trade that existed during that year. A decided drop, however, took place in 1809,[46] due probably to the increased activity of the French officials in that part of Europe.[47]

During 1810 a marked rise took place in the export of corn from Germany. A bountiful harvest and the need for grain in England were enough to break down all opposition on the

[44] *Parl. Pap.,* 1826, No. 159, p. 163; 1826–1827, No. 27; 1828, No. 258, pp. 71, 81. Oats were lower at Emden. Prices are also given in these sources for Mecklenburg-Schwerin, Mecklenburg-Strelitz and Oldenburg. For an account of the trade from Rostock and Wismer, see Stuhr, F., "Die Napoleonische Kontinentalsperre im Mecklenburg, 1806–1813," in *Jahrbuch des Vereins für Mecklenburgische Geschichte und Altertumskunde,* vol. LXXI, especially pp. 329, 331, 354–356, 361, 363. During the winter of 1808 and 1809 general misery was experienced by the poor, especially at Hamburg and Lübeck, due largely to the French army of occupation; prices of oats, the chief article of food, were very high: see Fisher, H. A. L., *Studies in Napoleonic Statesmanship,* Germany, p. 338.

[45] *London Times,* May 16, 1808.

[46] Imports from Heligoland:

	Wheat	Pease	Barley	Oats	Rye
1808	1,558 Q.	926 Q.	487 Q	12,130 Q	266 Q.
1809	841 Q.	0 Q.	0 Q.	1,090 Q.	24 Q.

See *Parl Pap.,* 1810, No. 67, Appendix, No. 1, pp. 2–9.

[47] The decline in the price of corn at Bremen and Hamburg, and throughout the provinces of Mecklenburg and Oldenburg, indicates the presence of a fair harvest: see *Parl. Pap.,* 1826–1827, No. 27, p. 27.

part of the French to this trade. Napoleon openly allowed the licenced export of wheat and flour from the Hanse towns, provided certain goods were imported into France on the return trip.[48] Merchants protected by these papers, as well as by British licences, engaged in this trade in perfect safety. It is interesting to note in passing that with few exceptions this trade was handled by foreign and not by British ships, and that the greater part of the ships docked at London. From Heligoland, however, the larger share went directly to London in British vessels.[49]

The following year a most astonishing decrease took place in the trade from Germany. In 1810 a total of 255,475 quarters had been shipped to Great Britain; in 1811, but 2,429 quarters were exported.[50] This drop, doubtless, was caused by the increased demands made upon this part of Europe by the French. Another factor of importance was the gathering of supplies for the future Russian campaign. It should be noticed that this decline in trade, therefore, had not been brought about by adverse harvest conditions in Germany. On the contrary, there is reason to believe that the crops were normal.[51] Prices, however, rapidly rose throughout the country. Wheat averaged in 1812 54*s.* 5*d.* at Hamburg, a price much higher than it had been for the last three years; other grains showed a similar

[48] Loyd, M., *New Letters of Napoleon*, No. 272; *London Times*, Sept. 17, 1810; and Melvin, F. E., *Napoleon's Navigation System*, pp. 242–243.

[49] See Customs 4: 6. During 1810, although several hundred licences were prepared for the Hanse towns, only a few seem to have been used: see Servières, G., *L'Allemagne Française sous Napoleon Ier*, pp. 137–138.

[50] Customs, 4: 7. As before, most of this corn was docked at London, and was carried in foreign rather than in British ships; the trade, moreover, from Heligoland shrank to 189 quarters: see Customs, 4: 7. During 1811, there appears to have been an increase in the use of the Hanse licences: see Servières, G., *op. cit.*, pp. 266–267. In the light of the export figures, however, it is doubtful whether many of these licences were used for the export of grain.

[51] For an account of the harvest of 1810, 1811 and 1812 within the Empire, see *Archives Parlementaire*, Second Series, XI: 254. In this source the returns from those parts of Germany included within the Empire are given, and show favorable harvests. Naturally Napoleon tapped this source of supply.

rise. At Bremen, wheat rose to 61*s.* 8*d.*, higher than it had been since 1806; other grains showed a similar rise.[52]

The huge demands made upon Germany by Napoleon to meet the wants of the Empire and of the Grand Army tended to check exportation and to increase prices. The following year, 1813, this army lay buried in the snows of Russia. This signal defeat of the heretofore invincible Napoleon caused Germany to rise and proclaim its freedom. Bit by bit the German nation regained its former political status. French armies and customs officers began a slow retreat towards the Rhine, and the Continental System ceased to exist in Germany. Unrestricted trade rapidly grew between the German people and the English. Especially was this true of the grain trade, which now was dependent upon the laws of supply and demand. Fortunately for all concerned the agricultural conditions in Germany were most favorable, which made possible the export of large quantities of corn to Britain.[53]

What was true of Germany was also true of Prussia. It will be recalled that during 1808 apparently not a single bushel of corn had escaped the watchfulness of the French customs for export to England. The next year matters improved but slightly; only 2,014 quarters of corn were exported to England.[54] This, of course, was contrary to the decrees of Napoleon who forbade

[52] This was also true of the Mecklenburgs and of Oldenburg: see *Parl. Pap.*, 1826–1827, No. 27, p. 27, and 1826, No. 159, p. 163; and also Consular Despatches, London, Oct. 18, 1811, June 15, 1812. See *Parl. Pap.*, 1828, No. 258, pp. 71, 74, for prices at Emden. A total of but 619 quarters of corn entered Britain from Germany in 1812, of which a few bushels came from Heligoland. Most of this trade was handled by foreign and not by British ships: see Customs, 4: 8.

[53] See Appendix No. 8. See also *Parl. Pap.*, 1826–1827, No. 27, p. 27, 1826, No. 159, p. 163, for prices throughout Germany. These prices show an improved condition of agriculture. The harvest of 1812 was much more bountiful than that for the past two years: see *Archives Parlementaire*, Second Series, XI: 254.

[54] See Appendix No. 8. Of this amount 1,527 quarters were of wheat and 487 quarters were of pease. Practically all of this wheat came from Poland, via Dantzic: see Customs, 4: 5. This is of particular interest in view of the fact that the European sources of information indicate that there was not a single bushel exported to England or elsewhere for that matter: see *Parl. Pap.*, 1826, No. 159, pp. 90, 128.

grain exports to the enemy. The permission, however, to ship to allied or neutral ports gave an opportunity which the itching palm of a few French agents could not fail to grasp.[55] The following despatch from Heinrich Hahn, British consul at Dantzic, is of interest in this respect:[56]

> Notwithstanding the many impediments laid in the way of trade, several ships have cleared out from these ports actually bound to Great Britain with cargoes of hemp, flax, linseed, staves etc. The French Consul takes a fee of 1 Pound for himself and a douseur to his Secretary for his *certificat d'origine.* Bonds are also given by the merchants for the return of the ships so that they did not go to a British port, that is of course only *pro forma.*

Instances of similar frauds multiplied during 1810, which accounts in part for the export of 316,223 quarters of corn to Great Britain.[57] Other factors explaining this trade were the presence of bountiful harvest in Prussia and an unusual demand on the part of the British.[58] Most of this trade, however, must have occurred after July 22, 1810. Before that time, export to the enemy was forbidden, but on that date a decree was issued providing for the Hanse licences. According to this decree, grain, among other commodities, might be exported to England under certain conditions as to the return cargo. "This," Napoleon remarked, "will rejoice the heart of Poland, which country is overflowing."[59]

[55] F. O., 64: 80, Advices from Hahn, May 16, July 27, 1809. Hahn was also British agent at Königsberg. During the war he assumed the name of Drusina: see *Letters of Sir T. B. Martin,* II: 25, 74–75. See also *Parl. Pap.,* 1826–1827, Nos. 20, 83, pp. 35–36, and No. 159, p. 25. During the years 1807 to 1814 Dantzic was in French hands, which created an unusual demand for wheat which of course caused an advance in price: see *Parl. Pap.,* 1813–1814, No. 339, p. 77.

[56] F. O., 64: 80, Advices from Hahn, May 19, 1809.

[57] Of this 296,756 quarters consisted of wheat. For instances of French consular frauds, see *Cor. de Nap.,* No. 16966.

[58] Proof of the existence of a bountiful harvest is to be found: first, in the large exports of that year; secondly, in the demand for grain on the part of France and Holland: see *Parl. Pap.,* 1826, No. 159, pp. 90, 91, 128.

[59] Loyd, M., *New Letters of Napoleon,* No. 272. See Melvin, F. E., *Napoleon's Navigation System,* pp. 242–244, for a detailed statement of this decree; see also *London Times,* Aug. 31, Sept, 17, 1810, and *Cor. de Nap.,* No. 16933. This decree was modified in August and December, but

Unfortunately, this trade was hampered by a very heavy export tax.[60] This hindrance was partially removed in July, 1811, when Bonaparte allowed this tax to be reduced by one half, and provided in addition special arrangements for Dantzic and the ports beyond the Oder.[61] The next month, the Prussian Government was allowed to grant licences, under certain conditions, permitting the export of corn and Silesian cloth.[62] During 1811, therefore, it would seem that the corn exports from Prussia were allowed according to the terms of the Licence System.[63] And yet, in spite of these inducements and the British licences which had been issued in large numbers, the corn exports dropped to 97,885 quarters. This decrease was due to the unusual demands that arose within the Empire, the heavy licence fees, and the export tax; and not by reason of any agricultural disturbance in Prussia.[64]

A continuation of these causes explains, in part, a further drop in 1812. During that year but 9,062 quarters of corn were shipped to Britain.[65] The sudden demand made upon Prussia to provision the Grand Army, as well as to replenish the diminished stocks of France and Denmark, were factors of significance.[66] The exact reverse took place in 1813, the year of the

not so as to alter the trade in corn. About one half the wheat imported from Prussia came from Poland by way of Dantzic. The entire import was in the hands of foreigners, and most of the shipments were to the port of London: see Customs, 4: 6.

[60] See Fisher, H. A. L., *Studies in Napoleonic Statesmanship, Germany,* p. 344, who quotes Gen. Rapp as saying that the heavy tax on grain and wood was responsible for the decay of that trade.

[61] Melvin, F. E., *op. cit.*, p. 244.

[62] *Cor. de Nap.*, No. 17974.

[63] See F. O., 64: 81, Advices from Drusina, and *Parl. Pap.*, 1826, No. 159, pp. 91, 129; 1826–1827, No. 83, p. 57.

[64] The price of wheat at Dantzic averaged as low as 36*s*. 3*d*. per quarter: see *Parl. Pap.*, 1826–1827, No. 83, p. 57. About one half of this trade came from Poland. All of it was carried by foreign ships and most of it entered London, although large quantities were docked in Scotland: see Customs, 4: 7.

[65] Of this 5,220 quarters came from Poland, and with the exception of 64 quarters, all was exported directly to London. The entire trade was handled by foreign ships: see Customs, 4: 8.

[66] See *Parl. Pap.*, 1826, No. 159, pp. 90, 129, 1826–1827, Nos. 20, 83, which show that exportation was forbidden at Dantzic.

War of German Liberation. Napoleonic despotism was a thing of the past. Trade and commerce were completely freed from the weight of the Continental System, the natural result of which was a great rise in the volume of corn exports to England.[67]

Had Napoleon kept out of Russia, the agricultural situation within the Empire would doubtless have been less acute. As it was, Western Europe was called upon to make new contributions in food as well as in men and money so as to force Russia to adhere to the Continental System. Tilsit, it will be remembered, had marked the adoption of this system by Russia. As a result of this alliance, as well as because of the nature of the war that had preceded it, the export of corn to Great Britain had steadily fallen during 1807 and 1808.[68] The next year this trade rose to 14,089 quarters.[69] This fall and rise in the corn trade is of decided interest, as it shows only too well the hold Napoleon had over the Czar Alexander, especially during 1807 and 1808. On the other hand the figures for 1809 show a slight departure from the spirit of the imperial decrees, as well as the presence of a fair harvest. These factors must have been exceedingly pleasing to the Englishman, who saw in this trade not merely a new source of food, but also a growing enmity between the Czar and Bonaparte.[70] And finally, although this relaxation in prohibition to export was in keeping with the system of licences granted that year in France, the fact remains that it stands as a clear instance of defection on the part of Russia from the Continental System.

During 1810, the Russian exports of corn to England rose to 66,868 quarters, of which 58,132 quarters were of wheat.[71]

[67] See Appendix No. 8.

[68] But 3,663 quarters of corn entered Great Britain in 1808 from Russia. This decline was also brought about by a partial harvest failure in Russia: see Mazade, C., *Correspondence du Mal Davout,* II: 64, 98, 188.

[69] Most of this entered London, and, with the exception of 795 quarters, was entirely of pease; only foreign ships engaged in this trade: see Customs, 4: 5.

[70] See *Monthly Mag.,* XXVII: 108–109, for British comment on the Russian trade.

[71] All of this was brought to London and the outports by foreign ships: see Customs, 4: 6; and also *Parl. Pap.,* 1826–1827, No. 27, for prices of grain in Russia.

The explanation for this is threefold: first, this export coincided with the French policy of permitting grain exports to England, and thus did not arouse any great objection on the part of Napoleon; secondly, an unusual demand for grain in England naturally drew supplies from Russia; thirdly, this trade was the outcome in part of the continued growth of an anti-French feeling in Russia.[72] These factors, therefore, tend to explain the tremendous rise in the Russian trade to Great Britain as well as to furnish one of the reasons why Napoleon undertook the ill-fated Russian campaign. The rapid occupation of Poland and western Russia by the French armies created an unusual demand for food supplies. As a result the Russian trade fell to 49,596 quarters, an amount greater, however, than the total exports for 1807, 1808 and 1809.[73] The next year, 1812, Russia was freed from the Napoleonic system.[74] Commerce grew by leaps and bounds. A total of 128,438 quarters of corn was shipped to England, of which 50,974 quarters consisted of wheat, and 60,342 quarters of rye.[75]

A similar state of affairs took place in the trade with the Scandinavian countries. During 1808 and 1809 only 13,369 quarters of corn were shipped thence to Britain. This was a decided drop over the volume of exports for 1807.[76] This decline had been caused, so far as Denmark was concerned, by the adoption on the part of that state of the imperial decrees. Economic conditions were another factor, a factor which probably also explains entirely the drop in exports from Norway and Sweden.

The policy of the Swedish Government, however, was not destined to keep Napoleon out of Swedish affairs. Like the neck

[72] See *Writings of J. Q. Adams* (ed. Ford), III: 400, 445, 458, 551, IV: 3–5, 14–16, 38–41, for references to the commercial situation in Russia.

[73] See Customs, 4: 7.

[74] See B. T., 5: 21, Sept. 28, 1812, for a letter from one Edward Cooke, Esq., stating that the Russian Government had opened its ports to the British by a Ukase of Aug. 16, 1812.

[75] During 1813, the Russian trade fell to 64,938 quarters of corn. It is interesting to note that in 1812 only 221 quarters of corn were brought to England in English ships: see Customs, 4: 8.

[76] See Appendix No. 8. In 1809, 1,269 quarters were imported by British ships: see Customs, 4: 5. See *Parl. Pap.*, 1826–1827, Nos. 27, 83, for prices of grain at Christiana and in Sweden.

of a huge bottle, Sweden was the avenue through which British goods entered Europe. This, of course, was not to the liking of Napoleon who clearly saw the imperative need of compelling Sweden to adopt his measure against Britain.[77] With extreme care and cunning, Bonaparte induced his most recent convert, Russia, to undertake this very disagreeable task. Military success crowned the efforts of the Russian Czar who wrenched from a defeated Sweden the district of Finland. Smarting under these humiliations, Sweden rapidly fell into the hands of a radical element. Military defeat plus commercial distress boiled the pot of revolutionary spirit to such a degree that it overflowed and swept Gustavus IV, king of Sweden, off his throne. The new monarch, Charles XIII, vainly tried to better matters by unwillingly accepting the Continental System in return for Pomerania and Rügen.[78] Again the scene shifted as Charles met an untimely death. To the astonishment of all, most of all to Bonaparte, the Swedish throne was offered to none other than the French Marshal Bernadotte. For the moment, the acceptance by Bernadotte had a most pleasing result, in that it gave to Napoleon the very cork which he needed to close up the long-necked bottle — Sweden. The glitter and the rustle of royal trappings, however, caused the new king to cast away his French baton. A new relationship at once sprang up between the former comrades in arms. The duty of a monarch, declared Bernadotte, was first to look out for the welfare of his subjects. The result was inevitable, namely, that the Continental System was but feebly enforced. Truly, Bonaparte needed a new cork. Aware of the numerous infractions of his decrees, the Emperor seized and occupied Pomerania. At once Sweden threw itself into the eager arms of Great Britain, and the Continental System, never completely accepted in Sweden, totally disappeared.[79]

[77] Cf. *Cor. de Nap.*, No. 13079.

[78] Martens, G. F., *Nouveau Recueil de Traités*, I: 19–29, 30, 232. See B. T., 5: 19, Jan. 19, 1810, in which reference may be found to a letter dated, Malmö, Oct. 26, 1809, in which the opinion is expressed that the Swedish Government intended to allow the export of corn; this, however, did not prove to be the case.

[79] Martens, G. F., *op. cit.*, I: 558–567.

During the swift progress of these events, the grain trade of Sweden reflected quite accurately the policy of Napoleon. Hardly had Sweden adopted the French decrees than violations followed in large numbers. Ranchoup, the French consul at Gottenburg, informed Napoleon late in the fall of 1810 that Gottenburg swarmed with foreign ships, chiefly American, which had brought in great cargoes of colonial produce.[80] Ranchoup also reported that American vessels convoyed by the British were engaged in an active trade between England and Sweden.[81] Alquier, the French ambassador to Sweden, strongly protested, and received vague promises that Sweden would mend its ways, and for a time matters did improve. Somewhat pleased, Napoleon opened his ports to Swedish goods, and allowed the export of French articles, including wheat, to Sweden.[82] This must have been of doubtful value to Sweden as it was then in no need of wheat. The late harvest had been so abundant that Sweden had more than it could possibly use. The result was an unprecedented export to Great Britain. The next two years, however, witnessed a return to normal conditions, and the Swedish grain trade diminished to a marked degree.[83]

Undoubtedly, the influence of the French was a factor in producing this drop in corn exports to Britain. It should not, however, be overemphasized. Sweden probably violated Napoleon's wishes more often than it obeyed them. No one was better informed of this than the faithful Alquier who promptly reported every infraction of his master's wishes. In July, 1811, this most conscientious servant openly took the Swedish Government to task for its departure from the Continental System. Ever since the British Admiral Saumerez had entered the Baltic, Alquier insisted, the Swedes had supplied him and the island of Anholt, and had allowed British ships to sail in safety for

[80] Archives des Affaires étrangères, Suède Correspondance, T. 249, fol. 294, quoted by Coquelle, P., "La Mission d'Alquier à Stockholm," in *Revue d'Histoire Diplomatique,* XIII: 199.

[81] *Ibid.,* p. 199.

[82] *Ibid.,* p. 207.

[83] The trade from Sweden was fairly well divided between London and the outports, and generally speaking was carried in foreign bottoms: see Customs, 4: 6, 7, 8.

England. A definite arrangement seems to have been made between the British admiral and the Swedes for that purpose.[84] This protest, however, fell on deaf ears as Sweden by that time was all but ready to hurl defiance at Napoleon. By this time, moreover, Napoleon was unable to give any more attention to Swedish affairs, as the Russian campaign was taking every ounce of strength. It is probable that Sweden had little surplus for export, and the amount furnished the fleet under Saumarez must have been quite small. The peculiar economic position occupied by that state prevented the excessive growth of corn.[85] Inadequate production, therefore, and not French influence, explains the drop in the volume of the corn trade during 1811 and 1812.[86]

In Denmark the French influence was more effective. In 1810, as a direct result of a favorable harvest, an extensive trade to England was allowed. The next year this trade slumped badly, probably because of a less favorable harvest, but also because of the general needs of the Empire. During 1812 and 1813 this trade increased slightly. By this time, however, French power was conspicuously absent, and the natural law of supply and demand took the place of the unnatural Continental System.[87]

[84] Coquelle, P., *op. cit.*, p. 226. See also Pinguard, Léonce, *Bernadotte, Napoléon et les Bourbons* (Paris, Plon-Nourrit, 1901), p. 116, and Mazade, C., *Correspondance du Mal Da out,* III: 243.

[85] Güinchard, J., *Sweden: Historical and Statistical Handbook,* II: 48, 49, 50, 54, 56, 510.

[86] During the years 1812–1814, not a single bushel was exported to Great Britain from Norway, although moderate amounts were shipped from Sweden.

[87] See Appendix No. 8. The trade from Spain, Portugal, Africa and the Mediterranean was small, and needs no discussion.

CHAPTER XI

CONCLUSIONS

The importance of the year 1812 — The effect of the Continental System upon the corn exports of Europe — The significance of the French Trade of 1810 — Could Napoleon have starved Great Britain into submission? — The importance of the North American supplies — England ruled the seas, but Napoleon dominated the continent — The remarkable increase in domestic production in the United Kingdom — Conditions in Great Britain during 1810 and 1811 — The crisis of 1812.

THE Napoleonic era has few years more significant than 1812. For the Corsican, it marks the beginning of the end. Oppressed Europe witnessed with unique satisfaction the débâcle of the Empire. A war of liberation seemed imminent. Napoleon, probably more than any other, realized the importance of the moment. With great concern he must have felt the earth quiver and shake with the tramp, tramp, tramp of a people mightier than the Imperial Guard. No one who has caught the bizarre effects of the Tschaikowsky masterpiece can fail to appreciate the awful meaning of that year. Frost-bitten and starved, deficient in numbers as in morale, the remains of the Grand Army camped in dread terror on the banks of the Niemen, while at Paris its leader was engaged in the Herculean task of defending the Empire. Napoleon, however, ceased to play the rôle of emperor. Casting aside the imperial trappings, he emerged once more as the brilliant military leader of his youth. All his unmatched ability, coupled with the resources of France, was devoted to measures of defense.

As a direct consequence of the Russian campaign and the events which immediately followed, the Continental System ceased to be the factor of importance that it had been. Only in France and in Holland does it appear that the corn trade received any particular attention. Even here it may seriously be questioned whether the underlying cause for the continued prohibition of exportation was the Continental Closure. The gravity of the situation as it existed at the beginning of 1813, the necessity of conserving all possible supply for the titanic struggle that was to take place, must have acted as a more powerful force in compelling non-exportation than did the Continental System. From these two states not a single bushel of wheat was shipped to Great Britain in 1813. Elsewhere on the continent a most pronounced increase took place in the export trade to England.[1]

The simple fact that exportation from Europe advanced so rapidly during 1813 is partial proof that before this year the prohibitory policy of Napoleon had been more or less successful. The extent to which the Continental System operated has already been observed by a somewhat detailed examination of the corn trade. At this point it seems best to attempt a composite picture of the entire trade, revealing its special relation with the imperial policy.

It is first imperative to determine a date at which the Napoleonic program began and when it ended. A fixed date might well be found in the Berlin Decree but for the fact that, although the system did not exist in name before that date, it did exist in point of fact. For the purpose of this study, it has been deemed best to view the year 1803 as the beginning and the year 1812 as the end. Tilsit provided a convenient and logical place to divide the period into two divisions. Before July, 1807, the corn trade of Europe, generally speaking, had not been interfered with to any great degree. Exception to this statement may be found in the trade from France, Flanders and Holland and partially from the Hanseatic towns. From Tilsit to 1810 the trade with the continent was considerably checked by the Napoleonic decrees, the activity of the Licence System being limited chiefly to France. During 1810, exportation was generally permitted by Napoleon, either through the medium of his licences or by non-interference with the trade itself, as was the

[1] The continental harvest of 1813 seems to have been good in quantity but poor in quality: see *Parl. Pap.*, 1814, No. 26, p. 10.

case with Russia. From then on to the close of 1812 the export trade to Great Britain was definitely restricted. Only in Sweden and Russia does it appear that the system was not rigorously enforced.

The essential characteristic of the Continental System was the cutting off of all trade, export as well as import, with Great Britain. Grain was denied the enemy as well as timber, naval stores, silk, linen, or other articles grown or manufactured in the Empire and the allied states. At least this was the theory. Napoleon at an early date wisely foresaw that while the law must be proclaimed as unalterable, exceptions, nevertheless, would have to be made. It was with this thought in mind that he allowed the export of cheese and other dairy products from Holland. It was also the peculiar conditions in France that had caused the creation of the Licence System. During the years 1809 and 1810 large numbers of these papers were issued. The Imperial Council meetings were most active in the discussions of this system. Numerous reports were presented, all of which received Napoleon's careful consideration. The *Correspondance* fairly bristles with frequent allusions to the enforcement of the system.[2] It is therefore no mere accident that 1,497,616 quarters of wheat were exported to Britain from the French Empire during these two years, out of a total of 2,023,112 quarters from the entire world.

As has already been pointed out, the cause prompting this unprecedented export was the presence of the bumper crops within the Empire. The incessant demand for a market, on the part of the agriculturists, had forced the Emperor to adopt the Licence System. The acceptance of this policy, although of infinite value to the landed classes, was not without distinct advantages for Napoleon. In the first place a decided increase in revenue took place, due to the export duties and the licence fees. This is revealed in the following remark of Napoleon: "You will perceive that this huge system will help to feed my ports, will make trade an exceptional one and will bring me in a

[2] Cf. Melvin, F. E., *Napoleon's Navigation System,* chaps. 4 to 10 inclusive.

considerable revenue. . . . Thus it is no piece of folly that I here undertake." [3]

Again, the export of grain to the enemy might fill the royal treasury in another way, namely, by providing for payment of this produce in gold or silver, rather than in articles of British growth or manufacture. It is very likely that the adoption of this mercantilistic idea was an afterthought on the part of Napoleon. As the volume of this trade waxed, however, the material advantages to be gained in this way played an important part in the Emperor's scheme. During 1810 and 1811, licences were granted on the express condition that the payment for the cargo exported should be in specie or bullion.[4] The import of this precious metal would also seriously undermine the financial condition of the enemy. Destruction of British credit, therefore, worked hand in hand with the policy of assisting the agriculturists and of filling the imperial treasury.[5]

It is of interest to note in passing how concerned the Englishman of that day became over the steady export of gold to pay for these and other purchases abroad. Thus the *Farmer's Magazine* remarked: "It is plain, that whilst the French Ruler kindly favored us with corn, he did it to promote his own convenience; and that, instead of accepting of payment in manufactures . . . nothing but bullion or specie would be received in return for the numerous cargoes shipped under his sanction." [6] Another leading periodical held that "The importation of corn from France into London, during six months has been such as to pro-

[3] Lecestre, L., *Lettres Inédites de Napoléon Ier,* No. 272; see also *Cor. de Nap.*, No. 19391.

[4] *Cor. de Nap.,* Nos. 16508, 17974; Servières, G., *L'Allemagne Française sous Napoléon Ier*, p. 136, note 2. See also Melvin, F. E., *Napoleon's Navigation System,* pp. 190–192, for a brief, though suggestive, treatment of this subject.

[5] Mr. Rose has commented rather freely on this mercantilistic phase of the grain trade, as has also Miss Audrey Cunningham. Both, however, overstate this matter by insisting that the destruction of British credit was the *raison d'être* for this trade. They apparently failed to see that the fundamental cause was the agricultural condition in the Empire: see also Rose, J. H., *Life of Napoleon* (eds. 1902, 1907, 1910), II: 204; also his articles in the *Cambridge Modern History,* IX: 372; *Monthly Rev.,* March, 1902; and Cunningham, Audrey, *British Credit in the Last Napoleonic War,* pp. 3–4.

[6] *Farmer's Mag.,* XI: 101.

duce the vast sum of 1,382,350 £ sterling. Such a traffic as this must undoubtedly drain the country of its specie, and pour wealth into the lap of the common enemy. . . ."[7] Similar ideas were expressed in Parliament.[8] Nor were these opinions void of truth. The reserves of the Bank of England in February, 1808, amounted to £7,855,470, and three years later they stood at £3,350,940.[9] The great concern expressed over this unfortunate trade balance shows very well the tremendous inroads Napoleon had made. It also discloses the hold mercantilism had over the English people at that time. Truly, the charge made against Napoleon of adhering to an antiquated system of mercantilism might with equal force be made against the British Government and people.

Another question, somewhat controversial in character, presents itself, namely, Could Napoleon have starved Great Britain into submission? A study of the various sources at hand fails to reveal the slightest indication that Napoleon ever held this idea. This is also the opinion of Rose.[10] Rose, however, goes one step further: [11]

> It is strange that he never sought to cut off our corn-supplies. They were then drawn almost entirely from the Baltic ports. The United States and Canada had as yet only sent us a few driblets of corn. . . . The plan of sealing up the corn-fields of Europe from Riga to Trieste, would have been feasible, at least for a few weeks . . . and an imperial decree forbidding the export of corn from France and her allied States to the United Kingdom could hardly have failed to reduce us to starvation and surrender in the very critical winter of 1810–1811.

In antithesis to this may be placed the remark of the American grain merchant Ellis: "We believe if he [Napoleon] saw the chance of starving Great Britain he would do it."[12] Which of these two views is correct?

[7] *Monthly Mag.*, XXIX: 405: see also *London Times,* Feb. 17, June 4, 1810.

[8] *Commons' Journal,* 65: 95–96; *Parl. Debates,* XIX: 940, 942, 943, s. vv. *Report of the Bullion Committee.*

[9] *Parl. Pap.*, 1832, No. 722, Appendix, pp. 19–20: see also *Parl. Pap.*, 1810, No. 349, pp. 4, 156, 157. Heavy drains were also made for other purposes: see Silberling, N. J., "Financial and Monetary Policy in Great Britain during the Napoleonic Wars," in *Quarterly Journal of Economics,* Feb., 1924.

[10] *Monthly Rev.*, March, 1902, p. 74.

[11] Rose, J. H., *Life of Napoleon* (eds. 1902, 1907, 1910), II: 204.

[12] Ellis and Allan to I. Stevens, May 4, 1809.

A careful investigation of the evidence at hand leads to the conclusion that any scheme of starving Great Britain into submission was almost impracticable. In the main, this thesis rests upon the following demonstrable facts: first, Great Britain had free access, so far as Bonaparte was concerned, to the cornfields of America; second, by increased acreage England had augmented its home production to a marked degree; third, a policy of retrenchment and substitution had given additional sources of supply.

Rose has stated that the Baltic ports, rather than those of America, were the chief sources of supply during the Napoleonic era. While there is much truth in this remark, it appears, however, to be overstated. The total import of wheat into Great Britain from these ports from 1800 to 1812 inclusive is as follows:

Prussia	3,017,471 quarters	Russia	644,767 quarters
United States ...	1,169,572 quarters	Canada	353,308 quarters
Germany	888,278 quarters		

From the Baltic, therefore, there were imported 4,550,516 quarters in contrast to 1,522,880 quarters from North America, or approximately 75 per cent and 25 per cent respectively.[13] One quarter of the total wheat imported into Great Britain from these ports came from North America. Comparing the wheat imports from the Baltic and from North America with the total amount of wheat imported from all parts during 1810–1812, one finds that approximately 53 per cent came from the Baltic and 18 per cent from North America. The very obvious conclusion to be deduced from these facts is that the trade from the United States and Canada was of considerable size and importance.

Over this trade and that from Ireland Napoleon had but little control. French privateers found it exceedingly dangerous to

[13] Contrasting these figures with the imports of other grains, and recalling that wheat was the chief article of consumption, one reaches the same conclusion. Ireland, furthermore, exported to Britain 1,014,679 quarters of domestic wheat, and 6,653 quarters of foreign wheat during the same period. Taking as a basis the imports from 1800 to 1814 inclusive, one finds that 77 per cent came from the Baltic, and 23 per cent from North America.

attempt any interference with ships sailing directly between the New World and Britain. It was, however, easier for the French to molest British or neutral ships en route from the continent. Any interference, to be effective, had to operate at the source of the supply and not at the means of transportation. The mastery of the sea lay with Britain, not with France; the mastery of the continent, however, lay with Bonaparte. The British fleet effectively prevented an enemy from cutting England off from American corn, but could not keep Napoleon from withholding European corn, so long as Europe kept faith with the Continental System. Fortunately for England, Napoleon never was able to be complete ruler of Europe at any one time. The task of whipping European governments and peoples into proper obedience to the imperial decrees was too great even for the Emperor. And so while it may appear possible for Napoleon to have sealed up the granaries of Europe, practically such a scheme was at no time possible. What effect an embargo of a few weeks might have had is very uncertain, especially when one recalls that in 1808 the Continental System actually placed a very effective embargo upon the grain trade, and yet did not stop the British import from Europe. An examination of the import figures shows the truth of this statement. In 1807, a total of 514,405 quarters of corn was shipped from Europe to Great Britain; the next year this fell to 65,529 quarters.[14] And although condi-

[14] The following table shows the more important imports:

		Prussia	Germany	Russia	Holland	France	Scandinavian states
		Q.	Q.	Q.	Q.	Q.	Q.
Oats	1807	10,750	130,355	2	222,248	96	61,070
Oats	1808	0	21,971	0	11,170	108	1
Wheat	1807	11,465	3,407	5,711	11,415	27,656	10,424
Wheat	1808	0	2,236	549	1,051	2,870	63
Barley	1807	0	2,151	201	108	78	417
Barley	1808	0	627	2	0	259	1,731
Beans	1807	655	3,465	0	2,368	1,412	1,834
Beans	1808	0	3,221	0	2,052	689	0
Rye	1807	0	0	265	8	2,816	0
Rye	1808	0	249	0	0	0	3
Pease	1807	20	2,157	4	1,374	53	410
Pease	1808	0	1,692	3,111	3,860	660	195
Total	1807	22,890	141,535	6,183	237,521	32,111	74,155
Total	1808	0	29,996	3,662	18,133	4,586	1,993
Net loss		22,890	111,539	2,521	219,388	27,525	62,162

See Appendix No. 8 for imports from Portugal and amounts taken by prize at sea.

tions in England were by no means as favorable as might have been desired, still the nation was able to overcome this as well as other difficulties. It should be noted, however, that conditions in 1808 were not as critical as during the winter of 1810–11. But even then it is highly questionable whether an imperial embargo of "at least a few weeks" could have forced Great Britain to terms.

During the year 1810 a grand total of 1,567,125 quarters of wheat was imported into Great Britain, of which 1,306,441 quarters came from the French Empire and its allied states. The explanation for this trade, as has already been pointed out, was the failure of the British harvest and the operation of the French Licence System. The value of this commerce to the Englishman must not be underestimated. It was well worth whatever treasure Napoleon exacted by way of payment. Without this importation there can be no doubt that prices would have risen still higher, and suffering would have increased at a most alarming rate. To insist, however, that an imperial embargo would have forced the British Government to its knees, is quite another matter.

Admitting, however, for the time being, that the European trade might have been closed during 1810, what would the effect have been in Great Britain? The answer to this will be found largely in another question, namely, What was the volume of the home production? Unfortunately, no definite statistics are available. There exist, nevertheless, certain methods of determining this amount.

Early in 1800 the Corn Committee of the House of Commons had estimated the home growth of wheat to be 6,700,000 quarters.[15] It will also be remembered that in 1801 Parliament enacted a *General Enclosure Act*. By 1810 over three quarters of a million acres had been brought under cultivation. During this decade the progress of agriculture had been tremendous. Scientific methods of farming as well as extensive improvements had stimulated a boom in agrarian circles. Capital invested freely. Societies for the advancement of agriculture were estab-

[15] *First Series,* IX: 125.

lished in all parts of the realm. Special magazines appeared devoting their entire space to the dissemination of agricultural knowledge. The daily newspapers often gave whole columns to a discussion of agricultural conditions. Popular magazines even devoted several pages of each issue to matters of interest to the farmer. The Board of Agriculture took the lead in offering prizes for improved crops or studies of investigation. This action brought as a reward a host of improvements and inventions. Land rents, values and wages all increased. There can be no doubt, therefore, that the domestic production had increased to a considerable degree.[16]

A more effective and convincing argument to show that there had been an increase in domestic production may be made in yet another fashion. In 1759, Mr. Charles Smith issued a pamphlet entitled *Tracts on the Corn Trade.*[17] It was the author's estimate that there were 6,000,000 people in England and that 3,750,000, or 62½ per cent, consumed an equivalent number of quarters of wheat. In addition to this quantity of home-grown wheat, some 90,000 quarters were annually produced for other purposes, which together with the amount exported made a total of 4,050,771 quarters. Of this, 4,168 quarters were imported, leaving as the total home production 4,046,603 quarters of wheat. Since 1759 there had been a gradual increase in the consumption of wheat, and a corresponding decrease in the use of oats, barley and rye.[18] How many people actually used wheat is a matter of conjecture. Arthur Young, whose opinion seems to have been generally accepted, stated, after applying Smith's tables to the population in 1810, that 8,500,000 people consumed an equivalent

[16] *Parl. Pap.*, 1814, No. 339, p. 3. Arthur Young estimated in 1814 that the yield per acre was 22 bushels. On the basis of the 750,000 acres that had been enclosed, the home production must have risen some 2,062,500 quarters; as it was, the home production increased 1,800,000 quarters: see *Parl. Pap.*, *ibid.*, p. 85.

[17] A new and revised edition of this work, edited by Chalmers, and containing marginal notes by Mr. Catherwood, general receiver of Corn Returns, appeared from the press of Stockdale, London, 1804.

[18] See Ashley, Sir Wm., "The Place of Rye in the History of English Food," in *Economic Journal,* Sept., 1921: see also Add. MSS., 35700, ff. 27–45, and Sheffield, Lord, *Remarks on the Deficiency of Grain,* p. 27; *Parl. Hist.,* XXXIV: 1490; *Commons' Journal,* 56: 211.

number of quarters of wheat. Having balanced the export and the import of wheat, Young then estimated that the total import was not quite equal to the demands of one sixth of the population.[19] Expressed in terms of weeks, the import amounted to a supply for eight and nine-tenths' weeks, leaving therefore, forty-three and one-tenth weeks' supply as the home production. Now whereas Smith estimated that $62\frac{1}{2}$ per cent consumed wheat in 1759, Young on the basis of a population of 10,791,115 people held that $78\frac{7}{10}$ per cent used wheat in 1810.[19a]

It must be remembered that of the 1,567,125 quarters of wheat imported in 1810, 260,684 quarters came from ports not under the control of Napoleon. Deducting from this amount the export trade of 73,431 quarters, we find that there is left a total of 187,253 quarters, or approximately one fifty-first of the total consumption. Expressed in terms of weeks this is a supply sufficient for one and one-tenth weeks. Now granting that Bonaparte might have prevented the export of all wheat from the continent, the total loss would have been an amount equal to a supply for seven and eight-tenths' weeks. To offset this loss, the English would have had access to other grains, and to the supplies saved by the distillation act, and would have increased the use of rice, and have adopted numerous substitutes, as had been done early in the century.[20] It seems quite likely, there-

[19] Add. MSS., 35700, ff. 236. Young estimated the import of 1810 at 1,530,691 quarters of wheat, whereas it actually was 1,567,125 quarters. He also estimated that the exports of wheat equalled 75,735 quarters; actually it was 73,431 quarters. There is no great difference in the result, namely, that the import equalled about one sixth of the amount consumed. In 1814 Parnell and Gascoyne estimated the total imports of all corn to be the equal of one twenty-fifth to one fortieth of the total consumption: see *Parl. Debates,* XXVII: 713, XXIX: 962, 967. See also Heckscher, E. F., *The Continental System,* pp. 337–338.

[19a] If we take 8,500,000 quarters as the amount of wheat consumed, one week's supply would have to average one fifty-second of that amount or 163,461 quarters. When the amount actually imported, 1,454,956 quarters, is divided by this weekly average, the result is a sum almost equal to a supply for eight and nine-tenths' weeks.

[20] See Appendix No. 8. In 1810 272,370 cwt. of rice were imported: see *Parl. Pap.,* 1814, No. 339, p. 127. See Heckscher, E. F., *op. cit.,* p. 338, for an interesting parallel between conditions in England during 1800–15 and in Sweden during the late World War.

fore, that the loss of continental wheat could not have forced the British to submission during the winter of 1810–11.

Conditions in Great Britain during this winter were by no means as severe as is generally supposed. One need only contrast this period with that of a decade earlier. During the first two years of the century the price of wheat in Great Britain was 100*s.* 5*d.* and 115*s.* 11*d.* per quarter respectively; and that in the face of the import of 1,264,520 quarters of wheat in 1800, and 1,424,765 quarters in 1801. In 1810, the price of wheat in Great Britain was 103*s.* 3*d.*, and in 1811, 92*s.* 5*d.* Imports in 1810 amounted to 1,567,125 quarters, and in 1811, to 336,130 quarters. The following table shows the average price in England and Wales during the winter months of 1800–01 and 1810–11:

1800–1801	*s.*	*d.*	1810–1811	*s.*	*d.*
Nov. 1	118	7	Nov. 3	99	11
Nov. 15	119	4	Nov. 17	100	9
Dec. 6	125	1	Dec. 1	99	4
Dec. 20	133	0	Dec. 15	97	1
Jan. 3	139	0	Jan. 5	94	7
Jan. 17	136	10	Jan. 19	96	0
Feb. 7	142	3	Feb. 2	95	6
Feb. 21	144	10	Feb. 16	95	0
March 7	152	1	March 2	94	1
March 14	156	2	March 16	92	7

Conditions, therefore, do not seem to have been as severe in the winter of 1810–11 as during the winter of 1800–01. In both years, 1800 and 1801, prices were higher during the winter months than in 1810 and 1811. Conditions were much more serious and more far-reaching measures were taken to afford relief in the winter of 1800–01 than in 1810–11. In spite of this, imports from foreign sources were less in 1800 than in 1810. Why then were prices lower in 1810? Because of an increase in the volume of imports over that of 1800? Partly, but not entirely. Prices were lower because the harvest of 1810 proved less disastrous than expected and because home production had increased during the past ten years.[21]

21 For Rose's views, see *Monthly Rev.*, March, 1902, pp. 71, 72. Here one notes that the critical time is the period of 1811–12. This idea also

Closer investigation leads to a still more interesting conclusion. It will be recalled that during the fall of 1810 Napoleon forbade the further export of corn from the Empire. Supplies from that source, therefore, were not available during the winter of 1810–11. And yet in the face of this and the growing trouble with America, prices actually fell in Great Britain. Is not this fact, that prices declined during the winter months of 1810–11, when foreign corn was being withheld by Napoleon, proof of great importance that the previous import of that year, plus the increase in domestic production, economy, and the use of substitutes, had been enough to feed a people during this crisis? This was, furthermore, a winter that experienced no such riots or acute distress as had occurred ten years before, or were to occur during the next year. If Great Britain did not go to the wall during the year 1812, it can hardly be believed that it would have done so during the previous winter, even though Napoleon had withheld supplies during the entire summer of 1810.[22]

And so it becomes apparent that had Napoleon had "the chance of starving Great Britain" he would have taken advantage of it. Unlike his successor in arms, the author of the Berlin Decree of 1917, Napoleon possessed no weapon capable of interfering with England's coastwise or overseas supplies of grain.[23] The England of 1810, however, was not the same England that she is today. At that time she was not so dependent upon foreign states for her food. Certainly, she had already ceased to be an exporting nation. She was able, however, by increased

---

appears in his *Napleonic Studies* (London, G. Bell & Sons, 1906), p. 216. In the 1902, 1907 and 1910 editions of the *Life of Napoleon,* II: 204, the date is that of the winter of 1810–11.

[22] See Heckscher, E. F., *op. cit.,* pp. 339–340, for an opinion that even in 1812, when food prices were very high, an absolute blockade of the continent would not have forced Britain to surrender. This view is very interesting, and contains, moreover, much that is true. It seems, however, that the author overlooks the extreme economic pressure that existed and which had been caused by the industrial and commercial crisis of that year.

[23] That Napoleon was keenly alive to this is evident from his remarks of June 24, 1811, for which see Tarle, E. V., *Kontinental'naja blokada,* I: 486, 494–495.

acreage, and by a careful policy of retrenchment and substitution, to augment her home supplies so that she could have been entirely self-sufficing, except for approximately seven weeks, even if Napoleon had possessed those deadly weapons of modern civilization, the submarine and the airplane.

APPENDICES

APPENDIX No. 1

A SELECTED LIST OF LAWS DEALING WITH THE CORN TRADE, PASSED DURING THE NAPOLEONIC PERIOD

(*Figures within the parentheses indicate the date of royal signature*)

39 and 40 Geo. 3, c. 8 (Oct. 12, 1799): Distillery Act for Scotland; to continue in force until March, 1800.
Continued by 39 and 40 Geo. 3, c. 21 (Feb. 28, 1800), to Feb. 1, 1801;
by 41 Geo. 3, c. 5 (Dec. 8, 1800), to Oct. 10, 1801;
by 42 Geo. 3, c. 5 (Dec. 11, 1801), to Jan. 1, 1802.

39 and 40 Geo. 3, c. 9 (Oct. 12, 1799): Distillery Act for England; to continue in force until June 1, 1800.

39 and 40 Geo. 3, c. 18 (Feb. 20, 1800): Stale Bread Act; to continue in force until six weeks after next session of Parliament.
Continued by 40 Geo. 3, c. 17 (Dec. 31, 1800);
Repealed by 42 Geo. 3, c. 4 (Nov. 21, 1801).

39 and 40 Geo. 3, c. 25 (March 25, 1800): Starch Act; to continue in force until Oct. 1, 1800.
Continued by 41 Geo. 3, c. 3 (Dec. 8, 1800), to Jan. 1, 1802.

39 and 40 Geo. 3, c. 29 (April 4, 1800): Wheat, Flour and Rice Bounty Act; to continue in force until Oct. 15, 1800.
Continued and amended by 41 Geo. 3, c. 10 (Dec. 15, 1800), to Oct. 1, 1801;
Explained by 41 Geo. 3, c. 19 (Dec. 31, 1800).
See also 41 Geo. 3, c. 13, U. K. (March 24, 1801).

39 and 40 Geo. 3, c. 35 (May 1, 1800): Oats Bounty Act; to continue in force until Oct. 15, 1800.

39 and 40 Geo. 3, c. 53 (June 30, 1800): Rye Bounty Act; to continue in force until Oct. 15, 1800.

39 Geo. 3, c. 87 (July 12, 1799): Act Granting Control over Corn Trade to the Crown; to continue in force until six weeks after next session of Parliament.
Continued by 39 and 40 Geo. 3, c. 9 (Oct. 12, 1799), to Sept. 30, 1800;
by 39 and 40 Geo. 3, c. 58 (June 30, 1800), to Dec. 21, 1800;

by 41 Geo. 3, c. 5 (Dec. 8, 1800), to Oct. 10, 1801;
by 42 Geo. 3, c. 13 (Dec. 11, 1801), to Jan. 1, 1803;
by 43 Geo. 3, c. 12 (Dec. 29, 1802), to Jan. 1, 1804;
by 44 Geo. 3, c. 4 (Dec. 15, 1803), to March 25, 1805;
by 45 Geo. 3, c. 26 (March 25, 1805), to March 25, 1806;
by 46 Geo. 3, c. 29 (April 2, 1806), to March 25, 1809;
by 49 Geo. 3, c. 23 (March 30, 1809), to March 25, 1810;
by 50 Geo. 3, c. 19 (April 6, 1810), to March 25, 1811;
by 51 Geo. 3, c. 14 (March 25, 1811), to six months after the ratification of peace.

39 and 40 Geo. 3, c. 91 (July 28, 1800): Act Forbidding the Exportation of Rice; to continue in force until Oct. 15, 1800.
Continued by 41 Geo. 3, c. 1 (Nov. 24, 1800), to Nov. 1, 1801.

41 Geo. 3, c. 2 (Nov. 24, 1800): Act Forbidding the Exportation of all Food; no time limit set.

41 Geo. 3, c. 3 (Dec. 8, 1800): Act Forbidding the Use of Corn in the Distillation of Spirits in England until Jan. 1, 1802.

41 Geo. 3, c. 16 (Dec. 31, 1800): Act Forbidding the Use of Fine Wheaten Flour or any Flour in the Manufacture of Bread; to continue in force until Nov. 6, 1801.
Suspended by 41 Geo. 3, c. 1, U. K. (Feb. 9, 1801), to March 25, 1801;
Repealed by 41 Geo. 3, c. 2, U. K. (Feb. 24, 1801), in respect to all other grain except wheat.

41 Geo. 3, c. 16, U. K. (March 24, 1800): Distillery Act for Ireland; to continue in force until March 25, 1801.

41 Geo. 3, c. 34, U. K. (April 30, 1800): Bounty Act for Ireland; to continue in force until Oct. 1, 1801.
See 41 Geo. 3, c. 92, U. K. (July 2, 1801).

41 Geo. 3, c. 36, U. K. (May 21, 1801): Act Granting Control over Corn Trade to the Lord Lieutenant of Ireland; to continue in force until six weeks after the next session of Parliament.
Continued by 42 Geo. 3, c. 13 (Dec. 11, 1801), to Jan. 1, 1803;
by 43 Geo. 3, c. 12 (Dec. 29, 1802), to Jan. 1, 1804;
by 44 Geo. 3, c. 12 (Dec. 15, 1803), to March 25, 1805;
by 45 Geo. 3, c. 26 (March 25, 1805), to March 25, 1806;
by 46 Geo. 3, c. 29 (April 2, 1806), to March 25, 1808;
by 48 Geo. 3, c. 27 (March 28, 1808), to March 25, 1809;
by 49 Geo. 3, c. 31 (April 28, 1809), to March 25, 1810;
by 50 Geo. 3, c. 16 (April 6, 1810), to March 25, 1811.

42 Geo. 3, c. 14 (Dec. 15, 1801): Act Permitting the Use of Rice and Potatoes in the Manufacture of Starch; to continue in force until July, 1802.

42 Geo. 3, c. 15 (Dec. 15, 1801): Distillery Act for Ireland;
Renewed by 44 Geo. 3, c. 11 (Dec. 5, 1803), to March 25, 1805;
Repealed by 44 Geo. 3, c. 89 (July 24, 1804).

42 Geo. 3, c. 35 (April 15, 1802): Act Regulating Trade between Great Britain and Ireland; to continue in force until Feb. 15, 1803.
Continued by 43 Geo. 3, c. 14 (Dec. 29, 1802), to July 1, 1803;
by 43 Geo. 3, c. 78 (July 4, 1803), to July 1, 1804;
by 44 Geo. 3, c. 65 (July 3, 1804), to July 1, 1805;
by 45 Geo. 3, c. 80 (July 2, 1805), to March 25, 1806;
by 46 Geo. 3, c. 29 (April 12, 1806), to March 25, 1808.

43 Geo. 3, c. 105 (July 27, 1803): Act Regulating the Exportation of Corn to the Channel Islands; to continue in force until July 27, 1805.
Made perpetual by 45 Geo. 3, c. 68 (June 27, 1805).

44 Geo. 3, c. 109 (July 30, 1804): General Corn Law for United Kingdom; no time limit set.
Explained and amended by 45 Geo. 3, c. 86 (July 10, 1805);
Explained by 46 Geo. 3, c. 11 (March 22, 1806).

46 Geo. 3, c. 97 (July 16, 1806): Act Establishing Free Trade in Corn between Great Britain and Ireland; no time limit set.
Explained by 47 Geo. 3, s. 2, c. 7 (Feb. 19, 1807).

48 Geo. 3, c. 69 (June 28, 1808): Sugar and Corn Trade Act for West Indies; to continue in force until March 25, 1810.
Continued by 50 Geo. 3, c. 13 (March 24, 1810), to March 25, 1813;
by 52 Geo. 3, c. 98 (July 9, 1812); no time limit set.

48 Geo. 3, c. 118 (June 30, 1808): Distillery Act for United Kingdom; to continue in force until Dec. 31, 1808.

48 Geo. 3, c. 125 (June 30, 1808): Corn Trade of West Indies; no time limit set.

49 Geo. 3, c. 7 (March 13, 1809): Distillery Act for United Kingdom; to continue in force until Dec. 31, 1809.
Continued by 50 Geo. 3, c. 5 (March 12, 1810), to Dec. 31, 1810;
by 52 Geo. 3, c. 3 (Feb. 7, 1812), to Dec. 31, 1812;
by 52 Geo. 3, c. 47 (May 5, 1812), to Dec. 31, 1812;
Amended by 52 Geo. 3, c. 118 (July 13, 1812);
Continued by 53 Geo. 3, c. 7 (Dec. 22, 1812), to Dec. 31, 1813.

52 Geo. 3, c. 127 (July 8, 1812): Starch Act; to continue in force until Nov. 1, 1812.
Continued by 53 Geo. 3, c. 2 (Dec. 16, 1812), to Oct. 1, 1813;
Repealed by 53 Geo. 3, c. 23 (March 23, 1813).

53 Geo. 3, c. 38 (April 15, 1813): Export Trade to British North American Colonies, as per 31 Geo. 3, c. 31; no time limit set.

54 Geo. 3, c. 69 (June 17, 1814): Corn Law of 1814; no time limit set.

55 Geo. 3, c. 26 (March 23, 1815): Corn Law of 1815; no time limit set.

ACTS OF AN ALLIED NATURE

41 Geo. 3, c. 12 (Dec. 22, 1800): Poor Relief; to continue in force until six weeks after next session of Parliament.

41 Geo. 3, c. 16 (Dec. 31, 1800): Assize Act; to continue in force until Nov. 6, 1801.
Repealed in part by 41 Geo. 3, c. 1, U. K. (Feb. 9, 1801);
Repealed altogether by 41 Geo. 3, c. 2, U. K. (Feb. 24, 1801).

41 Geo. 3, c. 18 (Dec. 31, 1800): Importation of Swedish Herring; to continue in force until Oct. 1, 1801.

41 Geo. 3, c. 11 (Dec. 15, 1800): Importation of Fish from Nova Scotia and other parts of British North America.

APPENDIX No. 2

TABLE SHOWING THE VARIOUS EXPORT DUTIES IN FORCE FROM 1791 TO 1815

From 1803 to 1814 a small ad valorem duty was collected.

31 Geo. 3, c. 30: 1791 — The exportation of corn, meal, flour, malt, bread, biscuit to foreign parts prohibited whenever the price at the port of exportation was at or above the following rates:

wheat	46*s*. per quarter.	
rye, beans, pease	30*s*. per quarter.	Duty Free,
barley, malt	23*s*. per quarter.	when prices
oats	15*s*. per quarter.	were lower.

33 Geo. 3, c. 65: 1793 — In addition to the foregoing, there was added oatmeal, which was prohibited when the price was at or above 14*s*. per boll. It also was duty free, when prices were lower.

44 Geo. 3, c. 109: 1804 — Exportation to foreign parts prohibited whenever the price at the port of exportation was at or above the following rates:

wheat	54*s*. per quarter.
rye, pease, beans	35*s*. per quarter.
barley, malt	31*s*. per quarter.
oats	19*s*. per quarter.

Duty free when prices were lower.

45 Geo. 3, c. 86: 1805 — No exportation from any district when the price in such district in the preceding week was at or above the import rates; otherwise exportation, duty free, was permitted.

54 Geo. 3, c. 69: 1814 — Corn, grain, meal and flour, bread and biscuit added by Treasury Order, might be exported at all times without payment of any duty or the granting of any bounty.

APPENDIX

TABLE SHOWING THE PROGRESSIVE

Species	Corn from Ireland and British North America	Corn from all other sources	Duty	From Nov. 15, 1791, by 31 Geo. 3, c. 30	
				s.	d.
				Per Quarter	
Wheat	Under 48*s*. per Q.	Under 50*s*.	High	24	3
	At or above 48*s*., but under 52*s*.	At or above 50*s*., but under 54*s*.	Low (1st)	2	6
	At or above 52*s*.	At or above 54*s*.	Low (2d)	0	6
Rye, Pease, Beans	Under 32*s*. per Q.	Under 34*s*.	High	22	0
	At or above 32*s*., but under 35*s*.	At or above 34*s*., but under 37*s*.	Low (1st)	1	6
	At or above 35*s*.	At or above 37*s*.	Low (2d)	0	3
Barley, Indian Corn	Under 24*s*. per Q.	Under 25*s*.	High	22	0
	At or above 24*s*., but under 26*s*.	At or above 25*s*., but under 27*s*.	Low (1st)	1	3
	At or above 26*s*.	At or above 27*s*.	Low (2d)	0	3
Oats	Under 16*s*. per Q.	Under 17*s*.	High	6	7
	At or above 16*s*., but under 17*s*.	At or above 17*s*., but under 18*s*.	Low (1st)	1	0
	At or above 17*s*.	At or above 18*s*.	Low (2d)	0	2
				Per	Cwt.
Wheat-meal or Flour	Under 48*s*. per Q.	Under 50*s*.	High	6	6
	At or above 48*s*., but under 52*s*.	At or above 50*s*., but under 54*s*.	Low (1st)	1	6
	At or above 52*s*.		Low (2d)	0	2
		At or above 54*s*.	Low (2d)	1	0
				Per	Boll
Oat-meal	Under 15*s*. per boll	Under 16*s*. per boll	High	8	0
	At or above 15*s*., but under 16*s*.	At or above 16*s*., but under 17*s*.	Low (1st)	1	0
	At or above 16*s*.		Low (2d)	0	2
		At or above 17*s*.	Low (2d)	0	6

Malt, and all ground corn, except wheat meal, flour, or oatmeal might not be imported after April 15, 1802. The trade from Ireland was changed by 42 Geo. 3, c. 35.

No. 3

INCREASE OF IMPORT DUTIES, 1791 TO 1814

From Dec. 31, 1796, with increase of 5 per cent by 37 Geo. 3, c. 15		From July 18, 1797, with increase of 5 per cent by 37 Geo. 3, c. 110		From July 5, 1803, with increase of $12\frac{1}{2}$ per cent by 43 Geo. 3, cc. 68, 70		From June 1, 1804, with increase of $12\frac{1}{2}$ per cent by 44 Geo. 3, c. 53	
s.	d.	s.	d.	s.	d.	s.	d.
Per Quarter		Per Quarter		Per Quarter		Per Quarter	
25	$5\frac{11}{20}$	26	$8\frac{1}{10}$	27	$3\frac{7}{20}$	30	$3\frac{3}{4}$
2	$7\frac{1}{2}$	2	9	2	$9\frac{3}{4}$	3	$1\frac{1}{2}$
0	$6\frac{6}{20}$	0	$6\frac{3}{5}$	0	$6\frac{3}{4}$	0	$7\frac{1}{2}$
23	$1\frac{1}{5}$	24	$2\frac{2}{5}$	24	9	27	6
1	$6\frac{9}{10}$	1	$7\frac{4}{5}$	1	$8\frac{1}{4}$	1	$10\frac{1}{2}$
0	$3\frac{3}{20}$	0	$3\frac{3}{10}$	0	$3\frac{7}{20}$	0	$3\frac{3}{4}$
23	$1\frac{1}{5}$	24	$2\frac{2}{5}$	24	9	27	6
1	$3\frac{3}{4}$	1	$4\frac{1}{2}$	1	$4\frac{17}{20}$	1	$6\frac{3}{4}$
0	$3\frac{3}{20}$	0	$3\frac{3}{10}$	0	$3\frac{7}{20}$	0	$3\frac{3}{4}$
6	$10\frac{19}{20}$	7	$2\frac{9}{10}$	7	$4\frac{17}{20}$	8	$2\frac{3}{4}$
1	$0\frac{3}{5}$	1	$1\frac{1}{5}$	1	$1\frac{1}{2}$	1	3
0	$2\frac{1}{10}$	0	$2\frac{1}{5}$	0	$2\frac{1}{4}$	0	$2\frac{1}{2}$
Per Cwt.		Per Cwt.		Per Cwt.		Per Cwt.	
6	$9\frac{9}{10}$	7	1	7	$3\frac{3}{4}$	8	$1\frac{1}{2}$
1	$6\frac{9}{10}$	1	$7\frac{4}{5}$	1	$8\frac{1}{4}$	1	$10\frac{1}{2}$
0	$2\frac{1}{10}$	0	$2\frac{1}{5}$	0	$2\frac{1}{4}$	0	$2\frac{1}{2}$
1	$0\frac{1}{2}$	1	$1\frac{1}{5}$	1	$1\frac{1}{2}$	1	3
Per Boll		Per Boll		Per Boll		Per Boll	
8	$4\frac{4}{5}$	8	$9\frac{3}{5}$	9	0	10	0
1	$0\frac{3}{5}$	1	$1\frac{1}{5}$	1	$1\frac{1}{2}$	1	3
0	$2\frac{1}{10}$	0	$2\frac{1}{5}$	0	$2\frac{1}{4}$	0	$2\frac{1}{2}$
0	$6\frac{3}{10}$	0	$6\frac{3}{5}$	0	$6\frac{3}{4}$	0	$7\frac{1}{2}$

The warehousing of corn without payment of duty was permitted, but when taken out for home consumption, in addition to the duties due at that time, those specified under the first low duty were also to be paid.

APPENDIX

TABLE SHOWING THE PROGRESSIVE

Species	Corn from British North America	Corn from all other sources	Duty	From Nov. 15, 1804, by 44 Geo. 3, c. 109, plus 12½ per cent by 44 Geo. 3, c. 53	
				s.	d.
				Per	Quarter
Wheat	Under 53*s.* per Q.	Under 63*s.* per Q.	High	30	3¾
	At or above 53*s.*, but under 56*s.*	At or above 63*s.*, but under 66*s.*	Low (1st)	3	1½
	At or above 56*s.*	At or above 66*s.*	Low (2d)	0	7½
Rye, Pease, Beans	Under 35*s.* per Q.	Under 42*s.* per Q.	High	27	6
	At or above 35*s.*, but under 37*s.*	At or above 42*s.*, but under 44*s.*	Low (1st)	1	10½
	At or above 37*s.*	At or above 44*s.*	Low (2d)	0	3¾
Barley, Indian Corn	Under 26*s.* per Q.	Under 31*s.* 6*d.* per Q.	High	27	6
	At or above 26*s.*, but under 28*s.*	At or above 31*s.* 6*d.*, but under 33*s.*	Low (1st)	1	6¾
	At or above 28*s.*	At or above 33*s.*	Low (2d)	0	3¾
Oats	Under 17*s.* per Q.	Under 21*s.* per Q.	High	8	2¾
	At or above 17*s.*, but under 18*s.*	At or above 21*s.*, but under 22*s.*	Low (1st)	1	3
	At or above 18*s.*	At or above 22*s.*	Low (2d)	0	2½
				Per	Cwt.
Wheat-meal or Flour	Under 53*s.* per Q.	Under 63*s.* per Q.	High	8	1½
	At or above 53*s.*, but under 56*s.*	At or above 63*s.*, but under 66*s.*	Low (1st)	1	10½
	At or above 56*s.*		Low (2d)	0	2½
		At or above 66*s.*	Low (2d)	1	3
				Per	Boll
Oat-meal	Under 16*s.* 6*d.* per boll...........	Under 20*s.* per boll	High	10	0
	At or above 16*s.* 6*d.*, but under 17*s.* 4*d.*	At or above 20*s.*, but under 21*s.*	Low (1st)	1	3
	At or above 17*s.* 4*d.*		Low (2d)	0	2½
		At or above 21*s.*	Low (2d)	0	7½

No. 3 (Continued)

INCREASE OF IMPORT DUTIES, 1791 TO 1814

From April 15, 1805, with increase of £2 10*s*. per cent by 45 Geo. 3, c. 29		From May 10, 1806, with increase of £8 6*s*. 8*d*. per cent by 46 Geo. 3, c. 42		From July 5, 1809, by Consolidation 49 Geo. 3, c. 98		From April 15, 1813, with increase of £25 per cent by 53 Geo. 3, c. 35	
s.	d.	s.	d.	s.	d.	s.	d.
Per Quarter		Per Quarter		Per Quarter		Per Quarter	
30	$11\frac{1}{40}$	32	$11\frac{11}{40}$	33	4	39	7
3	$2\frac{1}{4}$	3	$4\frac{3}{4}$	3	4	3	$11\frac{1}{2}$
0	$7\frac{13}{20}$	0	$8\frac{3}{20}$	0	8	0	$9\frac{1}{2}$
28	$0\frac{3}{5}$	29	$10\frac{3}{5}$	30	0	35	$7\frac{1}{2}$
1	$10\frac{19}{20}$	2	$0\frac{9}{20}$	2	0	2	$4\frac{1}{2}$
0	$3\frac{33}{40}$	0	$4\frac{3}{40}$	0	4	0	$4\frac{3}{4}$
28	$0\frac{3}{5}$	29	$10\frac{3}{5}$	30	0	35	$7\frac{1}{2}$
1	$7\frac{1}{8}$	1	$8\frac{3}{8}$	1	8	1	$11\frac{3}{4}$
0	$3\frac{33}{40}$	0	$4\frac{3}{40}$	0	4	0	$4\frac{3}{4}$
8	$4\frac{29}{40}$	8	$11\frac{37}{120}$	9	0	10	$8\frac{1}{4}$
1	$3\frac{3}{10}$	1	$4\frac{3}{10}$	1	4	1	7
0	$2\frac{11}{20}$	0	$2\frac{43}{60}$	0	4	0	$4\frac{3}{4}$
Per Cwt.		Per Cwt.		Per Cwt.		Per Cwt.	
8	$3\frac{9}{20}$	8	$9\frac{9}{20}$	9	0	10	$8\frac{1}{4}$
1	$10\frac{19}{20}$	2	$0\frac{9}{20}$	2	0	2	$4\frac{1}{2}$
0	$2\frac{11}{20}$	0	$2\frac{43}{60}$	0	4	0	$4\frac{3}{4}$
1	$3\frac{3}{10}$	1	$4\frac{3}{10}$	1	4	1	7
Per Boll		Per Boll		Per Boll		Per Boll	
10	$2\frac{2}{5}$	10	$10\frac{2}{5}$	11	0	13	$0\frac{3}{4}$
1	$3\frac{3}{10}$	1	$4\frac{3}{4}$	1	4	1	7
0	$2\frac{11}{20}$	0	$2\frac{43}{60}$	0	4	0	$4\frac{3}{4}$
0	$7\frac{13}{20}$	0	$8\frac{3}{20}$	0	8	0	$9\frac{1}{2}$

APPENDIX No. 4

AMOUNT OF DUTIES RECEIVED ON THE IMPORTATION OF CORN

(*Accounts and Papers*, 1898, vol. 34, pp. 258–259)

In the source used no distinction was made between England and Scotland before 1804. The first four entries under *England* represent, therefore, the duties for Great Britain.

Years ending January 5	England £	Scotland £	Ireland £	United Kingdom £
1800	936	No record	No record	No record
1801	0	....	....	....
1802	1,786	....	....	....
1803	30,398	....	....	....
1804	12,846	4,846	....	17,692
1805	17,557	3,812	1,367	22,736
1806	24,678	1,280	No record	25,958
1807	26,993	1,548	....	28,541
1808	36,112	2,581	....	38,693
1809	3,304	215	....	3,519
1810	33,718	2,262	....	35,980
1811	53,228	3,040	....	56,268
1812	6,971	843	....	7,814
1813	5,492	1,488	....	6,980
1814 *	—	—	—	—
1815	39,309	915	....	40,224

* Records destroyed by fire

APPENDIX No. 5

WEEKLY AVERAGE PRICE OF WHEAT PER QUARTER FOR ENGLAND AND WALES

(*Taken from the weekly averages for the inland and maritime counties as given in the London Gazette, 1800 to 1813*)

Week ending	s.	d.	Week ending	s.	d.	Week ending	s.	d.
1800			Sept. 6	107	3	April 25	148	6
Jan. 4	92	7	Sept. 13	108	1	May 2	143	11
Jan. 11	94	8	Sept. 20	107	0	May 9	135	8
Jan. 18	95	9	Sept. 27	101	0	May 16	127	4
Jan. 25	95	10	Oct. 4	99	6	May 23	120	5
Feb. 1	98	4	Oct. 11	103	8	May 30	124	4
Feb. 8	100	2	Oct. 18	108	7	June 6	126	8
Feb. 15	103	1	Oct. 25	114	5	June 13	129	1
Feb. 22	106	1	Nov. 1	118	7	June 20	129	11
March 1	107	6	Nov. 8	118	11	June 27	129	1
March 8	107	3	Nov. 15	119	4	July 4	129	8
March 15	108	10	Nov. 22	120	10	July 11	132	2
March 22	107	8	Nov. 29	123	6	July 18	136	11
March 29	108	3	Dec. 6	125	1	July 25	141	11
April 5	108	7	Dec. 13	128	5	Aug. 1	138	8
April 12	110	4	Dec. 20	133	0	Aug. 8	132	7
April 19	113	0	Dec. 27	137	0	Aug. 15	124	9
April 26	115	9				Aug. 22	113	5
May 3	119	2				Aug. 29	99	6
May 10	121	10	**1801**			Sept. 5	93	4
May 17	121	1	Jan. 3	139	0	Sept. 12	90	10
May 24	119	11	Jan. 10	138	11	Sept. 19	88	10
May 31	119	1	Jan. 17	136	10	Sept. 26	88	3
June 7	120	5	Jan. 24	136	8	Oct. 3	86	6
June 14	123	0	Jan. 31	140	0	Oct. 10	83	4
June 21	126	1	Feb. 7	142	3	Oct. 17	77	2
June 28	130	8	Feb. 14	144	10	Oct. 24	70	7
July 5	134	5	Feb. 21	146	8	Oct. 31	69	6
July 12	136	4	Feb. 28	149	5	Nov. 7	68	4
July 19	136	4	March 7	152	1	Nov. 14	69	4
July 26	132	3	March 14	155	2	Nov. 21	71	7
Aug. 2	121	11	March 21	156	2	Nov. 28	75	2
Aug. 9	107	10	March 28	154	2	Dec. 5	75	5
Aug. 16	96	2	April 4	154	8	Dec. 12	75	1
Aug. 23	92	5	April 11	153	4	Dec. 19	74	10
Aug 30	99	6	April 18	150	6	Dec. 26	76	5

APPENDIX No. 5 (Continued)

Week ending	s.	d.	Week ending	s.	d.	Week ending	s.	d.
1802			Oct. 9	61	10	July 2	60	4
Jan. 2	75	6	Oct. 16	61	8	July 9	59	7
Jan. 9	76	1	Oct. 23	60	9	July 16	*	*
Jan. 16	76	9	Oct. 30	60	6	July 23	57	7
Jan. 23	76	7	Nov. 6	60	0	July 30	56	10
Jan. 30	76	4	Nov. 13	59	7	Aug. 6	56	1
Feb. 6	76	2	Nov. 20	59	1	Aug. 13	55	9
Feb. 13	75	0	Nov. 27	59	2	Aug. 20	55	11
Feb. 20	73	7	Dec. 4	58	8	Aug. 27	56	10
Feb. 27	72	11	Dec. 11	58	2	Sept. 3	56	2
March 6	72	6	Dec. 18	58	0	Sept. 10	56	0
March 13	72	11	Dec. 25	57	3	Sept. 17	55	5
March 20	74	0				Sept. 24	54	9
March 27	74	8				Oct. 1	54	5
April 3	73	0	**1803**			Oct. 8	54	6
April 10	69	10	Jan. 1	57	1	Oct. 15	53	11
April 17	68	2	Jan. 8	56	9	Oct. 22	54	1
April 24	68	0	Jan. 15	56	9	Oct. 29	54	2
May 1	67	6	Jan. 22	56	8	Nov. 5	54	5
May 8	65	5	Jan. 29	56	7	Nov. 12	54	10
May 15	64	4	Feb. 5	57	2	Nov. 19	54	9
May 22	64	0	Feb. 12	56	8	Nov. 26	54	8
May 29	64	11	Feb. 19	56	5	Dec. 3	54	9
June 5	66	1	Feb. 26	56	1	Dec. 10	53	9
June 12	66	77	March 5	56	3	Dec. 17	53	8
June 19	67	10	March 12	55	8	Dec. 24	53	1
June 26	67	9	March 19	56	6	Dec. 31	52	5
July 3	67	5	March 26	56	10			
July 10	66	10	April 2	56	8			
July 17	67	1	April 9	56	9	**1804**		
July 24	67	4	April 16	56	5	Jan. 7	52	3
July 31	68	1	April 23	56	6	Jan. 14	51	10
Aug. 7	69	11	April 30	56	9	Jan. 21	51	4
Aug. 14	69	5	May 7	56	11	Jan. 28	51	3
Aug. 21	69	2	May 14	57	8	Feb. 4	50	7
Aug. 28	67	8	May 21	57	9	Feb. 11	50	2
Sept. 4	67	8	May 28	59	4	Feb. 18	50	2
Sept. 11	67	4	June 4	61	5	Feb. 25	49	8
Sept. 18	67	3	June 11	61	5	March 3	49	7
Sept. 25	66	11	June 18	61	8	March 10	50	0
Oct. 2	64	9	June 25	61	3	March 17	50	0

* The *London Gazette* showed no average for this week.

APPENDIX No. 5 (Continued)

Week Ending	s.	d.	Week Ending	s.	d.	Week Ending	s.	d.
March 24	50	7	**1805**			Oct. 19	81	4
March 31	50	8	Jan. 5	86	2	Oct. 26	77	11
April 7	50	9	Jan. 12	86	6	Nov. 2	78	10
April 14	51	10	Jan. 19	86	7	Nov. 9	78	7
April 21	51	6	Jan. 26	86	0	Nov. 16	78	7
April 28	51	7	Feb. 2	87	5	Nov. 23	78	5
May 5	51	9	Feb. 9	89	6	Nov. 30	77	1
May 12	51	9	Feb. 16	91	7	Dec. 7	76	0
May 19	51	7	Feb. 23	91	11	Dec. 14	75	5
May 26	51	8	March 2	91	8	Dec. 21	76	2
June 2	51	10	March 9	92	4	Dec. 28	76	6
June 9	51	10	March 16	93	0			
June 16	51	9	March 23	93	3			
June 23	52	2	March 30	93	2	**1806**		
June 30	52	4	April 6	91	11	Jan. 4	75	11
July 7	52	1	April 13	91	10	Jan. 11	75	7
July 14	52	10	April 20	91	8	Jan. 18	75	8
July 21	53	9	April 27	90	2	Jan. 25	75	5
July 28	54	10	May 4	89	5	Feb. 1	74	6
Aug. 4	56	4	May 11	87	6	Feb. 8	74	6
Aug. 11	57	8	May 18	87	8	Feb. 15	74	3
Aug. 18	60	1	May 25	88	8	Feb. 22	74	10
Aug. 25	64	11	June 1	90	1	March 1	74	7
Sept. 1	66	5	June 8	90	0	March 8	74	4
Sept. 8	65	6	June 15	89	11	March 15	74	4
Sept. 15	64	3	June 22	89	4	March 22	74	3
Sept. 22	64	6	June 29	89	2	March 29	74	7
Sept. 29	65	4	July 6	89	9	April 5	74	5
Oct. 6	65	10	July 13	90	1	April 12	75	4
Oct. 13	67	2	July 20	90	1	April 19	77	4
Oct. 20	68	8	July 27	93	5	April 26	81	1
Oct. 27	70	9	Aug. 3	95	8	May 3	82	10
Nov. 3	74	4	Aug. 10	98	6	May 10	84	10
Nov. 10	76	10	Aug. 17	100	0	May 17	84	6
Nov. 17	81	9	Aug. 24	98	3	May 24	84	6
Nov. 24	85	9	Aug. 31	95	7	May 31	84	11
Dec. 1	86	3	Sept. 7	90	10	June 7	84	5
Dec. 8	86	11	Sept. 14	89	11	June 14	84	8
Dec. 15	84	4	Sept. 21	88	10	June 21	84	0
Dec. 22	84	4	Sept. 28	87	1	June 28	82	11
Dec. 29	86	3	Oct. 5	84	11	July 5	81	10
			Oct. 12	83	4	July 12	81	6

APPENDIX No. 5 (Continued)

Week Ending	s.	d.	Week Ending	s.	d.	Week Ending	s.	d.
July 19	82	5	April 18	76	6	Jan. 16	68	11
July 26	83	0	April 25	75	11	Jan. 23	68	11
Aug. 2	83	5	May 2	75	9	Jan. 30	69	2
Aug. 9	82	9	May 9	75	1	Feb. 6	69	0
Aug. 16	81	7	May 16	75	6	Feb. 13	69	2
Aug. 23	80	9	May 23	75	8	Feb. 20	69	5
Aug. 30	80	7	May 30	75	1	Feb. 27	69	6
Sept. 6	80	8	June 6	74	3	March 5	69	4
Sept. 13	81	3	June 13	74	3	March 12	69	3
Sept. 20	80	8	June 20	74	6	March 19	69	8
Sept. 27	80	2	June 27	74	0	March 26	69	8
Oct. 4	80	2	July 4	73	5	April 2	70	1
Oct. 11	79	5	July 11	73	0	April 9	71	1
Oct. 18	78	8	July 18	73	6	April 16	71	0
Oct. 25	78	6	July 25	73	10	April 23	71	4
Nov. 1	78	0	Aug. 1	74	9	April 30	71	4
Nov. 8	77	8	Aug. 8	75	2	May 7	72	0
Nov. 15	77	4	Aug. 15	75	5	May 14	72	11
Nov. 22	77	0	Aug. 22	74	10	May 21	73	11
Nov. 29	76	9	Aug. 29	73	9	May 28	75	0
Dec. 6	76	0	Sept. 5	72	11	June 4	76	9
Dec. 13	76	7	Sept. 12	71	10	June 11	79	5
Dec. 20	77	6	Sept. 19	71	2	June 18	80	6
Dec. 27	77	7	Sept. 26	71	0	June 25	80	5
			Oct. 3	70	5	July 2	81	1
			Oct. 10	69	6	July 9	81	4
1807			Oct. 17	68	7	July 16	81	6
Jan. 3	76	9	Oct. 24	67	4	July 23	81	5
Jan. 10	77	1	Oct. 31	66	10	July 30	81	6
Jan. 17	77	0	Nov. 7	66	1	Aug. 6	81	3
Jan. 24	76	10	Nov. 14	65	9	Aug. 13	81	3
Jan. 31	76	9	Nov. 21	65	7	Aug. 20	81	3
Feb. 7	76	1	Nov. 28	66	8	Aug. 27	82	1
Feb. 14	75	8	Dec. 5	66	11	Sept. 3	82	7
Feb. 21	75	9	Dec. 12	67	4	Sept. 10	82	9
Feb. 28	76	6	Dec. 19	68	0	Sept. 17	84	1
March 7	76	7	Dec. 26	69	1	Sept. 24	86	9
March 14	77	0				Oct. 1	86	5
March 21	76	5				Oct. 8	85	0
March 28	76	10	**1808**			Oct. 15	85	5
April 4	76	10	Jan. 2	69	5	Oct. 22	87	0
April 11	76	11	Jan. 9	69	5	Oct. 29	89	1

APPENDIX No. 5 (Continued)

Week Ending	s.	d.	Week Ending	s.	d.	Week Ending	s.	d.
Nov. 5	90	9	July 29	89	9	April 21	105	4
Nov. 12	91	7	Aug. 5	91	5	April 28	106	4
Nov. 19	92	7	Aug. 12	93	4	May 5	106	8
Nov. 26	93	2	Aug. 19	94	3	May 12	108	2
Dec. 3	91	9	Aug. 26	95	9	May 19	110	1
Dec. 10	89	9	Sept. 2	98	8	May 26	112	8
Dec. 17	90	2	Sept. 9	100	1	June 2	115	4
Dec. 24	90	10	Sept. 16	101	9	June 9	116	9
Dec. 31	91	9	Sept. 23	103	10	June 16	*	
			Sept. 30	108	10	June 23	114	5
			Oct. 7	109	6	June 30	114	5
1809			Oct. 14	106	7	July 7	113	4
Jan. 7	90	4	Oct. 21	103	10	July 14	114	4
Jan. 14	89	10	Oct. 28	102	3	July 21	114	0
Jan. 21	90	6	Nov. 4	101	11	July 28	113	7
Jan. 28	91	7	Nov. 11	101	5	Aug. 4	115	0
Feb. 4	92	4	Nov. 18	101	9	Aug. 11	115	2
Feb. 11	92	7	Nov. 25	102	3	Aug. 18	116	2
Feb. 18	92	5	Dec. 2	102	7	Aug. 25	117	4
Feb. 25	93	7	Dec. 9	102	10	Sept. 1	115	7
March 4	94	9	Dec. 16	102	9	Sept. 8	113	6
March 11	95	7	Dec. 23	102	4	Sept. 15	109	11
March 18	94	9	Dec. 30	102	2	Sept. 22	107	6
March 25	94	11				Sept. 29	105	8
April 1	94	1				Oct. 6	104	1
April 8	92	7	**1810**			Oct. 13	102	10
April 15	92	4	Jan. 6	102	6	Oct. 20	101	1
April 22	93	6	Jan. 13	101	6	Oct. 27	99	7
April 29	93	10	Jan. 20	101	10	Nov. 3	99	11
May 6	94	2	Jan. 27	101	10	Nov. 10	100	2
May 13	92	10	Feb. 3	101	6	Nov. 17	100	9
May 20	90	3	Feb. 10	100	0	Nov. 24	100	0
May 27	89	5	Feb. 17	99	11	Dec. 1	99	4
June 3	89	4	Feb. 24	100	0	Dec. 8	98	7
June 10	88	6	March 3	100	1	Dec. 15	97	1
June 17	88	8	March 10	100	7	Dec. 22	95	11
June 24	87	0	March 17	102	3	Dec. 29	94	7
July 1	88	1	March 24	103	6			
July 8	87	9	March 31	104	8	**1811**		
July 15	87	11	April 7	104	4	Jan. 5	94	7
July 22	88	8	April 14	104	11	Jan. 12	95	9

* The *London Gazette* showed no average for this week.

APPENDIX No. 5 (Continued)

Week ending	s.	d.	Week ending	s.	d.	Week ending	s.	d.
Jan. 19	96	0	Nov. 9	103	7	Aug. 8	152	3
Jan. 26	95	11	Nov. 16	105	5	Aug. 15	155	0
Feb. 2	95	6	Nov. 23	107	10	Aug. 22	154	6
Feb. 9	95	1	Nov. 30	108	2	Aug. 29	151	8
Feb. 16	95	0	Dec. 7	107	1	Sept. 5	149	3
Feb. 23	94	2	Dec. 14	106	3	Sept. 12	141	2
March 2	94	1	Dec. 21	106	8	Sept. 19	132	9
March 9	93	4	Dec. 28	106	7	Sept. 26	123	0
March 16	92	7				Oct. 3	117	10
March 23	92	3				Oct. 10	112	4
March 30	91	1	**1812**			Oct. 17	110	1
April 6	91	0	Jan. 4	106	7	Oct. 24	111	11
April 13	88	11	Jan. 11	105	11	Oct. 31	115	11
April 20	88	7	Jan. 18	105	11	Nov. 7	120	1
April 27	87	4	Jan. 25	104	8	Nov. 14	122	8
May 4	87	6	Feb. 1	104	0	Nov. 21	121	8
May 11	87	7	Feb. 8	103	8	Nov. 28	121	5
May 18	88	9	Feb. 15	105	1	Dec. 5	121	5
May 25	88	6	Feb. 22	106	2	Dec. 12	120	10
June 1	88	5	Feb. 29	107	0	Dec. 19	121	0
June 8	87	9	March 7	108	8	Dec. 26	120	7
June 15	86	8	March 14	110	4			
June 22	86	8	March 21	113	1			
June 29	86	4	March 28	117	7	**1813**		
July 6	86	11	April 4	122	0	Jan. 2	119	10
July 13	86	10	April 11	123	7	Jan. 9	118	8
July 20	87	5	April 18	126	11	Jan. 16	118	9
July 27	87	6	April 25	129	5	Jan. 23	121	9
Aug. 3	88	3	May 2	130	8	Jan. 30	120	5
Aug. 10	89	3	May 9	132	4	Feb. 6	120	7
Aug. 17	91	1	May 16	133	7	Feb. 13	120	5
Aug. 24	93	0	May 23	132	10	Feb. 20	119	2
Aug. 31	94	3	May 30	133	1	Feb. 27	119	9
Sept. 7	95	6	June 6	132	3	March 6	120	5
Sept. 14	96	11	June 13	132	5	March 13	121	2
Sept. 21	97	11	June 20	133	10	March 20	122	8
Sept. 28	97	6	June 27	137	1	March 27	122	11
Oct. 5	98	9	July 4	140	9	April 3	122	2
Oct. 12	99	6	July 11	144	5	April 10	121	10
Oct. 19	100	4	July 18	146	0	April 17	119	11
Oct. 26	101	6	July 25	146	11	April 24	119	7
Nov. 2	102	4	Aug. 1	148	0	May 1	119	2

APPENDIX No. 5 (Continued)

Week ending	s.	d.	Week ending	s.	d.	Week ending	s.	d.
May 8	118	3	July 31	116	7	Oct. 23	93	5
May 15	117	5	Aug. 7	115	9	Oct. 30	91	10
May 22	117	4	Aug. 14	114	4	Nov. 6	90	0
May 29	117	1	Aug. 21	112	0	Nov. 13	87	5
June 5	117	11	Aug. 28	107	11	Nov. 20	85	1
June 12	118	5	Sept. 4	103	4	Nov. 27	82	4
June 19	117	10	Sept. 11	100	2	Dec. 4	77	9
June 26	117	5	Sept. 18	98	11	Dec. 11	72	7
July 3	116	3	Sept. 25	98	1	Dec. 18	73	6
July 10	115	11	Oct. 2	96	1	Dec. 25	75	10
July 17	116	5	Oct. 9	94	11			
July 24	116	1	Oct. 16	93	4			

The foregoing list of prices has been used generally throughout this work. Only when a particular discussion called for either an export or an import price were the maritime county averages used. It seemed wise to use the general average and not the maritime average for the reason that the former showed the price for each week, while only in the case of the maritime export price was the maritime average given for each week. Again, the maritime average was based solely upon the averages of the maritime counties, while the general average was based upon both the maritime and inland counties. The use of either the general or maritime average for England and Wales (and for Scotland, for that matter) is, without doubt, open to question. The lack of adequate machinery to administer in detail the numerous provisions of the act of 1791, which had determined the general scheme for fixing the prices, made possible the existence of many faults. The Commons' Committee for 1820, whose report may be found in *Parl. Pap.*, 1820, No. 255, showed very clearly the relative inadequacy of the existing methods of fixing prices. In spite of these faults, the averages as given in the *London Gazette* are probably a more accurate estimate than any of the record of prices kept by towns or schools. Again, the prices in the *Gazette* are for all England and Wales, not for a particular town, and were, moreover, the official prices upon which rested the grain trade of England.

Prior to the week ending Nov. 10, 1804, the prices as given in the *Gazette* showed (1) an individual weekly average for each inland county, and an individual average for the various parts of each maritime county in England and Wales; (2) a weekly average price for all the counties, inland and maritime, of England and Wales; (3) a weekly average price for each maritime county of England and Wales, which price determined the export trade of corn from each maritime county; and a quarterly average price, based upon an average of the averages of the past quarter, for each maritime county of England and Wales, which average price determined the import into each maritime county; (4) an individual weekly average price for all parts of Scotland; (5) a quarterly average price, based upon the average of the averages of the past quarter, for each maritime district of Scotland, which price determined the import of corn into each Scottish district; and an average price, made up every six weeks on the averages of the past six weeks, for each maritime district of Scotland, which price determined the export of corn from each Scottish district; (6) an average price for all Scotland, which price was made up every six weeks.

Beginning with the week ending Nov. 10, 1804, the various prices as given in the *Gazette* were changed as a result of 44 Geo. 3, c. 109. The *Gazette* now showed: (1) individual weekly prices continuing as above; (2) weekly average price for counties as above; (3) a weekly average price, based upon the weekly averages of the maritime counties, for all England and Wales, and this weekly average price determined the export of corn from all England and Wales, doing away with the weekly average price of each county which had determined the export from each maritime county as had been the case before the act of 1804; also a quarterly average price, based upon the average of the weekly maritime counties, for the past quarter, which quarterly average price determined the import of corn into all England and Wales, doing away with the former quarterly average price of each maritime county which had determined the import into each maritime county as had been the case before the act of 1804; (4) an individual average price for all parts of Scotland; (5) quarterly average price, based upon the average of the averages of the Scottish maritime districts for the past quarter, for all Scotland, which quarterly average price determined the import of corn into all Scotland, as opposed to the system which had existed before 1804; and an average price, made up every six weeks on the average of the averages of the past six weeks for all Scotland, which average price determined the export of corn from all Scotland as opposed to the system which had existed before the act of 1804; (6) an average price for all Scotland, which price was made up every six weeks.

According to the method adopted since Nov. 10, 1804, the quarterly average price of each maritime district either in England or Scotland had not been published; only the average of the averages of the maritime counties in England and Wales, and the average of the averages of the maritime districts in Scotland were printed every quarter. Beginning with the week ending Jan. 19, 1805, the quarterly average of each maritime district in both Scotland and England reappear. Quarterly averages of all the maritime districts in both Scotland and England continue to be published.

Beginning with the week ending Aug. 9, 1805, the *Gazette* showed an important change, as a result of 45 Geo. 3, c. 86. In accordance with the terms of this law, the quarterly average price, based upon the averages of all the maritime counties in England and Wales, and the weekly average price, based upon the averages of all the maritime counties in England and Wales, determine the export and the import of corn of Great Britain. This quarterly average price governing the import of corn, and this weekly average price determining the export of corn, are given in the *Gazette*. Quarterly average prices for each district are now left out. Weekly average prices for each district in England and in Scotland are still printed.

Amount of Duty Levied in England and Wales on the Import of Wheat, according to Quarterly Average Prices for Each Maritime County

DATE	DUTY
Feb. 15, 1800 May 10, 1800 Aug. 9, 1800 Nov. 15, 1800 Feb. 14, 1801 May 9, 1801 Aug. 15, 1801 Nov. 14, 1801 Feb. 13, 1802 May 15, 1802 Aug. 15, 1802 Nov. 13, 1802	In all the twelve maritime Districts of England and Wales, both foreign and colonial wheat paid the same duty of $6\frac{3}{5}$*d.* per quarter.
Feb. 12, 1803 May 14, 1803	In all of the Districts, except the 2d, 3d and 4th, both foreign and colonial wheat paid the duty of $6\frac{3}{5}$*d.* per quarter. In these three Districts foreign wheat paid the duty of 2*s.* 9*d.* per quarter, and colonial paid a duty of $6\frac{3}{5}$*d.*
Aug. 13, 1803	All Districts paid $6\frac{3}{4}$*d.* per quarter for both foreign and colonial wheat.
Nov. 12, 1803	Foreign and colonial wheat paid a duty of $6\frac{3}{4}$*d.* in Districts 1, 2, 4, 7, 8, 11. In Districts 5 and 6 a duty of 2*s.* $9\frac{3}{4}$*d.* was levied on both. In Districts 3, 9, 10, 12, foreign wheat paid 2*s.* $9\frac{3}{4}$*d.*, while colonial wheat paid $6\frac{3}{4}$*d.* per quarter.
Feb. 11, 1804	Foreign and colonial wheat paid 2*s.* $9\frac{3}{4}$*d.* per quarter in Districts 1, 9, 10, 12. In Districts 2, 3, 4 a duty of 27*s.* $3\frac{7}{20}$*d.* was levied on both. In Districts 7, 8–11 both foreign and colonial wheat paid $6\frac{3}{4}$*d.* per quarter. In District 5 foreign wheat paid a duty of 27*s.* $3\frac{7}{20}$*d.*, and colonial wheat paid but 2*s.* $9\frac{3}{4}$*d.* per quarter. In District 6, foreign wheat paid 2*s.* $9\frac{3}{4}$*d.* and colonial wheat paid $6\frac{3}{4}$*d.* per quarter.
Aug. 11, 1804	In Districts 1, 5, 6, 7, 8, 9, 11, 12 both foreign and colonial wheat was subject to $7\frac{1}{2}$*d.* per quarter. In Districts 2, 4, a duty of 3*s.* $1\frac{1}{2}$*d.* was levied on both foreign and colonial wheat. In District 3 a charge of 30*s.* $3\frac{3}{4}$*d.* per quarter was made on all foreign and colonial wheat. In District 10, foreign wheat paid 3*s.* $1\frac{1}{2}$*d.*, and colonial wheat paid but $7\frac{1}{2}$*d.*, per quarter.

AGGREGATE AVERAGE PRICE OF WHEAT OF THE TWELVE DISTRICTS OF ENGLAND

These prices are taken from the *London Gazette*. Prior to Nov. 10, 1804, the *Gazette* published the average price for each district; this, however, was rendered unnecessary by 44 Geo. 3, c. 109.

Date	Price per Quarter		Duty per Quarter: Foreign Wheat		Duty per Quarter: Colonial Wheat	
	s.	d.	s.	d.	s.	d.
Nov. 10, 1804	70	5		$7\frac{1}{2}$		$7\frac{1}{2}$
Feb. 9, 1805	87	8		$7\frac{1}{2}$		$7\frac{1}{2}$
May 11, 1805	90	6		$7\frac{13}{20}$		$7\frac{13}{20}$
Aug. 10, 1805	92	2		$7\frac{13}{20}$		$7\frac{13}{20}$
Nov. 9, 1805	78	8		$7\frac{13}{20}$		$7\frac{13}{20}$
Feb. 15, 1806	72	8		$7\frac{13}{20}$		$7\frac{13}{20}$
May 10, 1806	76	11		$8\frac{3}{20}$		$8\frac{3}{20}$
Aug. 9, 1806	80	2		$8\frac{3}{20}$		$8\frac{3}{20}$
Nov. 15, 1806	75	11		$8\frac{3}{20}$		$8\frac{3}{20}$
Feb. 4, 1807	76	1		$8\frac{3}{20}$		$8\frac{3}{20}$
May 9, 1807	75	11		$8\frac{3}{20}$		$8\frac{3}{20}$
Aug. 15, 1807	74	9		$8\frac{3}{20}$		$8\frac{3}{20}$
Nov. 14, 1807	67	2		$8\frac{3}{20}$		$8\frac{3}{20}$
Feb. 13, 1808	69	3		$8\frac{3}{20}$		$8\frac{3}{20}$
May 14, 1808	71	7		$8\frac{3}{20}$		$8\frac{3}{20}$
Aug. 13, 1808	81	4		$8\frac{3}{20}$		$8\frac{3}{20}$
Nov. 12, 1808	87	2		$8\frac{3}{20}$		$8\frac{3}{20}$
Feb. 11, 1809	91	7		$8\frac{3}{20}$		$8\frac{3}{20}$
May 13, 1809	92	9		$8\frac{3}{20}$		$8\frac{3}{20}$
July 12, 1809	89	3		8		8
Nov. 11, 1809	100	3		8		8
Feb. 10, 1810	98	7		8		8
May 12, 1810	102	9		8		8
Aug. 11, 1810	112	7		8		8
Nov. 10, 1810	97	2		8		8
Feb. 9, 1811	92	4		8		8
May 11, 1811	86	4		8		8
Aug. 10, 1811	87	1		8		8
Nov. 9, 1811	97	11		8		8
Feb. 15, 1812	102	3		8		8
May 9, 1812	124	5		8		8
Aug. 15, 1812	145	5		8		8
Nov. 14, 1812	112	3		8		8
Feb. 13, 1813	118	1		8		8
May 15, 1813	116	8		$9\frac{1}{2}$		$9\frac{1}{2}$
Aug. 14, 1813	112	6		$9\frac{1}{2}$		$9\frac{1}{2}$
Nov. 13, 1813	89	2		$9\frac{1}{2}$		$9\frac{1}{2}$

APPENDIX No. 6

A SELECTED LIST OF LICENCES AND ORDERS IN COUNCIL

FORM OF ORDER IN COUNCIL FOR LICENCES TO IMPORT AS SETTLED BY ADVOCATE GENERAL, MARCH 18, 1800

(*To be found among the Privy Council Unbound Papers, March, 1800*)

Whereas there was this day read at the Board the humble petition (here insert petitioners names) praying a Licence and passport to import from (name the place or places) on board (name of ship) a cargo of (insert the cargo or cargoes). Which petition being taken into consideration, it is hereby Ordered in Council that a Licence be accordingly granted to to import from on board (neutral ship or ships) although cleared out for a neutral port, such quantity of the above mentioned articles (being British or neutral property) as may be specified in (his or their) Bill of Lading to remain in force for the space of six months from the date hereof; provided that any person who shall claim the benefit of the Licence hereby granted shall take and have the same upon condition that if any question shall arise in any Court of Admiralty or elsewhere, whether the person or persons obtaining such Licence has or have in all points conformed thereto in all cases whatsoever, the proof shall lie on the person or persons obtaining or using such Licence or claiming the benefit thereof; And the Right Honourable Lord Pelham, one of His Majesty's Principal Secretaries of State, is to cause a Licence or Passport to be prepared for His Majesty's Royal Signature accordingly in case His Lordship should see no objection thereto.

A GENERAL IMPORT LICENCE, JUNE 29, 1803

(*This licence is to be found among the Privy Council Unbound Papers, 1803. Entries in italics appear in longhand in the original. See the licence granted Sept. 24, 1806, to Messrs. Hall & Co., a copy of which is given in this Appendix.*)

GEORGE R.

George the Third, by the Grace of God, of the United Kingdom of Great Britain and Ireland, Defender of the Faith etc. To all Commanders of our ships of War and Privateers, and to all others whom it may concern, Greeting:

Our will and pleasure is that you permit, *Messrs Campbell & Bowden & Co.*

on board *Three neutral vessels* (*the names of which they are unable to set forth*)

to import without molestation *from the Ports of Bordeaux, Charente, Rochelle Bayonne, Toulon, Marseilles and Cette to the ports of London, Hull, Bristol, Southampton, Guernsey, Jersey or Alderney*
Such quantities of *grain and salted provisions of all sorts, seeds, hops, starch, rags, turpentine, hides, skins, honey, wax, fruit, and raw materials, brandy, linseed cakes, tallow, weld, wine and verdigrease, bark, and naval stores* (*being British or neutral property*)
as may be specified in *their* bills of lading: Provided that the same shall be shipped as aforesaid. This Licence to remain in force for the space of *Six* months from the date hereof, and no longer; Provided also that any Person who shall claim the benefit of the Licence hereby granted, shall take and have the same upon condition, that if any question arises in any of our Courts of Admiralty or elsewhere, whether such Person or Persons hath or have not in all points conformed thereto in all cases whatsoever the proof shall lie on the Person or Persons using this our Licence or claiming the benefit hereof.

Given at our Court at St. James the *twenty-ninth*
Day of *June 1803* in the *forty-third*
Year of our Reign.

By His Majesty's Command

Pelham.

Order in Council, June 20, 1805

(*The following is a copy of an Order in Council issuing instructions to the ships of war and privateers. It is to be found under that date in the Privy Council Register, vol. 167.*)

In consideration of the present state of commerce, we are graciously pleased to direct that neutral vessels having on board the articles hereafter enumerated and trading directly or circuitously between the Ports of the United Kingdom and the enemy's Ports in Europe (such ports not being blockaded) shall not be interrupted in their voyages by our ships of War or Privateers on account of such articles or any of them being the property of our subjects trading with the Enemy, without having obtained our special licence for that purpose. And if any neutral vessel trading as aforesaid shall be brought into our ports for adjudication, such vessel shall be forthwith liberated by our Courts of Admiralty, together with the enumerated articles laden therein which shall be shewn to be British or Neutral property.

List of goods permitted to be exported to Holland, France and Spain: British manufactures (not naval or military stores) grocery, allum, annatta, sugar, tobacco, vitriol, elephants' teeth, pimento, cinnamon, nutnegs, cornelian stone, coffee, cocoa, callico, copperas, drugs (not dying drugs) rhubarb, spices, pepper, nankeens, East Indian bales, tortoise shell, cloves, red, green and yellow earthen ware, indigo (not exceeding 5 tons a vessel) woolens, rum, and prize goods not prohibited to be exported.

List of goods permitted to be imported, from Holland: Grain (if importable according to the Provisions of the Corn Laws) salted provisions of all sorts (not being salted Beef or Pork) oak bark, flax, flaxseed, clover and other seed, madder roots, salted hides and skins, leather, rushes, hops, saccharum-saturni, barilla, smalts, yarn, saffron, butter, cheese, quills, clinkers, Terrace Geneva, vinegar, white lead, oil, turpentine, pitch, hemp, bottles, wainscot-boards, raw materials, naval stores, lace and French cambrics and lawns. From France: Grain (if importable according to the Provisions of the Corn Laws) salted provisions of all sorts (not being salted Beef or Pork) seeds, saffron, rags, turpentine, hides, skins, honey, wax, fruit, raw materials, linseed cakes, tallow, weld, wine, lace, French cambrics, and lawns, vinegar and brandy. From Spain: Cochineal, barilla, fruit, orcella weed, Spanish wool, indigo, hides, skins, shumac, liquorice, juice seeds, saffron, silk, sweet almonds, Castile soap, raw materials, aniseed, wine, cork, black lead, naval stores, vinegar and brandy.
And we are further pleased to direct that the foregoing enumeration may be added to or altered by any Order of the Lords of the Council.

An Import Licence, Sept. 24, 1806

(*The following Import Licence is to be found among the Privy Council Unbound Papers, 1806. The licence itself consists of a prepared printed form with spaces left blank for the insertion of particular facts and data dealing with the individual nature of the contemplated trade. The material entered in longhand by the clerk is put in italics. The royal signature and that of Lord Spencer were also written in longhand.*)

GEORGE R.

George the Third, by the Grace of God of the United Kingdom of Great Britain and Ireland, Defender of the Faith etc. To all Commanders of our ships of war and privateers, and to all others whom it may concern Greeting:

Our will and pleasure is that you permit, *Messrs William Hall & Co. and other British Merchants*
on board one *neutral vessel* (*the name of which they are unable to set forth*) to *import one cargo* without molestation from *any Port of Prussia either directly or circuitously*
to *any port of Our United Kingdom*
Such quantity *of Grain, if importable according to the provisions of the Corn Laws, salted provisions of all sorts, salted beef and pork, oak bark, flax and flaxseed, clover and other seed, madder roots, salted hides and skins, lenthels, rustics, hoops, Saccharum-saturni, barilla, smalts, yarn, saffron, butterchurn, quilts, clinkers, Terrace Geneva, vinegar, white lead, oil, turpentine, pitch, hemp, bottles, wainscot-boards, deals, lathwood, clapboard, bleaching ashes, raw materials, naval stores, timber, ash, rafters, oak-plank, and staves being the property of the said person or some of them*
as may be specified in *their* bills of lading: Provided the same shall be shipped as aforesaid. This licence to remain in force for the space of

Six months from the date hereof, and no longer. Provided also, that any Person who shall claim the benefit of the Licence hereby granted, shall take and have the same upon condition, that if any question arises in any of our Courts of Admiralty or elsewhere, whether such Person or Persons hath or have in all points conformed thereto in all cases whatsoever, the proof shall lie on the Person or Persons using this our Licence or claiming the benefit hereof.

Given at our Court at St. James the *twenty-fourth* Day of *September 1806* in the *forty-sixth* Year of our Reign.

By His Majesty's Command,

Spencer.

A Special Licence

(*This special licence, the essential part of which is given below, was issued April 22, 1807, and is to be found among the Privy Council Unbound Papers. It appears to have been granted upon the receipt of a petition presented April 14, 1807, by James Currie, a London merchant, for the privilege of importing grain from France. An Order in Council granting this licence was issued April 22, 1807.*)

George the Third, by the Grace of God of the United Kingdom of Great Britain and Ireland, Defender of the Faith etc. To all Commanders of our ships of war and privateers, and to all others whom it may concern, Greeting:

Our will and pleasure is that you permit to proceed without molestation from any port in France, blockaded or otherwise, four ships having been Prussian or British Prize ships purchased by James Currie on behalf of himself or other British merchants and that such ships be allowed to go in ballast from the port in France they were in at the time they were purchased, to any other port for the purpose of taking cargoes of grain on board and that they may depart therefrom, or from the port they were purchased at, laden with grain, corn, meal or flour to any port in the United Kingdom for the purpose of delivering the said articles to the said James Currie or to the other British Merchants or Manufacturers, notwithstanding all the Documents which accompany such articles may represent the same to be destined to neutral or hostile ports, and notwithstanding the crews of the ship may not be composed of subjects of the state the vessels purport to belong to; and our further pleasure is that in case all or any of the ships so documented or laden and coming to this country should be detained and brought in by any of our ships of war or privateers, the said vessels and their cargoes shall be forthwith liberated (if proceeded against for adjudication) upon a claim being given by or on behalf of the said James Currie for the ships and cargoes, or other British merchants or manufacturers, the goods may be consigned to, and shall be finally restored upon proof being produced that such ships and their cargoes were really destined to and coming for importation to any port of this kingdom.

THE FORM AND CONTENT OF AN ORDER IN COUNCIL FOR AN EXPORT AND IMPORT BALTIC LICENCE

(*The following Order is to be found among the Privy Council Unbound Papers, November, 1807.*)

At the Council Chamber, Whitehall
the of 180
Present
The Lords of His Majesty's Most
Honourable Privy Council

Whereas there was this Day read at the Board the humble Petition of praying that a Licence may be granted to export on board any neutral vessel sailing under any Flag except the French from London to any Port in the Baltic a cargo of British Manufactures, Colonial Produce and
such goods as are permitted by virtue of His Majesty's Order in Council of the 11th of November 1807 to be *exported* and also to import on board any such vessel from a Port in the Baltic a cargo of such goods as are permitted by virtue of His Majesty's said Order in Council to be imported to *the* port of London, notwithstanding all the papers which accompany such cargo may represent the same to be bound to an hostile port, and that the Master may be permitted to receive his freight and return with his vessel and crew to any port not blockaded; Which Petition being taken into consideration, It is hereby Ordered in Council, that a Licence be granted to the Petitioner, for the purpose above set forth, notwithstanding all the documents which accompany the ship and cargo may represent the same bound to any other neutral or hostile port upon condition that before the vessel be permitted to depart, the name and tonnage of the vessel, the name of the master, and the time of her clearance from the port of London shall be endorsed on the said Licence by the proper officer of the Customs, and that before the vessel leaves her foreign port of lading on her return voyage, the tonnage of the vessel, the name of her master and the time of clearance from such foreign port shall also be endorsed on the said Licence. And that if any part of the return cargo of this vessel consist of naval stores, and be destined for any port of this kingdom lying to the south of the Port of Hull, the vessel importing the same shall, unless under the protection of convoy, stop at Dundee or Leith, and there obtain a fresh clearance for the port of her destination; and upon the further condition that such vessel shall not sail from Dundee or Leith without convoy, and shall proceed with such convoy and not desert the same, till her arrival at the Port of Destination, or as long as such convoy shall be instructed to protect her. Such Licence to remain in force for six months from the date hereof; and at the expiration of the said period or sooner if the voyage be completed, to be deposited as the case may be with the Commissioners of His Majesty's Customs at the port of London or with the Collector of the Customs at the Out Ports. And the Right Honourable Lord Hawkesbury, One of His Majesty's Principal Secretaries of State,

is hereby authorized to grant such licence, in case His Lordship shall see no objection thereto, annexing to such Licence, the duplicate of this Order herewith sent for that purpose.

An Order in Council for an Import Licence

(*It is believed that the following is a correct copy of the entry in Privy Council Register, April 22, 1808.*)

Order in Council for a Licence to John Lubboch and Co., on behalf of themselves and merchants, whether subjects of a neutral or enemy's country, permitting 6 vessels of any neutral or enemy's country, whether chartered here or elsewhere to proceed from Riga, Memel, St. Petersburg or any Ports in the Baltic or Russian ports of the Baltic though these ports may have been or now are in a state of blockade to any of the Ports of the United Kingdom, with such Russian produce as may be imported by Order in Council November 1807, and that the masters may receive their freight and return with vessel and crew to any unblockaded Port, provided that none of these carry to a blockaded port contraband and that if any vessels have naval stores they shall unless under convoy call at Dundee and obtain fresh clearances for any port of the United Kingdom. Licence to be in effect for six months.

The Form of an Order in Council for an Import Licence

(*The following Order in Council is to be found in the Privy Council Register, Vol. 176, May 5, 1808.*)

Whereas there was this day read at the Board the humble petition of James Currie of London merchant setting forth that he has long since purchased in France considerable quantities of grain, provisions and other goods permitted by His Majesty's Order in Council of the 11th of November 1807 to be imported, and chartered several vessels for the purpose of conveying the same to this country under the various flags, that one of the said vessels has been confiscated in consequence of having been boarded by a British cruiser and the rest laid under embargo; and therefore humbly praying that His Majesty's Licence may be granted for permitting six British or other Prize Vessels to be purchased by him in any of the ports of France (whether blockaded or not) to proceed in ballast from such ports of Lancon, Trequier, Painpool, Morlaix or St. Maloes there to load or if purchased at any of these ports to proceed direct from thence with 6 cargoes of grain, provisions and such goods as are permitted by virtue of His Majesty's aforesaid Order in Council to be imported and to proceed with the same under any flag or navigated in any manner calculated to facilitate their voyage to the Ports of Falmouth, Plymouth or Portsmouth and that on arrival at these ports, the masters may be permitted to receive their freight and return with their vessels and crew to any port not blockaded; Which petition being taken into consideration, it is hereby Ordered in Council that a Licence be granted to the petitioner for the purpose above set forth, by whatever documents the said cargoes may be accompanied; provided that if the cargo, or any part thereof of any of the said vessels be landed before its advance at the Port of Falmouth, Plymouth or Portsmouth the property on board such vessel shall not be entitled to the protection of His Majesty's Licence; such Licence to remain in force for 6 months from the date hereof; and the Right Honourable Lord Hawkesbury, One of His Majesty's Principal Secretaries of State is to cause a Licence or pass to be prepared for His Majesty's Royal Signature in case His Lordship shall see no objection thereto.

The Form and Content of an Order in Council for an Import Licence

(*The following Order in Council is to be found among the Privy Council Unbound Papers, April, 1809. Italics represent entries in longhand.*)

At the Council Chamber Whitehall,
the *3rd* day of *April 1809*
Present
The Lords of His Majesty's Most Honourable
Privy Council.

Whereas there was this day read at the Board, the humble petition of *Messrs Portman, Hullman and Ohrly*
It is Ordered in Council that a Licence be granted to the Petitioners for *permitting a vessel bearing any flag except the French to proceed with a cargo of*
Grain (if importable according to the Provisions of the Corn Laws) oak bark, flax, flaxseed, clove and other seeds, madder roots, salted hides and skins, rushes, hoops, saccharum-saturni, barilla, smalts, yarn, saffron, quilts, terrace, white lead, oil, turpentine, pitch, hemp, wainscot-boards, raw materials, naval stores,
from any Port between the Rivers Yadhe and Scheldt to any Port of Great Britain
the Master to be permitted to receive . . . freight and depart
vessel and crew to any port not blockaded, notwithstanding all the documents which accompany the ship and cargo may represent the same to be destined to any neutral or hostile port, and to whomsoever such property may appear to belong; upon condition that *the name and tonnage of the vessel, name of the master and time of her clearance from her Port of lading shall be endorsed on this Licence*
Such Licence to remain in force for *Six* months from the date hereof; and at the expiration of the said period, or sooner if the voyage be completed, to be deposited, as the case may be with the Commissioners of His Majesty's Customs at the Port of London or with the Collectors of the Custom at the Out Ports. And the Right Honourable, the Earl of Liverpool, One of His Majesty's Principal Secretaries of State, is hereby authorized to grant such Licence, in case His Lordship shall see no objection thereto, annexing to such Licence, the duplicate of this Order herewith sent for that purpose.

An Import Licence, Yadhe (*sic*), April 3, 1809

(*The following Licence is to be found among the Privy Council Unbound Papers, April, 1809. Italics represent entries in longhand.*)

To all Commanders of His Majesty's Ships of War and Privateers and to all others whom it may concern, Greeting:

I the undersigned, One of His Majesty's Principal Secretaries of State in pursuance of the Authority given to me by His Majesty by Order in Council under and by virtue of Powers given to His Majesty by an Act passed in the Forty-eighth year of His Majesty's Reign entitled, "An Act to permit Goods secured in warehouses in the Port of London to be removed to the out ports for exportation to any port of Europe; for empowering His Majesty to direct that Licences which His Majesty is authorized to grant under His Sign Manual, may be granted by One of the Principal Secretaries of State; and for enabling His Majesty to permit the exportation of goods in vessels of less burthen than are now allowed by Law during the present hostilites and until one month after the signature of the Preliminary Articles of Peace;" and in pursuance of an Order in Council specially authorizing the grant of this Licence a duplicate of which Order is hereunto annexed, do hereby grant this Licence for the purpose set forth in the said Order of Council, to *Messrs Portman, Hullman and Ohrly to import on board a vessel bearing any flag except the French*
a cargo of Grain (if importable according to the Provisions of the Corn Laws) oak bark, flax, flax seed, clove and other seeds, madder roots, salted hides and skins, rushes, hoops, saccharum-saturni, barilla, smalts, yarn, saffron, quilts, terrace, white lead, oil, turpentine, pitch, hemp, wainscot-boards, raw materials, naval stores.
from any Port between the Rivers Yadhe and Scheldt to any Port of Great Britain, the master to be permitted to receive freight and depart with vessel and crew to any port not blockaded, notwithstanding all documents which accompany the ship and cargo may represent the same to be destined to any neutral or hostile port, and to whosoever such property may appear to belong; provided that the *name and tonnage of the vessel, name of the master and time of her clearance from her port of lading shall be endorsed on this Licence*
This Licence to remain in force for 6 months from the date hereof; and at the expiration of the said period, or sooner if the voyage be completed, to be deposited, as the case may be with the Commissioners of His Majesty's Customs at the Port of London or with the Collectors of the Customs at the Out Ports.

Given at Whitehall, the *Third* day of *April 1809*
in the *Forty-ninth* year of His Majesty's Reign.

Liverpool.

A General Import Licence, April 7, 1809

(*This Licence is to be found among the Privy Council Unbound Papers, 1809. Entries in Italics appear in longhand in the original.*)

To all Commanders of His Majesty's Ships of War and Privateers, and to all others to whom it may concern, Greeting:

I the undersigned, One of His Majesty's Principal Secretaries of State, in pursuance of the Authority given to me by His Majesty by Order in Council under and by virtue of Powers given to his Majesty, by an Act passed in the Forty-eighth year of His Majesty's Reign entitled, " An Act to permit Goods secured in warehouses in the Port of London to be removed to the out ports for exportation to any port of Europe; for empowering His Majesty to direct that Licences which His Majesty is authorized to grant under His Sign Manual, may be granted by One of the Principal Secretaries of State; and for enabling His Majesty to permit the exportation of goods in vessels of less burthen than are now allowed by Law during the present hostilities, and until one month after the signature of the Preliminary Articles of Peace; " and in pursuance of an Order of Council specially authorizing the grant of this licence, a duplicate of which Order in Council is hereunto annexed, do hereby grant this Licence for the purpose set forth in the said Order of Council and do hereby permit *John Hall on behalf of himself and other Merchants to import on board Twelve Vessels, Twelve Cargoes of* Grain (if importable according to the Provisions of the Corn Laws) oak bark, flax, flaxseed, Clover, and other seed, madder roots, salted hides, and skins, rushes, hoops, saccharum-saturni, barilla, smalts, yarn, saffron, quilts, terrace, white lead, oil, turpentine, pitch, hemp, wainscot-boards, raw materials, naval stores *from any port in Holland to any port of the United Kingdom North of Dover*

The Masters to be permitted to receive *their* freight and depart with *their* vessel*s* and Crew*s* to any Port not blockaded notwithstanding all the Documents which accompany the Ship*s* and Cargo*es* may represent the same to be destined to any other Neutral or Hostile Port, and to whomsoever such Property may appear to belong; provided that *the Names and Tonnage of the Vessels, Names of their Masters and time of their clearance from the Port of Lading shall be endorsed on this Licence.*

This Licence to remain in force for *Six* months from the date hereof; and at the expiration of the said period or sooner if the voyage be completed, to be deposited, as the case may be with the Commissioners of His Majesty's Custom at the Port of London or with the Collector of the Customs at the Out Ports.

Given at Whitehall, the *Seventh* day of *April 1809*
in the *Forty-ninth* year of His Majesty's Reign.

Liverpool.

The Form and Content of an Order in Council for an Import Licence

(An Order in Council was necessary for every licence issued. A copy of the original order was supposed to be attached to every licence. The following Order is to be found among the Privy Council Unbound Papers, Sept., 1809. A notice of this Order will be found under the same date in the Privy Council Register. It should be observed that not every order appears in full in the Register. When licences were first issued the complete order was usually entered in the Register; however, as the number of licences increased, it became a physical impossibility to enter the lengthy order for each and every licence. In lieu therof a short condensed statement or notice was inserted.)

At the Council Chamber, Whitehall
the *29th* of *September 1809.*
Present
The Lords of His Majesty's Most
Honourable Privy Council.

Whereas there was this day read at the Board the humble petition of
Messrs Latham Price & Co. Dover for themselves and others
It is Ordered in Council that a Licence be granted to the Petitioner for permitting a vessel bearing any flag except the French, and that subject to the conditions herein after expressed, to
sail in ballast from any port of Holland and to import
a cargo of Grain, Meal or Flour, if importable according to the Provisions of the Corn Laws, and Burr Stones, from any Port of France
Between Boulogne to Conquet both inclusive
to any Port of the United Kingdom, the Master to be permitted to receive His freight and depart with his vessel and crew to any port not blockaded, notwithstanding all the Documents which accompany the ship and cargo may represent the same to be destined to any other neutral or Hostile port, and to whomsoever such property may appear to belong; upon condition that the Name of the Vessel; the Name of the Master, and the Time of her clearance from her Port of Lading shall be endorsed on the said Licence; that the Vessel shall be permitted to bear the French Flag, only until she is Two Leagues distant from her Port of Clearance, or the neighboring coast: Provided always that this Licence shall not be understood to protect any Vessel navigated by French Seamen or any vessel that shall appear to be French built, save and except French built vessels which may have been transferred into Foreign Possession prior to the Operation of the Order of the 11th of November 1807, or which may have been taken as Prize from the French, and shall not have returned again into French possession. Such Licence to remain in force for Four Months from the Date hereof and no longer; and at the expiration of the said period, or sooner if the voyage be completed, to be deposited as the case may be with the Commissioners of His Majesty's Customs at the Port of

London or with the Collector of the Customs at the Out Ports. And the Right Honourable the Earl of Liverpool, One of His Majesty's Principal Secretaries of State, is hereby specially authorized to grant such Licence in case His Lordship shall see no objection thereto, annexing to such Licence the duplicate of this Order herewith sent for that purpose.

An Import Licence, France

(*This Licence is to be found among the Privy Council Unbound Papers, 1809. Entries in italics appear in longhand.*)

To all Commanders of His Majesty's Ships of War and Privateers, and to all others to whom it may concern, Greeting:

I the undersigned, One of His Majesty's Principal Secretaries of State, in pursuance of the Authority given to me by His Majesty by Order in Council under and by virtue of Powers given to His Majesty, by an Act passed in the Forty-eighth year of His Majesty's Reign entitled, "An Act to permit Goods secured in warehouses in the Port of London to be removed to the out ports for exportation to any port of Europe; for empowering His Majesty to direct that Licences which His Majesty is authorized to grant under His Sign Manual, may be granted by One of the Principal Secretaries of State; and for enabling His Majesty to permit the exportation of goods in vessels of less burthen than are now allowed by Law during the present hostilities and until one month after the signature of the Preliminary Articles of Peace;" and in pursuance of an Order of Council specially authorizing the grant of this licence, a duplicate of which Order in Council is hereunto annexed, do hereby grant this Licence to *John Atkins of London, Merchant* and do hereby permit a vessel bearing any flag except the French, and that subject to the conditions hereinafter expressed *to sail in Ballast (if necessary) from any port of Holland or France to any port of France between Boulogne and Conquet both inclusive there to load* a cargo of Grain, Meal or Flour, if importable according to the provisions of the Corn Laws, and Burr Stones . . . *and to proceed with the same* to any Port of the United Kingdom, the Master to be permitted to receive his freight and depart with his vessel and crew to any port not blockaded, notwithstanding all the Documents which accompany the Ship and Cargo may represent the same to be destined to any other Hostile or Neutral port, and to whomsoever such Property may appear to belong; provided that the Name of the Vessel, the Name of the Master, Time of her clearance from her Port of Lading shall be endorsed on this Licence, that the vessel shall be permitted to bear the French Flag only until she is Two Leagues distant from her Foreign Port of Lading or the neighbouring coast: Provided always that this Licence shall not be understood to protect any vessel navigated by French Seamen, or any vessel that shall appear to be French built, save and except French built vessels, which may have been transferred into Foreign Possession prior to the Operation of the Order of the 11th of November 1807, or which may have been taken as Prize from the French, and shall not have returned again into French Possession. This Licence to remain in force for Four Months from date hereof, and no longer; and at the expiration of the said Period or sooner if the voyage be completed, to be deposited, as the case may be with the Commissioners of His Majesty's Customs at the Port of London, or with the Collector of the Customs at the Out Ports.

Given at Whitehall the *Fourth* day of *October 1809*
in the *Forty-ninth* year of His Majesty's Reign
Liverpool.

Endorsed: *The Brig Prussian Twee Gebruders of Emden L. Nosten Col. Denis Master, cleared out at the Customs house of Morlaix the 22nd January for Christiansand, sailed from Morlaix Road the 25th January 1810.*
L. Noster Col. Denis.

The Form and Content of an Order in Council for an Import Licence

(*The following Order is to be found among the Privy Council Unbound Papers for 1809.*)

At the Council Chamber Whitehall
the *11th* day of *October 1809*
Present
The Lords of His Majesty's Most Honourable
Privy Council

Whereas there was this day read at the Board, the humble petition of *John Hall and Co. and others*
It is Ordered in Council that a Licence be granted to the Petitioner for permitting a vessel bearing any flag except the French to proceed in ballast (if necessary) from any Enemy's Port North of the Island of Walcheren to her Port of Lading in Holland, and to import from any Port in Holland, north of the Island of Walcheren or west of the Island of Juist, a cargo of grain, corn, meal or flour, if importable according to the provisions of the Corn Laws . . . to any Port of this Kingdom, north of Dover, the Master to be permitted to receive his freight and depart with his vessel and crew to any port not blockaded, notwithstanding all the documents which accompany the ship and cargo may represent the same to be destined to any neutral or hostile port, and to whomsoever such property may appear to belong; upon condition that the name and tonnage of the vessel, the name of her master and the time of her clearance from her port of lading shall be endorsed on the said Licence. Such Licence to remain in force for three months from the date hereof and no longer: and at the expiration of the said period, or sooner if the voyage be completed, to be deposited, as the case may be with the Commissioners of His Majesty's Customs at the Port of London or with the Collectors of the Custom at the Out Ports. And the Right Honourable, the Earl of Liverpool, One of His Majesty's Principal Secretaries of State, is hereby

authorized to grant such Licence, in case His Lordships shall see no objection thereto, annexing to such Licence, the duplicate of this Order herewith sent for that purpose.

An Import Licence, Holland, October 11, 1809

(*This Licence is to be found among the Privy Council Unbound Papers October, 1809. Matter in italics appears in longhand in the original.*)

To all Commanders of His Majesty's Ships of War and Privateers, and to all others whom it may concern, Greeting:

I the undersigned, One of His Majesty's Principal Secretaries of State, in pursuance of the Authority given to me by His Majesty by Order in Council under and by virtue of Powers given to His Majesty by an Act passed in the Forty-eighth year of His Majesty's Reign entitled, "An Act to permit Goods secured in warehouses in the Port of London to be removed to the out ports for exportation to any port of Europe; for empowering His Majesty to direct that Licences which His Majesty is authorized to grant under His Sign Manual, may be granted by One of the Principal Secretaries of State; and for enabling His Majesty to permit the exportation of goods in vessels of less burthen than are now allowed by Law during the present hostilities, and until one month after the signature of the Preliminary Articles of Peace;" and in pursuance of an Order of Council specially authorizing the grant of this Licence, a duplicate of which Order in Council is hereunto annexed, do hereby grant this Licence for the purpose set forth in the said Order of Council, to
John Hall & Co. and others
and do hereby permit a vessel bearing any flag except the French to proceed in ballast, if necessary, from an Enemy's Port North of the Island of Walcheren to her Port of Lading in Holland; and to import from any Port in Holland, north of the Island of Walcheren or west of the island of Juist, a cargo of grain, corn, meal or flour, if importable according to the provisions of the Corn Laws, to any Port of this Kingdom north of Dover, the Master to be permitted to receive his freight and depart with his vessel and crew to any port not blockaded, notwithstanding all the documents which accompany the ship and cargo may represent the same to be destined to any neutral or hostile port, and to whomsoever such property may appear to belong; upon condition that the name and tonnage of the vessel, the name of her master and the time of her clearance from her port of lading shall be endorsed on the said Licence. Such Licence to remain in force for Three Months from the date hereof and no longer; and at the expiration of the said period, or sooner if the voyage be completed to be deposited, as the case may be with the Commissioners of the Customs at the Port of London or with the Collectors of the Customs at the Out Ports.

Given at Whitehall, the *Eleventh* day of *October 1809*
in the *Forty-ninth year of His Majesty's Reign.*
Liverpool.

The Form and Content of an Order in Council for an Import Licence

(*The following Order is to be found among the Privy Council Unbound Papers, February 8, 1810.*)

At the Council Chambers, Whitehall
the *8th* of *February 1810*
Present
The Lords of His Majesty's Most
Honourable Privy Council.

Whereas there was this day read at the Board the humble petition of *F. C. Zimmerman for himself and on behalf of others being foreign merchants*
It is Ordered in Council that a Licence be granted to the Petitioner to import into any Port of the United Kingdom on board the *Bremen Schooner "Weser"* bearing any Flag (except the French) from the United States direct a cargo of Flaxseed, ashes, staves, naval stores, cotton, tobacco, or any other article the produce of the United States, with liberty to touch at Amelia Island, or the Western Islands, or the Island of Madeira, or Lisbon or Cadiz, and if necessary to land the cargo at any of the said islands or places, and to reship the same, notwithstanding any change that may be made in the character of the vessel
And notwithstanding the said vessel and cargo may not be furnished with the proper papers to entitle her to an entry on arrival at a Port of the United Kingdom; and that the Master shall be permitted to receive his freight and depart with his vessel and crew to any port not blockaded, upon condition, that the name of the vessel, her tonnage, the name of the master and time of her clearance from her Port of Lading shall be endorsed on the said Licence. Such Licence to remain in force for the space of *nine* months from the date hereof, and no longer; and at the expiration of the said period, or sooner if the voyage be completed, to be deposited, as the case may be, with the Commissioners of His Majesty Customs at the Port of London, or with the Collector of the Customs at the Out Port. And the Right Honourable Richard Ryder, One of His Majesty's Principal Secretaries of State, is hereby specially authorized to grant such Licence in case His Lordship shall see no objection thereto, annexing to such Licence the duplicate of this Order herewith sent for that purpose.

APPENDIX No. 7

AN ACCOUNT OF THE NUMBER OF LICENCES ISSUED BY THE PRIVY COUNCIL FOR THE IMPORTATION OF FOREIGN CORN FROM 1803 TO APRIL, 1813

	General Licences	Special, for Corn only
1803	1,530	0
1804	889	0
1805	763	0
1806	849	0
1807	1,491	0
1808	3,528	0
1809	10,739	1,741
1810	14,970	923
1811	4,617	1,886
1812	4,970	470
April 5, 1813	65	26
Total	44,411	5,046

It is to be observed that in all General licences corn might be imported according to the terms of the Corn Laws. Special licences do not appear to have been issued before 1809. The foregoing information is taken from the report presented by Mr. Chetwynd, Clerk of the Privy Council, April 17, 1813, as given in *Parl. Pap.*, 1813, No. 184, p. 42. Contrast this data with the figures given by Mr. Melvin, *Napoleon's Navigation System*, p. 331.

APPENDIX No. 8

AN ACCOUNT OF THE CORN, MEAL AND FLOUR IMPORTED INTO GREAT BRITAIN

Sweden

Year	Wheat		Barley		Beans		Oats		Rye		Pease		Total	
	Q.	B.	Q.	B.	Q.	B.	Q.	B.	Q.	B.	Q.	B.	Q.	B.
1800	21,496	7	4,844	2	0	0	9,425	0	12,247	3	92	4	48,106	0
1801	13,194	1	3,565	1	0	0	8,987	6	39	3	588	7	26,375	2
1802	5,982	5	278	3	0	0	3,953	7	605	7	140	0	10,960	6
1803	0	0	0	0	0	0	0	0	0	0	540	0	540	0
1804	1,326	0	0	0	0	0	15,904	5	126	3	2,574	0	19,931	0
1805	18,810	3	4,519	7	0	0	2,282	0	0	0	247	0	25,859	2
1806	0	0	0	0	0	0	0	0	0	0	0	0	0	0
1807	0	0	0	0	0	0	0	0	0	0	110	4	110	4
1808	0	0	0	0	0	0	0	0	0	0	195	0	195	0
1809	780	4	0	0	0	0	0	0	369	3	745	7	1,895	6
1810	68,398	2	1,103	1	0	0	2,872	0	12,592	4	1,699	7	86,665	6
1811	19,038	3	10,613	1	0	0	2,577	1	5,324	5	1,884	3	39,437	5
1812	11,543	1	0	0	0	0	0	0	3,376	0	0	0	14,919	1
1813	66,088	0	0	0	0	0	3,508	0	997	0	1,039	0	71,632	0
1814	29,890	6	306	0	0	0	386	3	0	0	343	6	30,926	7
	256,549	0	25,229	7	0	0	49,896	6	35,678	4	10,200	6	377,554	7

							Norway and Denmark							
1800	20,950	2½	1,142	0	0	0	13,462	4	9,986	1	39	1	45,580	0½
1801	3,013	5	1,308	6	0	0	1,935	7	678	4	150	5	7,087	3
1802	110	0	34	5	0	0	3,658	1	0	0	78	5	3,881	3
1803	0	0	0	0	0	0	8,619	3	0	0	0	0	8,619	3
1804	4,147	6	50	0	0	0	26,537	6	0	0	93	0	30,828	4
1805	35,671	4	1,039	2	0	0	13,755	0	2,313	7	56	4	52,836	1
1806	1,386	0	190	0	0	0	8,708	1	0	0	0	0	10,284	1
1807	10,424	6	417	7	0	0	61,070	5	0	0	300	3	72,213	5
1808	63	5	1,731	4	0	0	1	0	3	0	0	0	1,799	1
	75,767	4½	5,914	0	0	0	137,748	3	12,981	4	718	2	233,129	5½
							Norway							
1809	0	0	155	0	0	0	297	0	0	0	0	0	452	0
1810	437	4	545	0	0	0	62	4	236	0	15	0	1,296	0
1811	955	2	0	0	0	0	0	0	0	0	0	0	955	2
1812	0	0	0	0	0	0	0	0	0	0	0	0	0	0
1813	0	0	0	0	0	0	0	0	0	0	0	0	0	0
1814	0	0	0	0	0	0	0	0	0	0	0	0	0	0
	1,392	6	700	0	0	0	359	4	236	0	15	0	2,703	2
							Denmark							
1809	8,846	0	0	0	0	0	90	0	0	0	91	4	9,027	4
1810	110,500	7	3,995	4	17	7	14,751	7	2,921	0	99	6	132,286	7
1811	18,008	5	8,416	5	0	0	6,917	2	11,146	6	638	3	45,127	5
1812	19,589	3	19,280	5	0	0	10,115	1	3,030	6	285	7	52,301	5
1813	19,815	3	9,750	0	382	0	27,013	0	1,864	0	48	0	58,872	4
1814	4,461	4	3,174	1	827	5	8,645	6	1,234	1	14	1	18,357	2
	181,221	6	44,616	7	3,261*	5	67,533	0	20,196	5	1,177	5	318,007*	4

* Includes 2,034 quarters and 1 bushel of beans imported from Denmark in 1804 and 1807.

APPENDIX No. 8 (Continued)

AN ACCOUNT OF THE CORN, MEAL AND FLOUR IMPORTED INTO GREAT BRITAIN

Spain, including the Canaries

Year	Wheat		Barley		Beans		Oats		Rye		Pease		Indian Corn		Total	
	Q.	B.	Q.	B.	Q.	B.	Q.	B.	Q.	B.	Q.	B.	Q.	B.	Q.	B.
1800	307	0	0	0	1,758	3	0	0	0	0	0	6	0	0	2,066	1
1801	8	7	0	0	0	0	0	0	0	0	0	0	0	0	8	7
1802	0	0	0	0	0	0	0	0	0	0	6	3	0	0	6	3
1803	0	0	0	0	0	0	0	0	0	0	62	1	0	0	62	1
1804	0	0	0	0	0	0	0	0	0	0	8	3	0	0	8	3
1805	645	0	0	0	0	0	0	0	0	0	0	0	0	0	645	0
1806	210	0	0	0	0	0	0	0	0	0	23	5	0	0	233	5
1807	0	0	0	0	0	0	0	0	0	0	0	0	0	0	0	0
1808	0	0	0	0	0	1	0	0	0	0	0	2	0	0	0	3
1809	0	0	0	0	0	0	0	0	0	0	2	0	10	0	12	0
1810	1,488	5	0	0	0	0	0	0	0	0	0	3	0	0	1,489	0
1811	99	3	0	0	0	0	0	0	0	0	0	4	0	0	99	7
1812	0	0	0	0	0	0	0	0	0	0	0	0	0	0	0	0
1813	0	0	0	0	0	0	0	0	0	0	0	0	0	0	0	0
1814	0	4	0	0	0	0	2,206	6	0	0	3	6	0	0	2,211	0
	2,759	3	0	0	1,758	4	2,206	6	0	0	108	1	10	0	6,842	6

Portugal, including the Azores and Madeira Islands

1800	3,661	3	0	0	0	0	0	0	0	0	0	3	0	0	3,661	6
1801	119	5	49	3	0	0	56	4	0	0	0	0	1	0	226	4
1802	0	0	0	0	0	0	0	0	0	0	0	0	14	4	14	4
1803	0	0	0	0	0	0	1,500	0	0	0	0	0	1	7	1,501	7
1804	0	0	0	0	0	0	0	0	0	0	0	0	0	2	0	2
1805	0	0	0	0	0	0	0	0	0	0	0	0	1	4	1	4
1806	768	7	0	0	0	0	0	0	0	0	0	0	0	3	769	2
1807	0	0	0	0	0	0	0	0	0	0	0	2	0	0	0	2
1808	611	4	94	6	2,341	0	0	0	0	0	4	0	4,095	3	7,146	5
1809	1,093	7	202	0	439	7	0	0	0	1	0	0	788	1	2,524	0
1810	12,381	1	454	6	0	0	2	7	0	0	1	7	11	2	12,851	7
1811	876	0	0	4	0	0	2	0	0	0	0	0	1	1	879	5
1812	7	7	0	0	0	0	0	0	0	0	0	0	2	2	10	1
1813	0	0	0	0	0	0	0	0	0	0	0	0	0	0	0	0
1814	0	0	0	0	0	0	0	0	0	0	0	1	0	0	0	1
	19,520	2	801	3	2,780	7	1,561	3	0	1	6	5	4,917	5	29,588	2

APPENDIX No. 8 (Continued)

AN ACCOUNT OF THE CORN, MEAL AND FLOUR IMPORTED INTO GREAT BRITAIN

Italy

Year	Wheat		Barley		Beans		Oats		Rye		Pease		Indian Corn		Total	
	Q.	B.	Q.	B.	Q.	B.	Q.	B.	Q.	B.	Q.	B.	Q.	B.	Q.	B.
1800	1	0	0	0	0	0	0	0	0	0	0	0	0	0	1	0
1801	61	7	0	0	0	0	70	7	0	0	0	0	0	0	132	6
1802	495	0	0	0	0	0	0	0	0	0	0	0	0	0	495	0
1803	0	0	0	0	0	0	0	0	0	0	0	0	0	0	0	0
1804	0	0	0	0	0	0	0	0	0	0	0	2	0	0	0	2
1805	0	0	0	0	0	0	0	0	0	0	0	0	0	0	0	0
1806	0	6	0	0	0	0	0	0	0	0	0	0	0	0	0	6
1807	0	0	0	0	0	0	0	0	0	0	0	0	0	0	0	0
1808	0	0	0	0	0	0	0	0	0	0	0	0	0	0	0	0
1809	2,391	1	0	0	0	0	0	0	0	0	2	0	0	0	2,393	1
1810	1	6	0	0	0	0	0	0	0	0	0	0	0	0	1	6
1811	0	0	0	0	0	0	0	0	0	0	0	0	0	0	0	0
1812	0	0	0	0	0	0	0	0	0	0	0	0	0	0	0	0
1813	0	0	0	0	0	0	0	0	0	0	0	0	0	0	0	0
1814	1	2	0	0	0	0	0	0	0	0	0	0	0	0	1	2
	2,952	6	0	0	0	0	70	7	0	0	2	2	0	0	3,025	7

France

Year	Wheat		Barley		Beans		Oats		Rye		Pease		Total	
	Q.	B.	Q.	B.	Q.	B.	Q.	B.	Q.	B.	Q.	B.	Q.	B.
1800	224	0	2	0	0	0	0	0	589	1	9	2	824	3
1801	0	2	0	0	374	5	70	0	0	0	1	2	446	1
1802	1,510	1½	0	0	5	5	0	0	0	0	0	4	1,516	2½
1803	0	0	0	0	0	0	0	0	0	0	0	2	0	2
1804	0	0	0	0	0	0	156	4	0	0	0	0	156	4
1805	2,089	6	0	0	0	0	0	0	0	0	0	0	2,089	6
1806	1,786	1	1,000	0	0	0	0	0	0	0	0	0	2,786	1
1807	27,656	7	78	0	1,412	0	96	0	2,816	1	53	4	32,112	4
1808	2,870	1	259	5	689	2	108	5	0	0	660	5	4,588	2
1809	25,058	2	0	0	27	0	0	0	395	0	14	7	25,495	1
1810	225,710	7	254	0	0	6	0	0	0	0	37	2	226,002	7
1811	4,186	5	0	0	0	0	0	0	0	0	0	0	4,186	5
1812	436	2	0	0	0	0	0	0	0	0	0	0	436	2
1813	0	0	0	0	0	0	0	0	0	0	0	0	0	0
1814	126,309	0	11,717	3	1,601	0	27,962	0	712	1	82	5	168,384	1
	417,838	2½	13,311	0	4,110	2	28,393	1	4,512	3	860	1	469,025	1½

APPENDIX No. 8 (Continued)

AN ACCOUNT OF THE CORN, MEAL AND FLOUR IMPORTED INTO GREAT BRITAIN

Flanders

Year	Wheat		Barley		Beans		Oats		Rye		Pease		Total	
	Q.	B.	Q.	B.	Q.	B.	Q.	B.	Q.	B.	Q.	B.	Q.	B.
1800	0	0	0	0	0	0	18	0	0	0	0	0	18	0
1801	1	6	0	0	0	0	0	0	7	3	1	0	10	1
1802	0	0	0	0	0	0	0	0	0	0	0	0	0	0
1803	0	0	0	0	0	0	0	0	0	0	0	0	0	0
1804	0	0	0	0	0	0	0	0	0	0	0	0	0	0
1805	0	0	0	0	0	0	0	0	0	0	0	0	0	0
1806	0	0	0	0	0	0	0	0	0	0	0	0	0	0
1807	0	0	0	0	0	0	0	0	0	0	0	0	0	0
1808	2	2	0	0	0	0	0	0	0	0	0	0	2	2
1809	20,198	1	0	0	0	0	420	0	0	0	5	5	20,623	6
1810	167,153	6	212	4	1	2	820	0	1,286	0	0	0	169,473	4
1811	0	0	0	0	0	0	0	0	0	0	0	0	0	0
1812	0	0	0	0	0	0	0	0	0	0	2	0	2	0
1813	0	0	0	0	0	0	0	0	0	0	0	0	0	0
1814	122,513	2	338	1	2,159	3	2,152	1	0	0	279	4	127,442	3
	309,869	1	550	5	2,160	5	3,410	1	1,293	3	288	1	317,572	0

Holland

1800	58,408	0	45,027	2	5,201	2	198,653	2	6,588	2	3,825	7½	317,703	7½
1801	93,824	5	12,068	1	6,607	5	221,402	4	15,979	7	1,438	6	351,321	4
1802	1,309	1	516	5	601	3	100,447	1	0	0	319	2	103,193	4
1803	525	6	0	2	84	6	80,974	3	0	0	172	2	81,757	3
1804	25,861	7	700	0	121	2	143,753	0	0	0	541	0	170,977	1
1805	9,636	4	3,004	0	1,344	5	58,504	0	0	0	27	2	72,516	3
1806	764	6	0	0	0	6	29,148	0	0	4	35	1	29,949	1
1807	11,415	4	108	5	2,368	3	222,248	5	8	0	1,374	0	237,523	1
1808	1,051	6	0	0	2,052	7	11,170	0	0	0	3,860	2	18,134	7
1809	94,266	6	1,212	0	10,881	1	188,869	3	3,063	0	9,665	1	307,957	3
1810	189,016	0	386	0	5,697	6	62,098	0	8,477	7	1,136	0	266,811	5
1811	0	0	0	0	0	0	0	0	0	0	0	0	0	0
1812	0	0	0	0	0	0	0	0	0	0	0	0	0	0
1813	0	0	0	0	0	0	0	0	0	0	0	0	0	0
1814	121,674	0	7,163	2	17,098	0	142,946	1	109	1	3,576	0	292,566	4
	607,754	5	70,186	1	52,059	6	1,460,214	3	34,226	5	25,970	7½	2,250,412	3½

APPENDIX No. 8 (Continued)

AN ACCOUNT OF THE CORN, MEAL AND FLOUR IMPORTED INTO GREAT BRITAIN

Prussia, including Poland

Year	Wheat		Barley		Beans		Oats		Rye		Pease		Total	
	Q.	B.	Q.	B.	Q.	B.	Q.	B.	Q.	B.	Q.	B.	Q.	B.
1800	665,955	5	7,221	0	4,751	6	64,247	4	32,079	6½	3,419	0	777,674	5½
1801	528,032	4	24,116	5	941	6	71,800	2	27,981	5	10,710	7	663,583	5
1802	334,829	6	2,652	7	1,974	6	16,239	6	12,634	5	9,652	5	377,984	3
1803	142,774	3	0	0	0	0	4,549	1	2,472	3	21,205	1	171,001	0
1804	320,745	2	6,183	6	6,820	6	184,528	5	697	7	12,387	4	531,363	6
1805	559,628	1½	10,123	4	5,405	7	117,461	6	2,097	0	7,889	3	702,605	5½
1806	51,523	6	685	0	442	4	37,368	4	0	0	20	0	90,039	6
1807	11,465	0	0	0	655	0	10,750	0	0	0	20	0	22,890	0
1808	0	0	0	0	0	0	0	0	0	0	0	0	0	0
1809	1,527	0	0	0	0	0	0	0	0	0	487	6	2,014	6
1810	296,756	7	264	0	0	0	875	0	15,014	4	3,313	0	316,223	3
1811	95,170	5	209	5	0	0	14	2	1,853	1	638	2	97,885	7
1812	9,062	4	0	0	0	0	0	0	0	0	0	0	9,062	4
1813	115,946	0	2,444	0	0	0	770	0	9,713	0	5,034	0	133,907	0
1814	133,106	1	2,689	6	7,101	7	38,698	4	1,692	3	2,952	2	186,240	7
	3,266,523	4½	56,590	1	28,094	2	547,303	2	106,236	2½	77,729	6	4,082,477	2

Russia

1800	81,707	7	20	0	0	0	10,498	1	2	4	78	7	92,307	3
1801	174,337	5	1,605	0	0	0	17,099	4	11,501	5	110	6	204,654	4
1802	8,665	3	93	0	0	0	3,962	0	150	0	0	0	12,870	3
1803	14,537	2	425	4	0	0	610	2	874	5	0	0	16,447	5
1804	7,108	2	576	7	0	0	470	0	0	0	60	0	8,215	1
1805	154,903	6	1,332	0	0	0	0	0	17,637	5	0	0	173,873	3
1806	56,732	7	183	0	0	0	0	1	499	5	0	0	57,415	5
1807	5,711	4	201	2	0	0	2	0	265	4	4	0	6,184	2
1808	549	5	2	0	0	0	0	0	0	0	3,111	5	3,663	2
1809	3,437	4	0	0	0	0	0	0	539	4	10,112	5	14,089	5
1810	58,132	5	331	0	0	0	5	6	6,792	7	1,606	3	66,868	5
1811	27,968	6	14,206	3	0	0	93	5	6,215	6	1,111	5	49,596	1
1812	50,974	1	15,294	3	0	0	1,778	7	60,342	1	48	4	128,438	0
1813	58,028	1	128	0	0	0	0	0	6,776	1	6	0	64,938	2
1814	8,432	2	0	0	0	0	990	7	337	1	0	0	9,760	2
	711,227	4	34,398	3	0	0	35,511	1	111,935	0	16,250	3	909,322	3

APPENDIX No. 8 (Continued)

AN ACCOUNT OF THE CORN, MEAL AND FLOUR IMPORTED INTO GREAT BRITAIN

Germany

Year	Wheat		Barley		Beans		Oats		Rye		Pease		Total	
	Q.	B.	Q.	B.	Q.	B.	Q.	B.	Q.	B.	Q.	B.	Q.	B.
1800	310,755	1½	72,221	3	4,033	6	246,298	4	81,416	3	19,300	7	734,026	0½
1801	289,789	3	69,786	7	8,295	5	259,891	5	40,608	1	30,968	2	699,339	7
1802	30,644	5	4,559	7	1,556	1	112,792	1	1,498	6	311	2	151,362	6
1803	1,487	3	0	0	0	0	158,327	4	0	0	1,331	6	161,146	5
1804	4,860	3	896	3	1,629	4	128,562	0	0	0	2,862	0	138,810	2
1805	32,827	7	7,250	1	1,869	5	81,953	4	1,983	2	262	2	126,146	5
1806	0	0	0	0	602	0	107,974	0	0	0	5	2	108,581	2
1807	3,407	3	2,151	0	3,465	1	130,355	6	0	0	2,157	3	141,536	5
1808	2,236	4	627	7	3,221	5	21,971	3	249	5	1,692	3	29,999	3
1809	33,575	0	7,913	5	15,806	0	102,551	5	4,553	0	5,052	0	169,451	2
1810	176,463	5	6,053	1	5,869	2	30,480	2	34,676	2	1,932	5	255,475	1
1811	1,628	0	217	6	315	7	0	0	242	4	25	0	2,429	1
1812	603	1	0	0	0	0	0	0	0	0	16	1	619	2
1813	79,365	2	3,657	0	568	0	26,159	0	14,019	0	1,388	0	125,156	2
1814	76,531	7	2,684	2	8,859	1	26,157	5	684	5	1,942	5	116,860	1
	1,044,175	4½	178,019	2	56,091	5	1,433,474	7	179,931	4	69,247	6	2,960,940	4½

The United States

Year	Wheat	Barley	Beans	Oats	Rye	Pease	Indian Corn	Total
1800	77,609 7	247 4	13 7	0 0	1,621 4	0 0	11,198 1½	90,690 7½
1801	245,371 4	390 0	20 1	49 5	49,165 1	84 1	77,069 5	372,150 1
1802	79,412 7	0 0	0 0	0 0	307 0	9 4	1,089 7	80,819 2
1803	109,131 0	0 0	0 4	0 0	0 0	0 0	700 2	109,831 6
1804	4,259 1	0 0	0 1	0 0	0 0	0 0	91 6	4,351 0
1805	13,453 4	0 0	0 0	0 0	0 0	0 0	22 2	13,475 6
1806	79,763 7	0 0	0 1	0 0	0 0	29 6	112 2	79,906 0
1807	249,712 4	0 0	0 1	0 0	0 0	414 3	738 0	250,865 0
1808	12,836 1	0 0	0 0	0 0	0 0	167 3	203 2	13,206 6
1809	170,939 0	0 0	143 4	0 0	0 0	1,441 6	354 2	172,878 4
1810	98,274 6	0 0	2 1	0 0	0 0	71 6	12 4	98,361 1
1811	18,011 3	0 2	0 0	0 0	0 0	71 7	13 7	18,097 3
1812	10,797 0	0 0	0 0	0 0	691 0	21 4	14 1	11,523 5
1813	810 5	0 0	0 0	0 0	0 0	0 0	282 1	1,092 6
1814	1 4	0 0	0 0	0 0	0 0	0 0	0 0	1 4
	1,170,384 5	637 6	180 4	49 5	51,784 5	2,312 0	91,902 2½	1,317,251 3½

APPENDIX No. 8 (Continued)

AN ACCOUNT OF THE CORN, MEAL AND FLOUR IMPORTED INTO GREAT BRITAIN

British North American Colonies

Year	Wheat		Barley		Beans		Oats		Rye		Pease		Indian Corn		Total	
	Q.	B.	Q.	B.	Q.	B.	Q.	B.	Q.	B.	Q.	B.	Q.	B.	Q.	B.
1800	21,258	4	170	0	0	0	0	0	0	0	10	5	0	0	21,439	1
1801	67,595	2	0	0	0	0	0	0	0	0	129	2	0	0	67,724	4
1802	75,164	5	0	0	0	0	0	0	0	0	8	0	0	0	75,172	5
1803	43,245	2	0	0	0	0	0	0	0	0	0	0	0	0	43,245	2
1804	21,213	6	0	0	0	0	0	0	0	0	0	0	0	0	21,213	6
1805	2,250	1	0	0	0	0	0	0	0	0	0	0	0	0	2,250	1
1806	9,800	2	0	0	0	0	0	0	0	0	0	0	0	7	9,801	1
1807	27,258	6	0	0	0	0	0	0	0	0	133	4	301	3	27,693	5
1808	18,489	1	0	0	0	0	0	0	1	0	3,010	3	6	2	21,506	6
1809	18,766	1	0	0	0	0	0	0	0	0	4,970	6	0	0	23,736	7
1810	24,202	4	0	0	0	2	0	0	0	0	1,734	6	0	1	25,937	5
1811	339	4	0	0	0	0	0	0	0	0	100	0	0	0	439	4
1812	23,724	3	0	0	16	2	0	0	0	0	33	1	0	4	23,774	2
1813	0	7	0	0	0	0	0	0	0	0	0	0	0	0	0	7
1814	2	5	0	0	0	0	0	0	0	0	0	0	0	0	2	5
	353,311	5	170	0	16	4	0	0	1	0	10,130	3	309	1	363,938	5

Channel Isles

1800	120	0	0	0	0	0	0	0	0	0	2	2	0	0	122	2
1801	0	0	0	0	0	0	0	0	0	0	0	4	0	0	0	4
1802	0	0	0	0	0	0	795	0	0	0	26	0	0	0	821	0
1803	2	4	45	0	0	0	226	0	0	0	53	7	0	0	327	3
1804	28	7	2	5	0	0	219	3	0	0	0	0	0	0	250	7
1805	775	6¾	0	3	0	0	952	7	0	0	52	0	0	0	1,781	0¾
1806	64	0	0	0	0	0	231	2	0	0	12	0	0	0	307	2
1807	7,950	2	77	0	0	0	124	2	0	0	25	0	0	0	8,176	4
1808	4	3	358	7	0	0	367	6	0	0	9	1	0	0	740	1
1809	502	5	185	2	0	0	1,124	6	0	0	70	2	0	0	1,882	7
1810	6,167	1	290	0	79	5	564	1	0	0	36	0	0	0	7,136	7
1811	598	0	6	0	1	3	11	4	1	4	33	0	0	0	651	3
1812	1,202	6	511	4	0	0	389	3	0	0	13	5	0	0	2,117	2
1813	1,697	0	0	0	0	0	15	7	0	0	11	0	0	0	1,723	7
1814	3,787	7	575	0	0	0	1,003	7	0	0	76	4	0	0	5,443	2
	22,901	1¾	2,051	5	81	0	6,026	0	1	4	421	1	0	0	31,482	3¾

APPENDIX No. 8 (Continued)

AN ACCOUNT OF THE CORN, MEAL AND FLOUR IMPORTED INTO GREAT BRITAIN

Ireland, Domestic Corn

Year	Wheat		Barley		Beans		Oats		Rye		Pease		Indian Corn		Total	
	Q.	B.	Q.	B.	Q.	B.	Q.	B.	Q.	B.	Q.	B.	Q.	B.	Q.	B.
1800	749	2	78	4	0	0	2,410	6	0	0	0	0	0	0	3,238	4
1801	150	4	0	0	0	0	374	6	0	0	0	0	0	0	525	2
1802	108,751	3	7,116	4	1,654	4	341,151	1	282	0	113	1	0	0	459,068	5
1803	61,267	2	12,879	3	1,652	4	266,358	6	752	4	611	2	0	0	343,521	5
1804	70,071	4	2,520	6	3,060	0	240,021	7	206	0	1,077	7	0	0	316,958	0
1805	84,087	2	15,656	0	2,009	4	203,302	0	235	0	1,633	7	0	0	306,923	5
1806	102,276	3	3,327	4	2,361	0	357,076	4	330	0	1,388	4	0	0	466,759	7
1807	44,899	4	23,048	3	3,777	0	389,649	1	431	4	1,390	4	0	0	463,196	0
1808	43,496	5	30,586	0	2,065	0	519,974	3	573	0	75	0	0	0	596,770	0
1809	66,943	6	16,619	0	2,669	1	845,782	7	425	0	37	7	0	0	932,477	5
1810	126,388	1	8,321	3	3,541	1	492,740	7	20	0	215	6	0	0	631,227	2
1811	147,245	2	2,713	0	4,081	0	275,756	5	21	0	50	2	0	0	429,867	1
1812	158,351	7	43,137	7	5,008	0	390,629	2	177	5	51	4	0	0	597,356	1
1813	217,153	5	63,560	0	4,455	0	691,498	4	420	0	77	0	0	0	977,164	1
1814	225,478	1	16,779	2	5,730	7	564,010	3	4	3	459	4	0	0	812,462	4
	1,457,310	3	246,343	4	42,064	5	5,580,737	6	3,878	0	7,182	0	0	0	7,337,516	2

Ireland, Foreign Corn

1800	0	0	0	0	0	0	0	0	0	0	0	0	0	0	0	0
1801	373	4	0	0	0	0	0	0	0	0	0	0	1	4	375	0
1802	767	5	0	0	0	0	780	0	0	0	0	0	4,148	2	5,695	7
1803	0	0	0	0	0	0	0	0	0	0	0	0	2	1	2	1
1804	0	0	0	0	0	0	0	0	0	0	0	0	0	0	0	0
1805	0	0	0	0	0	0	0	0	0	0	0	0	0	0	0	0
1806	186	5	0	0	0	0	0	0	0	0	0	0	0	0	186	5
1807	211	0	0	0	0	0	0	0	0	0	0	0	0	0	211	0
1808	0	0	0	0	0	0	0	0	0	0	0	0	0	0	0	0
1809	1,180	0	0	0	0	0	0	0	0	0	0	5	0	0	1,180	5
1810	1,121	7	0	0	0	0	490	0	0	0	0	0	9	6	1,621	5
1811	321	4	0	0	0	0	0	0	0	0	0	0	0	0	321	4
1812	2,490	6	124	4	0	0	297	0	0	0	0	0	0	0	2,912	2
1813	0	0	0	0	0	0	0	0	0	0	0	0	0	0	0	0
1814	342	6	0	0	0	0	0	0	0	0	0	0	0	0	342	6
	6,995	5	124	4	0	0	1,567	0	0	0	0	5	4,161	5	12,849	3

APPENDIX No. 8 (Continued)

By Prize

Year	Wheat		Barley		Beans		Oats		Rye		Pease		Indian Corn		Total	
	Q.	B.	Q.	B.	Q.	B.	Q.	B.	Q.	B.	Q.	B.	Q.	B.	Q.	B.
1800	1,315	4	2	2	37	5	4	3	0	0	15	6½	0	1	1,375	5½
1801	6,482	0	1,075	4	6	0	1,304	2	771	2	33	0	391	1	10,063	1
1802	20	2	0	0	0	0	0	0	0	0	2	4	0	6	23	4
1803	754	4	677	3	0	0	1	2	0	0	14	3	0	4	1,448	0
1804	1,514	4	665	2	96	4	239	7	1,613	5	43	4	151	7	4,325	1
1805	6,051	0	366	0	51	7	200	0	0	0	48	1	0	0	6,717	0
1806	5,077	4	0	0	0	0	0	0	183	7	45	0	0	0	5,306	3
1807	4,831	1	6	4	262	0	1,384	2	4,219	4	86	4	24	2	10,814	1
1808	2,672	5	1,589	0	369	4	1,060	6	4,470	6	95	2	2	2	10,260	1
1809	6,476	3	3,261	3	0	0	4,106	4	4,269	7	405	7	20	0	18,540	0
1810	3,223	5	4,106	1	16	0	3,446	2	8,965	2	367	7	0	0	20,125	1
1811	1,670	4	6,456	6	40	1	2,091	5	3,025	1	489	7	1	3	13,775	3
1812	1,904	6	5,309	1	0	2	2,825	4	5,202	3	234	0	0	0	15,476	0
1813	97	6	3,729	4	0	0	2,990	0	1,250	5	0	0	311	0	8,378	7
1814	22	3	604	3	7	3	1	0	1,270	7	110	2	1	0	2,017	2
	42,114	3	27,849	1	887	2	19,655	5	35,243	1	1,991	7½	904	2	128,645	5½

Miscellaneous Importations from Africa, Turkey, British West Indies, Foreign West Indies, Malta, Gibraltar, New Holland and Brazil

1800	0	0	0	0	0	0	0	0	0	0	1	0¾	0	2	1	2¾
1801	2,408	4	1	1	0	5	0	0	0	0	0	7	8	7	2,420	0
1802	0	0½	0	0	0	3	0	0	0	0	3	4	8	2	12	1½
1803	0	0	0	0	0	0	0	0	0	0	0	6	7	4	8	2
1804	2	4	0	0	0	0	0	0	0	0	0	4	0	6	3	6
1805	3	6	9	5	55	0	0	0	0	0	1	2	0	0	69	5
1806	0	2	0	1	0	0	0	0	0	0	0	2	0	1	0	6
1807	2	1	3	0	0	3	0	0	0	0	0	3	0	1	6	0
1808	4	4	0	4	0	0	0	0	0	0	1	0	1	2	7	2
1809	5	1	421	5	0	0	0	3	0	0	3	1½	89	6	520	0½
1810	1,305	7	2	0	0	0	0	0	0	0	0	4	3	0	1,311	3
1811	12	5	0	2	0	0	0	0	0	0	1	4	0	0	14	3
1812	21	6	0	0	0	0	0	0	0	0	6	0	0	0	27	6
1813	0	0	0	0	0	0	0	0	0	0	0	0	0	0	0	0
1814	10	7	0	1	0	0	0	0	0	0	0	3	0	2	11	5
	3,777	7½	438	3	56	3	0	3	0	0	21	1¼	120	1	4,414	2¾

APPENDIX No. 8 (Continued)

TOTAL IMPORTATIONS ACCORDING TO TYPE OF CORN

Year	Wheat		Oats		Barley		Rye		Beans		Indian Corn		Pease		Total	
	Q.	B.	Q.	B.	Q.	B.	Q.	B.	Q.	B.	Q.	B.	Q.	B.	Q.	B.
1800	1,264,520	3	545,018	0	130,976	1	144,531	0½	15,796	5	11,198	4½	26,796	3¾	2,138,837	1¾
1801	1,424,765	4	583,043	4	113,966	4	146,732	7	16,246	3	77,472	1	44,218	1	2,406,445	0
1802	647,663	4	583,779	1	15,251	7	15,478	2	5,792	6	5,261	5	10,671	2	1,283,898	3
1803	373,725	2	521,166	5	14,027	4	4,099	4	1,737	6	712	2	23,991	6	939,460	5
1804	461,139	6	740,393	5	11,595	5	2,643	7	11,928	1	244	5	19,648	0	1,247,593	5
1805	920,834	3¼	478,411	1	43,300	6	24,266	6	10,736	4	23	6	10,217	5	1,487,790	7¼
1806	310,342	0	540,506	4	5,385	5	1,014	0	3,406	3	113	5	1,559	4	862,328	5
1807	404,946	2	815,680	5	26,091	5	7,740	5	13,774	1	1,063	6	6,070	2	1,275,367	2
1808	84,888	6	554,653	7	35,250	1	5,297	3	10,739	3	4,308	3	12,882	2	708,020	1
1809	455,987	1	1,143,242	4	29,969	7	13,614	7	29,966	5	1,262	1	33,109	5½	1,707,152	6½
1810	1,567,125	6	609,209	4	26,318	4	90,982	2	15,226	0	36	5	12,268	6	2,321,167	3
1811	336,130	3	287,464	0	42,840	2	27,830	3	4,438	3	16	3	5,044	5	703,764	3
1812	290,709	5	406,035	1	83,658	0	72,819	7	5,024	4	16	7	712	2	858,976	2
1813	559,002	5	751,954	3	83,268	4	35,039	6	5,405	0	593	1	7,603	0	1,442,866	3
1814	852,566	5	815,161	3	46,031	5	6,044	6	43,385	2	1	2	9,841	3	1,773,031	2
	9,954,347	7¼	9,375,719	7	707,932	4	598,136	1½	193,603	6	102,325	0½	224,634	7¼	21,156,700	1½

GRAND TOTAL OF IMPORTATIONS

	Q.	B.
Wheat.	9,954,347	7¼
Oats.	9,375,719	7
Barley.	707,932	4
Rye.	598,136	1½
Beans.	193,603	6
Indian Corn.	102,325	0½
Pease.	224,634	7¼
Total.	21,156,700	1½

The foregoing data are to be found in *Parl. Pap.*, 1825, No. 227.

APPENDIX No. 9

THE AVERAGE PRICE OF WHEAT PER QUARTER IN GREAT BRITAIN, 1800–1814

Year	s.	d.	Year	s.	d.	Year	s.	d.
1800	110	5	1805	87	1	1810	103	3
1801	115	11	1806	76	9	1811	92	5
1802	67	9	1807	73	1	1812	122	8
1803	57	1	1808	78	11	1813	106	6
1804	60	5	1809	94	5	1814	72	1

For this and prices of barley, oats, pease, beans and rye, see *Parl. Pap.*, 1825, No. 227.

BIBLIOGRAPHY

The purpose of this bibliography is merely to present to the student and general reader a critical estimate of the more important sources used in the preparation of this study. No attempt has been made to indicate an exhaustive list of sources, or a record of each entry that may find a place in the footnotes. Doubtless the scheme of classification is not perfect; but what scheme is? The distinction between a primary and secondary source is often so fine or vague as to defy any definite arrangement. In the final analysis it is usually one's own individual opinion as to the nature of a particular source which determines its position in a bibliography. An attempt, however, has been made to follow a plan which at least will fill the requirements of this volume.

MANUSCRIPT MATERIAL

I. Archives

Board of Trade Papers. These are preserved at the British Record Office, London.

B. T., 1: In-Letters. Vols. 18 to 96 inclusive, covering the years from July, 1799, to April, 1815. A very helpful source, crowded with facts about trade and commerce. Vol. 92 contains interesting information on Amelia Island.

B. T., 3: Out-Letters. Vols. 6 to 12 inclusive, from Jan., 1799, to Dec., 1814. Practically all the material found in this group may be found in the Minutes of the Board.

B. T., 5: Minutes. Vols. 11 to 24 inclusive, covering the period from Sept., 1797, to May 31, 1816. Of considerable value. Frequent mention is made of the Corn Laws, the trade to the colonies, the fishing industry, and the leather trade.

B. T., 6: Miscellaneous. Vol. 88 deals with questions of trade between the British West Indies and North America, chiefly for the years

1804 and 1805. Vol. 136 furnishes an account of the imports of corn into the various ports of England from Jan., 1800, to July, 1802. It lists the port of entry, and distinguishes between domestic and foreign produce; it does not indicate the port of shipment. Vol. 139 contains the Corn Papers of 1800. This volume throws considerable light upon the operation and effects of the bounty on corn and upon the condition of the crops throughout the kingdom.

B. T., 8: Vol. 194 contains references and papers dealing with licences issued to neutral ships; most of these facts may be found in the Privy Council Register.—Vols. 195 to 211 inclusive furnish a record of licences granted from March, 1809, to July, 1813. The material contains the name of the petitioners, the subject of the petition, the date the petition was received, and the action taken by the Board.

Customs Papers. These are to be found at the British Record Office, London.

C., 4. Vols. 2 to 9 inclusive furnish an account of the imports and the exports from 1800 to 1814. Imports are listed as entering either London, the outports, or Scotland. The accounts are also entered stating whether the corn was imported in British or neutral vessels.

C., 5: This includes an account of imports into Great Britain, according to the articles imported, covering the years from 1811 to 1853.

C., 17: The State of Commerce and Navigation. Consulted vols. 22 to 29 inclusive, covering the years from 1800 to 1807 inclusive. These volumes contain import figures of all goods imported into Great Britain and are in agreement with the figures given by C. 4. Also, these volumes contain tables of tonnage that entered the United Kingdom, the British North American Colonies, and the West Indies, as well as an account of the tonnage of vessels constructed.

Foreign Office Papers. To be found at the British Record Office, London.

F. O., 5: America. Vol. 29 contains the letters from Mr. Robert Liston and Edward Thornton from Jan. to Dec., 1800. These letters are chiefly political and deal with conditions in America. Vols. 30, 33, 36, 39, 43, 46, 50, 53, 59, 65, 71, 78, 89 to 95, cover the period from 1800 to 1813 inclusive. These volumes contain the letters and despatches from the British consuls in America. The material is especially rich, throwing considerable light on commerce and trade, as well as political affairs in the United States before and during the War of 1812.

F. O., 22: Denmark. Vols. 36, 41, 42, 43, 50, 56 include the correspondence of the British consuls from Jan., 1800, to Dec., 1807, inclusive. Of little value for this study, although crowded with material on the commercial and political situation in general.

F. O., 27: France. Vols. 55 to 95 inclusive cover the period of this study. The material is chiefly of a political nature. Scant references may be found of commercial interest.

F. O., 33: Hamburg and the Hanse Towns. Vols. 38, 39, 40, 41 cover the period from Jan., 1807, to Dec., 1808. Of little value for this study. Crowded with information on the political, military and diplomatic situation.

F. O., 36: Heligoland. Vols. 1 to 7 inclusive. Scant reference to the grain trade. Rich in general commercial material.

F. O., 37: Holland. Vols. 60 to 64 cover the period from 1801 to 1804 inclusive. These volumes contain little information on the grain trade, although considerable stress is laid on the commercial conditions of that state.

F. O., 64: Prussia. Vols. 57 to 61, 72, 77 to 83 inclusive. Valuable consular despatches for the years 1800 to 1811 inclusive. A very important source, furnishing much of value on the Continental System.

F. O., 65: Russia. Consulted the volumes for the years 1800 to 1812 inclusive. A very disappointing source for this study; rich in other information.

F. O., 95: America. Letter books, registers, etc. Vols. 24, 28, 30, 31 contain in-letters and out-letters from British agents in America. Of some value.

Home Office Papers. These papers are preserved at the British Record Office, London.

H. O., 40: Vol. 1 throws much light upon the activities of the Luddite Riots of 1812. Vol. 2 furnishes the military reports of these disturbances.

H. O., 42: Domestic. Vols. 48 to 55 inclusive deal with the period from June, 1799, to Dec., 1800. Of very great importance. Crowded with valuable letters and papers of social, economic and political nature.

H. O., 43: Entry Books, Letters. Vols. 11 to 14, covering the years from Oct. 31, 1798, to July 21, 1804. A helpful source of a nature similar to that of H. O., 42.

H. O., 91: Entry Books. Vols. 1, 2 for the years 1805 to 1808. These volumes contain a record of the licences issued for export and import purposes. Especially full for the period ending 1806. The entries include a statement of the purpose of the licence, the full term and general scope of the licence. This source supplements, in part, the material to be found in the Privy Council Register.

Privy Council Register. This source is to be found at the British Record Office, London.

P. C., 2: Vols. 154 to 196 cover the period from Jan., 1800, to May 31, 1815. A very valuable collection. Matters of trade and commerce are treated at great length. Interesting facts on the Licence System, the state of the West Indies, and affairs in British North America. Legal material exists in great abundance.

PRIVY COUNCIL PAPERS. These are located in the Privy Council Office, Whitehall, London.

These papers are unbound and arranged, generally, according to years in small bundles; several bundles cover a month's record. In some instances the papers are numbered. Documents are frequently found in an unrelated packet or letter. There is, consequently, only one safe method of citing any reference, namely of indicating the particular piece or letter itself. These papers supplement the Registers, and contain valuable additional information. Here, may be found in full the letters and petitions addressed to the Council asking for this licence or that privilege. Frequently the petitions have highly suggestive endorsements by members of the Council. Statistical material of prime importance is very prominent. Drafts of orders, proclamations, opinions by the Advocate General and by the Board of Trade are to be found. Lists of vessels detained by reason of embargoes, military and clerical returns, and legal material are also scattered through these papers. Finally, one should note the rough and finished drafts of Council Minutes, which are of great value.

PRIVY COUNCIL. Miscellaneous Papers preserved in the Privy Council Office, Whitehall, London.

Out-Letters. A volume of letters dealing with the period from Jan., 1812, to Oct., 1812. These have a definite bearing on the licence trade.

Minutes. A volume containing a list of licences granted for export and import for March, May and June, 1808.

Minutes of Licences. 2 vols., covering the period from July 13 to Aug. 19, 1808, and June 1 to Dec. 31, 1805. Valuable for a detailed study of the licenced trade. Contains a statement of the petition with marginal references to the action taken by the Council.

Council Minutes. 4 vols., Jan. 14, 1808, to July 20, 1808; Jan. 1, 1807, to Dec. 31, 1807; 1806 to Dec. 20, 1806; 1800 to Dec. 20, 1800. These volumes contain information on questions of trade and commerce, the Licence System, legal matters, embargoes, and the like.

A volume dealing with the fees paid for licences. Each licence is listed separately with the date of issue and the amount paid. Covers the period from March 8, 1808, to Oct. 10, 1809 inclusive.

TREASURY PAPERS. To be found at the British Record Office, London.

T., 9: Out-Letters to the Privy Council. Vols. 3, 4, 5.

T., 11: Out-Letters to the Customs. Vols. 40 to 55.

T., 29: Minutes. Vols. 75 to 134.

A test was made of these three groups, but little material was found having a definite relation to this study.

CONSULAR DESPATCHES. Located at the State Department, Washington, D.C. Prof. W. E. Lingelbach has a suggestive account of these despatches in the *American Historical Review,* XIX: 257–281.

Amsterdam: 2 vols., 1790 to 1829. Rather diappointing for this study; rich in commercial material dealing with the trade to the United States.

Belfast: 1 vol., 1801 to 1806. There are but seven letters in this volume and they contain nothing of value on the grain trade.

Bordeaux: 3 vols., 1783 to 1815. Of some value, especially for a study of the Licence System.

Bristol: 1 vol., 1800 to 1815. Very complete and rich in economic and political material. Gives valuable information concerning the trade of Bristol and that of England in general.

Cork: 1 vol., 1800 to 1815. A collection of fifteen letters of no great importance for this work.

Dublin: 1 vol., 1805 to 1815. Contains but thirteen letters of little value for a treatment of the grain trade.

Falmouth: 1 vol., 1803 to 1813. Contains scattered information of various kinds.

Hamburg: 2 vols., 1790 to 1822. Very disappointing for this study. Contain much material of value for commercial and political matters.

Liverpool: 1 vol., 1801 to 1811. Important for the valuable information furnished relative to the agricultural, political and economic conditions in Great Britain.

London: 1 vol., 1804 to 1815. Very full and complete accounts. The most valuable of all the despatches for this period.

Paris: 5 vols., 1790 to 1826. Crowded with information, but unfortunately having little bearing on this problem.

Despatches from United States Ministers Abroad. These are to be found in the Department of State, Washington, D. C.

Consulted the volumes containing the correspondence of Rufus King, J. Q. Adams and William Monroe. These volumes contain many letters which are to be found in the printed collections of the writings of these men.

Customs Records, America. These are located in the Library of Congress, Washington, D. C.

A collection that invites the most careful investigation. At present the material is unclassified, and is not arranged except by names of ports. The Library of Congress possesses the Customs records of Alexandria, Philadelphia, New York, Georgetown, Perth Amboy and several other ports. An investigation of the records of Alexandria showed clearance and entry papers. Manifests of clearances from Alexandria appear to exist for all the years covered by this study except for 1800, 1803 and 1804. A test was also made of certain Customs papers, consisting of circulars and letters issued by the Treasury Department to the various collectors of the customs. Although this set appears to have distinct value, little was found relating to the grain trade.

II. Other Collections

The Board of Agriculture. The records of this body are preserved at the offices of the Board, Bedford Square, London.

Letter Book, March 31, 1810, to June 22, 1822. This volume furnishes copies of the out-letters, which are of little value for this study. General nature is similar to the minutes of the Board.

Minutes: 2 vols., Nov. 27, 1798, to May 28, 1808. These volumes contain the minutes of the Board sitting either as the Board or as the general committee of the Board. Of great value for an institutional study of the Board. These volumes abound in material dealing with the enclosure movement, with agricultural improvements, questions of scarcity, care of the stock, farm equipment and the like.

Rough Minutes: These minutes, similar in nature to those above, cover the period from Nov. 5, 1799, to Feb. 26, 1806.

Register of Letters: In-Letters, 1793 to 1819. Alphabetically arranged. A brief statement is given of the subject matter with the date of the receipt of the letter.

Auckland Papers. Add. MSS., British Museum, 34456.

This volume covers the years 1803 to 1806, and is but one of a large number of volumes. Little information was found relating to this study.

Barclay Correspondence. Preserved by the New York Historical Society, New York City.

A very valuable and extensive collection, containing accounts, lists of prisoners, letters to and from English agents at New York, New London, New Orleans and elsewhere. A mine of information on the War of 1812. Thomas Barclay for a time was the British consul at New York.

Bourne, Sylvanus, Letters. Preserved at the Library of Congress, Washington, D. C.

Two volumes which cover the years 1797 to 1813. Of little value for this work. Contain information on party and financial affairs, the slave trade and the Irish problem.

Great Britain, Foreign Office. New York Public Library.

Precis book of despatches sent from America by F. J. Jackson, J. Morier and A. J. Foster, addressed to George Canning, Earl Bathurst and Marquis Wellesley. 2 vols., covering the years 1809 to 1811. Contain information chiefly political in nature.

The Journal of the Life of Amos Wheeler. Located at Yale University, New Haven, Conn.

Covers the period from June, 1809, to Jan., 1811. Wheeler was a young lawyer who sought his fortune among the southern states, living for a time at Wilmington, N. C. His journal is exceedingly personal, and is crowded with interesting comments on the social and political life of the South.

ARTHUR YOUNG PAPERS. Add. MSS., British Museum, 35128 to 35131.

The original letters adressed to Arthur Young, with a few *holograph* draft replies. The entire collection numbers eight volumes, of which volumes three to six inclusive are of value for this work.

In addition to the foregoing manuscripts, I have consulted certain collections which proved rather disappointing. I had expected that the Francis Place Papers, at the British Museum, would reveal a mine of information, but such was not the case. I also sought to obtain some light on the rather interesting problem of the source of the large quantities of corn shipped from the port of New York. The archives at the Buffalo Historical Society and at the State Historical Society at Albany failed to furnish any information. The manuscript collection at Yale University proved of some value, as has already been mentioned. Certain other papers at New Haven, such as the Journal of Stephen Trowbridge and the Diary of Matthew R. Dutton, were consulted without obtaining any results of importance. The Burton Historical Library, Detroit, Michigan, possesses a valuable collection in the manuscripts of Dutilh, a Philadelphian firm which traded extensively with the West Indies and the Continent. A test was made of this collection; little, however, was found bearing on this work.

PRINTED SOURCES

I. GOVERNMENTAL PUBLICATIONS

American State Papers, Documents, Legislative and Executive. 38 vols., Washington, 1832 to 1861.

Vol. 3 of the series on *Foreign Affairs* gives considerable diplomatic and political information. Vol. 1 of the series on *Commerce and Navigation* furnishes statistical information. The export figures as given in this source do not agree with the import figures as given in the British Customs records. As this study is concerned with what was actually imported, the British and not the American figures have been adopted for this work.

Annals of Congress, 1789 to 1824. Washington, 1834 to 1856.
A compilation from press reports of the doings of Congress. I consulted the volumes covering the limits of this study.

Archives Parlementaires. Paris, 1860 ——
Consulted vols. I to XI of Series II. This source is based, in part, on the *Moniteur,* but contains much of additional value.

Documents Statistiques sur la France. Paris, 1835 ——
Published by the Ministère des Travaux Publics, de l'Agriculture et

du Commerce and others. A volume published in 1837 contains the price of wheat according to Departments from 1797 to 1835. Another volume, *Commerce Exterieur,* and one entitled *Territoire, Population,* Paris, 1837, 1838, contain valuable economic information.

Report of the Public Archives, Canada.
These have been published from 1881 to date. Contain much of value for an economic history of Canada.

Collection Complete des Lois, Décrets, Ordonnances, etc. Paris, 1788 to 1824.
This valuable collection is edited by J. B. Duvergier. Consulted the volumes covering the Revolution and Napoleonic era.

Gedenkstukken der algemeene geschiedenis von Nederland, van 1795 tot 1840. The Hague, 1905——
Edited by H. T. Colenbrander. Consulted the volumes covering the French domination in Holland. A very valuable source. This work is referred to as R. G. P.

Historical Manuscripts Commission.
Report on the Manuscripts of J. B. Fortescue Esq. Preserved at Dropmore. 9 vols., London, 1892 to 1915. A very helpful source. Contains the correspondence of Auckland, Pitt, Fox, Grenville and many others of this period. This source is referred to as *Dropmore Papers.*

The Manuscripts of Lord Kenyon. London, 1894. Certain facts of interest may be obtained from pages 551 to 563.

The Manuscripts of the Earl of Lonsdale. London, 1893. Certain suggestive material may be found for this period on pages 148 to 244.

Report on Manuscripts in Various Collections. Vol. 6, of this set contains the manuscripts of Cornwallis Wykeham-Martin, Esq., which, although not extensive, has several interesting comments on the social conditions of the period.

Journals of the House of Commons. 1799 to 1815.
Of particular interest for the various accounts and papers published in the appendix of each volume. A fair index.

Journals of the House of Lords. 1799 to 1815.
Contains little beyond a record of each day's proceedings.

Parliamentary Debates. London, 1812 to 1815, edited by T. C. Hansard. Vols. I to XXXI cover the years 1803 to 1815.

Parliamentary History. London, 1819 to 1820, edited by T. C. Hansard. Vols. XXXIV to XXXVI cover the years 1799 to 1803.

Parliamentary Papers.
Reports from Committees of the House of Commons, London, 1803. These are frequently referred to as the *First Series.* Vol. IX contains various reports dealing with the agricultural conditions from 1795 to March, 1802.

Report from the Committee on the Corn Trade. 1804, No. 96.

Report from the Committee on the re-committed report on the Corn Trade, June, 1804. 1804, No. 127.

Report from the Committee on the Corn Trade, May 14, 1805. 1805, No. 26.

Report from the Committee to whom the several petitions praying relief from the effects of the Act of 44 Geo. 3, c. 109 were referred. May, 1805. 1805, No. 154.

Report from the Committee on the Commercial State of the West India Colonies. 1807, No. 65.
This report is reprinted with the 1st Report of the Committee on Distillation, April 13, 1808.

Report from the Sugar Distillery Committee, Feb. 17, 1807. 1807, No. 83.

Orders in Council. A list of orders issued from Jan. to Dec., 1807. 1808, No. 5.

Minutes of Evidence taken at the Bar of the House of Lords to Consider the Orders in Council, March, 1808. 1808, No. 33.

Minutes of Evidence respecting the Orders in Council, March, 1808. 1808, No. 119.

Orders in Council. 1808, No. 127.

Report of the Committee on the Distillation of Sugar and Molasses, April 13, 1808. 1808, No. 178.

Second Report from the Committee on the Distillation of Sugar and Molasses. 1808, No. 278.

Third Report from the Committee on the Distillation of Sugar and Molasses, June 10, 1808. 1808, No. 300.

Fourth Report from the Committee on the Distillation of Sugar and Molasses, June 22, 1808. 1808, No. 318.

Minutes of Evidence taken from the Lords' Committee on the Prohibition of Distillation from Grain. 1810, No. 67.

Minutes of Evidence taken before a Committee of the Whole House of Commons to whom were referred the petitions against the Orders in Council. May 1812. 1812, No. 87.

Minutes of Evidence taken before a Committee of the Whole House of Commons relating to the Orders in Council. 1812, No. 210.

Report from the Select Committee appointed to inquire into the Corn Trade of the United Kingdom, May, 1813. 1813, No. 184.

Ibid., 1813–1814, No. 57. Ordered to be printed May 11, 1813, when it *appeared* as *Parl. Pap.*, 1813–1814, No. 184.

Report from the Select Committee on the Petitions relating to the Corn Laws. 1813–1814, No. 339.

Corn Laws. Report from the Lords. 1814–1815, No. 26.

Report from the Select Committee on Petitions complaining of Agricultural Distress, July 8, 1820. 1820, No. 225.

Account of the Grain of all sorts, meal and flour imported into Great Britain from Foreign Parts in each year from Jan. 5, 1800, to Jan. 5, 1825. 1825, No. 227.

I have checked the figures as given in this report with those found in the Customs' Papers, and find that they are in practical agreement. In view of this, and because of the better form and arrangement followed in the Parliamentary Paper, I have used the latter rather than the former.

Accounts from His Majesty's Consuls abroad relative to the Prices of Foreign Corn. 1826, No. 153.

Mr. Jacobs' report on the Trade in Corn and on the Agriculture of the North of Europe. 1826, No. 159.

Notes to the appendix, No. 24, of Mr. Jacobs' Report on the Trade in Corn and on the Agriculture of Northern Europe. 1826–1827, No. 20.

Foreign Corn. Growth and Average Prices of Foreign Corn 1700 to 1825. 1826–1827, No. 27.

Various accounts relating to Corn. 1826–1827, No. 50.

Foreign Corn. 1826–1827, No. 83.

Papers relative to regulations existing in Foreign Countries in respect to the Import and the Export of Grain, during the last Fifty Years. 1826–1827, No. 157.

Ibid., 1826–1827, No. 221. Continuation of *Parl. Pap.*, 1826–1827, No. 157.

Report from the Select Committee of the House of Lords, appointed to inquire into the Prices at which Foreign Corn may be shipped into Foreign Ports. 1826–1827, No. 333.

Mr. Jacobs' Second Report on the Trade in Corn and on the Agriculture of the North of Europe. 1828, No. 258.

Customs Tariffs of the United Kingdom, 1800 to 1897. 1898, vol. 34.

Report of a Committee of the Lords of the Privy Council. Washington, Dept. of State, 1888.

An interesting report on the trade of Great Britain with the United States.

Robinson, Christopher. *Report of Cases argued and determined in the High Court of Admiralty.* 8 vols., London, 1801–1812.

Statutes of the Realm. London, 1810–1828. 9 vols., and 2 vols. of index.

Statutes at Large. London, D. Pickering, 1762–1800; J. Raithby, 1815–1819.

Statutes at Large, Ireland, Dublin, G. Grierson, 1786–1801.

Verzameling van Placaaten enz., voor Vriesland. Leeuwarden, 1748–1810.
A very valuable collection of laws and decrees dealing with Holland but more particularly with Friesland. Consulted the volumes covering the period from March 30, 1799, to Oct. 18, 1810, which is as far as the source goes.

II. Semi-Official Material, Correspondence and Biography

No attempt has been made to estimate the value of some of the generally well known biographies and collections of writings of the English statesmen of this period. Most of these works are of interest chiefly for the political and diplomatic material contained, although references may be found to economic matters.

American Antiquarian Society, Proceedings of, N. S., vol. XXVII, pp. 83–177.
"Letters of Thomas B. Adams, 1799 to 1823." Most of this very interesting collection comes before 1807.

Auckland, Journal and Correspondence of Lord, 4 vols., London, 1861–1862.
Lord Auckland was Bishop of Bath, and his letters are of considerable interest and value.

Aulard, A., *Paris sous le Consulat.* 4 vols., Paris, 1903–1909.
An important source for a detailed study of the life of Paris. It contains a collection of documents, chief of which are the reports of the Minister of Police.

Bagot, J., *George Canning and His Friends.* 2 vols., London, 1909.

Bergh, A. E., *The Writings of Thomas Jefferson.* 20 vols., Washington, 1907.
A convenient collection of the various printed works of the correspondence and writings of Jefferson.

Bonaparte, Louis, *Documents Historiques et Réflexions sur le Gouvernement de la Hollande.* 3 vols., Paris, 1820.

Brotonne, Léonce de, *Dernières Lettres Inédites de Napoléon Ier.* 2 vols., Paris, 1903.

Brotonne, Léonce de, *Lettres Inédites de Napoléon Ier.* Paris, 1898.
These two works by Brotonne supplement in a most valuable way the *Correspondance de Napoléon.*

Colchester, Lord, *Diary and Correspondence of Charles Abbott, Lord Colchester.* 3 vols., London, 1861.

Correspondance de Napoléon Ier, Publiée par Ordre de l'Empereur Napoléon III. 32 vols., Paris, 1858–1870.
A very valuable source for a study of European history during the Napoleonic era.

Du Casse, A., *Mémoires et Correspondance du Roi Jérôme*. 7 vols., Paris, 1861–1866.

Francis, B., and Keary, E., *The Francis Letters*. 2 vols., London, 1901.
Of general social and economic interest, but of little help for this study.

Granville, Countess, *Private Correspondence of Lord Granville, Leveson-Gower*. 2 vols., London, 1916.
These two volumes are concerned chiefly with political and diplomatic affairs.

Hauterive, E. de, *La Police Secrète du Premier Empire*. 3 vols., Paris, 1908–1922.
An important collection for the period from 1804 to 1807 inclusive. Numerous references are made to the grain trade and to the agricultural conditions in France.

Ilchester, Earl, *The Journal of Elizabeth, Lady Holland*. 2 vols., London, 1908.
This very interesting journal covers the years from 1791 to 1811.

Jackson, Lady, *The Bath Archives*. 2 vols., London, 1873.
Covers the life of Sir George Jackson from 1809 to 1816.

Jackson, Lady, *The Diaries and Letters of Sir George Jackson*. 2 vols., London, 1872.
Covers the period from the Treaty of Amiens to the Battle of Talavera.

Jeffery, R. W., *Dyott's Diary*. 2 vols., London, 1907.
Chiefly military in nature.

King, C. R., *Life and Correspondence of Rufus King*. 6 vols., New York, 1894–1900.
Of value for the fact that King, for a time, was the American agent at London. Has many interesting comments on the agriculture of both England and America.

Lecestre, Léon, *Lettres Inédites Napoléon Ier*. 2 vols., Paris, 2d edition, 1897.
Of the same general nature as the collection by Brotonne.

Loyd, Lady Mary, *New Letters of Napoleon*. New York, 2d edition, 1898.
Based upon the work by Lecestre.

Malmesbury, Earl, *Diaries and Correspondence of James Harris, Earl of Malmesbury*. 4 vols., London, 2d edition, 1844.
Only the last volume covers the period of this study, and it is not of great value.

Martens, C. de, *Nouvelles Causes Célèbres du Droit des Gens*. 2 vols., Leipzic, 1843.

Martens, G. F. de et C. de, *Recueil des Principaux Traités d'Alliance, de Paix, etc., 1761–1808*. 8 vols., Göttingen, 1791–1835.

Idem, Nouveau Recueil des Traités, etc., 1808–1839. Paris, 1817–1842.

Massachusetts Historical Society Collections.

Commerce of Rhode Island. 2 vols., 7th Series, vols. IX and X. Vol. X covers the period from 1775 to 1800.

The Jefferson Papers, 7th Series, vol. I. Very few of these letters have any bearing on this subject; they are chiefly of a political nature.

Mazade, C. de, *Correspondance de Mal Davout, Prince d'Eckmühl, ses Commandements, son Ministère.* 4 vols., Paris, 1855.

A very helpful source; rich in military, political and economic material.

Melville, Lewis, *The Life and Letters of William Cobbett.* 2 vols., London, 1913. Of slight interest for this volume.

Navy Records Society.

Letters and Papers of Charles, Lord Barham, 1758–1813. 3 vols., edited by Sir J. K. Laughton, 1907–1911.

Letters and Papers of Sir Thomas B. Martin. 3 vols., edited by Sir R. V. Hamilton, 1898–1903. Of interest for the Baltic trade.

Letters of Admiral of the Fleet, The Earl of St. Vincent, 1801–1804. 1 vol., edited by D. B. Smith, 1922. Taken from Add. MSS., 31168–31170.

Paget, Sir Augustus, *Paget Papers.* 2 vols., London, 1896.

Largely diplomatic in nature.

Pellew, G., *Life and Correspondence of the Right Honble Henry Addington, First Viscount Sidmouth.* 3 vols., London, 1847.

Picard, E. et L. Tuetey, *Correspondance Inédite de Napoléon Ier, Conservée aux Archives de la Guerre.* 4 vols., Paris, 1912–1913.

A translation by L. S. Houghton, 3 vols., New York, 1913.

Romilly, S., *Memoirs of the Life of Sir Samuel Romilly.* 3 vols., London, 2d edition, 1840.

Written by Sir Samuel Romilly, but edited by his sons. Contains a selection of his correspondence.

Ross, C., *Life and Correspondence of Cornwallis.* 3 vols., London, 2d edition, 1854.

Russell, Lord J., *Memorials and Correspondence of Charles James Fox.* 3 vols., London, 1853–1854.

The third volume covers, in part, the limits of this work.

Stanhope, Earl, *Life of the Right Honourable Wm. Pitt.* 4 vols., London, 1861–1862.

Stapleton, A. G., *George Canning and His Times.* London, 1859.

The John P. Branch Historical Papers of Randolph-Macon College.

"*The Macon Papers.*" Vol. III, pp. 27–93, contains an interesting collection of papers of Nathaniel Bacon.

Letters of John Taylor of Caroline County, Va. Vol. II, pp. 252–353. Of little value for this study.

Leven-Powell Correspondence. Vol. I, pp. 217–256. A very suggestive collection containing some information on agriculture in the South.

Twiss, H., *The Public and Private Life of Lord Chancellor Elden.* 3 vols., London, 1844.

Vane, Charles, *Correspondence, Despatches and Other Papers of Viscount Castlereagh.* 4 vols., London, 1851.

Idem, Memoirs and Correspondence of Viscount Castlereagh. 4 vols., London, 1848–1849.

Vassal, Henry R., *Further Memoirs of the Whig Party.* London, 1905.

Vernon-Harcourt, Rev. L., *Diaries and Correspondence of Rt. Hon. George Rose.* 2 vols., London, 1860.

Walpole, S., *The Life of the Rt. Hon. Spencer Perceval.* 2 vols., London, 1874.

Rather disappointing. Contains selections of his correspondence.

Wilberforce, R. I. and S., *The Correspondence of William Wilberforce.* 5 vols., London, 1838.

Windham Papers, *The Life and Correspondence of Hon. Wm. Windham.* 2 vols., London, 1913.

III. Magazines and Newspapers

The following list of the many newspapers and magazines that appeared during the period under study is by no means exhaustive. A comparison of the several newspapers for a given year and for a given section of the country, will lead one to the conclusion that they tell pretty much the same story in about the same way. All the American papers, for example, clipped very extensively from one another as well as from the press of Europe. It appeared, therefore, unnecessary to go through columns of news items that usually read the same from Portsmouth and Savannah. Editorial opinion varied, and for that reason an attempt has been made to select from different years opinions that may be of value. For example, there are the views of the London press on the question of distillation. Where it was possible, I have noted the editor of the work used; further, I have indicated exactly what years or volumes have been read. Frequently the life of these papers extended backwards and forwards beyond the dates mentioned as having been read. The capital letter at the end of each reference indicates the location of the source: B.M., for British Museum; M., for the University of Michigan; W., for the Library of Congress; Y., for Yale University; P., for the University of Pennsylvania, and the Mercantile Library of Philadelphia, Pennsylvania.

The Agricultural Magazine. Series I: July, 1802, to June, 1806, 14 vols. Series II: July, 1806, to June, 1807, 2 vols., London.

This is a continuation of the *Commercial and Agricultural Magazine.* B.M.

The Agricultural Magazine or Farmers' Journal. July, 1807, to Dec., 1812, 11 vols. New Series, Jan., 1813, to Dec., 1815, 6 vols. Edited by R. W. Dickson, London.

A continuation of *The Agricultural Magazine.* B.M.

The Albany Register, 1811.
Of little value for this study. M.

Alexandria Advertiser and Commercial Intelligencer.
Used a volume of broken numbers, April 4, 1801, to July 30, 1801. Of value as Alexandria was a port from which large supplies of corn were shipped. W.

Annals of Agriculture. London, edited by A. Young.
Consulted volumes for 1800 and 1801. A magazine devoted to the advancement of farming. B.M.

Annual Register. London, edited by Wm. Otridge & Son.
Used the volumes from 1799 to 1815. Chiefly of value as indicating public opinion. Statements of facts should be used with care. The collection of state papers is of interest. M.

Anti-Jacobin Review. London, edited by J. R. Green.
Consulted the volumes from 1799 to 1815. A monthly review of political and literary opinion. M., Y.

Athenaeum. London, edited by J. Aiken.
Used volumes for 1807, 1808, 1809. A monthly review of general information; contains a section devoted to agriculture. W.

Bell's Weekly Messenger. London.
Used the volume for 1807. B.M.

Boston Gazette. Boston, edited by J. Russell.
Consulted the years 1810, 1811, and Jan. to June, 1812. M.

British Magazine. London.
Used the volumes for 1800 and 1801. P.

Cobbett's Annual Register. London, edited by Wm. Cobbett.
Consulted the volumes for period from Jan. 16, 1802, to Dec. 31, 1803. W.

Cobbett's Political Register. London, edited by Wm. Cobbett.
Used the volumes from 1804 to 1814. A weekly work of partisan nature. Editorials and contributions are of value. M.

Columbian Centinal. Boston, edited by B. Russell.
A semi-weekly devoted to the interests of the Federalist Party. Consulted broken files at the University of Michigan.

Commercial Advertiser. New York, edited by Noah Webster until 1803.
Used the volumes from Feb. 9, 1808, to Dec. 29, 1810, and from Jan. 2, 1812, to Oct. 31, 1812, when it was edited by Z. Lewis. W.

Commercial and Agricultural Magazine. London, edited by Griffith.
Consulted issues from Aug., 1799, to June, 1802. Of particular interest for this study. P.

Edinburgh Review. Edinburgh, 1802 ——
Used the volumes from 1802 to 1815. Devoted to literary and political affairs. Of little value for this study. M.

European Magazine. London, edited by the Philological Society.
Used the numbers that covered the period from Jan., 1801, to Dec., 1814. Chiefly interested in literary doings. Has a valuable section devoted to commercial and agricultural affairs. Y.

Examiner. London, edited by L. Hunt and others.
Consulted the issues for 1808, 1809, 1810. A weekly periodical, devoted to politics, domestic economics and theatrical affairs. B.M.

Farmer's Magazine. Edinburgh.
Consulted the numbers from 1800 to 1815. A very valuable source; devoted entirely to agricultural matters. Y.

Flower's Political Review and Monthly Register. London.
Used the volumes from Jan., 1807, to July, 1811. Decidedly anti-Tory in character. W.

Gentleman's Magazine. London.
Used the issues from 1799 to 1815, during which time the editor was J. Nicholas. Literary and political in nature with a section devoted to agriculture. M.

Independent Whig. London.
Used the volumes for 1807 to 1810. A weekly; very partisan in nature; similar to the *Examiner.*

Le Moniteur Universal. Paris.
The official journal of the Consulate and Empire. Used the issues from 1799 to 1815. Rather uninspiring and colorless, but still of value. Y.

Literary Panorama. London, edited by O. Taylor.
Used the numbers from 1806 to 1815. A review of current literature and a register of current events. Y.

Lloyd's List and Commercial Daily Chronicle. London.
Consulted the numbers for 1807 and 1808. Of little value for this study. Contains a brief description of boat arrivals, clearances, prices of stock, rates of exchange, etc. B.M.

London Gazette.
The official paper of the British Government. Used the issues from 1799 to 1815. Of prime importance. Contains official notices, orders, proclamations, etc. Valuable for official prices of foodstuffs. The Government, however, did not publish all of its orders, proclamations, etc. Many important omissions. The New York Public Library has a rather complete file of this paper; Yale University and the Library of Congress have broken files. I used chiefly the files at the New York Public Library.

London Morning Advertiser. London.
Consulted numbers at random for this period. B.M.

London Daily Courier. London.
Used the issues from 1810 to 1812. Of considerable value. B.M.

London Daily Times. London.
Used the volumes from 1800 to 1815. Of very great value for this study. Usually this paper reflected Government opinion. B.M.

London Morning Chronicle. London.
Used the numbers for 1807 and 1808. Similar to the *London Times.* B.M.

London News. London.
Consulted the numbers from Jan. 6, 1811, to Aug. 6, 1812. A weekly paper of interest for a résumé of the week's doings. W.

London Review. London, edited by R. Cumberland.
Used the volumes for 1809. Chiefly literary in character. B.M.

Monthly Magazine and British Review. London, edited by R. Phillips.
Used the issues from 1800 to 1815. A very valuable source. Has a section devoted to commerce and agriculture. M.

Monthly Register and Encyclopedia. London.
Consulted the issues for 1802 and 1803. Chiefly literary in character. P.

National Intelligencer. Washington, D. C.
Used the numbers for 1810, 1812, 1813. A tri-weekly; reflects governmental opinion. M.

New York Daily Advertiser. New York.
Used broken files from 1801 to 1812. M.

Philadelphia Gazette and Universal Daily Advertiser. Edited by S. Relf from 1801 to 1823.
Consulted the numbers from 1806 to 1810. P.

Providence Gazette. Providence, R. I., edited by J. Carter.
Consulted broken files for 1807, 1808, 1809, 1810, 1811. M.

Quarterly Review. London, 1809 ——
Used the numbers from 1809 to 1815. Similar to the *Edinburgh Review.* M.

Repository of Arts, Literature, Commerce and Manufactures.
Consulted the numbers for 1809. A most interesting magazine, containing valuable illustrated accounts of the various subjects treated. P.

Scott's Magazine. Edinburgh.
Used the numbers from 1799 to 1804. Is for Scotland what the *Gentleman's Magazine* is for England. Y.

United States Chronicle. Providence, R. I.
Used broken files for 1802. M.

Universal Gazette. Washington, D.C., edited by S. H. Smith.
Consulted broken files from 1802 to 1805. M.

Washington Federalist. Washington, D.C.
Used broken files for 1802 and 1808. A tri-weekly. M.

Weekly Register. Washington, D.C., edited by H. Niles.
Used the numbers from Sept., 1811, to March, 1814. A weekly register of national and domestic activities. M.

IV. Pamphlets

This section of the bibliography could be extended almost indefinitely, without, however, any important results. An attempt has been made to point out the relative importance of these tracts, especially in respect to the first years of the century. Pamphlets express personal or party opinion; as this study deals primarily with fact and not with opinion, I have not sought to exhaust this source of information.

Anon., *A Letter to the Earl of Liverpool,* London, 1814.
The author favors the Corn Bill of 1814.

Anon., *Thoughts of an Old Man.* London, 1800.
Speculation is assigned as the cause for the high prices.

Anon., *Thoughts on the Dearness of Provisions.* Oxford, Nov., 1800.
The author holds the farmers and the millers responsible for the high prices.

Blane, Sir Gilbert, *Inquiry into the Cause and Remedies of the late Present Scarcity and High Price of Provisions.* London, 1800.
The author ridicules the idea of a monopoly among the corn-factors and assigns as the cause for the high prices the unfavorable crops.

Colquhoun, P., *A Treatise on the Wealth, Power and Resources of the British Empire.* London, 1814.
Very suggestive, but should be used with caution.

Comber, W. T., *An Inquiry into the State of National Subsistence.* London, 1808.
An account of the Corn Laws and of their operation showing the dependence of Britain upon foreign grain.

Lang, Charles. *A Temperate discussion of the causes which have led to the present high price of bread.* London, 1800.
Denies the charge that combinations and monopoly have caused the high prices.

Lauderdale, Earl James, *A Letter on the Corn Laws.* London, 1814.

Malham, Rev. J., *The Scarcity of Wheat Considered.* Salisbury, 1800.
Places the blame upon the corn-factors.

Malthus, T. R., *An Investigation of the Cause of the Present High Price of Provisions.* London, 1800.
Places the blame upon the extension of the parish rates.

Oddy, J. J., *European Commerce.* 2 vols., Philadelphia, 1807.
Of great interest: shows the relative importance of the Baltic trade. Has a suggestive study of the corn trade. Has many tables of figures, but gives no authority. The work should be used with caution.

Phillimore, J., *Reflections on the Nature and Extent of the Licence System.* London, 1811, 2d edition.
Denounces the system as antagonistic to the Navigation Acts.

Reeves, J., *The Law of Shipping and Navigation from the time of Ed. III to the end of the year 1806.* London, 1807, 2d edition.
A most valuable, and on the whole, a very scholarly piece of work. For some time Reeves was Clerk to the Privy Council. His opinions are often noted among the Unbound Papers of the Privy Council.

Sheffield, Lord J., *Remarks on the Deficiency of Grain.* London, 1800.
Places the blame for the high prices on the failure of the crops of 1799.

Smith, Charles, *Tracts on the Corn Trade.* London, Stockdale, 1804.
This edition contains additions from the marginal notes by Mr. C. Catherwood, who for a time was General Receiver of the Corn Returns. A very capable work; one which influenced subsequent opinion and writing.

Stephen, James, *The Dangers of the Country.* London, 1807.
Demands retaliation against France because of the Berlin Decree.

Idem., War in Disquise: or the Fraud of the Neutral Flags. London, 1805.
See Melvin, F. E., *Napoleon's Navigation System,* pp. 402–403.

Symmons, John, *Thoughts on the Present Prices of Provisions.* London, 1800.
Assigns the failure of the harvest as the cause for the high prices.

The Whole Proceedings and Resolutions of the Freeholders of the County of Middlesex, Oct. 29, 1800. London, 1800.
The war is blamed for the high prices.

SECONDARY MATERIAL

Adams, Henry, *The History of the United States, 1801–1817.* 9 vols., New York, 1889–1891.
Decidedly anti-British in character. Vols. IV and VI are of value for this study.

Annuaire de l'Économie Politique. 1849.
An account of harvest failures is given on pp. 334–337 of this book.

Atton H., and Holland, H. H., *The King's Customs.* 2 vols., London, 1908–1910.
Vol.. II covers the period of this study; has suggestive material on the Corn Laws.

Barker, Arthur, *The British Corn Trade.* London, 1920.
The general nature of this work is suggestive rather than scholarly. Chapters four and five are of interest.

Bellot de Kergorre, Alexandre, *Un Commissaire des Guerres pendant Le Premier Empire.* Paris, 1899.

Rather disappointing for this study. Extremely interesting for its account of several of the important campaigns of Napoleon.

Du Casse, A., "Napoléon et Le Roi Jérôme," in *Revue Historique,* vols. XVIII to XXI.

Valuable for a study of the Kingdom of Westphalia.

Coquelle, P., "La Mission d'Alquier à Stockholm," in *Revue d'Histoire Diplomatique,* vol. XXIII.

During 1810 and 1811, Alquier filled the difficult rôle of French ambassador at Stockholm.

Cunningham, Audrey, *British Credit in the Last Napoleonic War.* Cambridge, 1910.

A very suggestive work.

Darmstädter, P., "Studien zur Napoleonischen Wirtschaftspolitk," in *Vierteljahrschrift für Sozial- und Wirtschaftsgeschichte,* vol. II, pp. 559–615.

Of little value for this study. The author appears to be interested chiefly in the industrial problem.

Davidson, John, *Commercial Federation and Colonial Trade Policy.* London, 1900.

Chapter one provides a convenient, although not altogether complete, account of English policy towards her colonies from 1763 to 1815.

Duboscq, André, *Louis Bonaparte en Hollande, d'après ses Lettres, 1806–1810.* Paris, 1911.

Fisher, H. A. L., *Studies in Napoleonic Statesmanship, Germany.* Oxford, 1903.

A very illuminating and valuable piece of historical research.

Gonner, E. C. K., *Common Land and Inclosure.* London, 1912.

Of great value for English economic history. Not of much help for this study.

Goulier, L., *Le Commerce du Blé, et Spécialement de son Organization en France.* Poitiers, 1909.

Very disappointing. Has little of value for this work.

Gras, N. S. B., *The Evolution of the English Corn Market from the Twelfth to the Eighteenth Century.* Cambridge, Harvard Press, 1915.

A scholarly presentation of the formative period of the English Corn Market.

Güinchard, J., *Sweden: Historical and Statistical Handbook.* 2 vols., Stockholm, 2d edition, 1914.

Contains several interesting and helpful chapters on Swedish agriculture.

Halévy, Elie, *Histoire du Peuple Anglais au XIXe Siècle.* Vol. I, Paris, 1913.

Contains an account of agricultural and industrial life during the period of this work.

Hammond, J. L., "The Agricultural Labourer in the Early 19th Century," in *Journal of the Minister of Agriculture,* vol. XXVII, pp. 586–597.
An account of the miserable lot of the average farm hand; not of great value for this study.

Hammond, J. L. and B., *The Village Labourer, 1760–1832.* London, 1913.
A very important contribution to our knowledge of social and economic conditions in English history.

Handelsman, Marcel, *Napoléon et la Pologne, 1806–1807.* Paris, 1909.
Chiefly concerned with the diplomatic and political relations between France and Poland. Of some value for this work.

Heckscher, Eli F., *The Continental System.* Oxford, 1922.
An economic interpretation. Based chiefly on printed material which was available to the author in Copenhagen. Of general interest and value. No attempt has been made to use the continental or British archives.

Hitzigrath, K. A. H., *Hamburg und die Kontinentalsperre.* Hamburg, 1900.
A short and suggestive account of thirty pages.

Hoekstra, P., *Thirty-Seven Years of Holland-American Relations.* Grand Rapids, Michigan, 1916.
A large part of this work is given to the Napoleonic era. Is distinctly well worth while.

Jaurès, J., *Histoire Socialiste.* 12 vols., Paris, 1900–1909.
Vol. VI, *Consulate et Empire,* by Paul Brousse and Henri Turot, contains a very good account of the agricultural condition of France under the Empire.

Lanzac de Laborie, L. de, *La Domination Française en Belgique.* 2 vols., Paris, 1895.
Of considerable value for political and diplomatic affairs.

Ibid., Paris sous Napoléon. Paris, 1908.
Contains a very full account of market conditions and food prices in Paris during the Napoleonic era.

Levasseur, P. E., *Histoire du Commerce de la France.* 2 vols., Paris, 1911–1912.
Vol. II, pp. 46–103, contains an account of the grain trade and economic life in France during the Empire.

Mavor, James, *An Economic History of Russia.* 2 vols., New York, 1914.
Of little value for this study.

Melvin, F. E., *Napoleon's Navigation System.* New York, 1919.
Of prime importance for every student of the Napoleonic period. The best account there is of the Continental System.

Murray, James, *Commercial Relations between England and Ireland, from the Restoration.* London, 1907.

Very deficient in its treatment of the grain trade between the two islands from 1800 to 1846.

Naudé, Wilhelm, " Die brandenburgish-preussiche Getreidehandelpolitik, vom 1713–1806," in *Jahrbuch für Gesetzgebung,* 1905.
The account for the nineteenth century is but a bare outline.

Nicholson, J. S., *The History of the English Corn Laws.* London, 1904.
A fair presentation of the history of these laws.

Peez, A., and Dehn, P., *England's Vorherrschaft,* vol. I, " Aus der Zeit der Kontinentalsperre." Leipsic, 1912.
A discussion on the English grain trade is given on pp. 303–309. The account depends to a great extent upon the works of J. H. Rose.

Pingaud, Léonce, *Bernadotte, Napoléon et les Bourbons.* Paris, 1901.
See pages 78–159 for an account of the relations between Sweden and France.

Porter, G. R., *The Progress of the Nation.* Revised edition, London, 1912.
A volume crowded with information; should be used with caution.

Prothero, R. E., *English Farming, Past and Present.* London, 1912.
A very careful and well written work. Contains an instructive discussion of the Corn Laws.

Rocquain, Félix, *Napoléon Ier et le Roi Louis.* Paris, 1875.
Supplements in many imporant instances the *Correspondance de Napoléon.*

Rose, J. H., *The Life of Napoleon.* 2 vols., New York, 1910.
Probably the best work in English on Napoleon.

Idem, Pitt and Napoleon. London, 1912.
Contains many heretofore unpublished letters of Pitt.

Idem, Wm. Pitt and the Great War. London, 1911.
Pages 431–559 contain some material of interest for this study.

Schmidt, Charles, *Le Grand-Duché de Berg, 1806–1813.* Paris, 1905.
A careful study of the French domination in the Grand Duchy of Berg. Of little value for this volume.

Idem, " Anvers et le Système Continental, 1792–1814," in *La Revue de Paris,* 1915, pp. 634–652.

Sears, L. M., " The Middle States and the Embargo of 1808," in *South Atlantic Quarterly,* April, 1912.
Has little or no relation to this study.

Servières, George, *L'Allemagne Française sous Napoléon Ier.* Paris, 1904.
A very important contribution. Of much value for this study.

Slater, Gilbert, *The English Peasantry and the Enclosure of Common Fields.* London, 1907.
A well written and careful account. Contains an appendix with a list of acres inclosed.

Smart, Wm., *Economic Annals of the Nineteenth Century.* 2 vols. London, 1910–1917.
Vol. 1 covers the period from 1801 to 1820. An annalistic account, based chiefly upon Hansard.

Stuhr, Friedrich, " Die Napoleonische Kontinentalsperre im Mecklenburg, 1806–1813," in *Jahrbuch des Vereins für Mecklenburgische Geschichte und Alterumskunde,* vol. LXXI.
Throws considerable light on the grain trade of this part of Europe.

Tarle, E. V., *Kontinental'naja blokada,* Moscow, 1913.
Contains an extensive and comprehensive bibliography. This volume deserves to be translated. I was unable to use it to any great extent, not having a knowledge of Russian.

Tooke, Thomas, *History of Prices.* 4 vols., London, 1838–1848.
Of value for general information. Extreme caution should be used when one employs the statistical matter presented in Tooke's work.

Thornton, Henry, *Historical Survey of the Corn Laws.* London, 1841.
This forms, in part, the basis for the account of the corn laws in *Accounts and Papers,* 1898, vol. 34.

ADDENDA TO MANUSCRIPT MATERIAL

Ellis and Allan Papers. Preserved at the Library of Congress, Washington, D. C.
Journals, accounts and letter-books of the Virginian firm of Ellis and Allan. A very valuable collection of mercantile papers, throwing much light upon agricultural conditions in America. Considerable information as to political and social matters may also be found.

Lawrason and Fowle Papers. Preserved at the New York Public Library.
Journals, accounts and letter-books of the Virginian firm of Lawrason and Fowle. Similar in nature to the Ellis and Allan Papers. A valuable source.

Lloyd Papers. Preserved at the Library of Congress, Washington, D. C.
A valuable collection of papers similar in nature to the Ellis and Allan Papers. Particularly rich in information pertaining to Virginia.

INDEX

UNIVERSITY OF MICHIGAN STUDIES

HUMANISTIC SERIES

General Editors: FRANCIS W. KELSEY AND HENRY A. SANDERS

Size, 22.7 × 15.2 cm. 8°. Bound in Cloth.

Vol. I. Roman Historical Sources and Institutions. Edited by Henry A. Sanders, University of Michigan. Pp. vii + 402. $2.50 net.

CONTENTS

1. The Myth about Tarpeia: Henry A. Sanders.
2. The Movements of the Chorus Chanting the Carmen Saeculare: Walter Dennison.
3. Studies in the Lives of Roman Empresses, Julia Mamaea: Mary Gilmore Williams, Mt. Holyoke College.
4. The Attitude of Dio Cassius toward Epigraphic Sources: Duane Reed Stuart, Princeton University.
5. The Lost Epitome of Livy: Henry A Sanders.
6. The Principales of the Early Empire: Joseph H. Drake, University of Michigan.
7. Centurions as Substitute Commanders of Auxiliary Corps: George H. Allen.

Vol. II. Word Formation in Provençal. By Edward L. Adams, University of Michigan. Pp. xvii + 607. $4.00 net.

Vol. III. Latin Philology. Edited by Clarence Linton Meader, University of Michigan. Pp. vii + 290. $2.00 net.

Parts Sold Separately in Paper Covers:

Part I. The Use of idem, ipse, and Words of Related Meaning. By Clarence L. Meader. Pp. 1–112. $0.75.

Part II. A Study in Latin Abstract Substantives. By Manson A. Stewart, Yankton College. Pp. 113–78. $0.40.

Part III. The Use of the Adjective as a Substantive in the De Rerum Natura of Lucretius. By Frederick T. Swan. Pp. 179–214. $0.40.

Part IV. Autobiographic Elements in Latin Inscriptions. By Henry H. Armstrong, Beloit College. Pp. 215–86. $0.40.

Vol. IV. Roman History and Mythology. Edited by Henry A. Sanders. Pp. viii + 427. $2.50 net.

Parts Sold Separately in Paper Covers:

Part I. Studies in the Life of Heliogabalus. By Orma Fitch Butler, University of Michigan. Pp. 1–169. $1.25 net.

Part II. The Myth of Hercules at Rome. By John G. Winter, University of Michigan. Pp. 171–273. $0.50 net.

Part III. Roman Law Studies in Livy. By Alvin E. Evans. Pp. 275–354. $0.40 net.

Part IV. Reminiscences of Ennius in Silius Italicus. By Loura B. Woodruff. Pp. 355–424. $0.40 net.

THE MACMILLAN COMPANY

Publishers 64–66 Fifth Avenue New York

VOL. V. SOURCES OF THE SYNOPTIC GOSPELS. By Rev. Dr. Carl S. Patton, First Congregational Church, Los Angeles, California. Pp. xiii + 263. $1.30 net.

Size, 28 × 18.5 cm. 4to.

VOL. VI. ATHENIAN LEKYTHOI WITH OUTLINE DRAWING IN GLAZE VARNISH ON A WHITE GROUND. By Arthur Fairbanks, Director of the Museum of Fine Arts, Boston. With 15 plates, and 57 illustrations in the text. Pp. viii + 371. Bound in cloth. $4.00 net.

VOL. VII. ATHENIAN LEKYTHOI WITH OUTLINE DRAWING IN MATT COLOR ON A WHITE GROUND, AND AN APPENDIX: ADDITIONAL LEKYTHOI WITH OUTLINE DRAWING IN GLAZE VARNISH ON A WHITE GROUND. By Arthur Fairbanks. With 41 plates. Pp. x + 275. Bound in cloth. $3.50 net.

VOL. VIII. THE OLD TESTAMENT MANUSCRIPTS IN THE FREER COLLECTION. By Henry A. Sanders, University of Michigan. With 9 plates showing pages of the Manuscripts in facsimile. Pp. viii + 357. Bound in cloth. $3.50 net.

Parts Sold Separately in Paper Covers:

Part I. THE WASHINGTON MANUSCRIPT OF DEUTERONOMY AND JOSHUA. With 3 folding plates. Pp. vi + 104. $1.25 net.

Part II. THE WASHINGTON MANUSCRIPT OF THE PSALMS. With 1 single plate and 5 folding plates. Pp. viii + 105–349. $2.00 net.

VOL. IX. THE NEW TESTAMENT MANUSCRIPTS IN THE FREER COLLECTION. By Henry A. Sanders, University of Michigan. With 8 plates showing pages of the Manuscripts in facsimile. Pp. x + 323. Bound in cloth. $3.50.

Parts Sold Separately in Paper Covers:

Part I. THE WASHINGTON MANUSCRIPT OF THE FOUR GOSPELS. With 5 plates. Pp. vii + 247. $2.00 net.

Part II. THE WASHINGTON MANUSCRIPT OF THE EPISTLES OF PAUL. With 3 plates. Pp. ix + 251–315. $1.25 net.

VOL. X. THE COPTIC MANUSCRIPTS IN THE FREER COLLECTION. By William H. Worrell, Hartford Seminary Foundation. With 12 plates. Pp. xxvi + 396. Bound in cloth. $4.75 net.

Parts Sold Separately in Paper Covers:

Part I. THE COPTIC PSALTER. The Coptic text in the Sahidic Dialect, with an Introduction, and with 6 plates showing pages of the Manuscript and Fragments in facsimile. Pp. xxvi + 112. $2.00 net.

Part II. A HOMILY ON THE ARCHANGEL GABRIEL BY CELESTINUS, BISHOP OF ROME, AND A HOMILY ON THE VIRGIN BY THEOPHILUS, ARCHBISHOP OF ALEXANDRIA, FROM MANUSCRIPT FRAGMENTS IN THE FREER COLLECTION AND THE BRITISH MUSEUM. The Coptic Text with an Introduction and Translation, and with 6 plates showing pages of the Manuscripts in facsimile. Pp. 113–396. $2.50 net.

THE MACMILLAN COMPANY

Publishers 64–66 Fifth Avenue New York

VOL. XI. CONTRIBUTIONS TO THE HISTORY OF SCIENCE.

Part I. ROBERT OF CHESTER'S LATIN TRANSLATION OF THE ALGEBRA OF AL-KHOWARIZMI. With an Introduction, Critical Notes, and an English Version. By Louis C. Karpinski, University of Michigan. With 4 plates showing pages of manuscripts in facsimile, and 25 diagrams in the text. Pp. vii + 164. Paper covers. $2.00 net.

Part II. THE PRODROMUS OF NICOLAUS STENO'S LATIN DISSERTATION CONCERNING A SOLID BODY ENCLOSED BY PROCESS OF NATURE WITHIN A SOLID. Translated into English by John G. Winter, University of Michigan, with a Foreword by Professor William H. Hobbs. With 7 plates. Pp. vii + 169–283. Paper covers. $1.30 net.

Part III. VESUVIUS IN ANTIQUITY. Passages of Ancient Authors, with a Translation and Elucidations. By Francis W. Kelsey. Illustrated. (*In preparation.*)

VOL. XII. STUDIES IN EAST CHRISTIAN AND ROMAN ART. By Charles R. Morey, Princeton University, and Walter Dennison. With 67 plates (10 colored) and 91 illustrations in the text. Pp. xiii + 175. $4.75 net.

Parts Sold Separately:

Part I. EAST CHRISTIAN PAINTINGS IN THE FREER COLLECTION. By Charles R. Morey. With 13 plates (10 colored) and 34 illustrations in the text. Pp. xiii + 86. Bound in cloth. $2.50 net.

Part II. A GOLD TREASURE OF THE LATE ROMAN PERIOD. By Walter Dennison. With 54 plates and 57 illustrations in the text. Pp. 89–175. Bound in cloth. $2.50 net.

VOL. XIII. DOCUMENTS FROM THE CAIRO GENIZAH IN THE FREER COLLECTION. Text, with Translation and an Introduction by Richard Gottheil, Columbia University. (*In press.*)

VOL. XIV. TWO STUDIES IN LATER ROMAN AND BYZANTINE ADMINISTRATION. By Arthur E. R. Boak and James E. Dunlap, University of Michigan. Pp. x + 324. Bound in cloth. $2.25 net.

Parts Sold Separately in Paper Covers:

Part I. THE MASTER OF THE OFFICES IN THE LATER ROMAN AND BYZANTINE EMPIRES. By Arthur E. R. Boak. Pp. x + 160. $1.00 net.

Part II. THE OFFICE OF THE GRAND CHAMBERLAIN IN THE LATER ROMAN AND BYZANTINE EMPIRES. By James E. Dunlap. Pp. 165–324. $1.00 net.

VOL. XV. GREEK THEMES IN MODERN MUSICAL SETTINGS. By Albert A. Stanley, University of Michigan. With 10 plates. Pp. xxii + 385. Bound in cloth. $4.00 net.

Parts Sold Separately in Paper Covers:

Part I. INCIDENTAL MUSIC TO PERCY MACKAYE'S DRAMA OF SAPPHO AND PHAON. Pp. 1–68. $0.90 net.

Part II. MUSIC TO THE ALCESTIS OF EURIPIDES WITH ENGLISH TEXT. Pp. 71–120. $0.80 net.

THE MACMILLAN COMPANY

Publishers 64–66 Fifth Avenue New York

Part III. Music to the Iphigenia among the Taurians by Euripides, with Greek Text. Pp. 123–190. $0.75 net.

Part IV. Two Fragments of Ancient Greek Music. Pp. 217–225. $0.30 net.

Part V. Music to Cantica of the Menaechmi of Plautus. Pp. 229–263. $0.60 net.

Part VI. Attis: A Symphonic Poem. Pp. 265–383. $1.00 net.

Vol. XVI. Nicomachus of Gerasa: Introduction to Arithmetic. Translated into English by Martin Luther D'Ooge, with Studies in Greek Arithmetic by Frank Egleston Robbins and Louis C. Karpinski. (*In press.*)

Vols. XVII, XVIII, XIX, XX. Royal Correspondence of the Assyrian Empire. Translated into English, with a transliteration of the text and a Commentary. By Leroy Waterman, University of Michigan. (*In press.*)

Vol. XXI. The Papyrus Minor Prophets in the Freer Collection and the Berlin Fragment of Genesis. By Henry A. Sanders, University of Michigan, and Carl Schmidt, University of Berlin. (*In press.*)

FACSIMILES OF MANUSCRIPTS

Size, 40.5 × 35 cm.

Facsimile of the Washington Manuscript of Deuteronomy and Joshua in the Freer Collection. With an Introduction by Henry A. Sanders. Pp. x; 201 heliotype plates. The University of Michigan. Ann Arbor, Michigan, 1910.

Limited edition, distributed only to Libraries, under certain conditions. A list of Libraries containing this Facsimile is printed in *University of Michigan Studies, Humanistic Series*, Volume VIII, pp. 351–353.

Size, 34 × 26 cm.

Facsimile of the Washington Manuscript of the Four Gospels in the Freer Collection. With an Introduction by Henry A. Sanders. Pp. x; 372 heliotype plates and 2 colored plates. The University of Michigan. Ann Arbor, Michigan, 1912.

Limited edition, distributed only to Libraries, under certain conditions. A list of Libraries containing this Facsimile is printed in *University of Michigan Studies, Humanistic Series*, Volume IX, pp. 317–320.

SCIENTIFIC SERIES

Size, 28 × 18.5 cm. 4°. Bound in Cloth.

Vol. I. The Circulation and Sleep. By John F. Shepard, University of Michigan. Pp. ix + 83, with an Atlas of 63 plates, bound separately. Text and Atlas, $2.50 net.

Vol. II. Studies on Divergent Series and Summability. By Walter B. Ford, University of Michigan. Pp. xi + 194. $2.50.

Vol. III. The Geology of the Netherlands East Indies. By H. A. Brouwer. With plates and text figures. (*In press.*)

THE MACMILLAN COMPANY

Publishers 64–66 Fifth Avenue New York

UNIVERSITY OF MICHIGAN PUBLICATIONS

HUMANISTIC PAPERS

General Editor: EUGENE S. McCARTNEY

Size, 22.7 × 15.2 cm. 8°. Bound in Cloth.

THE LIFE AND WORKS OF GEORGE SYLVESTER MORRIS. A CHAPTER IN THE HISTORY OF AMERICAN THOUGHT IN THE NINETEENTH CENTURY. By ROBERT M. WENLEY, University of Michigan. Pp. xv + 332. Cloth. $1.50 net.

LATIN AND GREEK IN AMERICAN EDUCATION, WITH SYMPOSIA ON THE VALUE OF HUMANISTIC STUDIES. Edited by FRANCIS W. KELSEY. Pp. x + 396. $1.50.

THE PRESENT POSITION OF LATIN AND GREEK, The Value of Latin and Greek as Educational Instruments, the Nature of Culture Studies.

SYMPOSIA ON THE VALUE OF HUMANISTIC, Particularly Classical, Studies as a Preparation for the Study of Medicine, Engineering, Law and Theology.

A SYMPOSIUM ON THE VALUE OF HUMANISTIC, Particularly Classical, Studies as a Training for Men of Affairs.

A SYMPOSIUM ON THE CLASSICS AND THE NEW EDUCATION.

A SYMPOSIUM ON THE DOCTRINE OF FORMAL DISCIPLINE IN THE LIGHT OF CONTEMPORARY PSYCHOLOGY.
(Out of print; new edition in preparation.)

THE MENAECHMI OF PLAUTUS. The Latin Text, with a Translation by JOSEPH H. DRAKE, University of Michigan. Pp. xi + 130. Paper, covers. $0.60.

PAPERS OF THE MICHIGAN ACADEMY OF SCIENCE, ARTS AND LETTERS

(containing Papers submitted at Annual Meetings)

Editors: PAUL S. WELCH and EUGENE S. McCARTNEY

Size, 24.2 × 16.5 cm. 8°. Bound in Cloth.

VOL. I (1921). With 38 plates and 5 maps. Pp. xi + 424. $2.00 net.
VOL. II (1922). With 11 plates. Pp. xi + 226. $2.00 net. Bound in paper $1.50 net.
VOL. III (1923). With 26 plates, 15 text figures and three maps. Pp. xii + 473. $3.00 net. Bound in paper, $2.25 net.

THE MACMILLAN COMPANY

Publishers 64–66 Fifth Avenue New York

Vol. IV (1924), Part I. With 27 plates, 22 text figures and 3 maps. Pp. xiii + 631. $3.00 net. Bound in paper, $2.25 net.

Vol. IV (1924), Part II. A Key to the Snakes of the United States, Canada and Lower California. By Frank N. Blanchard. With 78 text figures. Pp. xiii + 65. Cloth, $1.75.

LANGUAGE AND LITERATURE

Vol. I. Studies in Shakespeare, Milton and Donne. By Members of the English Department of the University of Michigan. Pp. viii + 232. Cloth. $2.50.

CONTRIBUTIONS FROM THE MUSEUM OF GEOLOGY

VOLUME I

The Stratigraphy and Fauna of the Hackberry Stage of the Upper Devonian. By Carroll Lane Fenton and Mildred Adams Fenton. With 45 plates, 9 text figures and one map. Pp. xi + 260. Cloth. $2.75.

VOLUME II

(*All communications relative to the Numbers of Volume II should be addressed to the Librarian, General Library, University of Michigan.*)

No. 1. A Possible Explanation of Fenestration in the Primitive Reptilian Skull, with Notes on the Temporal Region of the Genus Dimetrodon, by E. C. Case. Pp. 1–12, with five illustrations. $0.30.

No. 2. Occurrence of the Collingwood Formation in Michigan, by R. Ruedemann and G. M. Ehlers. Pp. 13–18. $0.15.

No. 3. Silurian Cephalopods of Northern Michigan, by Aug. F. Foerste. Pp. 19–86, with 17 plates. $1.00.

No. 4. A Specimen of *Stylemys nebrascensis* Leidy, with the Skull Preserved, by E. C. Case. Pages 87–91, with 7 text figures. Price, $0.20.

No. 5. Note on a New Species of the Eocene Crocodilian *Allognathosuchus*, *A. wartheni*, by E. C. Case. Pages 93–97, with 1 plate and 1 text figure. Price, $0.20.

No. 6. Two New Crinoids from the Devonian of Michigan, by G. M. Ehlers. Pages 99–104, with 1 plate. Price, $0.20.

THE MACMILLAN COMPANY

Publishers 64–66 Fifth Avenue New York

HISTORY AND POLITICAL SCIENCE

(The first three volumes of this series were published as "Historical Studies" under the direction of the Department of History. Volumes IV and V were published without numbers.)

Vol. I. A History of the President's Cabinet. By Mary Louise Hinsdale. Pp. ix + 355. Cloth. $2.00.

Vol. II. English Rule in Gascony, 1199–1259, with Special Reference to the Towns. By Frank Burr Marsh. Pp. xi + 178. Cloth. $1.25.

Vol. III. The Color Line in Ohio; A History of Race Prejudice in a Typical Northern State. By Frank Uriah Quillan. Pp. xvi + 178. Cloth. $1.50.

Vol. IV. The Senate and Treaties, 1789–1817. The Development of the Treaty-Making Functions of the United States Senate during Their Formative Period. By Ralston Hayden, University of Michigan. Pp. xvi + 237. Cloth $1.50 net.

Vol. V. William Plumer's Memorandum of Proceedings in the United States Senate, 1803–1807. Edited by Everett Somerville Brown, University of Michigan. Pp. xi + 673. Cloth. $3.50.

Vol. VI. The Grain Supply of England during the Napoleonic Period. By W. F. Galpin, University of Oklahoma. Pp. xi + 305. Cloth. $3.00.

Catalogue of the Stearns Collection of Musical Instruments (Second edition). By Albert A. Stanley. With 40 plates. Pp. 276. $4.00.

THE MACMILLAN COMPANY

Publishers 64–66 Fifth Avenue New York